Poets, Prophets, and Sages

Essays in Biblical Interpretation

Poets, Prophets, and Sages

Essays in Biblical Interpretation

Robert Gordis

INDIANA UNIVERSITY PRESS

Bloomington   London

Published in Canada by Fitzhenry & Whiteside Limited,
Don Mills, Ontario

Library of Congress catalog card number: 79–98984
ISBN: 253–16655–1

Manufactured in the United States of America

Contents

Preface

In contemplating the Bible one is inescapably driven to the use of superlatives. It may fairly be described as the greatest surviving monument of ancient culture. It is a collection of many of the most distinguished works of literature known to man. Finally, it is the supreme expression of religion of the human race, transcending by far the boundaries of sectarian loyalties. These aspects do not themselves fully reveal its singular claim to greatness. It is the fusing of these three elements of history, literature, and religion that makes the Bible truly unique. It remains perpetually fascinating and always elusive as each age discovers anew that it is eternally modern.

It is no wonder, therefore, that in approaching this Everest of the human spirit, men have contented themselves with attempting to climb only one of its slopes. All too often the Bible has been treated by the historian as a collection of convenient source materials, by the student of literature as an anthology of purple passages, and by the theologian and preacher as a corpus of edifying proof-texts. However inevitable this division of the Bible into areas of specialization may be, it has proved highly unfortunate. For it is precisely in this organic unity of the ideals of truth, beauty, and goodness that the ethos of the people of Israel has revealed itself throughout history, and never with greater clarity and power than in the Hebrew Bible. If we divide the Scriptures into separate compartments of history, literature, and religion, each is impoverished. What is most disastrous is that in the process we have destroyed the priceless contribution the Bible can make to the human quest for integrity and wholeness of spirit.

It is this sense of the unity of all its aspects, I believe, that informs the present work. Each of the chapters necessarily deals with a specific aspect but seeks to see it in relation to the others. The studies in this volume are all motivated by the conviction that biblical scholarship must be thorough and accurate in content and sound in methodology. But more is required if it is to have any genuine significance. It must ultimately contribute to answering the question, "What has the Bible to say to man today and tomorrow?"

To make manifest the abiding relevance of the Bible to the human condition now and always is the true justification and ultimate goal of all vital scholarship. To achieve this goal, learning alone is not enough.

The scholar must also be conscious of the fact that the reconstruction of the life and thought of past eras is as elusive a task as it is fascinating. Hence, a healthy dose of agnosticism is as essential for scholarship as it is for faith. If he is to be true to his professed ideals, the scholar must approach the material before him with humility, which is not merely a moral quality, but an indispensable intellectual virtue as well. The radical manipulation of the received text, the unwillingness to reckon with the testimony of tradition, the espousal of dogmatic views that ignore alternative positions—all such procedures, no matter how richly embellished by technical apparatus, are unworthy of genuine scholarship. Fortunately, this truth is becoming increasingly recognized and a more balanced and truly sound approach is more and more in evidence in contemporary biblical research.

Ever since my student days spent with an unforgettable master, the late Professor Max L. Margolis, biblical study has been one of the major concerns of my life. The products of this activity are embodied in a half-dozen books and several scores of papers that have appeared in periodicals in the United States, Europe, and Israel. For a long time, friends, colleagues, and students have urged that these papers, scattered in journals that are often inaccessible or out of print, be made available in book form.

In selecting the studies for this volume, I have omitted the more technical papers that deal with philological or exegetical subjects, on the assumption that scholars will be able to locate them in the journals. The present volume consists of studies of more comprehensive scope and, I hope, of more general interest.

While I have always been appreciative of the work of scholars who have preceded me, and reckoned with their conclusions, I have sought to build my conclusions on original research based on a study of each problem without prejudgment, whether theological or scholarly. I am gratified that several of the major insights in these pages have already won a substantial measure of agreement among contemporary scholars and readers.

It is a pleasure to acknowledge the kindness of the following editors and publishers who have granted permission to reprint studies which originally appeared under their auspices. My warmest thanks are extended to:

Dr. Louis Finkelstein and Harper & Row Publishers for the following papers:

"The Bible—Its Origin, Growth, and Meaning," which appeared as "The Bible as a Cultural Monument" in *The Jews*, ed. Louis Finkelstein (Harper & Row, 1949), pp. 783–822.

"Micah's Vision of the End-Time," from *Great Expressions of Human Rights*, ed. R. M. MacIver (Harper & Row, 1950), pp. 1–18.

"The Temptation of Job," which appeared as "The Temptation of Job—Tradition vs. Experience in Religion," in *Great Moral Dilemmas*, ed. R. M. MacIver (Cooper Square Publishers, 1964), pp. 155–78.

"Primitive Democracy in Ancient Israel," from the *Alexander Marx Jubilee Volumes* (Jewish Theological Seminary of America, 1959), pp. 369–88.

"The Song of Songs," from *Mordecai M. Kaplan Jubilee Volumes* (Jewish Theological Seminary of America, 1953), pp. 281–325.

"Isaiah of Jerusalem—Prophet, Thinker, World Statesman," from *The Samuel Friedland Lectures* (Jewish Theological Seminary of America, 1966), pp. 65–80.

Dr. Morton S. Enslin, Editor of the *Journal of Biblical Literature* and the *Society of Biblical Literature*, for the following papers:

"The Heptad as an Element of Biblical and Rabbinic Style," from *Journal of Biblical Literature*, vol. 62 (1943), pp. 17–26.

"The Knowledge of Good and Evil in the Old Testament and the Dead Sea Scrolls," from *Journal of Biblical Literature*, vol. 76 (1957), pp. 123–38.

Dr. Matitiyahu Tsevat, Editor of the *Hebrew Union College Annual*, for the following papers:

"The Social Background of Wisdom Literature," from *Hebrew Union College Annual*, vol. 18 (1944), pp. 77–118.

"Quotations in Biblical, Oriental, and Rabbinic Literature," from *Hebrew Union College Annual*, vol. 22 (1949), pp. 157–219.

"Hosea's Marriage and Message," from *Hebrew Union College Annual*, vol. 27 (1954), pp. 9–35.

Barr Thompson, Managing Editor of *Harvard Theological Review*, for:

"The Composition and Structure of Amos," from *Harvard Theological Review*, vol. 33 (1940), pp. 239–51, copyright by the President and Fellows of Harvard College.

Two of these papers, "The Wisdom of Koheleth" and "All Men's Book—An Introduction to Job," appeared in the *Menorah Journal* in 1943. "The Structure of Biblical Poetry," which appears here for the first time in an English translation, slightly modified from the Hebrew original, was published in *Sefer Hashanah Liyehudei Amerika* (5705 = 1945), pp. 136–59.

It should be noted that I have not subjected these studies to a complete revision, which would have necessitated virtually writing each paper anew. The changes consist basically of improvements in style, the omission of duplications, and the correction and updating of bibliographical references. Only at times have I introduced the results of later researches. Nevertheless, I would like to believe that readers will find a substantial measure of novelty, interest, and stimulation in these pages. In most instances, the translation of biblical and post-biblical passages are my own.

The papers that constitute the present volume are the products of research carried on during the course of a busy communal career, during which the author served on the faculties of Jewish Theological Seminary, Columbia University, and Union Theological Seminary in New York. That I was able to study and to learn, to write and to teach during these busy years was due in large measure to my dear wife, whose devotion and understanding made it possible for me to function not only in the public arena, but in the quiet of the study as well.

My erudite friend, Dr. Abraham I. Shinedling, who has been my collaborator in most of my literary projects, has again placed the readers and the author in his debt beyond the power of words to express by reading the proof and preparing the indices as a labor of love.

It is my hope that these studies, in spite of their imperfections, will help to shed new light on the great source of light which is the Book of Books.

New York, 1969   R. G.

POETS, PROPHETS, AND SAGES

Essays in Biblical Interpretation

1. THE BIBLE—ITS ORIGIN, GROWTH, AND MEANING

1. ATTITUDES TOWARD THE BIBLE—OLD AND NEW

The observation made some two centuries ago by Voltaire that *"La Bible est plus célèbre que connue"* is as true today as ever before. Many factors have conspired to produce this unfortunate situation, some superficial, others more fundamental. Many a prospective reader is deterred by the form in which the Bible is generally presented— the columns closely printed, the verses numbered as in a catalogue, with no distinction indicated between prose and poetry, between genealogical tables and exalted poetic utterances. A more basic hindrance to the widespread appreciation of the Bible today is, strangely enough, the veneration in which it is held as the Word of God. As a result, most readers turn to it with more devoutness than alertness and expect to be edified rather than stimulated by its contents.

The most important factor, however, leading to the neglect of the Book of Books in modern times is the confusion prevalent in men's attitude toward the Bible. In this respect, as in so many others, our age is a period of transition, with "one world dying, another powerless to be born." Two conceptions are to be met with today, one steadily losing ground, the other possessing implications as yet imperfectly understood. These contemporary attitudes reflect two stages in the development of Western thought.

For the greater part of its history, until the eighteenth century, Western civilization approached the Bible dogmatically through the theory of verbal inspiration. For nearly two millennia the Bible was regarded as the repository of God's messages to the human race, literal transcripts of His will revealed to worthy men through the ages. The role of the biblical authors was fundamentally passive. Their distinction lay in their moral and spiritual greatness, which made them worthy of receiving the Divine Revelation. Thus, in dealing with the closing verses of Deuteronomy, which describe the death and burial

3

of Moses, the Talmud declares: "The Holy One, blessed be He, was dictating and Moses was writing with a tear."[1]

As will be noted below, this conception of the literal inspiration of the Bible began undergoing reinterpretation as soon as it was subjected to scrutiny by talmudists, theologians and philosophers. But for the masses of the people it remained the regnant view. In large measure it has retained its hold upon devout believers in both Judaism and Christianity to the present day.

This attitude has several important implications. If Scripture is a literal transcript of God's Word, everything in it is of equal importance. As Maimonides quite rightly insisted, the genealogies of Esau in Genesis are no less sacred than the Ten Commandments or the *Shema*.

Moreover, everything within it is forever binding, being an emanation of the Eternal. Hence, many centuries after the composition of the Bible, the Puritans could adopt the Old Testament as the basis of their polity in the New World without the slightest doubt as to its relevance to their problems. At the same time, without any sense of anachronism, they could validate the burning of the witches in Salem by a reference to Ex. 22:17 which declares: "Thou shalt not suffer a witch to live."

The drawbacks inherent in this second implication were largely overcome in Judaism because of a third. Since the Bible is the Word of God, every apparently unimportant word and insignificant incident must have a deeper meaning. In order that the true intent of the Bible be revealed, the text is therefore in need of interpretation. Thus there developed various schools of biblical interpretation, which sought to reveal this hidden meaning of the text by finding important implications in the repetition of words and phrases, and by drawing deductions from each particle and copula, often from each syllable. The imposing development of the Talmud rests upon this method of textual interpretation. Given the premise, the conclusion was inescapably logical—a message coming directly from the Divine could have nothing accidental or superfluous, either in its content or in its form.

Whatever our attitude toward this approach to the Bible, it should be noted that the modern world owes it an incalculable debt, all too often ignored. In the first instance, it meant that the Bible remained a living and evolving law, keeping pace with new conditions and growing insights. Thus, to cite a few instances at random, almost two thousand years ago the rabbis had, by a process of biblical interpretation, virtually eliminated capital punishment, in spite of its frequent mention in the Pentateuch, and interpreted "an eye for an eye" to mean monetary compensation for damages. Similarly, talmudic law abolished the execution of "a stubborn and rebellious son," enjoined in Scripture (Deut. 21:18–21). It also modified the biblical prohibition of interest in order to meet the needs of commercial credit in an advanced society. Particularly noteworthy is the extension of the rights of women beyond the narrow limits of the ancient Orient. This was accomplished very simply. All the biblical passages which speak of a *na'arah*, or "girl," as being in the power of her father, who could sell her into slavery or marriage, were referred to a girl between the ages of twelve and twelve and a half! Before that age, she was a *ketanah*, or a "minor," and entitled to special protection. Above that age she was a *bogeret*, or "mature" woman and hence free from the *patria potestas.*

Moreover, this conception of the verbal inspiration of the Bible is to be credited with the creation of a fascinating literature in its own right. The vast nonlegal material in the Talmud and in the independent compilations of the Midrash called the Haggada consists of ethics, legends and folk wisdom of incomparable value and scope. Most of this literature takes the form of interpretations of biblical passages.

This conception of the literal inspiration of Scripture not only produced an evolving law and a rich ethical and religious literature. It also made possible the creation of religious philosophy in Judaism and in Christianity. In two periods, the traditional religion of the Western world came into contact with Greek philosophy. The first was at the beginning of the Common Era, when Alexandria was the cultural center of the world. The second came some eight or nine hundred years later. First in Bagdad and then in Spain, Arab scholars and thinkers, together with their Jewish confrères, were engaged in preserving and expounding the writings of the Greek philosophers, which were neglected and forgotten in Christian Europe. In addition, new discoveries in mathematics and the sciences were enriching and modifying the ideas to be found in these philosophic classics. From this vast and far-flung intellectual activity, there emerged a world view greatly at variance with traditional concepts found in the Bible.

The conflict was resolved by the allegorical interpretation of Scripture, which had been previously utilized with great skill by Philo of Alexandria in the first century. A great line of philosophically trained thinkers arose during the Middle Ages, who interpreted the biblical text so as to bring it into harmony with the "modern" thought of their age. In the process they broadened immeasurably the horizons of traditional religion, besides making many fruitful contributions to philosophy. It is paradoxical but true that the apparently naïve conception of the Bible as the direct dictation of God was the basis for the great medieval philosophical systems of Saadia, Maimonides, Crescas, and their associates.

The most important debt owing to this dogmatic attitude still remains to be noted: to it we owe the preservation of the Bible. At a time when the great classics of Greek and Latin literature were being neglected and in many instances lost in the West, the Bible was being preserved with loving care, both in the Hebrew original by Jewish scribes and in the Greek and Latin translations by Christian monks. The achievement of these Hebrew scribes, called *Masoretes* or "guardians of tradition," has not been sufficiently appreciated. These nameless scribes copied the Sacred Book with meticulous and loving care. Carefully they noted every letter and every detail of spelling, accentuation and musical notation, in order to prevent errors or changes in the text which they had received from earlier ages. They did not hesitate to count the letters and verses in each book, and noted every exceptional form in spelling or usage. The extent of their veneration for the Bible can be judged by their observation that the middle word of the entire Pentateuch was *darash* in Lev. 10:16 and that the middle letter of the entire Bible was the *yod* in the word *bayyir* in Jer. 6:7!

The development of talmudic law, the creation of the religio-ethical literature of the Rabbis, and the growth of medieval Jewish philosophy, as well as the physical preservation of the Bible, all rested upon the theory of literal inspiration. But the detailed study and analysis of the biblical text led to a recognition that there were differences within the Bible which could be explained only in terms of the human factor. The prophets and poets of the Bible were not mere passive vessels for the Divine, or their messages would have been identical in form and content. They were active participants in the process of Revelation, reflecting or refracting the Divine Light in accordance with the depth of their insight and their spiritual capacity. Thus the Talmud noted the differences in the theophanies described by the prophets Isaiah and Ezekiel. It explained that Isaiah's simple and majestic vision of God (ch. 6) was like the reaction of a city dweller accustomed to the proximity of the royal court, while Ezekiel's circumstantial and elaborate picture of the heavenly chariot (2:8) reflected the attitude of a rustic dazzled by the unwonted spectacle of royal splendor.[2] Similarly, Moses' pre-eminence over the later prophets was graphically expressed by comparing him to a star-gazer with a clear telescope while they had blurred instruments of vision.[3]

The talmudic Sages could not overlook the obvious fact that, while the Torah and the prophets seemed to be citing the words of the Deity ("The Lord spake to Moses saying," "Thus saith the Lord"), there were other books in the Bible which made no such claim and were obviously human in origin. The beloved book of Psalms consisted of hymns addressed by men to their Maker. Job was a flaming protest against the apparent miscarriage of justice in a world created and governed by God. The book of Esther does not so much as mention the Divine Name.

Hence, it was recognized early that there were different levels of inspiration in the Bible. The highest was represented by the Torah, the second by the Prophets, and the lowest by the Hagiographa. This distinction became a principle of talmudic jurisprudence: "Matters of law [Torah] are not deducible from other biblical books."[4] Similarly in its provisions for the handling and exchange of scrolls of the Torah and the Prophets, as well as in other legal enactments, the Mishna recognized the higher sanctity of the Torah.

Some influential teachers in the mishnaic period opposed the extremely painful forms of biblical interpretations which made elaborate deductions from particles or stylistic repetitions. Thus the school of Rabbi Ishmael laid down the principle that was destined to become very fruitful in later days, that "The Torah speaks in the language of man."[5] For all its fondness for homiletic and allegorical interpretations, the Talmud recognized that the literal meaning of a text must take precedence over its figurative interpretation, declaring, "The literal meaning of a verse may not be disregarded."[6]

Moreover, the Masoretes, whose principal activity followed the compilation of the Talmud, amassed a good deal of sound grammatical material during their ceaseless labors to protect the biblical text. In the tenth century the Gaon, Saadia ben Joseph, noticed the similarities of biblical and Rabbinic Hebrew. His contemporary, Judah ibn Koreish, recognized the resemblances of Hebrew to its sister tongues Aramaic and Arabic. Between them, these two scholars laid the foundations of comparative Semitic philology.

The scattered and unsystematic linguistic observations of the Masoretes were replaced by the scientific grammatical studies of brilliant philologists like Judah Hayyuj and Abulwalid ibn Janah and by the notable commentaries of gifted exegetes like Rashi, the Kimhis, Abraham ibn Ezra, and a host of others. Their scientific works attained a level of achievement that bears favorable comparison with those of our own day.

Thus, imperceptibly, the basis was laid for a human approach to the Bible that would regard it not as the dictation of God to men, but as the record of man's aspiration to God. Religious thinkers might still regard the Bible as the inspired Word of God, but man now became the agent and not merely the recipient of the Divine Revelation.

This revolutionary attitude toward the Bible began to dominate the thinking of most modern men in the eighteenth century. In the past the Bible had been regarded as great because it was holy. It was now regarded as holy because it was great. The lectures of Bishop Robert Lowth of Oxford on *The Sacred Poetry of the Hebrews* and on Isaiah, and the rhapsodic discourses of Johann Gottfried Herder in Germany on *The Oldest Sources of Humanity*, led to a new aesthetic appreciation of the Bible as literature, as the expression of the national spirit of Israel during its most creative period.

Resting upon the foundations of medieval learning, the modern age has built the imposing structure of biblical scholarship, which today includes a score of disciplines. Comparative philology has revealed the relation of Hebrew to other members of the Semitic group, the vocabulary and grammatical structure of which have shed light upon the biblical idiom. The text-critical study of the Bible has often revealed the true meaning of the text and in many instances faulty passages have been corrected. The higher critical study of the Bible has revealed a great deal concerning the sources, composition and mutual relationship of the various books and helped us understand the message of the biblical authors against the background of their times. Ancient civilizations have been brought to light whose literary and material remains have re-created the history of the ancient Orient and illumined almost every page of the Bible. Above all, archaeology and the allied sciences of comparative religion and anthropology have enlarged the frame within which the Bible is to be set.

Our conceptions regarding the development of biblical civilization and its literature are still in flux, to be sure. There are untold variations of attitude among contemporary scholars, varying all the way from the extremes of traditionalism to ultraradical criticism. Yet modern biblical research is beginning to achieve a new synthesis of critical approach and respect for tradition. In large measure this emerging point of view is the result of the extensive and fruitful excavations in the lands of the Fertile Crescent—Egypt, Palestine, Syria, and Iraq. The discoveries made there have offered welcome evidence of the essential credibility of the biblical writers and corrected the vagaries of some critics, who possess more acumen than sympathy and more analytical method than constructive imagination.

Our understanding of biblical tradition, history, law, ethics, poetry, prophecy and wisdom has been completely revolutionized by modern biblical and Semitic scholarship. But our debt to the past remains imponderable. If today a modern reader possesses the means for comprehending the Bible better than the greatest mind in medieval times, it is because we are dwarfs standing on the shoulders of giants.

What is the significance of the Bible for the modern age? On the most obvious level, the Bible is *literature*. Within its covers are found some of the world's greatest masterpieces in poetry and prose. There is scarcely a genre of literary art not represented by a distinguished example.

But the importance of the Bible goes deeper. It is an indispensable element in the *religious* and *moral* education of the human race. The Bible is the immortal record of God's Revelation through its various stages and forms, as embodied in the life and thought of the chosen spirits of Israel, who sought after God and the good life. Even this is not all. The importance of the Bible is more than historical—it is living religion. It contains the profound and ever-fruitful insights of lawgivers, prophets, poets, and sages who looked deep into the heart of man and the universe and recognized both as the handwork of God. The modern religious spirit finds God revealed far more impressively in the majestic harmony and order of the universe than in the miracles which earlier generations delighted to chronicle. Similarly,

the Bible as the achievement of man bears impressive testimony to
the divine inspiration that is its source.

Finally the Bible is *history*, vivid, revealing, unforgettable. It is the
thrilling record of the tragic yet glorious experience of the Jewish
people during its most vigorous period. Though Israel has always
been politically weak and physically negligible, the world has recognized its unique religious genius and moral power. As Santayana
has said, "He who does not know the past is doomed to repeat it."
A knowledge of this basic aspect of the world's spiritual development
is crucial today. In an age of multiple crises of mounting proportions,
one may well doubt whether mankind will have many more chances
to repeat the mistakes of yesterday. Hence, understanding the Bible
means not merely excavating the past, but laying the foundations of
the future.

2. THE BACKGROUND OF THE BIBLE

A true appreciation of the Bible as literature, religion and history
is predicated upon the recognition that it is not an anthology of
sacred texts or a collection of edifying tracts written by the like-
minded believers of a religious sect. It is, in the words of an acute
twentieth-century scholar, "a national literature upon a religious
foundation." The Bible reveals all the varied and even contradictory
intellectual currents and spiritual tendencies that characterized the
life of Israel during the first fifteen hundred years of its collective
experience. The biblical period begins with the emergence of the
Hebrew tribes upon the stage of history during the middle of the
second millennium B.C.E. and continues until the persecutions of
Antiochus, which preceded the Maccabean revolt (168 B.C.E.). Radical,
conservative and moderate, rationalist and mystic, believer and skeptic,
all have found their place within the canon of Scripture. The stimulating variety of attitudes and contents in the Bible is heightened by the
colorful influences of the older, neighboring cultures of Egypt, Syria
and Mesopotamia. The roots of the Bible are to be sought throughout
the Near East as surely as its fruits belong to the world.

A clue to the lively intellectual ferment within Israel that produced
the Bible is supplied by the traditional division of the Hebrew Bible
into three parts: the Torah, or Law, the Nebiim, or Prophets, and the

Ketubim, or Sacred Writings. This tripartite arrangement, which is very ancient, recalls the three principal cultural elements in biblical thought: the priest, or custodian of Torah, the prophet, or speaker of the Word, and the sage, the teacher of Wisdom. These groups are clearly delineated in two biblical passages. Jeremiah declares: "For instruction shall not perish from the priest, nor counsel from the wise, nor the word from the prophet" (18:18). Ezekiel utters his warning: "They shall seek a vision of the prophet, and instruction shall perish from the priest, and counsel from the elders" (7:26).

Each of these three elements must be understood in terms of its individual development, its relationship to the other two strands, and its ultimate incorporation into the common heritage of Israel.

3. TORAH—THE LAW

The Torah was the particular province of the priest. The Hebrew word *kohen*, "priest," and its Arabic cognate *kahin*, "seer of a spirit, diviner," bear witness to the earliest period of Semitic history. This stage of religion may have preceded the successive eruptions from the Arabian desert into the lands of the Fertile Crescent and Egypt that produced the different Semitic and Hamitic peoples. At all events, in this primitive period, whether before or after the emergence of distinct ethnic groups, there was only one functionary who met all the religious requirements of the clan. He was the diviner, consulted on all individual and group problems, as well as the custodian of the religious cult and the officiant at sacrifices.

With the growth of a more complex social system, and particularly with the transfer from a nomadic or seminomadic life to a settled agricultural economy, the functions of this dignitary were divided. The free spirit of the god, which ancient men believed was most evident and potent in hypnotic trances and similar transports, became the particular province of wandering seers or dervishes, who eked out a precarious existence from the bounty of those who consulted them on the future, particularly with reference to personal problems. On the other hand, more and more elaborate shrines, altars and temples now arose, which were ministered to by priests. The emoluments of the priests were more substantial and their position in society was more respected than that of the wandering seers. As a result, the

priesthood early became a hereditary caste, jealously protecting its
prerogatives as guardians of the sanctuary. As a matter of fact, the
functions of divining the future and revealing the will of the god or
gods were never completely surrendered by the priest. Yet more and
more his activities tended to become formalized through ritual
associated with the sacred objects of the shrine.

These priests naturally created and preserved the rites connected
with their sanctuaries. Being the only educated group, they became
the custodians of culture. The literature and science of ancient Egypt
and Mesopotamia was almost exclusively the work of the priesthood.
In Israel during the days of the First Temple, the priests were the
medical authorities, the judges in civil and criminal cases, and the
arbiters on all religious problems, as well as the custodians of the
ancient historical traditions.

The center of all this priestly activity lay in shrines and temples
like those at Shiloh, Beth-el, Gilgal, and, pre-eminently, the Temple
of Solomon in Jerusalem, which took precedence over these older
and lesser sanctuaries, but never succeeded in superseding them completely. In these sanctuaries, ancient historical records and manuals
of law were preserved, both for the practical guidance of the priests
and for the instruction of their youth.

The Bible contains many of these briefer *torot*, or legal manuals,
necessary to the functioning of the priesthood. Such is the torah of
the leper, forbidden foods, and the various sacrifices, all in Leviticus.
There were also more extensive legal and moral codes of hoary
antiquity, often combining ritual enactment, civil and criminal law,
moral exhortation and legal procedure. Such are the Book of the
Covenant (Ex. 21–23) and the Holiness Code (Lev. 17–26).

In II Kings 24, we read of an even more elaborate code discovered
during the reign of King Josiah (621 B.C.E.). Repairs had been undertaken of the Temple buildings and this Torah was found buried in
the foundations or hidden in the walls of the sanctuary, as was common in the ancient world. This code is generally identified today, in
whole or in part, with Deuteronomy, the fifth book of the Torah.
Doubtless, there were many other *torot* of briefer or more extensive
compass which have not reached us, especially those of the local
sanctuaries. The prophet Hosea seems to refer to such codes when
he says, "Though I write him ten thousand *torot*, they are foreign
to him" (8:12).[7]

What is the origin of the Five Books, or Pentateuch? To this question tradition gave a very definite answer. It was Moses, the great liberator of Israel, who had bestowed upon his people the Torah he had received from God.

There were, of course, manifest difficulties connected with this view. That Moses could have written the last verses of Deuteronomy, describing his own death, was a problem the Rabbis solved homiletically. Other passages, like Gen. 12:6 and 36:31, for example, which seemed to infer a post-Mosaic date, were noted by medieval Jewish exegetes. Their observations were repeated and extended by Spinoza in his *Tractatus Theologico-Politicus*, which was the direct stimulus to the modern Higher Criticism of the Pentateuch. Scholars found many repetitions and inconsistencies in the text and were led to the hypothesis of multiple sources embedded in the Torah. Once set in motion, the process of source analysis gained momentum. More and more contradictions in the text were being discovered which could be resolved only by the hypothesis of new sources, subsources, redactors, and redactional schools.

With the assumption that the Pentateuch consisted of multiple documents combined more or less skillfully by redactors, came the tendency to assign increasingly later dates both to the individual sources and to the composite product, many centuries after the Mosaic age. Moses became a legendary, if not mythical, figure and any resemblance between him and the traditional portrait was purely a matter of accident. The Priestly Code, the largest Pentateuchal source, was generally assigned to the days of the Second Temple, and its narratives and legislation were described as an artificial retroversion, or throwback, of Second Temple conditions into earlier ages.

It should be noted that the higher-critical study of the Torah has made important and enduring contributions to our understanding of biblical law and thought. These values need to be salvaged from the exaggerations and errors into which the critics were all too often betrayed. Their results cannot be dismissed as insignificant, a procedure often advocated today, particularly in nonscientific publications intended for the general reader.

Archaeological discoveries throughout the Near East brought to light law codes of high antiquity. The most important of these, the Babylonian Code of Hammurabi (20th or 18th century, B.C.E.), and the Assyrian, Hittite and Hurrian codes, possess many elements that shed light upon Pentateuchal law and tradition. Thus, aside from its many points of contact with the Code of Hammurabi, the Book of the Covenant (Ex. 21–23) contains much of the customary law of the Semitic peoples, and is, therefore, in part at least older than the Exodus from Egypt.

A similar situation obtains with regard to the most famous code of all, the Decalogue (Ex. 20; Deut. 5). It is, to be sure, unique in its simplicity and comprehensiveness and bears the unmistakable stamp of Israel's faith in one God, Whose likeness is not to be pictured by man. Nonetheless, the moral standards ordained in the Ten Commandments have their parallels in the Egyptian *Book of the Dead*, which describes the cross-examination that the dead undergo in the nether world.

For reasons of this kind, as well as larger historical considerations, scholars are recognizing increasingly that if there had been no tradition of a legislator like Moses it would have been necessary to invent one. Without such a dominating personality, it remains inconceivable how a band of slaves could have engineered a mass escape from a powerful country like Egypt. What is more, this group of cowed and oppressed helots were transformed into a mighty people, fired with the resolution to brave the hazards of the desert and carry on a long drawn-out struggle for the conquest of the strongly defended Promised Land. Moreover, this aggregation of clans possessed a strong sense of unity, a common historical memory and, underlying both, the worship of the same God. All this presupposed a liberator who was also a lawgiver. In order to impress upon the people the way of life they were to follow, what was required was not only the exalted principles of the Decalogue, but the more mundane and tangible details of ritual, civil and criminal law.

The great prophets of later times also bore testimony to the existence of an exalted religious and ethical tradition in Israel. Even Amos, the earliest among them, who spoke in the name of one living and universal God, enforcing His law of righteousness throughout the world, did not speak of himself as an innovator. On the contrary, the prophets called upon the people to "return" to their God and His law. Their denunciations of the people would be as pointless as they would be unfair, if the "knowledge of the Lord" which they demanded were not already part of the heritage of the people, however misunderstood or violated.

Many other features of the Pentateuch, in both its historical and legal sections, which had previously been dismissed as inventions of Second Temple writers, were seen to have very old parallels. This is true of the Tabernacle and the Ark in the wilderness, which have their analogies in the *mahmal* and the *'otfe*, sacred tentlike structures borne in the religious processions of various Arab tribes. So, too, with regard to the elaborate system of sacrifices described in Leviticus, the technical terms of which are known to us from Syrian and Punic documents. Another example, the *'edah* or *kahal*, inadequately rendered "congregation" in our current Bible translations, is discussed elsewhere in this volume.

Thus the conviction has been gaining ground among scholars that the tradition of the Mosaic authorship of the Pentateuch is not an invention. It may never be possible to establish the precise extent of legal material emanating from his period, but that the Torah contains the work of Moses appears certain.

The sanctuaries naturally served as the libraries for the legal codes that were necessary to the priest in carrying on his ritual and judicial duties. They would also be the natural locale for collecting the historical traditions of the people, especially since the lives of Abraham, Isaac, Jacob, Joseph, and Moses were bound up with the sacred sites and thus served to validate their sanctity. In addition to these national traditions there were others of even greater antiquity that Israel shared with its kinsmen, as part of their common Semitic heritage. Such were the narratives of Creation, the first human pair, the rise of sin, and the Flood. These tales, retold in Israel, were imperceptibly transformed by the alchemy of the Hebrew spirit to reflect the higher and profounder insights of Israelite religion.

All these traditions were originally repeated orally and probably were chanted in verse form. As time went on, however, poetry gave way to prose, and oral transmission to written forms. It is by no means easy to recapitulate the literary history of these historical traditions or to trace the origin and order of composition of the law codes now incorporated in our Torah. The process was undoubtedly long and complex. Yet for the reasons indicated, a new respect for the credibility of the biblical narratives and the antiquity of biblical law has developed.

In part, the difficulty that modern scholars have in reconstructing the steps leading to the compilation of the Torah stems from the fact that the composition and redaction of these codes and traditions proceeded slowly and anonymously over a period of centuries. Their final editing and integration into a single continuous work is most plausibly to be attributed to the impact of the destruction of the First Temple by the Babylonians and the exile of the people in 586 B.C.E. This catastrophe constituted a major threat to Jewish survival. Six centuries later, when the Second Temple was destroyed by the Romans, a similar crisis confronted Jewish leaders. At that time the traditions governing the Temple and its services were carefully collected in the mishnaic treatise *Middot*, lest they be forgotten in time. In very much the same spirit, the traditions and laws preserved by the priests of the First Temple seem now to have been assembled and codified in the Torah par excellence, the Five Books of Moses.

The collapse of the Babylonian Empire and the rise of Persia in its stead gave the Jewish people a new lease on life. Cyrus was magnanimous and farsighted in his policy toward subject peoples. He permitted those Jews who so desired to reconstitute their community life in Palestine, granting them religious and cultural autonomy. The Torah proved an incomparable instrument for uniting and governing the Jewish community. Three-quarters of a century after the Return, Ezra, who was a priest by birth and a *sofer*, or "scribe," by calling, persuaded the struggling Jewish settlement in Jerusalem to accept the Torah as its constitution for all time. Nor was this all. Though himself a priest, Ezra carried through a unique peaceful revolution, which stripped the priesthood of its position of religious and intellectual leadership, leaving it only the conduct of the Temple ritual as prescribed by law. The spectacle of moral corruption and degeneracy that a hereditary priesthood exhibited led Ezra to transfer the spiritual leadership of the people from the priests to the scholars, who represented a nonhereditary, democratic element recruited from all classes. The ritual ministrations of the priests in the Temple went on unimpaired, but the dynamic creative impulse in Judaism was henceforth centered in a less pretentious institution, the synagogue, at once a house of prayer, study and communal assembly.

The importance of this revolution, unparalleled in ancient religion, can scarcely be exaggerated. The Talmud gives Ezra little more than his due when it declares, "Ezra was worthy of giving the Torah had not Moses preceded him."[8] Ezra and his scholarly successors are to be credited, in large measure, with the progressive, evolving and democratic character of normative, traditional Judaism.[9]

The *Soferim* and the Rabbis not only preserved the Torah, they gave it new life. Their activity made the Bible relevant to the needs of new generations and thus prepared it to serve as the eternal charter of humanity. They gave the Jewish tradition some of its most noteworthy characteristics, its protean capacity for adjustment, and its fusing of realistic understanding and idealistic aspiration. These nameless scribes thus contributed in no small measure to the survival of the Jewish people. But their significance is not limited to the household of Israel. The Christian world, too, owes them a debt of gratitude. As founders of Rabbinic Judaism they helped create the background from which Christianity arose, formulating many of the basic teachings that both religions share in common.

Henceforth, the written Torah was complete, with nothing to be added or removed. The oral Torah would carry the growth and development of the Jewish religion forward to its new phase.

4. The Prophets of Israel

The second great division of the Bible is called "the Prophets." Like so many other aspects of Israelite life, the prophets represent a unique Hebrew development of elements common to all the Semitic peoples. Reference has been made above to the single official of the primitive Semites who exercised all religious functions which were later divided between the priest and the prophet. We have briefly traced the role of the priest, the custodian of Torah, who represents one line of development. The other is represented at its highest by the Hebrew prophet, the revealer of the Divine Word. In its origins, prophecy was infinitely less exalted.

Side by side with the formalized role of the priesthood, with its emphasis upon ritual, there arose a considerably more informal type of religious leadership, the diviner, soothsayer, or "seer," familiar today in the Arab dervish. Not being attached to a sanctuary, he had no fixed locale. He therefore had to depend upon the resources of his own personality for his maintenance and position. He functioned through trances or ecstatic spells, under the influence of which he would mutter or shout his message derived from his god. Self-hypnosis would be induced through dances, rhythmic swaying, music, ceaseless repetitions of the Divine Name, or self-laceration. The diviner was both feared because of his connection with the Divine and despised as a cross between beggar and lunatic. Throughout history, Semitic soothsayers remained on this low level and unquestionably had their counterparts in ancient Israel. Ecstasy, whatever the means by which it was induced, was the prime condition for the activity of the "seer."

In the Bible, however, this type of functionary is not to be met, except for a few stray allusions during the earlier period of the Judges and the Monarchy. This is due to two factors. In the first instance, the Bible is written from the incomparably higher vantage point of the great prophets, who despised these lowly practitioners of doubtful arts. In the second instance, in the biblical period this functionary had already evolved into a higher type, the *nabi*, or prophet. Other titles by which the prophet was known were *ro'eh* or *hozeh*, "seer," and *'ish ha'elōhim*, "man of God." The etymology of the word *nabi* is uncertain, being derived by some authorities from the meaning "mutter" and by others from the meaning "announce, proclaim." Probably both derivations are correct, reflecting different stages in the development of prophecy, which began as hypnotic utterances and became the respected announcement of the will of God.

The prophet was not merely the revealer of God to man; he was also man's intercessor before God. In his role as a prophet, Abraham prays for the recovery of Abimelech, the king of Gerar, exactly as in later periods Moses pleads for Miriam and Aaron, and Samuel prays for Saul. So, too, the sinful king Jeroboam implores "the man of God" to intercede for him, and Elijah and Elisha pray for humbler folk in distress (Gen. 20:7, 17; Num. 12:13; Deut. 9:20; I Sam. 15:11; I Kings 13:6; 17:21; II Kings 4:33).

When prophecy became national in scope, we find such diverse figures as Moses, Samuel, Amos, Isaiah and Jeremiah interceding for Israel (Ex. 15:25; 32:11; Deut. 9:18, 26 and elsewhere; I Sam. 7:5–9; 12:19; Jer. 42:2, 20; Amos 7:2, 5; Is. 37:4). Time and again, Jeremiah is commanded not to pray for his people (Jer. 7:16, 11:14, 14:11), proof positive that Israel's doom is sealed.

According to the Rabbis of the Talmud, the ritual of prayer was ordained as a substitute for the Temple sacrifices after the destruction of the sanctuary. But before prayer became fixed in form, "the service of the heart" was spontaneous and individual. In this sense, prayer may be traced back to the prophets as well as to the priests.

In general, the differentiation of function between prophet and priest was never absolute, each continuing to influence the other throughout the history of Israel.

Thus the Hebrew priest remained the custodian of the *Urim ve-Tumim* which were used as oracles to foretell the future. On the other hand, prophets like Samuel, especially in the earlier period, officiated at sacrifices. Moreover, several of the prophets were priests by descent and vocation. It should be added that the fixed ritual of the priesthood kept it within narrow limits. On the one hand, it prevented the priesthood's sinking to the level of irrationality and charlatanism that often characterized the soothsayer. On the other hand, it lacked the dynamic, personal character of the "seer," which reached its apogee in the great Hebrew prophets.

These great-souled teachers of humanity rejected with scorn the suggestion that they had anything in common with the soothsayers or their successors. Yet the techniques of the great prophets testify to their link with these lowly types. Many of the devices used to induce religious ecstasy are to be found among the greatest of the prophets. Frequently, the prophet would produce a sign as evidence of the truth of his message, or dramatize his theme by strange behavior. Nonetheless, these methods continued to lose ground among the great prophets. As time went on, the conviction among them grew that the truth of their revelation was evident in its content and did not require buttressing through ecstatic states or hypnotic seizures.

The successive stages of prophecy among the Hebrews may be reconstructed with tolerable completeness. The most primitive soothsayer or dervish is not described in the Bible, except by indirection. Doubtless, these wonder-working mendicants continued to ply their trade, side by side with the higher types of prophet, exactly as astrologists and fortunetellers are contemporaries of Freud and Einstein. Their activity, however, was limited to personal problems and their influence was almost surely local in extent.

From the ranks of the diviners, some individuals were evolving into leaders of tribal and national importance. These were prophets who spoke in the name of the God of Israel and proclaimed His will to the people. An example is the prophetess Deborah (twelfth century B.C.E.). It was she who nerved a spineless and disunited aggregate of tribes to unite against their common Canaanite foe in the north, inspiring the Hebrew leader Barak to his great victory at the Kishon River (Judg. 4–5). Another was Samuel (eleventh century), who still carried on the personal activities of a diviner, being consulted on matters as petty as the loss of a farmer's asses (I Sam. 9). But Samuel's functions far transcended this lowly role. Like Deborah, he served to unite the tribes against a dangerous enemy, this time the Philistines in the southwest (I Sam. 4:1). He also functioned as a judge and officiant at the rituals conducted at the principal sacred sites (I Sam. 7:15 ff.; 9). His greatest national role was as kingmaker and kingbreaker, a basic factor in the rise and fall of Saul and the ascendancy of David. Such dominating personalities tended to attract followers, who formed guilds called *Bnei Nebiim* (Sons of the Prophets). These schools of disciples traveled with their master and sought to learn his ways. The most gifted among them ultimately became leaders in their own right.

As the monarchy became a fixed institution, a king would attach a prophet to his court, so that he could be conveniently consulted on matters of state. In the very nature of things, these prophets would tend to be subservient to their masters, proclaiming the messages their overlords wanted to hear. The biblical historians have not transmitted the names of these typical court prophets for posterity. Only the memory of a heroic exception to the rule, a member of this group who proclaimed the truth to his royal master without fear, has been preserved to us. It is Nathan, who in his deeply moving parable dared to rebuke King David for his adulterous union with Bath-sheba, which he had sealed with the murder of her husband, Uriah (II Sam. 12:1 ff.).

Playing a role similar to that of the court prophets were others who were not attached to the royal court but remained independent figures. Some of them enjoyed great influence, like Ahijah (I Kings 11:31–39; 14:6–16), who set up Jeroboam's dynasty and later announced its doom. Not being completely dependent on the favor of an individual, these leaders could often be independent in attitude.

Incomparably the greatest of these independent figures was Elijah. He emerged suddenly from the wilderness and disappeared in a heavenly chariot. His meteoric career symbolized the two greatest Hebrew contributions to civilization, two that really are one: the faith in the One God and the passion for righteousness. In his contest with the priests of Baal on Mt. Carmel, he battled uncompromisingly against the degradation of the God-idea in Israel. In his encounter with the weak-willed King Ahab, whose greed had led him to murder, Elijah stood forth as the courageous champion of social justice. Elijah left no writings behind him. His dramatic actions were far more effective than words in recalling the erring people to the Living God and His teaching. For twenty-seven centuries the awesome figure of the prophet of Gilead has fired the imagination of men.

Such intrepidity of spirit was naturally rare. By and large, even the unattached prophets were responsive to the royal will or the pressure of mass opinion. They were the purveyors of popular religion, highly esteemed, well remunerated, and doubtless attracting many disciples. The prophet Elisha began his career as a follower of Elijah, and some of the latter's intransigence and truth-speaking clung to him. Before long, however, his path diverged from that of his great master. He was a wonder-worker, enjoying the gifts of the populace and the adulation of his followers. He fulfilled all too literally the curse pronounced by Elijah on Ahab's house, by anointing Jehu as king. It is true that Jehu's cold-blooded massacre of Ahab's family and followers may have been carried out without Elisha's knowledge or approval. Nonetheless, the prophet's career shows how easily even the personally independent seer tended to accommodate himself to the *status quo.*

Lacking any pretension to spiritual independence were men of the stamp of Zedekiah ben Kenaanah (I Kings 22:11), who was consulted by the kings of Israel and Judah as to the outcome of their projected war against Syria. For reply he fashioned two iron horns and unhesitatingly proclaimed, "Thus saith the Lord, with these you will gore the Arameans to destruction." Nearly two centuries later, Hananiah ben Azzur triumphantly proclaimed, "I have broken the yoke of the king of Babylonia" (Jer. 28:1 ff.). When Jeremiah, who saw the imminent ruin of the Judean kingdom, placed a yoke on his neck to underscore the need for political submission to the Babylonian Empire, Hananiah unhesitatingly smashed the symbol, doubtless to the resounding applause of the mob.

These enormously popular and, by their lights, influential prophets have gone down to infamy because they are described in the Bible as "false prophets," a judgment which not only they but virtually all their contemporaries would indignantly have rejected. This unflattering designation was attached to these well meaning preachers of conventional attitudes only because the Bible is written from the stand-point of a few rebels, who were disliked and despised in their own generation.

Almost from the very beginning of prophecy, there was a tradition of nonconformity in Israel. While the priests traced their functions and prerogatives back to Moses and Aaron, the High Priest, there were some spirits who saw in Moses the great prophet whose life was a flaming protest against slavery, tyranny and immorality. Deborah, Samuel, Nathan and Elijah stood in the same great line of opposition to the supineness, lust and greed of the people and its rulers.

These opponents of the *status quo* became especially articulate in the eighth century, the high-water mark of the kingdoms of Israel and Judah. During almost fifty years, the Northern Kingdom was ruled by perhaps its most capable king, Jeroboam II, while Judah enjoyed the presence of an equally able monarch in Azariah or Uzziah. Between them these kings restored the boundaries of the Solomonic kingdom by successful campaigns to the east, southeast and southwest. The fortifications of Jerusalem were strengthened and the country grew rich because of the spoils of victory, the tolls levied on the great trade routes linking Egypt and the Mesopotamian Valley, and the growing international trade. Luxury grew apace. Winter palaces, summer homes, elaborate furniture and expensive feminine attire became general. A strong sense of national confidence followed in the wake of prosperity. The present was secure; the future would be even more glorious.

The practical leaders, kings, generals, diplomats and merchants alike, did not recognize that the military victories were due to a brief interlude in the international scene, after the Syrian kingdom had fallen and before the new Assyrian power had risen to world dominion. Nor were these realistic observers interested to note that the prosperity was superficial, limited only to the upper levels of society. For the masses, there was ever growing insecurity and outright want. More and more, the independent farmers were being crowded out, their land foreclosed, their children sold into slavery for debt, and they themselves working as tenants on the fields they once had called their own. Moreover, international trade and diplomacy had introduced fashionable foreign cults. Their licentious rites were sapping the moral stamina of the people as surely as economic exploitation was undermining their stake in the country.

These portents of decline, political, social and religious, were so slight that they were noticed by only a few observers, and these, men of little standing or power in their day. In earlier and simpler days, the influence of the prophets had been widely felt. From Moses, through Deborah and Samuel, to Elijah and Elisha, they had been leaders in action. In later times, however, the prophets were looked upon as traitors and enemies of the people, or, more charitably, were dismissed as insane visionaries. As the national decline gathered momentum, the freedom of action of the prophets was restricted, though their freedom of speech could not be denied. Some were driven out, like Amos, or tried for treason, like Micah, or imprisoned, like Jeremiah. Some were killed through lynch law by hired thugs, as was the fate of Jeremiah's colleague, Urijah (Jer. 26:20–24). In rare instances, a member of this group might still influence the course of events. Such was the case with Isaiah, whose efforts were aided both by his aristocratic birth and connections and by the spiritual sensitivity of King Hezekiah. In general, however, these prophets found the door to effective action closed against them.

The period of literary prophecy now began. Several factors conspired to produce this change. The hostility or indifference of the people could not prevent the prophets from expressing God's truth. In Amos' words: "If a trumpet is blown in the city, will not the people tremble ? The Lord has spoken, who can but prophesy ?" (Amos 3:8).

Jeremiah has left a poignant description of the spiritual compulsion that drove him and his fellows to court men's hatred and even to face death:

> O Lord, Thou hast enticed me, and I was enticed,
> Thou hast overcome me, and hast prevailed;
> I am become a laughing stock all the day,
> Every one mocketh me.
> For as often as I speak, I must cry out,
> "Violence and spoil" do I shout,
> Because the word of the Lord is made a reproach unto me,
> A derision, all the day.
> If I say: "I will not make mention of Him,
> Nor speak any more in His name,"
> Then there is in my heart a burning fire,
> Shut up in my bones,
> Which I weary myself to hold in, but cannot (Jer. 20:7–9).

There were other motives for literary prophecy. Because the prophets exerted little influence on their contemporaries, they or their
disciples began writing down their striking utterances out of the very
human desire for vindication in the future (Is. 8:16; *cf.* Job 19:23).
Doubtless, too, there was the wish to instruct young disciples to
carry on the Lord's work, as well as the fear of reprisals for publicly
proclaiming the unpopular truth.

It required extraordinary courage for these men, generally despised
or ignored, to stigmatize the popular and influential prophets of their
day as "false." That position was not reached overnight. In the earlier
period, the rebel prophets did not deny the inspiration of their opponents. In the ninth century, Micaiah ben Imlah bravely contradicts
Zedekiah's optimistic prophecy, but he explains that his opponent
spoke as he did because God Himself has sent a lying spirit to
confuse and mislead the king (I Kings 22:19 ff.). A century later, the
Judean prophet Micah had outgrown this concept. For him, the false
prophets are hirelings, selling their wares to the highest bidder.
"When their maw is fed, they proclaim peace, but against him who
does not feed them, they declare war" (3:5). A hundred years later,
Jeremiah also denies their claim to divine inspiration and stigmatizes
his opponent as a liar (28:15).

The free prophets had no professional stake in their calling; theirs
was not the kind of message for which men paid. They therefore
resented any identification with the conventional prophets. When
Amos was called a *nabi* by the priest at Beth-el, he said: "I am neither
a prophet nor a member of the prophetic guild" (7:14). Yet poles
apart as the free prophets and their conventional rivals were in the
content of their message, their techniques, vocabulary and style were
similar. Their greatest divergence lay in their destiny. History, the
inexorable judge, consigned the conventional prophets to oblivion,
and raised the free prophets to immortality as transcendent spiritual
teachers of the human race. As critics of society and as heralds of a
nobler day, they remain perennially alive.

5. THE MESSAGE OF THE PROPHETS

The sources of prophetic thought, in both its negative and positive
aspects, are of genuine interest today. In attacking the evils of a

complex and decadent civilization, the prophets were convinced that they were not innovators, but rather restorers of the pristine tradition of Israel, which had fallen upon evil days. This conviction was fundamentally correct. Two great experiences had come to the Hebrews at the very inception of their history. As time passed by they would have receded in the national consciousness and ultimately been forgotten. That they have not become vague memories was basically the achievement of the prophets and their disciples.

The first great experience was the bondage in Egypt. The experience of common enslavement and liberation of the Hebrew tribes created a sense of the solidarity of Israel. But that was not all. Ever afterward, Hebrew tradition recalled the period of humiliation and suffering in Egypt, and utilized it to develop in the Hebrews a sense of community with the downtrodden and the oppressed. The prophets could count on this ready sense of identification with the underprivileged and the weak.

The second great factor in molding the life and thought of Israel was the desert period, the age of nomadism. Briefly put, the desert played as significant a role in Hebrew history as did the frontier in American history. Professor Turner has pointed out how the existence of untamed and unclaimed land in the United States throughout the eighteenth century influenced the psychology and institutions of the American people. Equally significant in its effect upon Hebrew ideals was the desert, which lies to the east and south of Palestine.

The influence of the desert, however, was complex, for it bore both a real and an ideal character. First and foremost, there was a period of wandering in the wilderness after the escape from Egypt. The well known biblical tradition places the period of wandering at forty years. Modern scholarship is disposed, however, to assume a much longer period before the settlement in Palestine. Whatever the duration, that period was remembered ever after, and as often happens with memory, was idealized by later generations, under the tutelage of the prophets.

The desert was more than a memory of the past. It was also a present reality to the Hebrews, even after the bulk of the tribes had settled in Palestine and progressed to an agricultural and even an urban economy. In Trans-Jordan and southern Palestine, nomadic conditions prevailed throughout the days of the Hebrew kingdoms and long beyond; in fact, down to the present. In describing the allocation of the territory among the twelve tribes, the Bible states that two or three clans at least remained as shepherds on the eastern bank of the Jordan. Thus the memories of nomadic life in the past were reinforced by the existence of similar conditions in the present. It was in the desert at Sinai that the God of Israel had revealed Himself to His people. His power was limitless, but His favorite abode was still the wilderness, vast and terrifying. Centuries after the Israelites had settled in Palestine, it was to the desert that the prophet Elijah fled, not only to seek escape from persecution but to rekindle his ardor for the God of Israel at His mountain.

The desert life, past and present, in both its real and its ideal aspect, exerted an enduring influence upon Hebraic ideals. The life of the Semitic shepherd, by no means lacking in crudity, possesses some noteworthy traits. Nomadic society is fiercely egalitarian. Within the tribe, complete social equality prevails; there are no kings or nobility, no ranks or classes. When a crisis or war threatens, the individual of superior sagacity or prowess emerges as a leader, but he is emphatically *primus inter pares*. When the emergency is over, he reverts to his normal place. The Book of Judges in the Bible is largely concerned with this type of leadership. It tells, too, of the attempt of an ambitious leader, Abimelech, to establish a hereditary kingship in its stead, an attempt which ended in ignominious failure.

Recent research has demonstrated that this type of primitive democracy was characteristic of all early Semitic societies, indeed of Indo-European groups as well.[10] Under this system, authority is vested in the entire adult male population, which decides questions of war and peace, chooses its leaders and deposes them, and is the supreme legislative and judicial power. In brief, it exercises all the functions of government. Unmistakable traces of this people's assembly (Akkadian *puḥrum*, Syriac *moʿed*) have been discovered in Babylonian epics and Assyrian legal documents, as well as in the Egyptian narrative of Wen-Amon which describes conditions in Syria in the twelfth century B.C.E.

With the evolution of more complex social and economic patterns, and the establishment of a monarchy, the democratic institution of the assembly disappeared, giving way to absolutism in the Babylonian and Assyrian Empires.

The existence of the people's assembly in Israel was overlooked. The terms by which it is referred to in the Bible, *ʿedah* and, secondarily, *kahal*, were erroneously translated "congregation," and thus suggested ecclesiastical connotations wide of the mark. These terms are better translated as "commonalty" or "people's assembly." When a monarchy was established in Palestine, its power was never absolute. During the days of the kingdom the "people's assembly" fought a slowly losing battle to retain its prerogatives. In many respects, the powers of the *'edah* remained effective to the end; in others, its role became largely symbolic. But the democratic impulse, which gave it birth and which in turn it nurtured, was never wiped out in Israel.

As significant as this primitive democracy is the fact that in the nomadic stage there is virtually no private ownership of wealth. The flocks are owned in common, and rights to wells and pasture grounds are vested in the tribe as a whole. Even later when nomadism had given way to settled agricultural life and private ownership of land had become the norm in ancient Israel, as everywhere else, the recollection of the earlier conditions of social equality and common ownership persisted among the Hebrews.

Finally, nomadic society is marked by a strong sense of mutual responsibility. "All for one and one for all" is the law of the tribe. Avenging a crime against any individual member is the duty of the entire tribe. The long-standing feuds among Arab tribes described in the chronicles represent the negative aspect of this conception of tribal brotherhood. The moral code did not extend beyond the tribe, but within the tribe it was all-powerful. Injustice, deception and dishonesty were hotly resented, and indignation found passionate expression in a society where every man was conscious of being the equal of everyone else.

Of themselves these factors—the period of the Egyptian bondage, the nomadic age and the old Semitic inheritance of a primitive democracy—could not have created the basic characteristics of biblical thought. Many peoples have had lowly origins, but most have preferred to forget their past or, better still, to distort it. As for nomadism, it represents a normal stage in social evolution, preceding an agricultural and commercial economy. Among most groups, the end of nomadism meant the surrender of nomadic ideals, and the democracy of the early period disappeared, leaving scarcely a trace.

That the same process did not take place in Israel was due to the activity of the prophets. Their role, as will be noted, is not limited to their own activity and writings. Their influence permeated the biblical

historians, who recounted the national past from the prophetic standpoint. It also deeply affected the legal codes by which Israelite society
was governed. Through history, law and exhortation the Hebrew
prophets made it impossible for their fellow countrymen ever to forget
that they had been slaves and shepherds. The prophets utilized the
Egyptian bondage to inspire the hearts of the people with humanitarian
sympathies. Contemporaries of an advanced and often corrupt culture,
they recalled the simple laws of justice, freedom and equality by which
their nomadic ancestors had lived, and declared those days to have
been the most glorious. "I remember for thee the kindness of thy
youth, the love of thy bridal state, when thou didst go after Me in
the wilderness, in a land unsown" (Jer. 2:1).

In the face of an effete and morally corrupt civilization, nostalgic
advocates of the past were not lacking in ancient Israel. There was a
clan or guild called the Rechabites, who sought mechanically to revert
to a simpler culture, by living only in tents and abstaining from wine,
the building of houses, the sowing of seed and the planting of vineyards. Somewhat similar was the institution of the Nazirites, "con-
secrated to the Lord," who took a vow not to cut their hair, and to
abstain from wine, besides avoiding defilement by contact with the
dead.

The prophets were at one with these groups in regarding the
nomadic period as a glorious tradition. But, unlike the Rechabites
and the Nazirites, the prophets were not ineffectual romantics. On
the contrary, they were creative geniuses of the first order, who knew
how to utilize the past for the vital needs of the present. Part of the
past was dead beyond recall, some of it could be retained, much of it
needed to be extended and deepened, while in other respects it had
to be transcended completely. The prophets did not urge a return to
nomadic conditions, nor did they forbid wine, the dwelling in houses,
or the practice of agriculture. They accepted the inevitable social
transformation of a settled life. But they demanded the practice of
those ideals of nomadism which are valid in every system of society:
its concrete sense of mutual responsibility, its passionate attachment
to freedom, its instinct for human equality. As Hosea put it, "Sow
to yourselves in righteousness, reap according to mercy, break up
your fallow ground. For it is time to seek the Lord, till He come and
cause righteousness to rain upon you" (10:12). How the prophets
treated the various elements of the nomadic way of life is of more

than historical interest. Their procedure points the way to the creative adjustment of tradition to the contemporary scene.

In a nomadic society the strict moral system rested ultimately on the principle of vengeance. When a murder was committed, the relatives of the dead man were enjoined and empowered to exact retribution from the killer and his kinsmen. The prophets transformed vengeance into justice and then proceeded to deepen its meaning to include mercy and loving-kindness. These, they taught, were the attributes of God and must govern the relations of men. More concretely, the Torah limited clan vengeance to cases of premeditated killing and established "the cities of refuge" for accidental murderers (Num. 33:9–34; Josh. 20:1–9). Thus began the long process of bringing human passions and self-interest under the sway of law, a process still incomplete today, as the tragic incidence of violence in our day all too abundantly testifies.

In another direction, also, the prophets transcended nomadic ideals. In the wilderness the clan or tribe is the largest recognized unit, beyond which morality does not apply. Doubtless, there were objective political and economic factors constantly at work breaking down the tribal distinctions in Israel, which were traced back to the twelve sons of the patriarch Jacob. But the process of creating a sense of national solidarity was not easy. Again and again centrifugal forces were in evidence, the most disastrous of which was the division of the kingdom after the death of Solomon. So powerful were these divisive factors that some scholars doubt whether there ever was a united kingdom. They regard the reigns of Saul, David and Solomon as a dual monarchy with a single head.

Whatever the truth of this view, it is undeniable that in stimulating the national spirit that ultimately emerged, the prophets played a significant role. They seldom refer to the individual tribes, and even the prime divisions into north and south they regard as a sin and a catastrophe. Amos was a Judean whose principal activity was in Israel, Hosea an Ephraimite who recalled the Davidic dynasty with affection. Jeremiah, who lived long after the destruction of Samaria, looked forward to the restoration of Ephraim to Divine favor, while Ezekiel foretold of a reunion of Judah with their kinsmen from the house of Joseph. The prophets broke the tribal barriers that hemmed Israel in and were therefore the fathers of Jewish nationalism.

In this process of extending the frontiers of solidarity, the Hebrew prophets went beyond the nation to a vision of a united humanity. Unity did not mean uniformity. For the prophets, nations were integral elements of God's plan, but their relationship to each other must be governed by His law—justice and mutual co-operation were binding upon all. To use a terminology they themselves would not have recognized, the prophets were the fathers of ethico-cultural nationalism. They pointed a way out for mankind between the Scylla of bloodthirsty chauvinism and the Charybdis of lifeless cosmopolitanism, which is sometimes suggested as its remedy. For they demonstrated in their life and thought that national loyalty, properly conceived, is the gateway, not a barrier, to human brotherhood.

It is impossible within the confines of a paper to discuss adequately the insights of Hebrew prophecy in general and the particular contributions of individual figures to such eternal issues as the relationship of God and man, the meaning of history, Israel's role among the nations, the future of society and the character of faith.[11] On these and other problems the prophets have profound contemporary significance, which is all too often ignored through the combination of adulation and neglect which has overtaken the Bible as a whole.

Of the stirring activity of the great prophets, the Bible has preserved only magnificent fragments. It is certain that the prophets whose words have survived must have produced much more than the few hundred verses that have come down to us. There are, moreover, good grounds for assuming that others, less fortunate but perhaps equally worthy, have been completely forgotten. All that has reached us are four books containing prophetic addresses: Isaiah, Jeremiah, Ezekiel, and the Twelve, or Minor, Prophets.

The first three prophetic books follow a broad chronological order. Isaiah belongs to the late eighth century, Jeremiah to the late seventh and early sixth, while Ezekiel is a somewhat younger contemporary of Jeremiah.

Nonetheless, the internal arrangement of these books is not based on historical grounds. Scholars diverge greatly in their views as to the extent of interpolation undergone by each book, Ezekiel in particular being the subject of acute controversy at present. It is, however, universally recognized that beginning with Chapter 40, the Book of Isaiah contains the work of one (and perhaps more than one) unknown prophet, who lived nearly two hundred years later, during the Babylonian Exile. In profundity of thought and grandeur of style, this unknown prophet, often called Deutero-Isaiah, eminently deserves his place by the side of Isaiah ben Amoz, who was probably the mightiest intellect among the prophets of Israel. The closing chapters of the Book of Jeremiah consist of oracles against the neighboring nations, which are probably from another hand. The bulk of the book, however, reveals the soul of Jeremiah with a poignant clarity unmatched by any other biblical author.

That historical considerations were not the guiding principle in the arrangement of the prophetic books becomes especially clear in the fourth book of this group. The Hebrew title, the Twelve, is apter than the common English designation, the Minor Prophets. For several of these are minor only in point of size, not significance. The Talmud correctly indicates the reason for joining the work of these twelve prophets, "because each is small, it might have been lost."[12]

This statement is a clue to a principle which has not been adequately evaluated in the arrangement of biblical writings. Since each document was preserved on a scroll, the scribe's tendency was to write the longer text first and then append, often on the remaining section of the same scroll, shorter material, whether or not related in theme. Thus also in the Koran, the longer suras, recognized as later, come first, and the shorter chapters, indubitably the oldest visions of Mohammed, come last. This principle, which sheds light on the organization of material within each biblical book, may explain the position of the Minor Prophets after Isaiah, Jeremiah, and Ezekiel.

The Twelve Prophets include the two earliest literary prophets, Amos and Hosea (middle of the eighth century), and Micah, a younger contemporary of Isaiah. These prophets are among the greatest of the immortal company. The Book of Jonah is an acute satire on the attitude of the popular chauvinist prophets which takes the historical figure of Jonah ben Amittai as its hero to drive home a profound and lasting truth. Others, like Joel, Obadiah, Nahum, Habakkuk, and Zephaniah, belong to the middle period, while Haggai, Zechariah, and Malachi are representative of the last stage of prophecy in the Persian period, shortly before its disappearance.

These four books, containing the addresses and writings of the prophets, are preceded in the Hebrew Bible by four historical books, Joshua, Judges, Samuel, and Kings, called the Former Prophets. Together, these eight books constitute the second section of the Bible, *Nebiim*, or Prophets. The four historical books contain the history of

the Hebrew people from their entrance into Palestine until the Babylonian Exile. Superb examples of historical narrative, these works
interpret the past experience of Israel in terms of prophetic ideals.
They are far more concerned with the religious conditions and the
activity of the prophets than with political and economic factors or
military and diplomatic events. Thus, the two greatest kings of Judah
and Israel, Uzziah and Jeroboam the Second, are dismissed in fourteen verses (II Kings 14:23–15:7), while the prophet Elijah receives
more than five chapters (I Kings 17–21) and Elisha eight (II Kings
2–9).

The anonymous historians who created these works, from still
older sources now lost, were, on the one hand, disciples of the prophets. On the other, they were deeply influenced by the Torah and
its norms for national life, as will be noted below. Hence the historical
books, or Former Prophets, which continue the history of Israel
begun in the Torah and supply the background for the activity of
the prophets, are an ideal link between these two spiritual tendencies.

Both Torah and prophecy find their foil and their complement in
the third strand of Hebrew thought, called *Wisdom*.

6. The Voice of Wisdom

The Hebrew priests and prophets have their analogues among all
the Semitic peoples, as we have seen. Fundamentally, however, their
work was concerned with the life of Israel and therefore it reflects
specific national characteristics. Wisdom, on the other hand, is broadly
human, dealing with the individual as such. It is therefore even more
closely linked to the culture pattern of the ancient Orient.

The connotations of the Hebrew *Hokmah* are far wider than the
English rendering "Wisdom" would imply. *Hokmah* may be defined
as a realistic approach to the problems of life, including all the
practical skills and the technical arts of civilization. The term *hakam*,
"sage, wise man," is accordingly applied to the artist, the musician,
the singer. Bezalel, the skilled craftsman who built the Tabernacle
and its appointments in the wilderness, as well as all his associates,
are called "wise of heart" (Ex. 28:3; 35:31; 36:1). Weavers (Ex. 35:25),
goldsmiths (Jer. 10:9), and sailors (Ez. 27:8; Ps. 107:27) are *hakamim*.

Above all, the term is applied to the arts of poetry and song, vocal
and instrumental. The song in ancient Israel was coextensive with life

itself. Harvest and vintage, the royal coronation and the conqueror's return, courtship and marriage, were all accompanied by song and dance. The earliest traditions dealing with the exploits of tribal and national heroes were embodied in song. Snatches of these poems are preserved in the later prose narratives, some being explicitly quoted from older collections, like *The Book of the Wars of the Lord* (Num. 21:14) and *The Book of the Just* (Josh. 10:13; II Sam. 1:18; I Kings 8:53 in the Greek).

The guilds of singers in the Temple, the women skilled in lamentation (Jer. 9:16), the magicians and soothsayers with all their occult arts, are described by the same epithet, "wise" (Gen. 40:8; I Kings 5:10–12; Is. 44:25; Jer. 9:16). Skill in the conduct of war and in the administration of the state (Is. 10:13; 29:14; Jer. 49:7) is also an integral aspect of Wisdom.

All these phases have disappeared with the destruction of the material substratum of ancient Hebrew life. What has remained of Wisdom is its literary incarnation, concerned not so much with the arts of living as with developing a sane, workable attitude toward life. To convey its truths, Wisdom created an educational method and a literature generally couched in the form of the *mashal*, the parable or proverb, brief, picturesque, unforgettable.

It may be noted that the third section of the Bible, called *Ketubim*, the Sacred Writings or Hagiographa, is not a miscellaneous collection, but, on the contrary, has an underlying unity. Basically, it is the repository of Wisdom. The Book of Psalms is a great collection of religious poetry, most of which was chanted at the Temple service with musical accompaniment. Both the composition and the rendition of the Psalms required a high degree of that technical skill which is *Hokmah*. Moreover, in point of content, many Psalms (like 37, 49, 112, 128) have close affinities with the proverbial lore of the Wisdom teachers.

Three other books, Proverbs, Job and Ecclesiastes, obviously belong in a Wisdom collection. So does Ben Sira, or Ecclesiasticus, which was not included in the canon of Scripture, because it clearly betrayed its late origin. Lamentations is a product of *Hokmah* in its technical sense. The Song of Songs is included, not merely because it is traditionally ascribed to King Solomon, the symbol and traditional source of Hebrew Wisdom, but because these songs, whether sung at weddings or at other celebrations, were also a branch of technical song.

It has also been suggested that the Song of Songs entered the Wisdom collection because it was regarded as an allegory of the relationship of love subsisting between God and Israel. From this point of view, it would be a *mashal*, which means "allegory" or "fable" as well as "proverb." The Book of Daniel, the wise interpreter of dreams, obviously is in place among the Wisdom books.

The reason for the inclusion of Ruth and Esther is not quite as evident. Perhaps they were included here because both reveal practical sagacity, Esther in saving her people from destruction and Ruth in securing a desirable husband! The three closing books of the Bible, which survey history from Adam to the Persian period, are really parts of one larger work, Chronicles-Ezra-Nehemiah. It is possible that they may have been included in the Wisdom section merely because they were placed at the end as an appendix to the Bible as a whole. The place of these last-named books in *Ketubim* has also been explained differently. It has been suggested that Chronicles (with its adjuncts) is really an appendix to Psalms, since one of its principal concerns is to describe in detail the establishment of the Temple ritual. Ruth may then have been a supplement to the Psalms, since it concludes with the genealogy of David, the traditional author of the Psalter. Esther may be an appendix to Chronicles, the style of which it seeks to imitate. These links, however tenuous they may appear to the Western mind, will not seem farfetched to anyone familiar with the Semitic logic of association, evidence for which is plentiful in the redaction of the Bible and in the organization of the Mishnah and the Talmud.

Wisdom literature in its narrower sense, as it appears in Proverbs or Ecclesiastes, for example, impresses the modern reader as the most secular element in the Bible, being based on clear, realistic observation and logical inference and deduction, rather than on tradition and revelation. Yet in an age permeated by the religious consciousness, the devotee of Wisdom was both unable and unwilling to surrender his claim to Divine inspiration. Thus the *hakam* took his place by the side of the *kohen*, who derived his authority from the Divine Law revealed by Moses, and the *nabi* who spoke out under the direct impact of the Divine. Hence the "wise man," in all the ramifications of the term, could be described, as was Bezalel the craftsman, as "filled with the spirit of God, with wisdom, understanding, knowledge and all manner of skill" (Ex. 31:3).

This conception was given a metaphysical form as well. Each cultivator of Wisdom is endowed with a portion of the transcendental, Divine Wisdom, dwelling in Heaven. This supernal *Hokmah* is described in various poetic figures. Wisdom is the instrument by which God has created the world, or the pattern He has followed in fashioning the universe. She is the beloved playmate of His leisure hours, or the gracious hostess inviting men on the highway to enter her seven-pillared palace (Pr. 8:1 ff.; 8:22 ff.; 9:1 ff.; Ecclus. 1:8 ff. and *passim*). This Hebrew conception of Wisdom as a semidivine figure doubtless draws upon ancient Oriental ideas. In turn it has had wide influence upon such varied elements of thought as Philonian philosophy, Rabbinic speculation, Christian theology, and Gnosticism.

Biblical Wisdom itself was a true Oriental product that had been cultivated for centuries throughout the lands of the Fertile Crescent, Egypt, Palestine, Syria and Babylonia. Everywhere its purposes were similar: the preparation of youth for success in government, agriculture and commerce. Thus Wisdom was part of the cultural inheritance of the Semitic-Hamitic world, which the Hebrews shared with their neighbors and kinsmen.

The tradition that King Solomon was "the wisest of men" and the author of the Song of Songs, Proverbs and Ecclesiastes is no longer airily dismissed by scholars as a mere figment of the folk imagination. It is seen to reflect the historical fact that the intensive cultivation of Wisdom goes back to his reign, when wide international contacts and internal prosperity contributed to the flowering of culture. Its origins are even more ancient. Embedded in the historical books are gems of Wisdom literature older than Solomon: Jotham's biting fable of the trees and the thornbush (Judg. 9:7), Nathan's parable of the poor man's lamb (II Sam. 12:1), the melancholy comment on the transitoriness of life by the "wise woman of Tekoa" (II Sam. 14:14), not to speak of the later parable of King Joash (II Kings 14:9). Moreover, it is increasingly recognized that the Books of Psalms, Proverbs, and the Song of Songs are anthologies containing a great deal of pre-exilic material, for which parallels of considerable antiquity have been discovered in Babylonia, Syria and Egypt.

Nonetheless, the Golden Age of Hebrew Wisdom literature is the first half of the Second Temple period, roughly between the fifth and the second century B.C.E. This flowering was fostered by both positive and negative factors. After the Babylonian Exile, a far reaching change had taken place in the spirit of the people. It was a chastened folk that returned to Jerusalem after the Proclamation of Cyrus, to rebuild the shattered foundations of the national life. The tragedy of exile had convinced them of the truth of the prophetic message and had imbued them with the desire to fulfil the will of God as revealed in the Torah. Hence, one of the first concerns of the returning settlers was the rebuilding of the Temple. Here, as has been noted, the priests resumed their function as officiants at the ritual, but the spiritual hegemony passed to the scholars, the expounders of the Law.

Prophecy, like the written Torah, had passed its creative phase. It declined and finally ceased to function in the days of the Second Temple. Ultimately the impulse reasserted itself in a strange, "underground" form, to produce the apocalyptic writings. Various factors contributed to the disappearance of prophecy. The postexilic period as a whole was well described as "an age of small things," with little to stir men's hearts to ecstasy or to wrath. There was neither stimulus nor need for the grand prophetic vision. The Jews were a struggling community under the domination of successive foreign rulers, Persian, Greek, Egyptian and Syrian. The unyielding insistence of the prophets upon national righteousness as the basic premise of national well-being was now an accepted element of Jewish thought, but it was neither particularly novel nor especially relevant to the problems of the hour. For there was little prospect of national greatness and power for Jewish life either in the present or in the recognizable future.

A fundamental revolution in men's thinking now took place. The ancient Semitic outlook, which was shared by the Hebrews, had placed the well-being or decline of the group, be it family, tribe or nation, in the center of men's thoughts. This collective viewpoint now gave way to a heightened interest in the individual. Prosperity and freedom for a tiny weak people was not likely to be achieved in a world of mighty empires. All that remained was for each human being to strive to attain his personal happiness. What qualities were needed, what pitfalls had to be avoided by a man seeking to achieve success and a respectable place in society? To these perennially modern and recurrent questions, Wisdom now addressed itself with zeal and skill.

The Wisdom literature of the First Temple was sedulously collected and augmented. All signs point to its cultivation by the conservative, upper classes in society, just as the Oral Law was the particular province of the lower and middle classes. These upper strata of society, even the high priestly families among them, whose position and income derived from their services in the Temple, were concerned less with the Will of God than with the way of the world. Their goal in education was utilitarian, the training of youth for careers as merchant princes, landed gentry or government officials. To satisfy this need, a special type of preceptor arose, principally, if not exclusively, in Jerusalem, the capital. Like the Sophists in classical Greek, who performed a similar function for the upper class youth of Greek society, these teachers taught "Wisdom" (Hebrew *Hokmah*, Greek *Sophia*).

The Hebrew Wisdom teachers sought to inculcate the virtues of hard work, zeal, prudence, sexual moderation, sobriety, loyalty to authority, and religious conformity—all the elements of a morality making for worldly success. What is more, they did not hesitate to urge less positive virtues on their youthful charges, such as holding one's tongue, and even bribery, as aids in making one's way:

> Where words abound, sin is not wanting,
> But he that controls his tongue is a wise man. (Prov. 10:19)
>
> A man's gift makes room for him,
> It brings him before great men. (Prov. 18:16)

In brief, this lower, conventional, practical Wisdom represented a hardheaded, matter-of-fact, "safe and sane" approach to the problems of living. Of this practical Wisdom the literary repositories are Proverbs in the Bible and Ben Sira or Ecclesiasticus, in the Apocrypha. Both works contain aphorisms and injunctions and observations on life designed to direct youth. Proverbs is more original in style; Ben Sira more derivative. On the other hand, while the literary unit in Proverbs is generally a single verse, Ben Sira has expanded it to a larger form, bordering on our essay.

Among the many preceptors of Wisdom, however, were some whose restless minds refused to be satisfied with these practical goals of what may be termed the lower Wisdom. They sought to penetrate to the great abiding issues: the meaning of life, the purpose of creation, the nature of death, the mystery of evil. In grappling with these ultimate problems they insisted on using the same instruments of observation and common sense that they applied to daily concerns, rather than religious authority and conventional doctrines. Like so many rationalist minds since their day, however, they found unaided human reason incapable of solving these issues. Some, no doubt, finally made their peace with the traditional religion of their day. But others, more tough minded, refused to take on faith what their reason could not demonstrate. Hence their writings reveal various degrees and types of skepticism and heterodoxy.

Several of these devotees of the higher or speculative Wisdom were highly fortunate, for it was given them to transmute the frustration and pain of their quest into some of the world's greatest masterpieces, notably Job and Kohelet. Job is the immortal protest of man against the mystery of suffering. Kohelet expresses the tragic recognition that the basic truth of the universe is beyond men's ken, so that all that remains in life is the achievement of happiness, itself illusory and fleeting. Thus, Wisdom, which began with practical and down-to-earth matters, ended by grappling with the profoundest and most abiding issues of life.

7. The Higher Unity of the Bible

The three principal types of religious and cultural activity in ancient Israel were obviously distinct in purpose, emphasis, and technique. Torah and prophecy were principally concerned with the group; Wisdom almost exclusively with the individual. On the other hand, Torah and Wisdom had their gaze fixed on the present, while the prophets used their vision of the ideal world of the future as a touchstone for evaluating the real world of today.

For the priests, ritual was the central feature of the religious life. The Wisdom teachers regarded the Temple service as part of the accepted order of things, but not as especially significant. The prophets, on the other hand, saw righteousness as the goal of religion, and differed among themselves in their attitudes toward ritual. In the brief Book of Amos no favorable reference to sacrifice is to be found. On the other hand, the prophet Ezekiel, himself a priest, drew up a manual on Temple worship after the destruction of the sanctuary. Midway between them stood Isaiah and probably most of the prophets. Isaiah sharply criticized the unholy alliance of piety and plunder in his day. On the other hand, he recognized the Temple in Jerusalem as the seat of God's glory, where he himself had experienced his inaugural vision (ch. 6). In the critical hour when Sennacherib besieged Jerusalem, Isaiah boldly declared that the city of God was inviolate. For the moderate Prophets, ritual was not an end in itself; if it proved a gateway to righteousness, it was acceptable; otherwise it was a snare and a delusion.

It is clear that the activities of priest, prophet, and sage were not carried on in mutual isolation or antagonism. On the contrary, there was a very lively intellectual interchange among them. As a result, the Bible is pervaded by a higher unity, all the more striking because it rests upon the diversity of its component elements.

Doubtless, there were priests in Israel whose interests were purely professional, and for whom religious duty was exhausted in the punctilious fulfillment of the ritual. But the Torah is not the work of priests of this character. On the contrary, it is deeply impregnated with the prophetic spirit. It is profoundly significant that the Torah bears the name of Moses, who is the first of the prophets, "trusted in God's house" beyond any of his successors (Num. 12:7, 8). The great moment of Moses' life is the Divine Revelation on Sinai. His hope for his people is "would that all the Lord's people were prophets" (Num. 11:29)!

Moreover, the Torah goes beyond the abstract ethical and religious demands of the prophets and translates these ideals into concrete institutions. The Sabbath law for the protection of the slaves, the six-year period of bond service, the sabbatical year of release from debt, the Jubilee Year for the restoration of real property, the ordinances regarding poor relief, these and countless other elements of biblical legislation are a signal contribution to righteousness in human affairs. All these are explicitly or implicitly motivated by the memories of Egyptian bondage and by the ideals of equality and justice inherited from the wilderness period, the recollection of which the prophets kept alive in the consciousness of the people.

The Ten Commandments are proclaimed in the name of God, who is described as the Redeemer of Israel from the land of bondage, and not as the Creator of heaven and earth, a fact that the medieval philosopher Judah Ha-Levi noted in another connection. The Sabbath rest was enjoined not only upon the Jew, but also upon the slave, "for thou wast a slave in the land of Egypt." The stranger, who in those days, even more than today, had no rights, was not to be oppressed, nor his life embittered, "for ye know the soul of the stranger, for ye were strangers in the land of Egypt" (Ex. 23:9). On the contrary, as is emphasized no less than thirty-six times in the Torah, one law was to be binding upon the alien and the citizen alike. The Golden Rule, "Thou shalt love thy neighbor as thyself" (Lev. 19:18), has its even nobler counterpart in the same chapter, which commands: "And if a stranger sojourn with thee in your land, ye shall not do him wrong. The stranger that sojourneth with you shall be unto you as the home-born among you, and thou shalt love him as thyself; for ye were strangers in the land of Egypt: I am the Lord your God" (Lev. 19:33 f.). Undoubtedly, the persistent effort to limit slavery and the hostility toward the institution manifested by biblical law are the end products of the Hebrews' experience with Egyptian slavery. With extraordinary courage, one biblical code goes further and demands that the Hebrew should not hate the Egyptian, "for thou wast a stranger in his land" (Deut. 23:8). As the Bible became accepted as sacred, these doctrines exerted a continuous educative influence upon the people, giving them a sympathy for the oppressed and a passionate attachment to liberty which was intensified by their later tribulations.

Obviously, these exalted ideals were never universally realized and were often flouted in life. But their enunciation is itself a great achievement. We have only to contrast the Bible with such exalted writings as Plato's *Republic*, which pictures the ideal state of the future as protected by a standing army perpetually on guard against the non-Greek barbarians, or Aristotle's *Politics*, with its reasoned defense of human slavery.

In sum, the spirit of the Torah is best described as "priestly-prophetic." The world's most categorical ethical ideals are to be found in the Decalogue, side by side with ritual enactments. Within the Book of Leviticus, which contains the priestly regulations, the Holiness Code (chs. 17–26) is embedded. Aside from countless ritual ordinances, this code contains the Golden Rule, the demand for loving the stranger, the Jubilee legislation to prevent monopoly in land, and the great commandment which highlights the cardinal sin of the twentieth century, "You shall not stand idly by the blood of your neighbor" (Lev. 19:16, 18, 33 f.; 25:1–34).

The interplay of both prophetic and priestly elements is particularly evident in Deuteronomy. The insistence upon a single sanctuary (ch. 12 and *passim*) doubtless harmonized with the interests of the Jerusalemite priesthood, though it had obvious religious and moral advantages. On the other hand, the highly varied legislation throughout the book (as *e.g.*, 15, 20, 21, 27) reflects a sympathy for the poor, a hatred of tyranny, and a compassion for the weak, the underprivileged and the alien that is genuinely prophetic in spirit.

Prophecy likewise reveals an intimate relationship with both Torah and Wisdom. The fundamental emphasis of the biblical historians is on the prophetic doctrine that disaster is the inescapable consequence of sin and that national well-being rests upon national righteousness. Interestingly enough, this doctrine is formulated most clearly in Wisdom literature: "Righteousness exalts a people but sin is the shame of a nation" (Prov. 14:34). In retelling the history of Israel in the spirit of the prophets, the Books of Joshua, Judges, Samuel and Kings continue the historical narratives in the Torah. Hence, many scholars refer to the Pentateuch and Joshua as the Hexateuch, while some go even further and include all the historical books under the name Octateuch.

The predilection of the prophets for the techniques of Wisdom needs no elaborate demonstration. The prophets used parables and apothegms with telling effect. Most of their oracles and other addresses are poetic in structure and much of it must have been chanted to musical accompaniment. Prayers and psalms are by no means uncommon in the prophetic books. Moreover, the searching issues that troubled the unconventional Wisdom teachers could not have been overlooked by the profound spirit of the prophets. Jeremiah, Ezekiel and Deutero-Isaiah, in particular, grappled with the agonizing problem of the undeserved suffering of the righteous, both individually and in the collective experience of Israel.

The attitude of Wisdom to the Torah and prophets has already been indicated. Doubtless the Sages looked askance at the emotional basis of prophetic activity, and were skeptical about the prophets' extravagant hopes for the future. Nevertheless, prophetic attitudes penetrated even into their rationalistic circles. Witness the hatred of injustice in Ecclesiastes and Job, the emphasis upon morality as the heart of religion in Psalms 50 and 81, the triumphant affirmation of the coming Divine Judgment on evil in Psalms 75 and 82, and the passionate yearning for purity and freedom from sin throughout the Book of Psalms.

The Bible possesses a unity fashioned out of every current of

Hebrew thought and action. It is inexhaustible in the wealth and variety of its contents. Priest, prophet, historian, poet and sage rub shoulders with one another within its covers, as they actually did in their own lifetimes, differing, arguing and influencing one another and unconsciously collaborating in producing the greatest spiritual force in the history of mankind. The prophets' magnificent faith in God's justice, and Job's equally noble protest against undeserved suffering, the Psalmists' mystical absorption in God, and the practical counsel of the Sages in Proverbs, the love of life and the life of love hymned in the Song of Songs and in the melancholy reflections of Ecclesiastes—all were authentic expressions of the genius of Israel.

8. The Bible as Literature

The nobility and eternal relevance of the Bible are heightened by its superb literary form. The Bible is a library of masterpieces written by men who are artists not for art's sake, a conception which they would not have favored had they known it, but for life's sake. They were impelled by a single purpose, to tell their message as directly and effectively as possible. With the sure instinct of genius, they utilized the literary techniques and forms of their day and developed them to perfection. Unbeknown to themselves, they produced a gallery of classics in which deceptive simplicity conceals the highest art.

Tolstoy has called the Joseph saga in Genesis the greatest narrative in the world, unrivaled for dramatic power and psychological finesse. Throughout the four books of the Torah in which Moses is the guiding spirit, no formal description of the great leader is to be met with, except for one brief passage where he is described as the "humblest of men" (Num. 12:3). Nonetheless, the character of Moses is one of the most vivid ever drawn. The trajectory of his career is traced through mounting trials and crises with an art as consummate as it is unconscious, an art that Boswell might well have envied but could not surpass.

Over and beyond the sheer perfection of its elements is the architectural structure of Genesis. The majestic opening verse, "In the beginning, God created the heaven and the earth," takes the cosmos as its background. Immediately thereafter, with characteristic Jewish realism, heaven is let alone and the narrative turns to the earth.

Concerning itself with the human race, it traces the origin of mankind, its trials and sins culminating in the Flood, from which only Noah and his family survive (2–9). The offspring of two of his sons, Ham and Japhet, are briefly listed and dismissed (10:1–20), so that the descendants of Shem may be treated at greater length (10:21 ff.; 11:10 ff.). This serves as a preface to the career of Abraham, with whom the history of Israel begins (12–24). Of his two sons, Ishmael's descendants are briefly noted (25:12 ff.), and the narrative concentrates on Isaac (25:19–27). He, too, has two sons, Esau whose stock is dismissed in one chapter (36), and Jacob, whose personal fortunes and family misfortunes become the fundamental theme of the rest of the book. The Joseph saga then prepares the way for the bondage in Egypt, the liberation by Moses and the giving of the Law at Sinai. With unsurpassed literary art, the Book of Genesis has thus linked Creation and Revelation.

The historian-author of Samuel has painted an unforgettable portrait in the life story of Saul, with its bright early promise and the cloud of mental instability and ruin later descending upon him. At least equally notable is the vivid narrative of David's life with its bright ascendancy, its glorious noonday and its tragic dusk. Surrounding these two principal figures stands an immortal gallery of human nature, Samuel and Jonathan, Michal and Bath-Sheba, Nathan and Solomon, Absalom and Barzillai. Ruth has been described as the most perfect short story ever written. Jonah has been justly called by C. H. Cornill the "noblest book in the Old Testament." For sheer storytelling art, it belongs with the Elijah cycle and Esther. The memoirs of Nehemiah are a revealing picture of the period of the Restoration, with the problems strikingly similar to our own. Oratory has suffered in esteem in modern times, but the tenderness of Deuteronomy, the majesty of Isaiah, and the heartrending pathos of Jeremiah will never lose their power, because they speak from the heart and deep calls to deep.

The poetry of the Bible is perhaps its crowning glory. The moral fervor of the prophets, the passionate tenderness of the love lyrics in the Song of Songs, the grief of Lamentations, and all the human impulses reflected in the Book of Psalms have never been surpassed and rarely equaled. Faith and doubt, victory and defeat, hatred and doom, rebellion and submission, all find matchless expression in the Psalter, the world's most beloved songster. The nature poetry in

Psalms (19 and 104) and the great God-speeches in Job have been acclaimed by figures as various as Herder and von Humboldt. The common sense of Proverbs will never cease to charm as well as to instruct young and old, while mature minds grappling with the mystery of life and the existence of evil will find both comradeship and comfort in Ecclesiastes and Job. The one was called by Renan, "the most charming book ever written by a Jew." The other was pronounced by Carlyle, "the grandest book ever written with pen."

Earlier generations were admonished with regard to the Bible, "Turn it over and over, for everything is in it, and grow old and gray in it, but do not swerve from it."[13] That judgment is vindicated anew, as men penetrate ever more deeply into its spirit. For the Bible's goal is righteousness, its weapon is truth, and its achievement is beauty.

NOTES

1. Baba Batra 15a.
2. Hagigah 13b.
3. Yebamot 49b.
4. Baba Kamma 2b and parallel passages.
5. Berakot 31b and parallel passages.
6. Shabbat 63a and parallel passages.
7. Reading, with the Kethib, *ribbo' tōrōthai*.
8. Sanhedrin 21b.
9. Cf. R. Gordis, *Judaism for the Modern Age* (New York, 1955), Section II, pp. 127-214.
10. Cf. the next study in this volume, "Primitive Democracy in Ancient Israel."
11. For more detailed evaluations of the life and work of the Prophets, see the studies below on Amos, Hosea, Isaiah and Micah.
12. Baba Batra 15b.
13. Abot 5:22.

2. PRIMITIVE DEMOCRACY IN ANCIENT ISRAEL

I

One of the most interesting by-products of recent trends in Biblical studies has been the rehabilitation of several Biblical writers, whose reputation for credibility had fallen very low during the past half century. Thus, the Chronicler was dismissed as a Midrash on the Book of Kings, who was not needed when he repeated the same sources and was not believed when he differed from, or supplemented, the older historian. Basically, he had concocted an artificial construction of Biblical history, reading into First Temple days the characteristic religious institutions of the Second Temple. Recent scholars, on the other hand, like Alt, von Rad, Albright and Noth now approach the material in Chronicles with new respect for its credibility, or at least for its importance.[1]

The same process of restitution is due the sections in the Pentateuch attributed by the critics to the "Priestly Code." These narratives of the Wilderness period were described as a *Rückbildung* from Second Temple days and the legal enactments were discounted as lacking any historical validity for pre-exilic Israel. In accordance with the dominant critical view of post-exilic Judaism as a church-state, the Biblical terms *'ēdāh* and *kāhāl* were taken to mean "the community of Israel collectively regarded as a congregation."[2] According to Driver, P's aim is to present "an ideal picture of the Mosaic Age, constructed indeed upon a genuine traditional basis, but so conceived as to exemplify the principles by which an ideal theocracy should be regulated."[3] Pfeiffer, in his indispensable *Introduction*, summarizes the critical view by describing P as "the constitution of the Jewish theocratic state," whose purpose it was "to make a holy nation out of the Jews, a church within the Empire," "a sort of monastic order." Pfeiffer naturally has a low opinion of P's credibility: "even though some of the characters in P's story, like Moses, are genuine, the work

45

as a whole is dogmatic rather than historical. It is an account of the establishment of an imaginary Utopia."[4] In similar vein, George Foot Moore, commenting on Judges 20:1, disregards the obviously primitive character of the incidents of the concubine of Gibeah and of the war of reprisal against Benjamin, and says, "Every word betrays the post-exilic author—the congregation, the religious assembly takes the place of the people."[5]

This conception of the late date of the oldest Biblical traditions was first shaken, shortly after its classic formulation, through the discovery of Babylonian parallels to the Creation Story, the Flood and other Biblical traditions and allusions. When the evidence could no longer be ignored, it was explained that during the Babylonian Exile the Jews had access to Babylonian sources whence they drew these traditions and some mythological references. But the mass of material recently accumulating in Ugaritic literature from the second millennium has made this explanation increasingly untenable.[6]

The breach in the hyper-critical attitude toward the Pentateuchal narratives has continued to widen. The portable Tabernacle and the Ark of the Covenant, originally dismissed as inventions of Second Temple writers, were now discovered to have authentic parallels in the portable Ark of the nomadic Arabs,[7] and to be completely out of keeping with a sedentary agricultural society in Canaan. Thus, as Albright has indicated, a Mosaic date for the Ark and the Tabernacle, both as a whole and in many of the details, provides the best theory for their origin.[8]

The elaborate sacrificial system enjoined in Leviticus was once confidently explained as a late construction based upon the Second Temple cult, manifestly out of question for an early period. But the Tariff of Sacrificial Dues found at the Carthaginian Temple of Baal Zephon[9] speaks of the *'ōlāh*, *šᵉlāmīm* and the *minḥāh*. These sacrifices are obviously far older than the 5th or 4th century date of the inscription, and doubtless reflect the age-old practice of the mother country, Phoenicia. This conclusion is now validated by Ugaritic literature where *šᵉlāmīm* and other offerings are referred to.[10]

As a matter of fact, it should have been recognized long ago that this conception of the post-exilic Jewish community as a church-state rested on exceedingly weak foundations. The new community was so little a church that it rebelled at least once against Persian suzerainty under Zerubbabel, and enjoyed sufficient autonomy to have its own coins with the designation יהד in Hebrew letters.[11] The group antagonisms revealed by the Book of Nehemiah are ethnic rather than religious and his complaint about intermarriage is that "the children spake half in the speech of Ashdod and could not speak in the language of the Jews" (Neh. 13:24). This people, too, carried on a long and bitter war against the Seleucide empire, not only for religious freedom but for political independence as well. While the Temple cult was, to be sure, carried on by priests, as in all ancient religions, a new democratic, non-hierarchical institution, the synagogue, had come into being. Within its confines, there grew up the imposing corpus of the Oral Law, by which the masses of the people lived and in the development of which the priests played no part. The sects of the Second Commonwealth differed politically and socially as well as religiously. Obviously religion penetrated every aspect of the national life, but the life was national, not merely ecclesiastical. In sum, whether the Jewish community of Second Temple days enjoyed independence, as under the Hasmoneans and Herod, or merely autonomy, as under Persian, Ptolemaic, Seleucide and Roman suzerainty, it constituted a religio-ethnic group, a people.

II

Thus, there was no *ecclesia* in the post-exilic period which could serve as a prototype for the Biblical author's conception of Israel in pre-exilic and even in Canaanite days. A careful study of the Biblical usage of *'ēdāh* and *kāhāl* makes it clear that in the vast majority of instances, neither represents a *congregatio*. Far from being an artificial construction of a later age, these terms shed light upon the earliest form of community life in Israel. A clue to their true meaning may be found in the usage of a kindred Semitic community, that of Mesopotamia, studied by Thorkild Jacobsen.[12]

Defining democracy as a form of government in which internal sovereignty resides in a large proportion of the governed, namely in all free adult male citizens without distinction of fortune or class (p. 159), he points out that in historic times (roughly from the second millennium onward), autocracy prevailed in Mesopotamia, with one individual uniting in himself the legislative, judicial and executive powers (p. 160). All the more remarkable, therefore, are the unmistakable evidences of democracy in that civilization. Thus, in the Assyrian merchant colonies in Asia Minor, the judicial power was vested in a general assembly of all the colonists, *kārum ṣaḥir rabi*, "the colony, (lit. the quay), young and old." Even in the centralized structure of the old Babylonian Empire, where the king is the supreme judge, the town (*alum*) or the assembly (*puḥrum*) heard cases, cited the parties and executed judgment in trials (p. 162).

It is obvious that this democratic spirit in the judiciary institution is thoroughly at variance with the dominant autocracy. Was it the result of new tendencies just beginning to gain a foothold, or the vestigial remains of earlier times? Jacobsen decides very plausibly that the latter is the case, for he finds evidence that in the older traditions, the assembly enjoys greater powers than merely the judicial. Thus the assembly in the days of the kings of Akkad chose the king (p. 165), while the Gilgamesh epic indicates that King Agga of Kish does not declare war until the "elders" of Uruk and the men of the town have given their approval.

Moreover, Mesopotamian mythology, which pictures the gods in human form, describes an assembly of all the gods (*i-puuh-ri kala i-li, p. 167*). When a decision had to be reached, the gods would assemble, stimulate their faculties by strong drink and then take to the business in hand, with the *ilu rabiutum*, "the great (or senior) gods" having the first, but by no means the only voice. The final decision lay in a group of "seven gods who determine destiny."

We may supplement Jacobsen's data by citing the graphic picture of the assembly of the gods as the basic source of authority, which is given in the Babylonian epic *Enûma Elish*. After both Ea and Anu have failed to conquer Ti'âmat, Anshar, father of the gods, charges Marduk with the task. Marduk exults in the words of his father, but he demands that the assembly of gods delegate its authority to him (Note the words in italics below):

"If I am to be your champion,
To vanquish Ti'âmat and to keep you alive,
Summon a meeting, make my lot unsurpassable and proclaim it.
When ye are joyfully seated in the Assembly Hall,
May I through the utterance of my mouth determine the destinies, *instead
    of you.*
Whatever I create shall remain unaltered,
The command of my lips shall not return (void), it shall not be changed."[13]

The condition laid down by Marduk recalls Jephthah's demand that the elders and the people appoint him their head and captain, before he consents to lead them against the Ammonites (Judg. 11:9–11).

Among the Sumerians, the royal rule was limited to a *bala* or term of office. Hence, the assembly of the gods had the authority not only to confer kingship, but also to withdraw it at will.

This type of assembly is met with in another area of the Semitic world, in Syria. Professor John A. Wilson has shown that such an assembly bearing the name of *mō'ed*, with at least consultative powers, existed in Byblos.[14] In the Egyptian tale of Wen-Amon (c. 1100 B.C.), the wandering hero tells that when he was about to leave Gebal, certain enemies, the Theker, demanded his arrest. The beginning of the hearing is described in these words (2:70 f.): "When morning came, he (Zakar-ba'al, the prince of Gebal) had his *mw'd* summoned, and he stood in their midst and he said to the Theker, 'Why have ye come?' "

This primitive democracy has been noted also in the Teutonic folk-moot, the institutions of Homeric Greece and among the Hittites.[15]

III

Is there any evidence for a similar institution among the ancient Hebrews?[16] The evidence, too long disregarded, lies in the frequent Biblical use of *'ēdāh* and *kāhāl*.[17]

While modern scholars have seen in these terms evidence of a church-state conception of Israel, earlier students sought to discover fine-spun differences between the two terms. Thus, in Augustine's distinction between the Greek ἐκκλησία, Latin *convocatio* and the Greek συναγωγή, Latin *congregatio*, the theological animus is clear from his remark that the former is the nobler term, since it is used only of human beings, while the latter may be applied to cattle![18] Vitringa defines *kāhāl* (= *ecclesia*) as *universam alicuius populi multitudinem* and *'ēdāh* (συναγωγή, *congregatio*) as *quemcumque hominum coetum et conventum*.[19] LXX generally renders *'ēdāh* by συναγωγή and *kāhāl* by ἐκκλησία (so in Deut., Josh., Judg., Sam., Kings., Chron.-Ezra-Neh., Ps.)[20] but *kāhāl* is translated συναγωγή in Ex., Lev., Num.

Actually no genuine distinction in meaning exists between these two terms, different writers preferring one or another term. Thus

Driver notes that *'ēdāh* is used in P and rarely in the Historical Books (Judg. 20:1; 21:10, 13, 16; 1 Kings 8:5 = 2 Ch 5:6), while *kāhāl* is used in Deut. and Chron.-Ezra-Neh. This is no more than a stylistic predilection, as is evident from the fact that both words are used interchangeably throughout the Psalms, as well as in many parallel phrases such as *'adat^h yisrā'ēl* (Ex. 12:3) || *k^ehal yisrā'ēl* (Deut. 31:30); *'adat^h JHVH* (Num. 27:17) || *k^ehal JHVH* (Num. 16:3; 20:4) || *k^ehal 'elōhīm* (Neh. 13:1). That this preference is not absolute is clear from the existence of such compound phrases as *kāhāl v^e'ēdāh* (Prov. 5:14); *k^ehal 'adat^h yisrā'ēl* (Ex. 12:6), etc.

The etymology of both words also indicates their synonymous character—*kāhāl* from *kāhal* "to gather, assemble" and *'ēdāh* from *yā'ad* "meet, come together," exactly like the Akkadian *puḥrum* from *puḫḫurum* "assemble (cf. Ugaritic פֹחר—"assembly of the gods) and the 12 cent. Inscription of Yeḥawmilk of Byblos (מפחרת אל).

That both terms refer to the same institution is evident from the fact that they occur within the same passages, as e. g. the sacrificial code in Lev. 4 (vv. 13, 15 *'ēdāh*, v. 14 *'kāhāl*), the Korah rebellion (Num. 16:2, 3) and the narrative in Judges ch. 20, 21 (*'ēdāh* 20:1; 21:10, 13, 16; *k^ehal 'ām* 20:2; *kāhāl* 21:5). This use of two distinct terms for the same institution is parallelled by the Babylonian use of *alum* "town" and *puḥrum* "assembly" as alternatives.[21] That both *'ēdāh* and *kāhāl* could be used interchangeably for each other and often for *'ām* "people" is additional evidence, if any were required, that this "public assembly" was really "the commonalty, the citizenry," coinciding with the entire male adult population.

On the other hand, it seems clear from a detailed study of the Biblical usage of both terms, that *'ēdāh* is the original technical term for "assembly" while *kāhāl* means "the people" as a collective unit. The root *yā'ad* means not merely "to gather" but "to meet by appointment" cf. Amos 3:3 הֲיֵלְכוּ שְׁנַיִם יַחְדָּו בִּלְתִּי אִם נוֹעָדוּ; Josh. 11:5 וַיִּוָּעֲדוּ כֹּל הַמְּלָכִים הָאֵלֶּה, also Ps. 48:5; Job. 2:11 and passim. Hence, *'ēdāh* means "public assembly specifically convened." This nuance of conscious meeting is lacking in the root *kāhāl*. The Akkadian usage is highly instructive here. While, as has been noted, the two terms *alum* "town" and *puḥrum* "assembly" are used interchangeably, it is clear that the basic term for "public assembly" is the latter, while the former is a borrowed epithet.

Moreover, in such passages as Lev. ch. 4 and Judges ch. 20–21, 'ēdāh is primary and kāhāl is secondary in terms of frequency and of importance ('ēdāh 6 times, kāhāl 3). So too, in the legal and quasi-legal passages discussed below, where the precise technical term would tend to be preferred, 'ēdāh occurs 13 times as against 5 times for kāhāl.[22]

A passage like 1 Kings 12:20 is instructive in indicating that 'ēdāh represents the "people's assembly" in its technical sense: וַיְהִי כִּשְׁמֹעַ כָּל־יִשְׂרָאֵל כִּי־שָׁב יָרָבְעָם וַיִּשְׁלְחוּ וַיִּקְרְאוּ אֹתוֹ אֶל־הָעֵדָה וַיַּמְלִיכוּ אֹתוֹ עַל־כָּל־יִשְׂרָאֵל (Note the use of kol yisrā'el by the side of 'ēdāh and the phrase "they called him to the 'ēdāh).''

Finally, the verb generally used for "convening" is hakhel, ya'ad frequently bearing the connotation of "meeting with hostile intent."[23] The former verb is used 9 times with 'ēdāh, הקהל את העדה (6 times in the Hiphil, 3 in the Niphal)[24] while it occurs with kāhāl only 3 times (הקהל את הקהל).[25] On the basis of all these considerations, it seems clear that 'ēdāh is the authentic term for the "public assembly" in ancient Israel.

IV

Before seeking to trace the history of the institution in Israel, it is important to note the various categories in which kāhāl and 'ēdāh are used in Biblical literature:

A—*As common nouns*, meaning "multitude, crowd." This non-technical use is quite natural, cf. the use as common nouns of English words like "congress," "assembly," by the side of their use as proper nouns.

'Ēdāh is the usual designation for Korah's band (Num. 17:7, 10, 11; 26:9, 10 and passim). It is used even of a cluster of bees (Judg. 14:15), and in many poetic phrases: עֲדַת מְרֵעִים (Ps. 22:17); עֲדַת חָנֵף (Job 15:34); עֲדַת צַדִּיקִים (Ps. 1:5); בְּסוֹד יְשָׁרִים וְעֵדָה (Ps. 111:1); עֲדַת עָרִיצִים (Ps. 86:14); עֲדַת אַבִּירִים (Ps. 68:31); לְאֻמִּים (Ps. 7:8).

Kāhāl is also a common noun in fixed phrases as: קְהַל עַמִּים (Ezek. 32:3 a. e.); קְהַל גּוֹיִם (Gen. 35:11; Jer. 50:9;) קְהַל קְדֹשִׁים Ps. 89:6. The phrase kᵉhal JHVH represents the entire people viewed as a sacred assembly and hence required to maintain itself free from contamination (Deut. 23:2 ff. a. e.; cf. also Lam. 1:10).

B—The use of ʿēdāh and kāhāl in the *narratives of Pentateuch and the Historical Books* to refer to "the commonalty, the people assembled." It is the ʿēdāh which figures in the report of the Ten Spies (Num. 14:1 and passim, parallel to ʿam), in the incident at Meribah (Num. 20:1 ff.), the death of Aaron (Num. 20:22 ff.) and the avenging act of Phineas (Num. 25:6 ff.). Moses and the leaders are commanded to convene the assembly (hakhēl ʾet haʿēdāh) for the census (Num. 1:18). For gathering the commonalty, trumpets are ordained (מִקְרָא הָעֵדָה Num. 10:2; הַקְהֵל אֶת הַקָּהָל Num. 10:7; cf. Joel 2:16 קַדְּשׁוּ קָהָל).

The Sabbath violator is brought before Moses, Aaron and the ʿēdāh (Num. 15:33 ff.) and it is they who execute the blasphemer (Lev. 24:14 ff.). That the ʿēdāh is judicial rather than ecclesiastical in character is clear from the fact that the daughters of Zelophehad appear before Moses, Eleazar, the princes and all the ʿēdāh to demand their rights of inheritance (Num. 27:2 ff.), as do the Transjordan tribes bringing their plea for pasture land (Num. 32:2 ff.).

The judicial function of the ʿēdāh is illustrated by Ps. 82:1, where the poet makes use of mythological overtones that are familiar from Akkadian and Ugaritic literature: אֱלֹהִים נִצָּב בַּעֲדַת־אֵל בְּקֶרֶב אֱלֹהִים יִשְׁפֹּט "God (originally JHVH) stands in the divine assembly, in the midst of the gods will He judge.[26]

This divine assembly is convened in Isa. 14:13 on *har mōʿēd* "the mount of assembly" and was believed to take place in the "uttermost north." This synonymous use of *mōʿēd* and ʿēdāh apparently occurs also in Num. 16:2, nᵉśīʾēi ʿēdāh, kᵉruʾēi mōʿēd. It has its parallel also in the use of *mōʿēd* for assembly in Byblos.

All this would suggest a reconsideration of the familiar term ʾōhel mōʿēd, used over 150 times in the Pentateuch and the Historical Books. In consonance with the theory of ʿēdāh as a congregation, the phrase has been generally rendered as "tent of meeting" (RV) mainly for the purpose of declaring God's will to His people, hence practically equivalent to "the tent of revelation."[27]

It is, of course, obvious that God's will was made known there, but such passages as Ex. 25:22 וְנוֹעַדְתִּי לְךָ שָׁם (cf. 30:36), by the side of 29:43 וְנוֹעַדְתִּי שָׁמָּה לִבְנֵי יִשְׂרָאֵל (cf. 29:42;) indicate that basically it is "the place of meeting between God and the assembled people, the ʿēdāh." Cf. II Chron. 1:3, ʾōhel mōʿēd hā ʿelōhim lit. "the tent for meeting God" (objective genitive). The people might be represented

by its leaders, Moses or Joshua,[28] by its religious functionaries, the
Aaronides or the Levites at sacrifices and other ritual occasions,[29] or
by its "princes" or "elders" at judicial and other governmental functions.[30] For obvious physical reasons, these dignitaries probably did
duty for the *ēdāh*, as a whole, even in those cases where our sources
speak of a gathering before the Tent of Meeting of the entire commonalty.[31] While the primitive democracy of the *ʿēdāh* was limited
to males, it is interesting to note that the women also gathered at
ʾōhel mōʿēd (haṣṣōbhᵉʾōth, Ex. 30:8; I Sam. 2:22), probably for religious
purposes only.

The *ʿēdāh* requires a leader "who will go out and come in before
them" in war (Num. 27:16 ff.). In the war against Midian (ibid.
31:12, 13), the spoils are divided between the warriors in combat
and the rest of the *ʿēdāh* (31:27). The commonalty as a military
entity is referred to as *kāhāl* by Balak of Moab עַתָּה יְלַחֲכוּ הַקָּהָל אֶת־כָּל
סְבִיבֹתֵינוּ (Num. 22:4), by David before Goliath (1 Sam. 17:47), and
in the days of Jehoshaphat (II Chron. 20:5, 14).

Treaty-making is closely associated with the waging of war. The
princes of the *ʿēdāh* made the treaty with the Gibeonites (Josh. 9:15
ff.). In the feud with Benjamin, as well as in the partial restitution
made at the expense of the Jabesh-Gileadites, it is the *ʿēdāh* (or
kāhāl) which operates (Judg. 20:1 ff; 21:5, 10 ff.).

C—*The most technical use of both terms* is to be found in legal and
quasi-legal sections, *to refer to "the people's assembly."* Such are the
sections dealing with the sin-offering for an error in judgment (Lev.
4:13, 15 *edāh*; 4:14; Num. 15:24 *kāhāl*), the trial of a murderer (Num.
35:12, 24, 25; Josh. 20:6, 9) and the division of the spoils of battle
(Num. 31:26 ff.). The Paschal law is addressed to *kol ʿadatʰ Yisrāʾēl*
(Ex. 12:3, 6, 19 and *passim*) as is the Holiness Code (Lev. 19:2). The
great law of the equality of the alien and the citizen is addressed to
the *kāhāl* (Num. 15:15 vocative הַקָּהָל). The Day of Revelation at Sinai
is called *yōm hakkāhāl* in Deut. (9:10; 10:4; 18:16), a phrase which
emphasizes the binding character of the Law as accepted by the
assembled commonalty of Israel. Similarly Moses recites his Farewell
Song, as Joshua reads the Torah, before the *kāhāl* (Deut. 31:30; Josh.
8:35).

Obviously, in the ancient world, all these functions, most of which
would today be described as secular, being concerned with political,

judicial, economic and military affairs, were conducted under the aegis of religion, with appropriate rites and ceremonies. Nonetheless, the *'ēdāh* and *kāhāl* was not a congregation, a church, or a religious fellowship. It was the people's assembly, the supreme arbiter in all phases of the national life.

V

It is now possible to reconstruct the history of this "public assembly" or "commonalty" in Israel, at least in its broadest outlines. Its existence in Mesopotamia, as well as analogies in non-Semitic societies like that of the Hittites and the Teutonic tribes, validates the Pentateuchal tradition which assigns it to the earliest stage of Israelite history. Its origins are to be sought for in nomadic society, in which a strong egalitarianism prevails and where no hierarchy of rulers or complex governmental structure is permitted to arise.[32]

Here each member is as important as any other, and has the right and opportunity of making his voice felt at the "assembly." Within it, to be sure, the elders, who are presumed to have wisdom as well as age, play a dominant role and their opinions carry great weight, particularly since no formal vote is taken, but rather a consensus is reached on issues confronting the group, *viva voce*. It is doubtful whether the elders are to be regarded as a distinct body or Senate. They are rather *primi inter pares*, deriving their powers from the "commonalty" by popular consent.

Our sources speak of other leaders, perhaps more official in character and hence more permanent. These are referred to as *nesī'ē hā'ēdāh* (Ex. 16:22; Num. 16:2) *kerī'ē hā'ēdāh* (Num. 1:16; 26:9) *kerī'ē mō'ed* "called to the meeting" (Num. 16:2).

Religious functionaries also derive their authority from the same source, at least in a formal sense: The Levites are ordained by *'adat^h benēi yisrā'ēl* (Num. 8:9 f.). In the case of the priests, who possess a higher degree of sanctity, the *'ēdāh* is convened to *witness* their consecration (Lev. 8:3 f.; 9:5).

Doubtless such "assemblies" existed in each tribe, but when the tribes unite, a larger commonalty emerges. In such cases, the tribal individuality does not disappear completely, but is expressed at least symbolically by the *rōš* or *nesī' hammatteh* (Num. 1:4, 16; 13:2). The 'ēdāh remains a vital force throughout the Wilderness period and the Conquest, when nomadism was either a reality or a recent memory.

As the supreme authority, representing the entire people, the assembly has an important role to play in the allocation of the land to the various tribes, since the decision is regarded as a kind of social contract in which all the tribes are equal. Moses had allocated the land to the Transjordan clans, with the approval of the 'ēdāh (Num. 32:2 ff.; Josh. 22:12 ff.). Joshua and the heads of the tribes (Josh. 24:1 f.) cast lots for the portions of Judah (ibid. 15:1) and the Joseph tribes (16:1; 17:1 ff.). When these most powerful aggregations have been satisfied, the entire 'ēdāh under Joshua's leadership arranges for the division among the seven remaining tribes (Josh. 18:1 ff.).

As has already been noted, our Pentateuchal sources indicate that the 'ēdāh served as the judiciary in cases involving capital punishment. Thus it sits in judgment on murder cases (Num. 35:12, 24, 25), Sabbath violation (Num. 15:33 ff.), and the blasphemer (Lev. 24:16). From Ezek. 16:40; 23:46 f., it is clear that it executed judgment on the adulterer, *kahal* being the term used by the prophet here.

The executive functions of the assembly include the making of war, wherein, of course, the priests are consulted for the will of God, the division of the spoils (Num. 31:26 ff.) and the making of treaties (Josh. 9:15 ff.). In the punishment of the Benjaminites, the 'ēdāh performs two of its principal functions: it judges the guilty and decides on war.

As a settled agricultural society develops and the population grows, the 'ēdāh becomes increasingly difficult to convene and unwieldy to conduct. Under somewhat similar circumstances, the New England town meeting developed from direct to representative democracy. In the ancient Near East, as the history of the Mesopotamian empires indicates, the primitive democratic structure evolved into a centralized monarchy. In Israel, to be sure, the king never attained to the absolute power of the Babylonian or Assyrian rulers. Nevertheless, the establishment of the monarchy meant the progressive weakening and ultimate disappearance of the old order, which included the tribal system, the blood feud and the public assembly.

The first casualty is doubtless the judicial power, which must be transferred to the throne if the monarchy is to have any strength. In addition to his own activity, the king sets up judges in the gates of the cities.[33]

Nonetheless, the process is gradual. Exactly as the ʿēdāh had brought the Ark to Shiloh in Joshua's day (Josh. 18:1), David invites the kāhāl to participate in bringing the Ark up from Kiryat Yearim (1 Chron. 13:2) and in making preparation for the building of the sanctuary (1 Chron. 29:1 ff.). The testimony of the Chronicler is in harmony with the report in I Kings (8:5 = II Chron. 5:6) of the participation of the ēdah at the dedication of Solomon's Temple. After his death, it is the assembly that crowns Jeroboam king of Israel (1 Kings 12:3 kāhāl; 12:21 ʿēdāh).

It is uniquely characteristic of Israel that unlike other Semitic peoples, it retained the strong democratic impulse derived from the nomadic stage in the agricultural and urbanized culture of monarchical days. In addition to ancient historical memories, there was the ever-present example of the Transjordan tribes to recall "the kindness of Israel's youth, the love of its bridal state" (Jer. 2:1). There were such institutions as the Nazirate and such movements as the Rechabites that strove to revert to the past, albeit mechanically. In prophetism, the ideals of the nomadic stage were restated and deepened to meet the needs of a more advanced society.

In line with this strong democratic tendency, the ʿēdāh or kāhāl, the ancient public assembly, managed to survive. It is possible that its role at coronations was largely ceremonial, intended to give symbolic expression to the idea that the king was the legitimate ruler of the people, having been chosen by the commonalty. The example of the medieval German kings being crowned as rulers of the Holy Roman Empire is somewhat analogous. On the other hand, the fact that the assembly appears in moments of national crisis, religious or political, would imply that it still commanded prestige and that its consent, at the very least, was required to give a decision binding force. Thus according to our sources, the "assembly" participates in the restoration of the Davidic dynasty in the person of Jehoash after the assassination of Athaliah (2 Chron. 23:3), and in the Reformation and Passover of Hezekiah (2 Chron. 29:28 ff.; 30:2 ff.), as well as in the post-exilic decisions to separate from foreign wives (Ez. 10:12, 14) and to restore fields and vineyards taken on pledge (Neh. 5:13) in the days of Nehemiah. As at Sinai, the Reading of the Torah is carried out by the entire commonalty of Israel (Neh. 8:2 ff.).

The collective assembly of ancient Israel was never formally abolished. New conditions led to the diminution of its functions so that ultimately it was convened only in hours of critical importance.[34] But the positive democratic spirit which actuated it in its earliest period never died in Israel, and through the Bible, it entered the fabric of Western civilization.

NOTES

1. Cf. von Rad, *Das Geschichtsbild der Chronistischen Werke* (Stuttgart, 1930); Martin Noth, *Ueberlieferungsgeschichtliche Studien* (Halle, 1943); W. F. Albright, *From the Stone Age to Christianity* (Baltimore, 1940), p. 208.

2. Cf. J. Wellhausen, *Die Composition des Hexateuchs*, p. 205; J. A. Selbie, in Hastings, *Dictionary of the Bible*, p. 467 a.

3. Cf. S. R. Driver, *Intr. to Lit. of O. T.* (12 ed.), 1906, p. 128.

4. R. H. Pfeiffer, *Introduction to O. T.* (1941). Our quotations will be found on pp. 208, 190 and 191.

5. G. F. Moore, *ICC on Judges*, p. 423.

6. Cf. *inter alia*, J. H. Patton, *Canaanite Parallels in the Book of Psalms* (Balt., 1944), esp. p. 27 f.; W. F. Albright, *Yahveh and the Gods of Canaan* (New York, 1968), *inter alia*.

7. Cf. H. Lammens, "Le culte des bétyles et les processions réligieuses chez les Arabes pré-Islamiques" in *Bull. Inst. Franc. Arch. Orient.* XVII (Cairo 1917); J. Morgenstern, "The Ark, the Ephod and the Tent of Meeting," in *HUCA*, 1942-3, 1944 and separately.

8. Albright, op. cit., p. 203, declares : "It is captious to refuse them a Mosaic date." This is queried by T. J. Meek, *JNES*, Vol. II, 1943, pp. 123.

9. Cf. *CIS*, I, no. 165; G. A. Barton, *Archaeology and the Bible*, seventh ed. (Phila., 1937), pp. 439 ff.

10. Cf. H. L. Ginsberg, *Kitbe Ugarit* (Jerusalem, 1936), pp. 111 f., 116.

11. Cf. E. L. Sukenik, "The Oldest Coin of Judea" in *Journ. Pal. Orient. Soc.*, Vol. XIV, 1934, pp. 78 ff.; Vol. XV, 1935, pp. 341 ff.

12. Primitive Democracy in Ancient Mesopotamia" in *JNES*, Vol. II, 1943, pp. 159-172. All page references are to this paper.

13. *Enûma Elish*, Tablet II, ll. 123–29 repeated verbatim in Tablet III, ll. 58–64. The translation is that of A. Heidel, *The Babylonian Genesis* (Chicago, 1942), pp. 20, 23.

14. Cf. J. A. Wilson, "The Assembly of a Phoenician City," in *JNES*, Vol. IV, 1945, p. 245. In notes 2 and 5, Prof. Wilson cites Gardiner's tentative suggestion that the word in question means "bodyguard" and his doubts about the identification with "assembly." The evidence adduced in the present paper on the Hebrew terms *'ēdāh* and *mō'ēd* strongly supports Wilson's view.

15. Jacobsen (op. cit. n. 72) cites W. J. Shepard, *Encyclopedia of the Social Sciences*, IX, 355; also VII, p. 11 and O. Schrader, *Reallexikon der indogermanischen Altertumskunde* (2nd. ed. Leipzig, 1917-29) art. "König" and "Volks-

versammlung" for Europe; Glotz, *The Greek City and its Institutions* (New York, 1930), pp. 39-57, for the Greeks, and Hardy "The Old Hittite Kingdom," *AJSL, LVIII*, 1941, pp. 214 f. for the Hittites.

16. It is the merit of Abram Menes (*Die Vorexilischen Gesetze Israels, Beiheft 50, ZATW*, Giessen, 1921) to have noted the existence of a *Volksversammlung* in Israel and to have made some illuminating observations about it (pp. 21–3, 88–96). However, a fresh and fuller treatment of the subject is in order, for several reasons which can be indicated only briefly. Though Menes recognizes the technical use of *hakhēl* "to convene (the assembly)" (p. 21) he fails to note that *'ēdāh* and secondarily *kāhāl* are the technical names for this group. Lacking the evidence now available to us, he declares that such an institution is "zwar dem vorderen Orient sonst unbekannt" (ibid.). Perhaps because he is under the influence of the Wellhausen school, which treats Pentateuchal data with suspicion unless attested to by the Historical Books, he inverts the entire history of the institution, declaring "die antike Demokratie konnte sich nur in einem Stadtstaat behaupten" (p. 88) but not in an agricultural civilization. That its true provenance might lie in a nomadic society does not occur to him. Hence for him, the people's assembly begins to attain importance in Deuteronomy and "die Kompetenz der Volksversammlung in deuteronomischer Zeit bedeutend erweitert wurde" (p. 89). He interprets the stress in Deut. (and for that matter in Ex.) upon the acceptance of the Law at Sinai by the entire people as a throwback to early conditions (ibid.) from the monarchical period, when the people's assembly was considered the highest organ of the state (p. 90). Noting the existence of the "elders" as a kind of senate in the folk assembly, he regards them as generally friendly toward the larger body (for which he compares II Kings 23:1 ff.) but sometimes as hostile (p. 9). For this latter attitude he finds evidence in a contrast he draws between Ex. 24:7 and 24:9, but the proof is unconvincing. The *šōfᵉtîm* or judges frequently referred to in Deuteronomy, he regards as a democratic institution (p. 92) since the people are bidden to select them (16:18). It seems more plausible to assume that the judges represent the extension of the royal power, which generally attempted to break down the autonomy of the tribes and of such older institutions as the folk-assembly, in which the elders played a significant role. Menes may perhaps be correct in regarding the judicial function of the priests as a later development (p. 93), but the problem is a vexing one and requires further study. Notwithstanding these criticisms, his treatment is a highly suggestive and valuable contribution to the subject.

It should be added that our own paper was projected in 1943 and its reading was announced in the program of the Annual Meeting of the Society of Biblical Literature in December of that year. Due first to illness and then to other commitments, it was not read until the 1946 Meeting of SBL. At that time, Dr. C. Umhau Wolf of Chicago Lutheran Seminary was kind enough to inform me that he had been working on the same theme, and that his paper was scheduled to appear in *JNES*. Upon exchanging copies of our manuscripts, we both found that while there were naturally points of resemblance, there was complete independence in the approach and in many of the conclusions, particularly with regard to '*ēdāh* and *kāhāl*, which, as Dr. Wolf wrote, he had not touched. His paper has since been published in *JNES*.

17. '*Ēdāh* (including suffixes) occurs 145 times, aside from Hos. 7:12, which is probably corrupt. *Kāhāl* is nearly as frequent, occurring 124 times. The verb *kāhal* occurs 19 times in the *Niphal* and 20 in the *Hiphil*. *Kehillah* occurs twice, in Neh. 5:7, where it is probably a metaplastic form for *kol* "voice" (cf. F. Zimmermann in *JBL* 1931, Vol. 50, pp. 311 f.) and in Deut. 33:4, on which see the interesting suggestion of H. Torczyner "The Words of Koheleth" in *Studies in Memory of Moses Schorr* (Hebrew) p. 149 ff. *Makhēlīm* and *makhēlōth* occur once each (Ps. 26:12; 68:27).

18. Cf. J. A. Selbie in Hastings, *Dictionary of the Bible*, vol. 1, p. 466a; A. R. S. Kennedy, *ibid.*, vol. 1, p. 17.

19. Cf. *De Synagoga Vetere* (2nd. ed.) 1726, pp. 80, 88.

20. Except that in Deut. 5:19 and Ps. 40:11, *kahal* is rendered by συναγωγή (but in v. 10, it is given as ἐκκλησία).

21. Cf. Jacobsen, op. cit., p. 162 f.

22. '*Ēdāh* occurs in Ex. 12:3, 6, 19; Lev. 4:13, 15; 19:2; Num. 31:26, 27; 35:12, 24, 25; Josh. 20:6, 9. *Kāhāl* occurs in Lev. 4:14; Num. 15:15; 24; Deut. 31:30; Josh. 8:35.

23. Cf. Num. 14:35; 16:11; 27:3. The use of *yā'ad* is neutral in Num. 10:4; 1 Kings 8:5 = II Chron. 5:6.

24. Hiphil — Ex. 35:1; Lev. 8:3; Num. 1:18; 8:9; 16:19; 20:8; Niphal — Lev. 8:4; Num. 17:7; Judg. 20:1.

25. Num. 10:7; 20:10; Ezek. 38:13. Of these three verses, the last is in a poetic passage, and the other two are in sections where '*ēdāh* is common and the writer may have wished to vary his style. Thus in Num. 10:1-7 '*ēdāh* occurs twice (vv. 1,3) before he uses *kāhāl* (v. 7). In Num. 20:7-13, '*ēdāh* occurs twice in v. 8, before *kāhāl* is used in v. 10, while '*ēdāh* again occurs in v. 11 and *kāhāl* again in v. 12. For the sake of completeness, it may be added that *hakhēl* occurs with '*am* (Deut. 4:10; 31:12), with *z^ekenim* (Deut. 31:28; 1 Kings 8:1 = 2 Chron. 5:2), with *bēth y^ehudāh* (1 Kings:12:21 = 2 Chron. 11:1) and with *kol yisrā'ēl* (1 Chron. 13:5; 15:3).

26. This Psalm is in the so-called "Elohistic Collection," Ps. 51-72, 42-49, 50, 73-83, where *JHVH* has been replaced by '*elōhīm*. On Psalm 82, see the detailed study by Julian Morgenstern, "The Mythological Background of Psalm 82," *HUCA*, vol. XIV, 1939—pp. 29-126, esp. p. 39 ff. See his note 22 for his interpretation of this verse.

27. Cf. Brown-Driver-Briggs, *Lexicon*, p. 418a; Driver, *ICC on Deuteronomy*, p. 339. Less widely accepted are the views of Zimmern, *Beiträge zur Kenntnis der Babylonischen Religion*, p. 88, n. 2, who interprets it as "Orakelzelt," i. e. "the place where the proper time for an undertaking is determined" and of Meinhold, *Die Lade Jahvehs* (1900), p. 3 f. who interprets it as equivalent to אֹהֶל הָעֵדוּת, "the tent of testimony," and therefore regards LXX as correct in rendering both phrases by σκηνὴ τοῦ μαρτυρίου.

28. Cf. e. g. Ex. 25:22; 30:36; Lev. 1:1; 10:9; Num. 1:1; 7:89; 12:4; Deut. 16:10.

29. E. g. Ex. 40:31 f.; Num. Ch. 4, passim. Priests or Levites are mentioned in connection with 'ōhel mō'ēd about 45 times, and sacrifices nearly as frequently.

30. Num. 11:16; 27:2; Josh. 19:5.

31. Lev. 8:3 f.; 9:5, 23 (hā'ām); Num. 10:3; 14:10; 16:19; 17:17; 25:6; 27:2; Josh. 18:1.

32. Cf. the classic treatment of K. Budde, "The Nomadic Ideal in the O. T." in *New World*, 1895, pp. 726-45; J. W. Flight, "The Nomadic Idea and Ideal in the O. T." in *JBL*, Vol. 42, 1923, pp. 158 ff. A brief treatment of this subject is to be found in the opening study of this volume. To be sure, this idea has been challenged more recently, but its basic validity is, in my opinion, unassailable.

33. Cf. Deut. 17:18; 21:19; 22:15; II Sam. 15:2: Amos 5:12, 19; Isa. 29:21; Prov. 24:7; 31:22; Job 5:4; 31:21; Ruth 4:1, 11.

34. It is tempting to note the resemblances between these irregular convenings of the 'ēdāh and kāhāl in the Later Monarchy and the period of the Return on the one hand and the view propounded by Professor Solomon Zeitlin on the other concerning the post-exilic k'neset hagg'dōlāh (from kānas — "gather," cf. yā'ad, kāhal). According to his view, the "Great Assembly" frequently referred to in Rabbinic literature, in Josephus and the Apocrypha, was also convened only at critical moments in Jewish history. Doubtless the k'neset hagg'dōlāh was representative rather than all-inclusive, but that must have also been true of the 'ēdāh in the later periods, at least. Cf. the discussion of this institution in S. Zeitlin, "The Origin of the Synagogue," in *Proc. Am. Acad. for Jew. Research*, 1930-31, pp. 79 f.

3. THE STRUCTURE OF BIBLICAL POETRY

For many centuries the theory of the verbal inspiration of the Bible, both among Jews and among Christians, held sway. During this long period, it was not to be expected that an aesthetic appreciation of the Bible and an understanding of its literary characteristics would develop. This is not to underrate the extent of the debt that the modern age owes to these earlier, pious generations. As we have noted above, the entire body of rabbinic law, or Halachah, and the rich religio-ethical teaching of the Aggadah, which are embodied in the Talmud and the Midrash as well as in the New Testament, rest upon the basis of literal revelation. The structure of religious philosophy initiated by Philo of Alexandria and developed by medieval thinkers, both Jewish and Christian, was derived from the same theory. Most important of all, we owe the meticulous preservation of the biblical text itself in the face of wars, expulsions, and other man-made disasters to the upholders of the doctrine of verbal inspiration, who regarded everything in the Bible as holy and nothing as superfluous or meaningless. The time for aesthetic appreciation had not yet come.

One or two illustrations may indicate how the ancients failed to recognize the existence of parallelism, the repetition of the same idea in different words, which is the very foundation of biblical poetry. Thus, in the ancient Song of Triumph of Lamech (Gen. 4:23), we find two parallel stichs:

> A-mán have-I-sláin for-woundíng-me
>
> And-a-lád for-bruisíng-me.

The Midrash refers the words *man* and *lad* to two distinct individuals—the first being Cain and the second being Tubalcain, his descendant.

Another example may be drawn from the Gospels, which may be described as a Midrash seeking to interpret the Messianic prophecies of the Old Testament as fulfilled in the life and career of Jesus. One famous Messianic passage occurs in Zechariah 9:9 where the Savior is described as "poor, and riding on a donkey; upon a colt, the foal of an ass." Unaware of the parallelism employed here, Matthew 21:7 tells us that the messengers were commanded to bring Jesus two animals, and he rode both of them at once: "They brought the ass and the colt and put on them their garments and he sat thereon."

This literalistic approach was dominant during the Talmudic and medieval eras. Nevertheless, even during these centuries some voices were raised against it. In the second century, Rabbi Ishmael expressed his viewpoint in a classic formulation: "The Torah speaks in the language of man" (B. Berakhot 31b; B. Sanhedrin 56a, etc.). Even sharper was his pronouncement against Rabbi Akiba's painfully precise deductions from every detail of the biblical text: "Because you press the meaning of the *Vav* in *ubhat* ("and the daughter" in Lev. 21:9), shall this woman be put to death by fire?" (B. Sanhedrin 51b).

Actually, adumbrations of an aesthetic appreciation of the Bible may be found in the Talmud. Thus, a rabbinic law ordains that certain sections, like the Song of the Sea (Ex., chap. 15), Moses' Farewell Song (Deut., chap. 32), and the Song of Deborah (Judg., chap. 5) are to be written by the scribe in poetic lines in the scrolls (J. Meg. 3d; B. Meg. 16b; B. Shab. 103b). To be sure, this insight was not consistently applied. The poetic elements in the Hebrew Bible are by no means limited to these few sections but include many ancient fragments embedded in the Torah and the Historical Books, the bulk of the Prophetic writings, all of the Psalms and Proverbs, the Dialogues of Job, the Song of Songs and Lamentations, as well as parts of Ecclesiastes and Daniel in the Hagiographa.

Following in the footsteps of the Talmudic sages, the Masoretes, who were not lacking in poetic instinct, created a special system of accentuation for the three poetic books of Psalms, Proverbs, and Job, which is distinct from the notation established for the other "twenty-one" prose books.[1] They also created the *metheg* (secondary accent) and the *maqqeph* (hyphen), which, in addition to other functions, helped to define the meter in biblical poetry, as will be noted below.

Scattered references to the poetic character of the Bible may be found in other ancient writers, like Josephus, who sought to win the admiration of the Greek and Roman world for his people and its achievements. Thus, he compares *The Song of the Sea* and Moses'

Farewell Song to classical poems written in hexameters. He declares that David wrote poems in various meters, such as tristichs and pentastichs (Antiquities ii, 16, 4; iv, 8, 44; vii, 12, 3). The Church Fathers Origen and Jerome recognized the poetic structure of several parts of the Bible and identified them with the meters common in Greek and Latin literature.

The highest accolade for the aesthetic qualities of the Bible was paid in the treatise, "On the Sublime," attributed to the Greek rhetorician Longinus, who lived in the third century c.e In particular, he cannot sufficiently extol the simplicity and sublimity of the verse, "And the Lord said, 'Let there be light and there was light.' "

The medieval Hebrew poets recognized that the structure of their writings was totally different from the form of biblical poetry. Many of them complained that the Arabic meter-patterns had all but preempted the field in the Middle Ages, but they did not attempt to analyze the character of biblical poetry. Only a handful of commentators—Abraham ibn Ezra, David Kimhi, and Gersonides—recognized parallelism as the fundamental principle of biblical poetry.[2] Their comments, however, were scattered observations which were never united into an organized system or subjected to further analysis.

The Renaissance was marked by a new sense of the aesthetic. The newfound appreciation of the beauty in the Greek and Latin classics led some scholars to compare these masterpieces of antiquity with ancient Hebrew literature. This was the age of the pioneer of critical Jewish scholarship, Rabbi Azariah de Rossi (1513–1574), who paid the penalty for living before his age by being virtually forgotten until the nineteenth century. In his uniquely original work, *Me'or Einayim*, which appeared in the year 1575, he established his title as the founder of scientific research into biblical poetry. The closing chapter of his work (chap. 60) is dedicated to the theme of biblical prosody. In it he discovered the second principle of biblical poetry, that of meter. Two hundred years later, in 1778, the English scholar Bishop Robert Lowth recognized the originality of de Rossi's ideas and included the bulk of his chapter in the *Commentary on Isaiah*. Yet all too often, scholars even today who cite Lowth ignore de Rossi![3]

In the same year, 1778, the well-known German humanist, Johann Gottfried Herder, published his book *The Earliest Sources of Mankind*, in which he described the Bible as the repository of the ancient remains of nature poetry and the national traditions of the Hebrew people.

From the eighteenth century to our day, the basic ideas of de Rossi and Lowth have been repeated with few important additions. To be sure, various extreme views on the structure of biblical poetry were proposed, like those of Ley, Grimme, Sievers, and others. By and large, however, these theories rested upon radical procedures involving frequent deletions, transpositions and far-reaching emendations of the received text. For this reason these theories have won few adherents.[4]

In recent years, attempts have been made to establish the "original" Hebrew meter-patterns by reconstructing a pre-Masoretic biblical text on the basis of preclassical Hebrew morphology and phonology. In spite of the value of these efforts, there inheres in them a substantial measure of uncertainty with regard to both the assumed text and the proposed metrical patterns.[5]

Not all new efforts in this area have been in vain. As in all other branches of scholarship, considerable progress has been registered and more is to be expected, if the subject is approached with sound methods and genuine insight.

A. The Stich

In his pioneering work, Azariah de Rossi recognized that the stich in biblical poetry differs from that in most other literatures, where the meter depends upon a fixed number of syllables. In Greek and Latin poetry, the rhythm pattern depends upon the number and sequence of long and short syllables used by the poet. The same principle is basic in medieval Arabic poetry, which was imitated by the Hebrew poets of Spain and the Arab-speaking world.

In modern literature the stich also depends upon a fixed number of syllables, except in free verse. What is crucial here, however, is not their quantity, but their quality, that is to say, not whether they be long or short, but whether they be accented or unaccented syllables.

In contradistinction to both these types of meter, biblical prosody depends not upon the form of the words employed, but upon the ideas they express. In other words, the stich does not depend upon the number and order of syllables, whether long or short, as in classical poetry, or accented or unaccented, as in modern verse. The meter in Hebrew poetry is determined by the number of important words, each of which constitutes a thought unit, with each normally receiving one accent, irrespective of the number of syllables it contains. Biblical poetry, therefore, exhibits stichs of varying length:

(2 beat stich)   Saíd the-fóe ‖ I-shall-pursúe, I-shall-overtáke. (Ex. 15:9)

(3 beat stich)   The-córds of-Sheól have-surroúnded-me ‖ The-tráps of-deáth have-mét-me. (II Sam. 22:6)

This principle was clearly expressed by de Rossi: "Without doubt, there are modes and patterns for the sacred poems we have mentioned, but they are not dependent upon the number of complete or partial vowels. . . . Their modes and patterns depend upon the number of subjects and their sections, whether subject or object, and what is associated with them in each spoken or written utterance."[6]

It will often happen that a subordinate and unimportant word will be linked to the adjoining, more significant word in order to create a single thought unit. In this instance, the secondary word receives no accent of its own. The Masoretes, who created our system of accentuation, seem to have grasped this principle intuitively. They, therefore, created the *Maqqeph* (hyphen), which links the secondary word to its more important neighbor:

Heár, O Heáven, and-I-shall-spéak ‖ and-let-the-eárth heár the-words-of-My-moúth. (Deut. 32:1)

Here the two Hebrew words, *'imrei-phi* ("the words of My mouth") receive only one accent.

This insight of the Masoretes is basically sound. It is important to note, however, that since they were not consciously aware of biblical meter, one cannot always rely upon the use or absence of the *maqqeph* to establish the number of beats in a given line.

Thus, according to the Masorah we read in Psalm 2:6:

Va'anī ñasakhtī malkī ‖ *'al-ṣiōn har-qodši*

But I have established My king ‖ upon Zion My holy mountain.

Though the Masorah places a *maqqeph* between the last two words, it would seem that the word *har*, "mountain," deserves an accent of its

own, with the result that the verse consists of two stichs of three
beats each.[7]

With regard to this principle, there is little doubt. However, there
is no unanimity with regard to its opposite: Is it possible for one word
in a stich, if it is long and important, to receive two accents? We
believe that this question is to be answered in the affirmative. A few
examples will illustrate the principle:

Al-tir'ū ḥerpat 'enōš || *ūmiggidūphōthām 'al-tēḥātū.* (Isa. 51:7)

Do-not-fear the-contempt of-men || And-before their-curses

be-not-dismayed.

An examination of the entire section makes it clear that the prophet
employs three-beat stichs throughout. It is therefore clear that the
long word *ūmiggidūphōthām* should receive two beats—the primary
stress on the last syllable and the secondary one upon the fourth. This
principle, too, was recognized by the Masoretic guardians of the
traditional text. They therefore created the *metheg*, serving a variety
of functions, one of the most important being to mark the secondary
accent.

Even where the Masorah has not inserted a *metheg*, the meter will
at times clearly require two stresses:

'Az yedabbēr 'eilēimō be'appō || *ūbhaḥⁿrōnō yebhaḥⁿlēmō.* (Ps. 2:5)

Then-He-will-speak to-them in-His-anger || And-in-His wrath

He-will-affright-them.

It is clear that in stich b, which consists of two long words, one of
them must be given a secondary accent, so that the meter pattern will
be 3:3, exactly as in verses 2, 3, 4, 8, and 9.

A particularly instructive example is to be found in Psalm 2:3:

Nenatteqāh 'eth mōsrōthēmō || *venašlīkhāh mimmennū 'abhōthēmō*

Let-us-break their-bands-asunder || And-cast-away their-cords from-us.

If we do not give two stresses to the word *mōsrōthēmō*, the verse
would emerge with two beats in stich a and three in stich b. Not
only does this differ from the meter pattern of the entire psalm, but
the opening stich would be shorter than the closing one. This form

is extremely rare in our received text. In our judgment, the existence
of a shorter stich followed by a longer stich is highly questionable
wherever it occurs, with one important exception to be presented
below.

It is therefore clear that for rhythmic purposes an unimportant
word may appear without a stress or an important one may receive
two stresses. The impact of the rhythm, however, is even greater.
For metric reasons, even two important words may appear with a
single stress, especially when the thought unit in the parallel stich
consists of one word with one beat. One instance may be cited here:

'Azbhū 'eth-YHVH ‖ ni'ªṣṣu 'eth qᵉdōš-Yisrā'ēl ‖ nāzŏrū 'aḥŏr (Isa. 1:4)

They-have-forsaken the-Lord, they-have-despised the-Holy-One-of-Israel,

they-are-turned-away backward.

Here the phrase "qᵉdōš Yisrā'ēl" in stich b corresponds to YHVH in
stich a, and therefore it receives only one stress, so that the verse is
in 2:2:2 meter. Other examples of the phenomenon of two words
receiving only one stress may be found in Numbers 23:7 and Micah
6:7.

Just as the meter has the power at times to deny stress to an important word, so it may, at times, give a stress to an unimportant
word, particularly if there are other long words in the same stich:

Lō' 'yithyaṣṣᵉbhū hōlᵉlīm ‖ lᵉneged 'einekhā (Ps. 5:6)

Revelers shall-not stand ‖ in Your-sight.

This entire psalm is written in the *qinah* rhythm (3:2), which will be
discussed below.[8] Hence the short word *lō* requires a stress of its own.
Other instances may be found in Psalms 27:5[9] and Micah 6:8.[10]

From these examples it is clear that the biblical stich may consist
of a varying number of stresses. We therefore encounter two-beat,
three-beat, four-beat, and five-beat stichs. The two-beat stich, the
shortest of all, is marked by high emotional tension and energy, as in
Isaiah 21:5. This two-beat meter is the most frequent in Babylonian
poetry, as in the Creation myth and the Gilgamesh epic.

In biblical poetry it is the three-beat stich which is by far the basic
meter, as in Moses' Farewell Song in Deuteronomy 32, most of the
book of Psalms, and the book of Job. Stichs of four beats and five

are not as common, but they do occur. Thus, Job's opening line in his complaint (3:3) is in four-beat rhythm and Psalms 42:3 exhibits the 5:5 meter.

In the case of these latter meters, a question arises. It is possible that the four-beat stich is to be divided into two stichs of two beats each, and each five-beat stich likewise into two stichs, one of three and the other of two stresses.

In all these instances (2:2; 3:3; 4:4; 5:5), the verse consists of two or three stichs containing an identical number of stressed thought units. Over eighty years ago, the German scholar Karl Budde discovered that in biblical elegies the opening stich was often longer than the closing, so that the verse generally exhibited a 3:2 meter pattern. He gave the name *qināh* rhythm to this meter, which is marked by a longer opening and a shorter closing stich.[11] Examples are to be found in Lamentations 2:1 and passim, Isaiah 1:21, etc. The term applied to this meter by Budde has remained in use, even though it is not limited to laments and occurs in hymns and love songs as well, as in Psalm 27:1 ff., and Song of Songs 5:10 ff.

It should be understood that the *qināh* rhythm is not limited to the 3:2 pattern. What is basic is that the closing stich or stichs be shorter than the opening. Actually, any number of changes may be wrought upon this fundamental principle. The meter may be 4:3 or 4:2, and it may be extended to 4:4 ‖ 3:3, or 4:4:3 ‖ 3:3:2, etc. The book of Lamentations avoids the monotony of a single pattern by utilizing all these and similar variations of the *qināh* rhythm.

B. CHANGE OF METER IN BIBLICAL POETRY

When the principles of parallelism and rhythm were formulated, some scholars proceeded in their textual criticism on the assumption that a poem beginning with a given meter could not vary from it during its entire course. When, therefore, a variation was encountered, scholars proceeded to "correct" the text by emendations, deletions, and additions. Thus the German scholar Bernhard Duhm expressed the view that the tragic prophet Jeremiah used only the *qināh* rhythm. Duhm then proceeded to place the biblical text on the Procrustean bed of his preconceived notions and to operate accordingly. The

English scholars Oesterley and Robinson were more moderate, but they, too, accepted the principle that "the Hebrew poet used only one meter in any given poem."[12] This assumption was particularly prevalent in the study of Job, where most of the verses consist of two stichs of three stresses each. Wherever commentators found a change either in the character or in the number of stichs in the verse, they did not hesitate to remove the "superfluous" words.

As we have already noted, the recognition of the meter pattern may be a highly valuable instrument in textual criticism, but only when there are other grounds for assuming an error in the text. A priori, one would assume that a poet would vary his meter in order to increase the beauty of his poem and its interest. Thus, the Song of the Sea (Ex., chap. 15) exhibits virtually every conceivable meter: 4:4 (v. 1), 3:3 (v. 2), 5:5 (v. 4), 2:2 (v. 9). The poetry of Egypt and Babylonia also contains varying rhythm patterns, as was demonstrated long ago.[13] During the past two decades, extensive remains of Canaanite literature of the fifteenth century B.E. have been found in Ugarit. These include mythological poems and substantial sections of epics depicting the lives of the gods and goddesses of the Canaanite pantheon. These poems, written in a dialect closely related to Hebrew, clearly demonstrate that the poet varies his rhythm as he chooses.[14] Here there is obviously no possibility of attributing the changes to the multiplicity of sources or to late glossators.

A simple example of the proper use of meter as a tool of textual criticism is to be found in Psalms 4:7, 8. In the Masoretic text, verse 8 is now in 3:4 rhythm, which, as we have indicated above, we regard as highly dubious. Moreover, in verse 7, which precedes it, the rhythm pattern is 4:5. As many commentators have noted, one has only to attach the last word of verse 7, *YHVH*, to verse 8 and both verses emerge with the entirely regular 4:4 meter.

In the Blessing of Moses (Deut., chap. 33), verse 21 contains the incomprehensible word *ṣāphūn* and the anomalous form *vayētē*. In addition, the verse in the Masoretic text exhibits a meter pattern of 3:4:3:3:3. Both anomalous forms, *ṣāphūn* and *vayētē*, which are adjacent to each other, need only to be reversed and joined together as one word to create the verb *vayyith'as^ephūn* ("and they gathered together"), for which Deuteronomy 32:5 offers an exact parallel. When that is done, verse 21 emerges in completely regular three-beat stichs.[15]

The most dangerous foe of the poetic spirit is a slavish attachment
to rules. It is therefore impossible to lay down hard and fast principles
with regard to the use of meter and its variations. Nevertheless, it is
obvious that psychological factors find expression in literary phenomena. Thus, there is a natural tendency for writers as well as for
speakers to bring a discourse to a close on a strong note in order to
leave a more powerful and lasting impression on the reader or listener.
Similarly, in music a composer will end his piece on a higher note or
with increased volume, *crescendo* or *fortissimo*.

The biblical poets were no different in this respect. We therefore
find a tendency, not hitherto noticed, to complete a psalm or a poetic
speech (as in the book of Job) with greater power. This purpose is
achieved by the lengthening of the meter in a variety of ways. When
this principle is recognized, many alleged difficulties in the text and
meter-pattern disappear.

The following principal techniques are utilized to achieve this goal:

1. *Increasing the number of stichs in the closing verse.* When the rest
of the poem consists of verses containing two stichs each, the poet
may conclude with a verse of three stichs (Ps. 13, 14, 16, 18, 19, 37,
47, 53, 55, 63, 73, 90, 94, 103, 104, 111, 119, 125, 129, 148; Job 10,
11, 19, 26[16]).

2. *Increasing the number of syllables in the last verse,* either by the
use of longer words or by a larger number of short ones (Ps. 17, 26,
41,[17] 45, 71, 81, 91, 116; Job 5, 17, 18, 21, 41).

3. *Lengthening the meter in the last verse.* When the poem is written
basically in the *qinah* rhythm (3:2 meter), the closing verse will exhibit
a longer meter. Thus, Psalms 42–43 end in a 4:4:3 meter.[18] Similarly,
Psalm 27, which is also written in a 3:2 pattern ends in the first half
(v. 6) with a 4:3 rhythm.[19] Psalm 48 also ends in a 4:3 meter.

When the poem is constructed of stichs of three beats each, the last
verse may be lengthened either to a five-beat meter (Ps. 98, 106) or,
more commonly, to a four-beat meter (Ps. 19:11,[20] 24, 34; 51:19,[21] 82,
89, 90, 149, 150).

Micah's unforgettable definition of religion (6:6–8) is predominantly
in the three-beat meter. In v. 8, which is the climax, the prophet
continues to use a 3:3 meter for the first two stichs, but concludes
with 4:4 meter in the two final stichs:

He-has-told-you O-man what-is-good

And-what-the-Lord requires of-you:

Only-to-do justice and-to-love mercy

And-to-walk humbly with your-God.[22]

4. *Lengthening the meter in the last stich only.* When this technique is used, the closing stich will emerge longer than the opening, a phenomenon which is otherwise extremely rare and the existence of which we regard as highly doubtful. In order to make the closing stich longer, the poet may, at times, shorten the opening stich. Thus, the closing verse of Psalms 8, 20,[23] 62, 67, 84, consists of an opening stich of two beats and a closing stich of four. Similarly, the last verse of Psalm 66 contains an opening stich of two beats and a closing stich of five.

A closing stich of four beats after an opening stich of three occurs in the last verse of Psalms 13, 15, 47, 59, 63, 86, 123. A closing stich of five beats occurs after an opening stich of three, in the closing verse of Psalms 10, 50, 52, 145, and after an opening stich of four beats in Psalm 4.

It seems that the poetic word *Halleluyah*, which occurs profusely in the Psalms, serves among other purposes to lengthen the closing stich, as in 113, 117, 145, and 147.

5. In order to bring the composition to a powerful close, the poet at times may use two of these techniques simultaneously. Thus, Psalm 47, constructed basically of verses containing two stichs each of three beats, ends with a verse consisting of three stichs in 3:3:4 meter.

Underlying all these variations in prosody is the psychological need to bring the composition to a powerful and impressive conclusion.

C. PARALLELISM

Since the days of Lowth, it has been recognized that the essence of biblical poetry resides not in rhyme or syllabic meter, but in the parallelism of stichs (poetic clauses). Lowth himself recognized three forms of parallelism, a number which subsequent research has amplified.

1. *Synonymous parallelism*

In synonymous parallelism—the basic form—the idea expressed in the opening stich (stich a) is repeated in the closing stich (stich b) in different words. The parallelism is *total* when every element of stich a has its parallel in stich b. For example:

(stich a) How shall I curse, whom God has not cursed?
(stich b) How shall I execrate, whom the Lord has not execrated?
           (Num. 23:8)

The parallelism is *partial* when part of the idea expressed in stich a is not expressed in stich b, but is understood. For example:

(stich a) Sun, stand still on Gibeon,
(stich b) And moon, in the valley of Aijalon. (Jos. 10:12)

Here there is no verb expressed in stich b parallel to *stand still*, but essentially the two stichs are parallel, because the verb from stich a is understood in stich b.

2. *Antithetic parallelism*

Antithetic parallelism is particularly frequent in Wisdom literature. It is common among the authors of Proverbs, who wish to teach a principle by setting forth a doctrine both positively and negatively. For example:

(stich a) The memory of the righteous is a blessing,
(stich b) But the name of the wicked rots. (Prov. 10:7)

(stich a) Folly is enthroned on the great heights,
(stich b) But the rich sit in the low places. (Eccl. 10:6)

Incidentally, the antithetic parallelism in this latter passage is highly significant with regard to the attitude of Koheleth toward the social classes of his time! To be sure, antithetic parallelism is not lacking in other branches of biblical poetry:

(stich a) They are bowed down and fallen,
(stich b) But we are risen and stand upright. (Ps. 20:6)

These two forms of parallelism are the foundation stones of biblical poetry. However, particularly in a long poem, there is a danger of monotony in this constant repetition. In order to avoid this peril, the biblical poet uses various devices.

One method is to change the order of the words in stich a and b. Thus the poet in Deuteronomy, chapter 32, begins with the same word order in both stichs in the opening verses. Thus, verse 2 literally rendered reads:

(stich a) I-will-drop as-the-rain My-doctrine

(stich b) I-will-distil as-the-dew My-word.

The order here is verb-noun-object in both stichs. In the very next verse, however, the order in stich a (object-verb) differs from that in stich b (verb-object):

(stich a) For-upon-the-name of-the-Lord I-shall-call,

(stich b) Ascribe greatness to-our-God.

The longer the given stich is, the greater the opportunity for variations in the order of the words. Thus, if stich a consists of three stressed words, stich b may occur in one of six variations: a, b, c; a, c, b; b, a, c; b, c, a; c, a, b; c, b, a. All these patterns are found in biblical poetry.

The second method for avoiding monotony has already been noted: partial parallelism, in which stich b avoids repeating all the details of stich a, thus adding new life and variety to the poem. Thus, the order may be categorized as follows: a, b, c ‖ b, c. Compare:

(stich a) I shall-restore your-judges as-at-the-first,

(stich b) And-your-counselors as-at-the-beginning. (Isa. 1:26)

In this case, however, stich b is shorter than stich a. When the poet wishes to fill out the lacuna, he will use a phrase in stich b longer than its parallel in stich a:

(stich a) Her-hand she-put to-the-tent-pin,

(stich b) Her-right-hand to-the-workman's hammer. (Jud. 5:26)

Here there is no verb in stich b paralleling the verb in stich a. Instead, the longer phrase, "the workman's hammer," which is parallel to "tent-pin," receives two beats, so that stich b has three beats like stich a. The added "ballast" serves to fill out the stich.

In all these variations, parallelism retains its authentic character: no new ideas are introduced in stich b which are lacking in stich a.

The next step is entirely natural. In order to raise the level of interest in the poem, the author may introduce a new idea in stich b. This creates the third category in parallelism.

3. *Complementary parallelism*

In complementary parallelism, stich b repeats and completes the idea expressed in stich a. Scholars have generally called this type *climactic parallelism*. We prefer the term *complementary*. It may be categorized as a, b, c, ‖ a, b, d. This type is particularly common in exalted poetry:

(stich a)   Ascríbe to-the-Lórd, Heavénly Béings

(stich b)   Ascríbe to-the-Lórd glóry and stréngth. (Ps. 29:1)

(stich a)   O Gód of vengeánce, O Lórd,

(stich b)   O Gód of-vengeance, shine-fórth. (Ps. 94:1)

(stich a)   For ló, your-enémies, O Lórd,

(stich b)   For-ló, your-enémies shall-pérish. (Ps. 92:10)

This third category appears frequently in the Ugaritic epics. Hence some scholars have regarded this type in Hebrew poetry as a direct borrowing from the Canaanites. In a few instances, they have argued that certain Psalms are foreign in origin and have entered into Hebrew literature with only a slight reworking, if any at all. One is reminded of the contention of earlier scholars that parallelism was a borrowing from the Babylonians.[24]

It is perhaps natural for scholars to seek foreign influence wherever there are resemblances, real or apparent, between the culture of Israel and its Near Eastern environment. What is overlooked is the fact that the Hebrew people were part of the Semitic world, possessing authentic roots in the cultural background common to the entire area. Unless there are strong grounds for assuming direct borrowing, it is methodologically sounder to postulate the parallel or divergent development of a common heritage.[25]

The recognition of this type of parallelism may also prove very useful for dealing with the biblical text. This category affords some striking examples.

In Hosea 8:11 the Masoretic text is rendered:

(stich a)   For Ephraím has-multiplíed altárs to-sín,

(stich b)   The-altárs have-served-hím for-sín.

This verse suffers in part from a rhythmic imbalance, but its basic weakness lies in its content. For stich b contains neither a repetition of the ideas of stich a in different words nor an addition in thought. Scholars have, therefore, made the suggestion to re-vocalize *laḥᵃtō'* ("to sin") in stich a, as *lᵉḥattē'* ("to purify"). This privative use of the verb, which is highly technical, does not commend itself here.

A better procedure is to recognize that *laḥᵃtō'* in stich a is a dittography from stich b, where it also occurs after *mizbᵉḥōt* ("altars"). Removing it in stich a simultaneously improves both the meter and the content, for the verse emerges as a perfect example of complementary parallelism in 3:3 meter:

(stich a)   For-Ephraím has-multiplíed altárs,

(stich b)   The-altárs have-served-hím for-sín.

A similar error occurs in another passage, which also is improved by the removal of one superfluous word. The Masoretic text in Job 20:29 should be translated:

(stich a)   Thís is the-lót of a-wicked-mán from-Gód,

(stich b)   And-the-inheritánce of-an-evíldoer from-Gód.[26]

The meter of the verse can be improved and the complementary parallelism restored by recognizing that *mē'elōhīm* ("from God") in stich a should be deleted as a dittography from *mē'ēl* ("from God") in stich b. The sense of the verse and its rhythm (3:3 meter) are now clear:

(stich a)   Thís is-the-lót of a-wicked-mán,

(stich b)   And-the inheritánce of-an-evíldoer from-Gód.

4. *Formal parallelism*

Another step forward in the use of parallelism is to be found in a fourth category. Here no vestige remains of synonymous parallelism —nothing is repeated in stich b from stich a. The closing stich continues to develop the idea of the opening one or to explain it. Only the rhythm of the verse, particularly when seen within the poetic context in which it occurs, or the unusual word order testifies that we have poetry and not prose before us. In general, there is no iron curtain between prose and poetry in the ancient world. Even if we do not accept the view proposed by Cassuto and Tur-Sinai that the prose narratives of the Bible were originally a poetic epic, it is clear that even prose tales were declaimed and sung.

Scholars have called this type of parallelism *synthetic* or *constructive*, since both halves of the verse constitute a single idea. We believe that these terms, however, obscure the specific characteristics of this type —*that there is no parallelism of thought at all.* We therefore prefer the term *formal* or *external* parallelism to describe it. A few examples:

(stich a)   For-Í have-estáblished my-Kíng

(stich b)   Upon-Zíon, My-holy-mountáin. (Ps. 2:6)

(stich a)   Do-not-ánswer a-foól according-to-his-fólly

(stich b)   Lést you-toó resémble-him. (Prov. 26:4)

This category is also to be found in an ancient poetic fragment imbedded in Genesis 21:7. Here the inverted word order in stich b and the use of the poetic word *millēl* ("spoke") in stich a, as well as the 3:3 rhythm of the tristich, testify that it is poetry and not prose:

Mí millēl l'abhrāhām ‖ *heiníqah bhānim sārāh* ‖ *ki-yaladti bén liz^equnāv.*

A literal rendering of the verse would be:

(stich a)   Whó would-have-saíd to-Abrahám,

(stich b)   Gíven-to-súck sóns has-Saráh,

(stich c)   Fór-I-have-bórn a-són in-his-óld-age.

5. *Anadiplosis*

A unique type of parallelism is to be found in some of the Psalms, particularly in the Song of Degrees collection (Ps. 120–34). As is well known, the Hebrew term *šīr hamma'alōt* has never been satisfactorily explained. Many interpretations of *ma'alōt* have been offered, such as the returning exiles from Babylonia (Ezra 7:9), the regular festival pilgrimages to Jerusalem, or the fifteen steps between the Court of the Israelites and the Court of the Women in the Second Temple (M. Middot 2:5; B. Tal. Sukkah 51b).

In the nineteenth century Gesenius and Delitzsch rejected all these suggestions. They sought to explain the term as referring to a unique type of parallelism which resembles steps by carrying the idea forward and upward from stich to stich and from verse to verse. That this is the meaning of the phrase *šīr hammaʿalōt* ("The Song of Degrees") is scarcely likely, since at the time the book of Psalms was edited, there was no clear-cut knowledge of the forms of biblical poetry. Moreover, there are psalms in this collection, like Psalm 132, where this type of parallelism is entirely lacking. The term *anadiplosis* (i.e., lit. rising and doubling) is, however, an accurate description of this category. In essence, it is a combination of synonymous, complementary, and formal parallelism. Psalm 121 illustrates this composite category very clearly, particularly the repetition in form or content *from verse to verse*:

I will-lift-up my-eyes to-the mountains,

Whence shall-my-help come?   (formal)

My-help is-from the-Lord,

The-Maker of-heaven and-earth.   (complementary)

He-will-not-suffer your-foot to-stumble,

He-who-keeps-you does-not slumber.   (synonymous)

Behold he-does-not-slumber or-sleep

The-Guardian of-Israel.

The-Lord is-your-keeper, the-Lord is-your-shade

Upon your-right-hand.   (formal)

By-day the-sun shall-not-smite-you

Nor-the-moon by-night.   (synonymous)

The-Lord will-guard-you from-all-evil,

He-will-guard your-soul.   (complementary)

The-Lord will-guard your-going-out and-your-coming-in,

From-this-time-forth and-forever.

            (formal and complementary with previous verse)

It should be added that this type of parallelism is rarely carried through an entire literary unit.

The close relationship between biblical prose and poetry may be seen in the existence of this type of parallelism in biblical prose, including legal pericopes. We may cite the following examples where the closing clause both repeats and completes the opening one:

Make yourself an ark of gopherwood,
With rooms shall you make the ark. (Gen. 6:14)

The field I give you,
And the cave that is in it I give it to you, too.
In the presence of the sons of My people, do I give it to you. (Gen. 23:11)

May they take for Me an offering,
From every man whose heart is willing shall you take My offering. (Ex. 25:2)

You shall eat of the produce, the old store,
Until the ninth year, until its produce comes in, you shall eat the old store.
    (Lev. 25:22)

Seven weeks shall you count for yourself,
From the time the sickle is first put to the standing corn, you shall begin
    to count seven weeks. (Deut. 16:9)

When parallelism in biblical prose was recognized, it was attributed to the Pentateuchal source P. This usage is to be found in Aramaic as well as in the Bauer-Meissner papyrus.[27] Our concern here is to demonstrate the similarity between this usage in prose and anadiplosis in poetry, though to be sure, with different effects. In legal prose it is used for exactness; in poetry it adds an element of sublimity. What is common to both is that this usage emphasizes an idea and clarifies it.

D. THE ORDER OF STICHS

1. *Consecutive Structure*

In the various types of structure discussed above, the successive stichs have been related to each other in direct order. That is to say, the opening and the closing stich of each verse have been directly linked to each other by the repetition, completion, or antithesis of an idea. This order of stichs, which is by all odds the most common in the Hebrew Bible, may be described as *consecutive*. In a passage consisting of four stichs, for example, the customary order would be for stich a to parallel b and for c to parallel d. There is no need to illustrate this most common type by citing examples. Indeed, most of the passages quoted in this chapter fall into this category.

There are, however, some rarer forms which deserve special attention, because of the light their recognition sheds on difficult passages.

2. *Alternate structure*

In alternate structure, stich a corresponds to stich c and b to d. Consider Hosea 5:3:

> (stich a)   I know Ephraim,
> (stich b)   And Israel is not hidden from Me.
> (stich c)   For now, O Ephraim, you have committed harlotry,
> (stich d)   Israel is defiled.

An even more interesting instance is to be found in Psalms 33:20–21:

> (stich a)   Our soul has waited for the Lord,
> (stich b)   He is our help and our shield,
> (stich c)   Because in Him our heart rejoices,
> (stich d)   Because in His holy name we have trusted.

Many commentators have deleted the first *kī*, "because," in 21a (stich c) or transposed it to 20b on the basis of the *Septuagint* and the *Pešita*. Actually, there is no evidence for these transpositions from the Versions, because they preserve the *kī* in 21a as well. The clue to the understanding of this passage is to be found in Ehrlich, who points out that 21a gives the reason for 20a, and 21b, the reason for 20b. We have here an instance of alternate parallelism, the sense of the passage being:

> Our soul has waited for the Lord,
> Because in Him our heart rejoices.
> He is our help and our shield,
> Because in His holy name we have trusted.

This stylistic trait is also to be found in biblical prose. Ehrlich quotes Exodus 29:27, where once again section c corresponds to a, and section d to b:

a) You shall sanctify the breast of the wave offering, b) and the thigh of the heave offering c) which is waved d) and which is heaved up of the ram of consecration.

A more elaborate and striking illustration of this usage occurs in Deuteronomy 22:25–27, which deals with the violation of a betrothed girl in the open field:

But if the man find the betrothed girl in the open field . . . a) then the man shall die. b) But to the girl you shall do nothing, c) for as though a man were to rise against his neighbor and murder him is this case, d) for the girl must have cried out, but there was none to save her.

The reasons for the punishment of the man and the exoneration of his victim are set forth in two successive clauses, each introduced by *kī*, "for."

Alternate structure is the key to understanding an interesting passage in Ecclesiastes. In chapter 5, verses 17–19, Koheleth emphasizes his fundamental view that man should enjoy life, for this is the will of God and it is He who makes it possible for man to find happiness in his existence. In this passage we encounter two statements (vv. 17, 18) followed by two additional verses, each beginning with *kī*, "because" (vv. 19a, b). When it is noted that this is an instance of alternate parallelism, it becomes clear that verse 19a gives the reason for 17 and 19b for 18:

(stich a—v. 17)	Here is what I have discovered: It is meet and proper for a man to eat, drink and enjoy himself in return for the toil he undergoes under the sun in the scant years that God has given him, for that is man's portion.
(stich b—v. 18)	Indeed, every man to whom God has given wealth and possessions and granted the power to enjoy them taking his share in rejoicing in his labor, that is the gift of God.
(stich c—v. 19a)	For that is man's portion and not long will he remember the days of his life.
(stich d—v. 19b)	For it is God who provides him with the joy in his heart.

3. *Chiastic structure*

In this less common order, stich a corresponds to d, and b to c. An example is to be found in Proverbs 23:15–16:

(stich a)	My son, if your heart is wise,
(stich b)	My heart, too, will be glad;
(stich c)	My reins will rejoice,
(stich d)	When your lips speak right things.

The difficult passage in Job 20:2–3 also receives its due interpretation, when its chiastic structure is recognized:

(stich a)   Indeed, my thoughts force me to answer,
(stich b)   Because of the feelings within me.
(stich c)   I hear censure which insults me,
(stich d)· And my spirit of understanding impels me to reply.

Another instance of chiastic parallelism is the clue to the understanding of the passage in Lamentations 2:13, which we have discussed elsewhere.[28]

The beautiful formula of betrothal in Hosea (2:21–22) is also an
instance of chiastic parallelism:

(stich a)   And I will betroth you to me forever.
(stich b)   I will betroth you to me in righteousness and justice,
(stich c)   In steadfast love and in compassion,
(stich d)   And I will betroth you to me in faithfulness,
(stich e)   And you shall know the Lord.

Here, "forever" corresponds to "faithfulness," and "righteousness
and justice" to "steadfast love and compassion."

Once more, a poetic usage proves useful in the understanding of
prose as well. In Ecclesiastes (11:3–4) a passage occurs that is deleted
in whole or in part by many commentators. In this chapter, Koheleth
offers practical counsel with regard to labor and business. Thus, he
suggests that the merchant diversify his possessions:

Send your bread upon the waters . . .
Divide your means into seven or eight portions,
For you cannot tell what calamity will come upon the earth.

He also warns the farmer against laziness which he would try to
justify on the ground that he is waiting for the rain and the wind.
This excuse for indolence Koheleth refutes ironically by observing
that there is no value or need for sitting idly by. When the clouds are
filled with water, they will empty it upon the earth, and if the wind
casts a tree down to earth, it will remain there without human "help."
This observation is expressed chiastically: a and d refer to the rain,
while b and c refer to the wind:

a) If the clouds are filled with rain, they will empty it upon the earth. b) If
a tree is blown down by a wind in the south or in the north, wherever it

falls, there it lies. c) Therefore, *on with your work*, for he who watches the wind will never sow, d) and he who gapes at the clouds will never reap.

In Hosea 8:14 many commentators delete stich b as a later addition. This becomes unnecessary if we recognize the existence of chiastic structure in the verse; b and e refer to palaces, while c and d refer to cities:

> (stich a)   For Israel has forgotten his Maker.
> (stich b)   He has built palaces,
> (stich c)   While Judah has multiplied fortified cities;
> (stich d)   But I will send a fire upon its cities,
> (stich e)   And it will devour its castles.

One more instance of this structure occurs in Psalm 1:5–6, where stich a and d refer to the sinners and b and c to the righteous:

> (stich a)   Therefore the wicked shall not stand in judgment,
> (stich b)   Nor sinners in the community of the righteous,
> (stich c)   For the Lord knows the way of the righteous,
> (stich d)   But the way of the wicked must perish.

Chiasmus also develops more extended and complex forms, the recognition of which is of inestimable value in the exegesis of some difficult and enigmatic passages. Job, chap. 8, is a striking case in point. Bildad wishes to state his conviction that Divine justice operates in the world. He does so by presenting a parable, not of one plant, as has often been assumed, but of two. One appears to be fresh and verdant, but it dries up quickly (vv. 12–15)—the symbol of the wicked. The other survives even under adversity and renews itself (vv. 16–19)—the symbol of the righteous. Bildad then sets forth his conclusion in v. 20:

> Indeed God will not spurn the blameless,
> Nor will He uphold the evil-doers.

The whole passage has a chiastic structure: a—the evil-doer (vv. 12–15), b—the righteous (vv. 16–19); b^1—the righteous (v. 20a), a^1—the evil-doer (v. 20b).[29]

E. OTHER CHARACTERISTICS OF BIBLICAL POETRY

All biblical readers are familiar with the fact that there are alphabetic acrostics in the book of Psalms (chaps. 9–10, 25, 34, 37, 111,

119, 145), in Lamentations (chaps. 1–4), and in the book of Proverbs (31:10–31). It is also certain that the first chapter of Nahum was originally an alphabetic acrostic which suffered radical errors in transmission.[30] Scholarly consensus has it that the acrostic is a late characteristic of biblical poetry, but the existence of acrostics in Akkadian literature casts uncertainty upon this view. It would seem that this usage derives originally from the desire to aid the memory. With the passing of time, it became a literary convention which served as a challenge to the ingenuity and skill of the writer, as happened in the Hebrew poetry of the Middle Ages.

It should be noted that in Lamentations (chaps. 2–4) the letter *Pe* comes before the *Ayin*. This would seem to have been either an older or an alternate order in the alphabet. In fact, the effort has been made to demonstrate that the development of the letters of the Hebrew alphabet requires this order.[31] Be this as it may, it is clear that in Psalm 34, the original order was *Pe* before *Ayin*. Thus, the difficulty in the sequence of vv. 16–18 in our present text is obviated. For the restored order now is:

(v. 17)   The face of the Lord is against the evil doer . . . .
(v. 16)   The eyes of the Lord are toward the righteous . . . .
(v. 18)   They cry and the Lord hears them.

It should be added that two alphabetic Psalms (25 and 34), following the conclusion of the alphabet, add another verse beginning with *Pe*. There are grounds for assuming that this second *Pe* originally existed in Hebrew, like the two *Pe* consonants in classical Ethiopic.

Aside from these alphabetic acrostics, some scholars have sought to find acrostics bearing the name of some individual in the opening letters of consecutive verses. The use of acrostics to indicate the name of the author occurs in Akkadian verse of the 2nd millennium B.C.E. and in Latin literature, as Cicero informs us.[32] The practice became a commonplace in medieval Hebrew poetry. During the heyday of the Maccabean dating of the Psalms, it was suggested that the opening letters of each verse in Psalm 2:2–4 contain "Yannai," the name of the Maccabean king, Alexander Jannaeus. Similarly, it has been proposed that in Psalm 110 beginning with verse 1b (Hebrew *šēbh*), we have an acrostic containing the name of Simon the Maccabee. For many cogent reasons this view has few adherents today.

Another issue which continues to arouse considerable interest is the question of the existence of strophes in biblical poetry. For over a century, some scholars have sought to defend the view that biblical poems may be divided into regular stanzas consisting of several verses each. This position has recently been urged with new vigor by scholars like Kissane, Skehan, and Terrien in their studies of Job.[33] Obviously, a poem could—and should—be divided into sections according to the various themes treated by the author. However, if the term *strophe* is to have any significance in this context, it must mean that the poem falls into sections *of equal length*. The existence of stanzas is clear in the relatively rare instances in biblical verse where a refrain occurs and is repeated at regular intervals, sometimes with minor changes. Such is the case in Psalms 42–43 (refrain in 42:6, 12; 43:5), Psalm 49 (refrain in vv. 13, 21), and Job, chapter 28 (refrain in vv. 12, 20 and perhaps originally also at the beginning of the "Hymn to Wisdom"). In Psalm 107, the refrain consists of two verses with a different verse inserted between them each time (vv. 6–8, 13–15, 19–21, 27–31).

On the other hand, where no such refrain exists in the text, the theory of strophes proves abortive. Thus, the effort of scholars to divide the speeches in the book of Job into strophes collides with one stubborn fact: The alleged sections are not uniform in length. In order to save the theory, some scholars have not hesitated to delete, transpose, and emend the text solely for metric reasons. Others, conscious that such procedures are methodologically unwarranted, argue that the strophes in any given speech may not be uniform in length, but may vary within limits.[34] But even if one were to grant the legitimacy of applying the term *strophe* to sections of varying lengths, the theory suffers from another fundamental drawback. An examination of the text makes it clear that in order to arrive at this pattern of irregular regularity, Kissane is compelled to divide the text arbitrarily, separating verses that obviously belong together and ignoring the sections into which the thought naturally falls.

The only conclusion that may legitimately be drawn from the extant text of Job is the one arrived at by Budde, who long ago denied the existence of strophes as an unproved and improbable theory. Similarly, Dhorme confesses that he was compelled to give up his initial efforts to divide the speeches into strophes because the theory can counter to the facts.[35]

Biblical poetry has sufficient resources at its command without the necessity of introducing dubious devices for which genuine objective evidence is lacking.

The question of rhyme in biblical poetry has also aroused interest. Though we may be sure that popular poetry found delight in rhyme, it is clear that this was not a significant trait in the work of the great poets who have left the products of their genius in the Bible. Perhaps this lack of interest in rhyme as a literary device derives from the basic characteristic of biblical poetry, which makes content primary and form secondary. Only in the remnants of folk poetry is rhyme to be met with, as for example in Samson's riddle (Jud. 17:18) and in the women's song of greeting to David on his triumphant return from battle (I Sam. 18:7; 21:12; 29:5). On the other hand, the examples of rhyme in some love poems (Song of Songs 5:6, 7) give the impression of being purely accidental.

F. Parallelism in Post-Biblical Poetry

One of the major obstacles to the full appreciation and understanding of the Bible has been the tendency to establish a dichotomy between the biblical and post-biblical eras. Today it is increasingly recognized that the biblical epoch constitutes the first period in the spiritual development of Israel, directly related to later eras in the life, thought, and faith of the Jewish people. Hence, both the biblical and post-biblical periods can shed mutual light upon each other.

A study of post-biblical literature makes it clear that biblical meter and parallelism did not come to an end with the close of the biblical era. The books of the Apocrypha and Pseudepigrapha, the bulk of which were written in Hebrew and Aramaic, reveal even in the Greek, Latin, Coptic, or Slavonic translations in which they have reached us, all the poetic traits to be found in the Bible. The Thanksgiving Hymns found at Qumran, which are unabashedly imitative of biblical poetry, naturally exhibit the same phenomena. G. B. Gray was astonished at the fact that the apocryphal book, The Wisdom of Solomon, was composed completely in parallelism, since most scholars believe that it was written in Greek.[36] A reexamination of the original language of this striking work may well be in order.

Even after the apocryphal period, the forms of biblical poetry retained their hold upon Hebrew writers. Its fundamental principles

—meter and parallelism—survived in three areas in the rabbinic period: a) in proverbs and apothegms similar in spirit and form to biblical proverbs; b) in a few lyrical fragments imbedded in the Talmud, such as elegies on dead scholars, which in some degree resemble biblical lamentations; and c) in the oldest, basic prayers of the Jewish liturgy, which were composed before the rise of the involved *piyyut* of Eleazar Kalir (8th or 9th century) and his contemporaries.[37]

The Mishnic treatise Abot, frequently called "The Ethics of the Fathers," contains a rich collection of utterances which parallel the basic principles of biblical poetry. Thus it is possible to find stichs of every type:[38]

(2-beat meter)   He-who-increases flesh, increases worms. (2:8)

(Qinah meter)   If-I am-not for-myself,

who will-be-for-me?

And-if-I-am only-for-myself,

what am-I?

And-if not now,

when? *('eimāthay)* (1:14)

(3-beat meter)   Be deliberate in-judgment,

and-set-up many pupils,

and-make a-fence for-the-Torah. (1:1)

(3-beat meter)   Let-your-house be-open wide

and-let the-poor be of-your-household,

and-do-not-multiply conversation with-a-woman. (1:5)

(4-beat meter)   Upon-three things the-world stands:

Upon-Torah, upon-worship, and-upon-deeds of-loving-

kindness. (1:2)

Another phenomenon noted above in biblical poetry—the desire to end on a strong and impressive note—reappears in these rabbinic utterances in a variety of techniques:

1. *The tendency to begin with a shorter meter and to lengthen the meter at the conclusion.* Thus in Abot 3:24 the meter changes from two beats to three:

Everything is-foreseen

but-free-will is-given.

And-in-goodness is-the world judged

and-everything is-according-to-the-preponderance of-one's actions.

In Abot 2:6 the apothegm begins in a three-beat meter, goes over to a four-beat meter, and ends in a five-beat meter.

2. *The entire maxim will be written in one meter, and only the closing stich is lengthened.* Compare the famous observation of Rabbi Tarphon (2:19), which is couched in a two-beat meter ending in a three-beat stich:

The-day is-short,

but-the-work is-great,

The-workers are-lazy,

but-the-reward is-great.

And-the-master of-the-house is-urgent.

In 3:1 the utterance begins with three-beat stichs and ends with a six-beat stich:

Observe three things,

and-you will-not-come to-transgression:

Know whence you-come,

and-whither you are-going,

and-before-Whom you are-destined to-render account and-judgment.

In 1:6 we have three-beat stichs with a closing stich of four or five beats:

> Choose for-yourself a-master
>
> and-acquire for-yourself a-friend,
>
> and-judge every-man in-the-scale of-merit.

This same phenomenon may be found in Abot 1:16, where the meter is 3:4:5, and in 2:6 where the meter is 3:3:3:3:4:5.

3. *The meter remains unchanged, but the closing stich consists of longer words.*

We may note Abot 1:17, which is written in a 3:3:3 meter:

> Stay-far from-a-bad neighbor,
>
> and do-not associate with-the-wicked.
>
> and-do-not-give-up-hope of-retribution.

In this utterance, stichs a and b consist of six syllables each, while stich c contains nine.

The oldest Hebrew prayers, which emanate from the Talmudic period, also exhibit the various rhythm patterns, as well as the tendency to end with a longer meter, as in this passage of the High Holy Day liturgy:

> (2-beat meter) Therefore give
>
> glory to-your-people,
>
> praise to-those-who-revere-You,
>
> hope to-those-who-seek-You,
>
> (3-beat meter) and-free speech to-those-who-trust-in-You.

The following prayer, the conclusion of the daily Silent Prayer, begins with three-beat stichs and ends in the four-beat meter:

> O-my-God,
>
> keep my-tongue from-evil,
>
> and-my-lips from-speaking falsehood,
>
> and-to-those-who-curse-me may-my-soul be-silent,
>
> and-may-my-soul be like-dust to-everyone.

It would appear that the three-beat meter, which is by far the most common in biblical poetry, gave ground in the Talmudic period to the four-beat meter, which seems to predominate, as in the following examples of the traditional liturgy:

It-is-for-us to-give-praise to-the-Lord of-all,

to-render greatness to-the-Creator of-the-world.

> (Daily and High Holy Day Service)

God, Lord over-all creatures,

blessed and-praised in-the-mouth of-every-soul.

> (Sabbath Morning Service)

God, blessed, great in-knowledge

He-fashioned and-created the-light of-the sun. *(ibid.)*

You-ordained the-Sabbath; You-desired its-offerings

You-commanded its-observances with-its-order of-oblations. *(ibid.)*

Most of the examples we have adduced from rabbinic literature exhibit synonymous parallelism, total or partial. Alternate structure is also to be found, as in the moving elegy pronounced over the Talmudic sage, Raba (B. Moed Qatan 25b):

> If among the cedars the flame has fallen,
> What can the hyssops of the wall do?
> Leviathan has been caught in a trap,
> What can the fish of the pond do?
> Upon the sweeping stream drought has fallen,
> What can the waters of the creek do?

Formal parallelism is also not lacking, as in the elegy pronounced over the two scholars, Rabbah Bar Bar Huna and Rab Hamnuna (*ibid.*):

> The stock of ancients has come up from Babylon,
> and with it the Book of the Wars of God.

Thus, the characteristics of biblical poetry continued to survive centuries after the close of the biblical canon. Ultimately, however, the Hebrew language ceased to be spoken even among the scholars in the academies and alien influences began to predominate, Biblical meter patterns and parallelism then gave way to the new involved medieval *Piyyut*, which intrigued both the poets and the people by its complicated structure. In the period of the Jewish-Arab symbiosis in Spain, the complex metric patterns of Arabic poetry became the model for the medieval Hebrew poets, of whom Solomon ibn Gabirol, Moses ibn Ezra, and Judah Halevi were the most distinguished.

This study has obviously dealt only with the technical aspects of biblical poetry. It goes without saying that creativity is far more than the mastery of technique. The inferior writer is trapped by rules; the genius uses them and rises above them to scale the heights. The great poets whose works have survived in the Bible were literary craftsmen unconcerned with literature. Utilizing the forms of biblical meter and parallelism, they created immortal poetry which transcended the frontiers of the beautiful and entered into the precincts of the holy.

NOTES

1. *Cf.* W. Wickes, *A Treatise on the Accentuation of the Poetical Books of the O.T.* (Oxford, 1889); S. Baer, *Ta'amei 'Emet* (Roedelheim, 1852).

2. *Cf.* ibn Ezra's commentary on Gen. 49:6, where he agrees with Moses Giqattila that the nouns *nefĕš* ("soul") and *kābhōd* ("glory") in this verse are identical in meaning, "because the meaning is repeated as in the prophecies of Moses and Balaam (in Deut. 32:7 and Num. 23:8)." *Cf.* also ibn Ezra's comment on Deut. 32:7. David Kimhi explained Isa. 19:8 as *kippūl 'inyān bᵉmillōt šōnōt*, "the repetition of the subject in different words." The philosopher and commentator, Gersonides, described this usage as "a rhetorical usage" (*derekh ṣaḥōt*) and pointed out that it was to be found in the poetry of the Arabs.

3. *Cf.* Karl Budde, art. "Poetry" in Hastings *Dictionary of the Bible* (New York, 1899-1902) vol. iv, pp. 3-13; G. B. Gray, *The Forms of Hebrew Poetry* (London, 1915). On the other hand, cf. C. F. Burney, *Poetry of our Lord* (Oxford, 1925), pp. 59, 62, which is an extremely valuable study of biblical poetry, both in the Old and the New Testaments, as well as in rabbinic literature.

4. A summary and criticism of these systems is to be found in Budde's article and Gray's book mentioned above, as well as E. Koenig, *Stilistik Rhetorik Poetik* (Leipzig, 1900); W. H. Cobb, *A Criticism of Hebrew Meter* (Oxford, 1905), whose severe comment, p. vii, is thoroughly justified : "How strange it is to see how far these critics have gone with their systems, which transform the exalted poetry of the Bible to inferior prose, so that thorns grow instead of wheat and thistles instead of barley!"

5. For some of these studies, cf. the papers of W. F. Albright in *JPOS* (1922), vol. 2 and *JBL* (1944), vol. 63; F. M. Cross, Jr. and D. M. Freedman,

BASOR (1947), no. 108; *JBL* (1948), vol. 67; *JBL* (1953), vol. 72; *JNES* (1955), vol. 14. This method and some of its results are now presented in accessible form in W. F. Albright, *Yahveh and the Gods of Canaan* (New York, 1968), pp. 1–52. In spite of the frequency and the assurance with which their conclusions are presented by advocates of this approach, a good deal of doubt, in varying degree, remains concerning a) the "reconstructed" text and its vocalization, b) the newly rediscovered vocabulary and the proposed novel exegesis, c) the dating of these linguistic and phonological phenomena and, consequently, d) the meters suggested for the "original" songs. Thus, to cite one instance, Albright (*op. cit.*, p. 12) proposes a meter-pattern for Ex. 15:11 which is based on his view of Hebrew pronunciation in vogue "a little *before* the time of Moses" (italics added).

Our present study is concerned with classical biblical poetry in the form in which it has come down to us. This approach has two basic advantages : First, it deals with an actual *datum*, both consonantal and vocalic, and not merely a hypothetical text. Second, the metrical analysis of the received biblical text, when the methodology employed is sound, helps to elucidate one of the most significant bodies of poetry in world literature, which deserves to be appreciated in its own right, whatever its "pre-history," real or assumed, may have been.

6. *Cf. Me'or Einayim*, ed. Zunz, p. 208.

7. In this verse, it is possible to scan the meter as 3:2. However, the rest of the Psalm (see vv. 2, 3, 4, 8, 9) has a three-beat meter in each closing stich. Verses 2 and 5 are also to be regarded as containing three beat stichs, on the basis of principles enunciated later in our discussion.

8. *Cf.* vv. 2, 3, 8, 9, 10, 11. The other verses cannot be analyzed here.

9. Here *ki* must receive a stress (unless *yiṣp^enēnī* be given two beats) to create a 3:3 meter.

10. Here *'im* in the closing stich must receive a stress, to carry out the 4:4 meter. The rhythm pattern is analyzed below.

11. *Cf. Zeitschrift der alttestamentlichen Wissenschaft*, 1882, pp. 4 ff.

12. *Cf.* W. O. E. Oesterley and T. H. Robinson, *Introduction to the Books of the Old Testament* (London, 1934), p. 146.

13. For Egypt, *cf.* Max Mueller, *Die Liebespoesie der alten Aegypter* (Leipzig, 1899), p. 11; for Babylonia, see A. Zimmern in *Zeitschrift für Assyriologie*, vol. 12, p. 382.

14. This has been noted by W. F. Albright, C. H. Gordon, and many other scholars.

15. On this and other passages in this song, *cf.* Gordis, "Critical Notes on the Blessing of Moses" in *Journal of Theological Studies*, vol. 34, 1933, pp. 390 ff.

16. Though 26:14 does not appear as Job's closing line, since he continues to speak in 27:2 ff. (cf. 27:1), it is clear that 26:14 marks the end of the description of the might of the Lord. There are convincing grounds for regarding 26:14 as the end of Bildad's speech. *Cf.* Gordis, *The Book of God and Man, A Study of Job* (Chicago, 1965) (= BGM), pp. 96 ff., p. 274 f.

17. The verse is 41:13. Verse 14 is of course a doxology added to mark the end

of Book I of the Psalms, a procedure followed in all five subdivisions of the Psalter.

18. In Ps. 42:6, the word *'elohai* is to be joined to *pānāv* and to be read *panay v'elohai*, as in 42:12 and 43:5.

19. Many commentators divide Ps. 27 into two distinct units after v. 6. We do not share this view. (See the study on quotations in the present volume.) It is, however, clear that a new section begins with v. 7.

20. Many critics divide Ps. 19 into three distinct poems (2–7, 8–11, and 12–15). This atomization of the Psalm not only destroys the integrity of the poem, but eliminates the basic idea of the unity of God, whose greatness is revealed in nature (vv. 2–7), in the Torah (5–11) and in the human spirit's striving after purity (vv. 9–15). When the poetic technique indicated in our text is recognized, there is no need for emendations of v. 11, like that of Z. P. Chayes (*Pērūš Madai Tillim*), *ad loc.*, which are designed to make it conform to the meter of the preceding verses.

21. The two closing verses of Ps. 51 are an obvious addition, intended to make the Psalm appropriate for worship purposes in the Temple, as Mowinckel and many others have recognized. Note the obvious contradiction between v. 12 and v. 21.

22. The vocable *'im*, "with," which is incidentally highly significant in spite of its brevity, receives a stress in accordance with the principle pointed out in section A of this paper. See note 10 above.

23. The recognition of this technique obviates the need of emending the verse to read *'Adonai hōšiāh hammelekh*, || *va'anēnū* (or *'adonai 'anēnū*) *beyōm qor'ēnū*.

24. This was the contention of Schrader and Briggs. See the refutation by Budde in his article "Poetry," in Hastings, *Dictionary of the Bible*, already cited.

25. Such criteria for direct borrowing would be a) an objective evidence of contact between the two culture areas at the period indicated; b) an unusual or extensive similarity in the sequence of the two literary documents; c) a striking or unexpected turn of phrase in both texts; d) an unconventional idea not likely to have arisen independently in distinct culture areas.

26. To be sure, stich b is generally rendered "the heritage appointed him by God" (*'imrō* being derived from the Hebrew word *'ōmer*, "word, decree"). As we have already noted, there is a tendency for an author to complete his poem with a longer stich. Here, on the contrary, we have a 4:3 meter, which is not what we would expect at the conclusion. It is also clear that this rendering of *'imrō* is inappropriate here, especially if we compare two parallel passages :

> Surely such are the dwellings of the evildoer,
> And this the place of him who knows not God.   (Job 18:21)

and

> This is the sinner's portion from God,
> The heritage the oppressors receive from the Almighty.   (Job 27:13)

It is therefore better to interpret *'imrō* from the Arabic *'imru^un*, "man," as was pointed out by Eitan and David Yellin (*Hiqrē Miqra*, Job 5686 = 1927, p. 52).

The noun then would be parallel to *'ādām*, "man," in stich a and the idea of "wicked" would be understood in stich b. The parallelism would then be a,b,c, || a,b,d.

However, we prefer to interpret *'imrō* from the Arabic, *'āmīr* = "prince, ruler," from the root *'amara*, "to command," a meaning which the root also has in Hebrew (cf. I Ki. 11:18 and see *BDB*, Lexicon *s.v. 'āmar*, sec. 4, p. 56b, as well as its repeated use in the opening chapter of Genesis). If we interpret *'imrō* as "a powerful one, tyrant," it would be exactly parallel to *'ādām rašā'*, "wicked man," in stich a. The *Vav* in *'imrō* is the petrified suffix of the original nominative case as in *bᵉnō šippōr* ("son of Zippor"), Nu. 23:18; *be'no be'ōr* ("son of Beor"), Nu. 24:3; and *hay'tō sāday* ("beasts of the field"), Ps. 104:11, 20 and elsewhere.

27. Cf. H. L. Ginsberg in *JAOS*, vol. 62, 1942, pp. 230 ff.

28. Cf. Gordis, "A Note on Lamentations 2:13" in *Journal of Theological Studies*, vol. 34, 1933, pp. 163 ff., and *idem, A Commentary on the Text of Lamentations* (New York, 1968), pp. 15 ff., for an analysis of this passage.

29. On this widely misunderstood passage, see BGM, pp. 206 and notes, 246 f. The full discussion must be reserved for our *Commentary on Job*, now in preparation.

30. See the commentaries *ad loc.* and Gray, *op. cit.*, chap. 7.

31. Cf. Bauer-Leander, *Historische Grammatik der hebraeischen Sprache des A.T.* (Hildesheim, 1962), Intro.

32. Cf. B. Landsberger in *Zeitschrift für Assyriologie*, 1936, p. 33; R. Marcus in *Journal of Near Eastern Studies*, vol. 6, 1947, p. 109; S. Lieberman, *Hellenism in Jewish Palestine* (New York, 1950) pp. 79 f.

33. For the literature on the strophe, cf. F. B. Köster, "Die Strophen" in *Theologische Studien und Kritiken*, vol. IV, 1831, pp. 40-114; G. Bickell, "*Das Buch Hiob nach Anleitung der Strophik*" (Vienna, 1894); K. Budde, art. "Poetry" in Hastings *Dictionary of the Bible*; G. B. Gray, *Forms of Hebrew Poetry* (London, 1915); A. Condamin, *Poèmes de la Bible* (Paris, 1933); K. Moeller, "Strophenbau in den Psalmen," *ZATW*, 1932, pp. 56 ff.; W. A. Irwin, "Poetic Structure in the Book of Job," *JNES*, vol. 5, 1946, pp. 26-39; E. J. Kissane, *Commentary on Job* (Dublin, 1939) pp. lvi-lx; P. J. Skehan, "Strophic Patterns in the Book of Job," *Catholic Biblical Quarterly*, vol. 23, 1961, pp. 125–42; *idem*, "Job's Final Plea and the Lord's Reply," *Biblica*, vol. 45, 1904, pp. 64 ff.; S. L. Terrien, *Job* (Neuchâtel, 1963), pp. 33 f.

34. Thus, Kissane maintains the following strophic pattern for the First Cycle in Job (chaps. 3–14) : Job's First Reply to Eliphaz (chaps. 6–7) consists of strophes alternating between six and seven verses; Job's reply to Bildad's First Speech (chaps. 9-10) consists entirely of strophes of six verses each; Job's answer to Zophar's First Speech (chaps. 12–14) consists of strophes of five or six verses each; Eliphaz's First Speech (chaps. 4–5) consists entirely of strophes of five verses each; while Bildad's First Speech consists of three-verse strophes.

35. Cf. *Le Livre de Job* (Paris, 1926), p. ci. This is also the conclusion of M. H. Pope, *Anchor Bible—Job* (New York, 1965), pp. xlviii ff.

36. See Gray, *op. cit.*, p. 32.

37. These characteristics of post-biblical Hebrew poetry have generally been unrecognized or insufficiently appreciated. Burney, *op. cit.*, notes the existence of parallelism in the *Mishnah Abot*, but since his basic concern is the New Testament, he devotes only a page and a half to examples from Rabbinic literature. The musicologist A. Z. Idelsohn in his paper *"Han^eginah Haš^equlah B^eyisrā'ēl"* in the Hebrew annual *Sepher Hašānāh Liyehūdeī Ameriqāh* (5698 = 1938) pp. 141 ff., calls attention to parallelism in the Jewish liturgy.

38. It should, of course, be clear that our conclusions with regard to meter and stress in the passages cited refer not to the English version, but to the Hebrew original, which should be consulted by the interested reader.

4. THE HEPTAD AS AN ELEMENT
OF BIBLICAL AND RABBINIC STYLE

Among all peoples certain numbers have played more significant roles than others, for reasons we cannot always understand. Such are the numbers "three," "five"[1] and "ten." Pre-eminent above all others in Semitic life and thought is the number "seven." For the Israelites, one has only to recall the seven days of Creation and the Sabbath, the Sabbatical year, the Jubilee, the Feast of Weeks, the seven days of Passover and Tabernacles, and the seven-branched candlestick. One can easily add the tradition of the seven Canaanite peoples, the seven processions around Jericho, the seventy weeks in Daniel, the "seven eyes" in Zechariah, and countless other instances from Bible, Apocrypha, New Testament and Talmud.[2]

A closely related usage is that of "three and a half," which is half of seven. This use occurs in apocalyptic literature, as e. g. "time, times and a half" (Dan. 7:23; 12:7; Rev. 12:14) and in post-Biblical references to the famine in the days of Elijah, which is described as lasting three years and six months (Luke 4:25; James 5:17; *Seder Olam Rabba*, ed. Ratner, p. 71, Oxford ms. reading).

These examples have been regarded by many exegetes as "broken sevens" and hence "mystic numbers." G. Kittel (*Rabbinica*, pp. 31 ff.) points out that three and a half is used not infrequently in Rabbinic literature and argues that it is merely a round number, equivalent to "a few." A study of available examples indicates, however, that "three and a half" is used predominantly, if not exclusively, of tragic or un-fortunate events.[3] This would support the view that it is an "unlucky number," and that its use as a symbol of evil preceded its neutral use as a round number, if the latter use existed at all. At all events, its relationship to the basic number "seven" is indisputable.

It has not been noted that this widespread predilection for the number "seven" has made it a favorite number for grouping literary material in heptads or units of seven. When this practice is recognized, it becomes a useful instrument for dealing with critical questions regarding the authenticity and unity of given passages, not alone to be sure, but in conjunction with other factors. A few examples of the heptad as a literary unit in the O. T. may be cited.

The call Abram receives from God takes the form of a blessing (Gen. 12:1–3). It is noteworthy that the blessing proper, exclusive of the command in v. 1, contains seven clauses:

> I *will make* of thee a great nation,
> And I *will bless* thee,
> And *make* thy name *great*;
> And *be* thou a blessing.
> I *will bless* them that bless thee,
> And him that curseth thee *will* I *curse*;
> In thee shall all the families of the earth *be blessed*.

The Midrash notes this fact and develops a series of homiletic interpretations on "the three promises of greatness and the four blessings" here given (*Bereshit Rabbah* 39:11).

Isaac, the least colorful of the Patriarchs, receives no special blessing. When, however, he is led to bless Jacob, his benediction, after the introduction, again takes the form of a heptad (Gen. 27:28 f.):

> So God *give* thee of the dew of heaven,
> And of the fat places of the earth,
> And plenty of corn and wine.
> Let peoples *serve* thee,
> And nations *bow* down to thee.
> *Be* lord over thy brethren,
> And let thy mother's sons *bow* down to thee.
> *Cursed* be every one that curses thee,
> And *blessed be* every one that blesseth thee.

The use of "seven" seems apparently to have been particularly popular with Amos, who has recourse to it no less than three times in his brief book.

In 3:3–7, we have a series of seven questions: (v. 3) a meeting of two men, (v. 4) the lion (2 instances), (v. 5) the bird in the trap (2 instances), (v. 6) the trumpet, (v. 7) the prophet.

In 4:6–13, the prophet enumerates a series of calamities, which also total seven in number: (1) hunger (v. 6), (2) drought of the crop (v. 7), (3) lack of drinking water (vv. 7, 8), (4) diseases of the crop (v. 9), (5) the locust (v. 9), (6) the plague (v. 10), (7) the earthquake (v. 11).

This third instance has bearing on the critical questions raised by Amos' "Arraignment of the Nations" (chaps. 1, 2). Many scholars have eliminated one or more of the sections on Philistia, Tyre, Edom, and Judah, though with little unanimity.[4] As Sellin explicitly recognizes, there are no conclusive grounds for these excisions. These being the facts, it should be noted in favor of the integrity of the received text, that the prophet arraigns seven nations, Damascus, Philistia, Tyre, Edom, Ammon, Moab, and Judah, before turning to his major concern, the kingdom of Israel.

Another Biblical writer who employs "seven" as a stylistic device is Ecclesiastes. The famous "Catalogue of Seasons" in 3:1–8 consists of twenty-eight stichs, or four times seven. Quite correctly, Hertzberg notes that this number is no accident.[5]

Of interest for our theme, though, strictly speaking, irrelevant, is the fact that the Midrash (*Koheleth Rabbah*, ad loc.) refers Koheleth's theme, "Vanity of vanities, says Koheleth, vanity of vanities, all is vanity" (1:2) to the seven ages of man, by counting each singular noun as one and each plural as two, in characteristic Talmudic fashion!

Koheleth also exhibits the use of seven as a stylistic element, in conjunction with another literary device. Most of the book consists of reflections extending over several verses. In 7:1–14, however, we encounter a collection of proverbial statements, generally similar to those in Proverbs with respect to their subject-matter, the use of parallelism, and the lack of logical connection between the sayings. For these reasons, scholars have tended to excise many of these verses as being later additions, inserted by a single editor (L. Lave, Jastrow), by two (Barton, Podechard, McNeile), or by several (Siegfried); but there has been little agreement on the deletions.[6] On the other hand, several recent students of the book, like L. Levy and W. Hertzberg, have argued for the genuineness of the entire passage; but, in their effort to find unity of thought in the section, they have been led to propose far-fetched interpretations.

We believe that a clue to the understanding of the passage is to be found in the gnomic structure of most of the verses, as evidenced by the use of synonymous parallelism (vv. 1, 7, 8), antithetic parallelism (v. 4) and comparisons (vv. 2, 3, 5). Pointing in the same direction are the conventional ideas expressed in some of the verses (vv. 3, 4, 5, 7, 8, etc.). At the same time, the spirit and style are characteristic

of Koheleth. This is exactly what we should expect, if we remember
that Koheleth was not only an original thinker, but also, and perhaps
principally, a teacher of traditional Wisdom in the schools. What we
have here is a collection of proverbs, reflecting both the original and
the traditional elements in Koheleth's thought, the whole refracted
through his unique personality.

How is this material organized? The nexus of these verses is to be
sought not in the realm of ideas, but in their purely formal similarity.
We have here a prose heptad, a collection of *seven utterances*, each
beginning with *tōbh* (vv. 1, 2, 3, 5, 8, 11), (*tōbʰāh*), 14 (*beyōm tōbʰāh*).
In v. 8, we have two apothegms beginning with *tōbh*, so that the
heptad may be conceived of as extending from v. 1 to v. 11, without
the need to include *beyōm tōbʰāh* in v. 14 as part of the rubric. In
most instances, these maxims have been amplified by related comments, which generally follow, but in one case (v. 13) precede the
maxim.

The practice of organizing material on the basis of similarity of
form, rather than relevancy of contents, is frequent in later Rabbinic
literature. The Mishnah offers many illustrations, as in *Eduyot*, chap.
6–9, where unrelated matters are associated under the rubric *heʿid*
"he testified that," and in *Yadaim* chap. 4, where *bo bayom* "on that
day" is the introductory formula.

A translation of Ecc. 7:1–14 will illustrate the literary structure of
the passage:

Better a good name than good oil, and so the day of death rather than
the day of one's birth.

Better to go to a house of mourning than to a banquet hall, for that is
the end of all men and the living may take the lesson to heart.

Better sorrow than laughter, for through a serious mien, the understanding
improves. Therefore wise men prefer the house of mourning and fools the
house of joy.

Better to hear the reproof of a wise man than the praise of fools. For
like the sound of thorns crackling under the pot, the laughter of fools grates
on the ear. But even the wise man's reproof is vanity, for a gift turns the
wise man into a fool and a bribe destroys the understanding.

Better to judge a matter at its end rather than at its beginning, and therefore
better patience than pride. Hence do not be quick to rouse your temper,
for anger lodges in the bosom of fools. Do not say, "What has happened?
The earlier days were better than these!" For not wisely have you asked
the question.

Better is wisdom with an inheritance—an advantage to all who see the sun, for there is the double protection of wisdom and money, and the advantage of knowing that wisdom preserves the life of those who possess it.

Observe the work of God, for who can straighten out what He has made crooked? In the day of *good fortune*, enjoy it, and in the day of trouble consider that God has made the one over against the other, so that man may not discover anything that happens after he is gone.

In Rabbinic literature, "seven" is also utilized as a stylistic device, though not as commonly as "three" or "five." As in the case of the other preferred numbers, the statement is often explicitly made that seven items will be enumerated. Such are the seven marks of a fool (Ab 5:7), the seven types of calamity (*ibid.* 5:8), the three kings and four commoners who have no share in the world to come (Sanh. 10:2), the seven things created before the world (Pes. 54a), the seven matters hidden from man (*ibid.* 54b), the seven types of man estranged from God (*ibid.* 113b).[7]

Of greater interest is the heptad, where the number is not indicated as such. Recognition of the heptad as a literary unit is useful in the critical study of Rabbinic sources. Thus in Sanh. 10:3–6, the Mishnah considers those who are beyond redemption. As each illustration is given, various opinions are cited. The structure becomes clear when the heptad is noticed.

The seven examples quoted are: 1) the generation of the Flood, 2) the inhabitants of Sodom, 3) the Ten Spies,[8] 4) the generation of the Wilderness, 5) the adherents of Korah, 6) the Ten Tribes, 7) the inhabitants of the Corrupted City (cf. Deut. 13:13–18).

That this use of the heptad is not accidental is strikingly confirmed by a comparison with the corresponding *Tosefta*. The *Tosefta* flatly denies that an instance of a Corrupted City ever took place,[9] and thus has only six of the seven instances left. It therefore adds another, "the generation of the Tower of Babel," and thus completes the heptad![10]

So, too, the Mishnah (Sanh. 11:1) lists the crimes punishable by strangulation, which total seven. So do the seven forms of worship that constitutes the sin of idolatry (*ibid.* 7:6). The crimes punishable by stoning are given in a double heptad, under fourteen categories (*ibid.* 7:4): 1) incest, 2) homosexuality, 3) sodomy, 4) a woman's sodomy, 5) blasphemy, 6) idolatry, 7) child sacrifice, 8) necromancy, 9) violation of the Sabbath, 10) cursing of parents, 11) rape, 12) seduction to idolatry (cf. Deut. 13:7, 13–18),[11] 13) practice of magic, 14) rebellion of a son (cf. Deut. 21:18 ff.).

With less assurance, attention may be called to the Mishnah Eduyot 4:1–6, which cites thirteen instances where the Shammaites adopt a more lenient position than the Hillelites, contrary to the general rule. Some editor has added to the ordinary texts a special category (4:2), perhaps to supply fourteen instances.[12] Following this group, additional points of issue between the two schools are listed: they total fourteen (*ibid.* 4:7–12).[13]

The Mishnah *Aboth* offers examples both of the heptad and the double heptad. The former occurs in ch. 2, which contains extremely interesting examples of the use of numbers five, seven, and ten as an element of style. In 2:4b, Hillel is cited in five sayings. In 2:7 another saying of Hillel's is cited and includes ten clauses. Between the five and the ten, we have a statement with six sections, followed by an Aramaic utterance which is the seventh and concluding number of the heptad (2:5, 6). The double heptad occurs in the description of the various ages of man from five to one hundred, numbering fourteen (5:21).

The *Baraita de Rabbi Meir*, usually appended to *Aboth*, likewise offers illustrations of the heptad and the double heptad. The beautiful description of the physical hardships of the scholar's life (6:4) contains seven clauses:

> This is the path of Torah:
> A morsel with salt *shall you eat*,
> And water by measure *shall you drink*,
> And upon the ground *shall you sleep*,
> And a life of pain *shall you live*,
> And in the Torah *shall you labor*.
> If you do so, happy *shall you be*.
> And *it will be well* with you,
> Happy in this world,
> And well in the world to come!

So too, seven Biblical verses are cited in praise of the Torah (6:7). Rabbi Meir's magnificent paean on the effect of the study of Torah upon human character (6:1) is a double heptad of fourteen clauses.[14]

Finally, it may be pointed out that this use of the heptad as a stylistic device may perhaps shed light on the critical problems connected with two of the greatest passages in the New Testament.

From St. Augustine to modern times, the Lord's Prayer has been regarded as consisting of seven petitions.[15] Yet it has been objected that these are really only six petitions, since "lead us not into temptation, but deliver us from the evil one" are merely the positive and negative expressions of the same idea. However, the Genesis passages quoted above, where the identical idea is expressed through synonymous (12:2; 27:28, 29 abcd) or antithetic parallelism (12:3; 27:29 ef), make it clear that the Lord's Prayer is a true heptad, containing not seven distinct petitions, but rather seven *clauses*, with the same idea repeated through parallelism.[16]

Another striking example of a heptad occurs in the *Beatitudes*. Montefiore remarks truly that "the effect which they produce in Matt. (5:3–11) is much greater than the effect produced by the shorter form of them in Luke 6:20–23."[17] The present text in Matthew actually contains nine $\mu\alpha\kappa\alpha\rho\iota\sigma\mu oi$. However, v. 11 is generally eliminated from the number, being regarded by some authorities as part of v. 10. More probably, it originally stood elsewhere, since unlike all the other Beatitudes in Matthew and like those in Luke, it is in second person ("Blessed are ye") rather than in third ("Blessed are they"). In addition to v. 11, v. 5, "Blessed are the meek, for they shall inherit the earth" is almost surely to be eliminated, as a doublet to v. 3, "Blessed are the poor in spirit," obviously based on Ps. 37:11. It is well-known that *'anavim* (humble) and *'aniyim* (poor) are often interchangeable in the Old Testament, in the double sense of the "lowly in estate" and the "humble of spirit."[18] Both v. 5 and the phrase $\tau\hat{\omega}\ \pi\nu\epsilon\acute{u}\mu\alpha\tau\iota$ in v. 3, represent editorial glosses to transmit the O.T. sense of "poor" to readers lacking the Jewish background of Jesus' original audience.[19]

These independent arguments for the deletion of vv. 5 and 11 are reenforced by the consideration that when they are eliminated, the Beatitudes in Matthew constitute a heptad, and thus illustrate once again the use of seven as an element of Biblical style.[20]

NOTES

1. The importance of "five" as a round number in Rabbinic literature and the N.T. is the subject of an excellent study by G. Kittel, *Rabbinica* (Leipzig, 1920) pp. 39 ff.; cf. also S. Lieberman, *Greek in Jewish Palestine* (New York, 1942) p. 31, n. 18. I am deeply grateful to my colleague, Prof. Saul Lieberman,

for calling my attention to Kittel's study, and for the opportunity of discussing several of my conclusions with him. Kittel also notes the use of "five" as a stylistic device. For the Bible, he could have called attention to the use of "five" in the Joseph story (Gen 43:34; 45:6, 11, 22; 47:2), possibly due to Egyptian influence. Prof. Leroy Waterman has shown that the "Book of Covenant" (Ex., chaps. 21–22) is constructed of paragraphs, each containing a pentad (AJSL, vol. 38, pp. 36–54).

2. For a succinct account of the use of "seven," see E. König in Hastings, *Dictionary of the Bible*, vol. III, pp. 562, 565.

3. In addition to the Biblical examples cited in the text, all of which bear this character, the Divine Presence is said to have waited in vain for the sinners to repent during three and a half years. (*Echah Rabbati, Petihta*, ed. Buber, p. 30). In the text of *Midrash Mishle*, 1:24, published by Buber, the reading, "*šeš šanim umeḥeṣâh*" should be corrected to "*šaloš šanim umeḥeṣâh*" which is vouched for by the Roman ms., cf. Buber's note *ad loc*. So too, three and a half years is the period of the siege of Jerusalem by Nebuchadnezzar (*Echah Rabbati, Petihta*, ed. Buber, p. 33) and by Vespasian (*Echah Rabbati* 1, 5), as well Hadrian's beleaguering of Beter in Bar Kokhba's unsuccessful revolt (*ibid*. 2:2; *Seder Olam*, ed. Ratner, p. 146). Hadrian's futile attempt to discover the extent of the Adriatic Sea, which also lasted the same length of time (*Mid. Tehillim* 93:4, ed. Buber, p. 416) was doubtless regarded with disfavor, both because of his own wickedness and the impiety of seeking to fathom God's ways. The instance of the Athenian who tried unsuccessfully for three and a half years to learn the language of Wisdom (*Mid. Echah Rabbati*, 1:1, §12) is probably to be interpreted similarly. In *Y. Shab*. vii, 9c, R. Johanan and Resh Lakish try, for the same period of time to deduce forty-nine sub-categories of forbidden labor on the Sabbath from each of the forty-nine major categories, an effort also unsuccessful. The number "three and a half" seems therefore restricted in use to misfortunes and failures in Rabbinic as well as in Biblical literature.

4. Harper, *ICC on Amos*, p. cxxxi; Eissfeldt, *Einleitung in das A.T.* (Tübingen, 1934), p. 444 "probably," and R. H. Pfeiffer, *Introd. to the O.T.* (New York, 1941), p. 579, delete Tyre, Edom, Judah, and possibly Philistia. Sellin, *Zwölf-prophetenbuch* (Leipzig, 1922) p. 165 ff., who dismisses all the arguments advanced against the authenticity of the various sections, finally deletes Tyre, Edom, and Judah on metric grounds. Concerning his views, and the entire issue, see "The Composition and Structure of Amos" in this volume.

5. *Der Prediger*, KAT (Leipzig, 1932) p. 84.

6. E. g. Jastrow deletes vv. 1a, 2c, 3, 5, 6a, 7, 8b, 9, 11, 12; Barton, 1a, 3, 5, 9–12; McNeile, 1a, 4, 5, 6, 7, 8, 10, 11, 12. For a detailed analysis of this passage, see R. Gordis, *Koheleth—The Man and His World*, 3rd ed. (New York, 1968), pp. 265–75 (= KMW).

7. The Midrashic miscellany, *Pirke Rabbenu Hakadosh*, which assembles rabbinic sayings based upon numbers, gives no less than twenty-two examples of the use of the number "seven" in chap. 5. The work has been published by M. Higger in *Horeb*, Vol. VI, No. 11–12 (New York, Nov. 1941).

8. It should be noted that the Ten Spies are lacking in the Mishnah of the

Palestinian Talmud (ed. Lowe, *ad loc.*) and that there is only a brief discussion about them in our texts of the Babylonian Talmud (Sanh. 109b). Moreover, Rabbinovicz (*Variae Lectiones, ad loc.*, vol. 9, p. 352) cites a variant, where this discussion is introduced by the formula characteristic of a *Baraita*, "*teno rabbanan.*" The paragraph in the Mishnah may therefore not be authentic. The Spies are, however, given in the Tosefta. Professor Lieberman suggests that the *Baraita* may differ from the Mishnah in citing the Biblical verse which the latter lacks, a frequent phenomenon in Tannaitic literature. If it is not authentic, a later editor is responsible for the rubric of seven.

9. עיר הנידחת לא היתה ולא עתידה להיות. (*Tos. Sanh.* 14:1, ed. Zuckermandl, p. 436).

10. *Tos. Sanh.* 13:6–12; *ibid.*, pp. 434 f.

11. The Mishnah uses two distinct nouns, *mesit* "the seducer" (cf. Deut. 13:7) and *maddiaḥ* "he who leads astray" (cf. Deut. 13:13–15). While the Talmud draws some distinctions between the two (*Y. Sanh.* vii, 25d, *B. Sanh.* 67a), the laws are really one in character, as well as in their Biblical source; on this basis, we may regard *hamesit vehamadiaḥ* as a single phrase.

12. The catchwords are: 1) ביצה, 2) שאור, 3) השוחט, 4) הבקר, 5) עומרי, עוללות, 10) פרט, 9) ביעור, 8) כרם רבעי—חומש 7) העומר, 6) השדה, 11) חבית, 12) שמן טהור, 13) שמן טמא. The additional instance, apparently taken from a *Baraita* (cf. *B. Betzah* 6b), is בהמה שנולדה ביום טוב.

13. The catchwords are: 1) האשה, 2) גט ישן, 3) המגרש, 4) צרות, 5) חלצו, כלכלת השבת 11) סדין, 10) המפלת, 9) המדיר, 8) ב' אחים, 7) נתיבמו 6) אדם תחת הסדק, 14) ב' כיתי עדים, 13) מי שנדר 12).

14. The verbs are: 1) זוכה, 2) כדאי הוא, 3) נקרא, 4) מלבשתו, 5) מכשרתו, והווה 12) ונעשה, 11) ומגלין, 10) נותנת, 9) ונהנין, 8) מקרבתו, 7) מרחקתו 6) ומרוממתו 14) ומגדלתו 13).

15. A. Plummer in Hastings, *Dictionary of the Bible*, III, p. 142b.

16. On parallelism in the N.T. cf. C. F. Burney, *The Poetry of Our Lord* (Oxford, 1925), pp. 63–69.

17. C. G. Montefiore; *Rabbinic Literature and Gospel Teachings* (London, 1930) p. 1.

18. Cf. Rahlfs, *Ani—Anav in den Psalmen*; Driver, art. "Poor" in Hastings, *Dictionary on the Bible*; Burney, *op. cit.*, p. 167.

19. Burney, *ibid.*, drops the phrase in v. 3 on rhythmic grounds.

20. When this paper was originally published in *JBL*, Professor R. H. Pfeiffer called my attention to the fact that the number *seven* is also used rhetorically in the Wisdom of Solomon: twenty-one (7×3) attributes of Wisdom are enumerated (7:17–18); seven wise men lived from Adam to Moses (ch. 10); seven sounds terrified the Egyptians (17:18–19 [LXX, 17:17–18]); the contrasts between Egyptians and Israelites are exactly seven (chs. 11 and 16–19).

5. QUOTATIONS IN BIBLICAL, ORIENTAL, AND RABBINIC LITERATURE

I

Recent discoveries of Egyptian and Babylonian Wisdom literature have stimulated a renewed and fruitful interest in Biblical Wisdom and shed light on countless features of this fascinating aspect of Hebrew thought and creativity. Yet, as is to be expected, there still remain many unsolved problems in this field where a fresh approach, coupled with light from our new Oriental sources, can prove highly helpful.

Particularly striking are the many passages, pre-eminently in Ecclesiastes and to a lesser degree in Job, which scholars have found irrelevant and even contradictory to the tenor of the book in question. Thus the problem of Ecclesiastes has a long history and has been met in varying ways in modern times.[1] In the eighteenth century, the view was prevalent that the book of Koheleth is a dialogue between a refined sensualist and a sensual worldling, or between a pupil and a teacher, or a record of conflicting views of academies of learned men.[2] Another way of accounting for the apparent contradictions of the book is the theory, first suggested by Van der Palm, adopted by Graetz, and elaborated by Bickell, that the book was written on leaves that were subsequently disarranged. More recently, the theory of composite authorship was tentatively advanced by Haupt, and worked out by Siegfried, who divided the book among nine authors.

Today the critical theory is less extreme. It argues that the essentially heterodox and unconventional writings of Koheleth were subjected to wide and persistent interpolation, in order to make them acceptable to the orthodox. Jastrow finds over 120 interpolations in a book of 222 verses; Barton claims that a *Hasid* glossator is responsible for 15 important additions, and that a *Hokmah* interpolater is the author of 30 more, aside from many minor changes. Volz eliminates an equal number of passages, which do not, however, coincide with Barton's. Eissfeldt protests against the assumption of composite authorship, and assumes only nine pious additions. However, he saves the authenticity of the text only by assuming that there is no clear-cut, integrated philosophy in Koheleth, merely a series of rambling reflections that often contradict one another.[3]

In Job, there are more complex problems, such as the integrity of the various sections and the obvious disorder and lacunae of the Third Cycle (chap. 22–31), which cannot be solved merely by excision. Far-reaching rearrangements of material have been suggested.[4] Nonetheless, the assumption of interpolations has been widely held. Thus in chapter 12, which contains 25 verses, Grill and Siegfried eliminate twenty-two, Driver-Gray delete nine, Jastrow omits twelve in whole or in part, while Volz retains only five verses of the total.[5] In Job ch. 21, widespread excision and emendation have been resorted to in order to make vv. 19–34 relevant and intelligible, the net result often being the creation of impossible Hebrew.[6]

This theory of widespread interpolation by uncomprehending or hostile readers, is losing ground increasingly among contemporary scholars.[7] Thus Aage Bentzen observes: "The separation of sources is sometimes driven to a caricature, as in *Ecclesiastes* and *Job*. The British pun: Is the Pentateuch Mosaic or a Mosaic? is not only characteristic for the sentiment among opponents of literary criticism, but also among the younger generation of scholars as a whole."[8]

Over two decades ago, the present writer was led to reject the practice of wholesale deletions in the text of the Wisdom books as being unnecessary and therefore unconvincing.[9] The considerations that justify this conclusion are both general and specific:

1. In many instances the ratio of "interpolations" to "authentic" material is extremely high, as has been noted above. That the superstructure is more extensive than the foundation is theoretically possible, but not likely, if another, less complicated explanation is available.

2. A convincing motivation for these alleged interpolations is lacking. What need was there for making the heterodox verses of Ecclesiastes palatable to the orthodox, when the entire book might just as easily have been ignored or consigned to the *genizah*? This happened with the Apocryphal and Pseudepigraphic books, many of which were far less objectionable to the alleged orthodox sentiment of the time.

3. The lack of textual proof for the theory. All the Versions, including LXX, the earliest witness, offer no support for the assumption, but reproduce, as faithfully as their resources permit, these allegedly interpolated passages in their translations. This is particularly true of Ecclesiastes,[10] which has been most exposed to the theory of interpolation, and where LXX is as meticulously exact as Aquila in rendering the text, with no lacunae.[11] There is no evidence of a recension differing from our Masoretic text underlying the Greek Versions of either Job or Ecclesiastes, as is the case with Jeremiah[12] and Ezekiel.[13]

4. Since the Wisdom books were written in the post-exilic period, the theory must crowd many steps into a relatively short span of time. These include the composition of the book, its attaining to popularity, its arousing objections among conventional readers, the addition of interpolations, and finally their integration and acceptance as part of the original text, so that the work would be accepted as canonical and hence translated into Greek as Scripture. All this must be assumed to have occurred within some three centuries. For at the Council of Jamnia 90 C.E., the position of Job and Ecclesiastes might be theoretically discussed, but they could not be dislodged from the Canon,[14] and the LXX translation of Job and Ecclesiastes are dated at 100 B.C.E. and at the very latest, 150 C.E., respectively.[15]

5. In most instances, the alleged interpolations in Biblical Wisdom books cannot be removed without leaving the rest of the passage hanging in the air. Cf. e. g. Eccl. 2:13, 14: וראיתי אני שיש יתרון לחכמה מן הסכלות כיתרון האור מן החשך: החכם עיניו בראשו והכסיל בחשך הולך וידעתי גם אני שמקרה אחד יקרה את כלם To remove 13 and 14a, leaves וידעתי גם אני, which is adversative, as גם indicates, without any connection or meaning.[16]

An even more complex situation exists in Eccl. 8:11–14: אשר אין־נעשה פתגם מעשה הרעה מהרה על כן מלא לב בני־האדם בהם לעשות רע: אשר חטא עשה רע מאת ומאריך לו כי גם־יודע אני אשר יהיה־ טוב ליראי האלהים אשר ייראו מלפניו: וטוב לא־יהיה לרשע ולא־יאריך ימים כצל אשר איננו ירא מלפניו האלהים: יש הבל אשר נעשה על הארץ אשר יש צדיקים אשר מגיע אליהם כמעשה הרשעים וגו'. Here vv. 11 and 12a express the idea, appropriate to Koheleth, that retribution is slow, and v. 14 that it is uncertain, some righteous men receiving the penalty due the wicked and vice versa. Vv. 12b and 13, on the other hand, express the conventional idea that those who fear God will fare well, and those who do not, will not live long. It is easy to delete these latter verses on the ground that they are the interpolations of a pious reader, but that does not meet the issue, for several reasons:

a) The ideas in vv. 11, 12a and 14 are not really heterodox. That retribution is slow and not without seeming exceptions could be conceded by a conventional believer; in fact, it is part of the theodicy of Job's Friends (Job 8:12 ff.; 15:20 ff.; 18:5 ff.; 20:4 ff.). It does not follow, therefore, that a pious reader would feel the need for a refutation. On the other hand, the idea expressed in v. 14 that the righteous and the wicked may meet the same fate, is much more uncompromisingly expressed in 9:2: הכל כאשר לכל מקרה אחד לצדיק ולרשע לטוב ולטהור לטמא ולזבח ולאשר איננו זבח כטוב כחטא הנשבע כאשר שבועה ירא. The interpolation would have been much more appropriate here, yet here none occurs!

b) The style of vv. 12b and 13 is replete with characteristics of Koheleth; כי גם (cf. 8:16; 9:12); יודע אני (cf. 2:14) אשר אלהים יראי ייראו מלפניו (cf. 2:26; 7:18, also 9:7) כצל (cf. 6:12).

c) The removal of 12b and 13 leaves 12a isolated in the context.

These objections made it increasingly clear that the assumption of widespread interpolations in Biblical Wisdom literature could no longer be maintained. A new approach was required which would reckon with the complete background of the Wisdom writers, and take into account the wider horizons revealed by Oriental Wisdom as a whole.

II

Basically, Hebrew Wisdom consists of two categories: the *practical* or lower *Wisdom*, conventional in attitude and dedicated to the cultivation of the virtues making for success and personal happiness, and the *metaphysical* or *higher Wisdom*, concerned with problems like the purpose of life, the meaning of death and the problem of evil. Not only the writers of Proverbs and Ben Sira, but also the authors of Job and Ecclesiastes, were teachers of Wisdom, and as such, accustomed to use the *māšāl* form in their ordinary pedagogic activity, as well as when they grappled with larger metaphysical issues.[17] Both these types of literature have their counterparts in Babylonian and

Egyptian Wisdom. The *proverb-collections* parallel the Hebrew *Proverbs* and *Ben Sira*, while the *meditations and complaints* are the counterparts of *Job*, *Ecclesiastes* and *Agur ben Jakeh* (Prov. ch. 30).

There is, however, no wall of separation between the lower and the higher Wisdom. Thus Erman points out that the Egyptian writings bearing the name *sbōyet* "instruction" include two literary genres a) "discourses on worldly prudence and wisdom intended merely for schools" and b) "writings far exceeding the bounds of school philosophy."[18] In Babylonian Wisdom, fewer examples of which have survived, the same two types are also to be met with.[19]

Similarly, there is no line of demarcation between the lower and the higher *Hokmah* in Israel. Since the unconventional Wisdom was an outgrowth of the practical school and was cultivated by Wisdom teachers, proverbial passages are to be regarded as authentic unless and until it is demonstrated that they cannot belong to the book. For the relationship of these unconventional Wise Men to the culture of their day was essentially complex. Within their world-view were elements of the completely conventional, the modified old, and the radically new. They doubtless accepted many aspects of the practical Wisdom as expounded in the schools, where they were educated and in which they probably themselves taught. As teachers of Wisdom they quoted conventional proverbs or composed original sayings of their own, which were not different in form or spirit from those of their more down-to-earth colleagues. Other ideas they accepted in modified form, while still others they opposed entirely.

Hence, quotations would be particularly congenial to the *hākām*, who unlike the prophet, lays no claim to direct supernatural revelation, but depends on careful and patient observation and logical deduction. Each generation of Sages would find in the extant proverbial literature of the past a body of lore created by their predecessors or their contemporaries, whose observations on life appealed to them as vital and true. Moreover, Babylonian and Egyptian Wisdom offers illustrations of quotations generally proverbial in form, cited for different purposes by the writers. These will be adduced below.

Because of these considerations, both positive and negative in character, the writer was led several years ago[20] to recognize the existence of quotations in Biblical Wisdom literature, which were utilized by the authors in various ways to express and expand the ideas they were seeking to promulgate. These quotations are naturally not indicated by a system of punctuation, which did not exist in ancient times, and often they may lack an introductory verb of speaking or thinking. That the passage is indeed a quotation must be understood by the reader, who is called upon in Semitic literature to supply not only punctuation but vocalization as well. The tendency to omit the verb of speaking or thinking is particularly common in a double quotation, where the verb may be used in one passage and omitted in the next, or vice versa.

It is noteworthy that this technique of quotations is not limited to the Wisdom books. On the contrary, it is to be met with in the Bible, in non-Hebrew Oriental sources, and in Rabbinic literature. This abundance of material not only demonstrates the validity of the usage postulated for the Bible, but sheds welcome light on the variety of techniques employed.

Before setting forth the evidence, several points should be made clear. The term "quotations" refers to *words which do not reflect the present sentiments of the author of the literary composition in which they are found, but have been introduced by the author to convey the standpoint of another person or situation.* These quotations include, but are not limited to, citations of previously existing literature, whether written or oral. In other words, the term, as employed in this paper, refers to passages that cite the speech or thought of a subject, actual or hypothetical, past or present, which is distinct from the context in which it is embedded. It will also become evident that the various types of quotations do not represent distinct categories, but constitute closely related developments of the same basic technique.

III

A. *Direct quotations of speech by the subject.* Hence a *verbum dicendi* must be understood or supplied.

1. *The words of enemies*

Ps. 2:2 f.

יתיצבו מלכי־ארץ ורוזנים נוסדו־יחד
על־ה׳ ועל־משיחו
ננתקה את־מוסרותימו ונשליכה ממנו עבתימו

The kings of the earth stand up,
And the rulers take counsel together,
Against the Lord, and against His anointed
saying:
"Let us break their bands asunder
And cast their cords from us."

Ps. 22:8 f.

כל־ראי ילעגו לי יפטירו בשפה יניעו ראש
גל אל־ה׳ יפלטהו יצילהו כי חפץ בו

All they that see me laugh me to scorn;
They shoot out the lip, they shake the head,
Saying:
"Commit thyself unto the Lord!"
"Let Him rescue and deliver him,
For He delighteth in him."[21]

This is a very interesting example of two quotations spoken by the Psalmist's foes; the first, addressed directly to him hypocritically, urges him to have faith in God; the second, like the Elizabethan "aside," sarcastically expresses their real wish to see his downfall.

That this is the intent of the passage seems clear from the verse now to be adduced.

Ps. 55:22 f.

חלקו מחמאות פיו	וקרב לבו
רכו דבריו משמן	והמה פתחות
השלך על־ה׳ יהבך	והוא יכלכלך
לא יתן לעולם	מוט לצדיק

Smoother than cream[22] were the speeches of his mouth,
But his heart was war;
His words were softer than oil,
Yet were they keen-edged swords,
As he said,
"Cast thy lot upon the Lord and He will maintain thee;
He will never permit the righteous to stumble."

Another insincere counsel addressed to the Psalmist by his false friends, which therefore evokes his imprecation in the next verse (55:24).

A. Ps. 109:5–20

ושנאה תחת אהבתי	5· וישימו עלי רעה תחת טובה
ושטן יעמד על־ימינו	6· הפקד עליו רשע
ותפלתו תהיה לחטאה	7· בהשפטו יצא רשע
ולמוזח תמיד יחגרה	19· תהי לו כבגד יעטה
והדברים רע על נפשי	20· זאת פעלת שטני מאת ה'

They requited me evil for good
And hatred for my love,
Saying: "Set Thou a wicked man over him;
And let an adversary stand at his right hand.
When he is judged, let him go forth condemned;
And let his prayer be turned into sin.[22a]
Let it be unto him as the garment which he putteth on,
Like the girdle with which he is girded continually."
This is the result my enemies hope from the Lord[23]
Who speak evil against my soul.

This entire passage cannot be the sentiment of the Psalmist who speaks of his foes in the plural throughout (vv. 2–5, cf. v. 20).[24] It is a quotation of the imprecation pronounced upon the Psalmist by his foes.[25] This avoids the necessity of assuming that the singular refers to one of the Psalmist's foes suddenly singled out without reason[26] or that the passage is a fragment of a "curse which should be deleted from the Psalter."[27]

2. *The words of the righteous*

Ps. 52:8, 9

ועליו ישחקו	ויראו צדיקים וייראו
אלהים מעוזו	הנה הגבר לא ישים
יעז בהותו	ויבטח ברב עשרו

The righteous also shall see and fear,
And shall laugh at him,

Saying:

"Lo, that is the man that made not God his stronghold
But trusted in the abundance of his richness,
And strengthened himself in his wickedness."

3. *The words of God*

Ps. 75:10 f.

אזמרה לאלהי יעקב   ואני אגיד לעלם
תרוממנה קרנות צדיק   וכל קרני רשעים אגדע

But as for me, I will declare for ever,
I will sing praises to the God of Jacob,
Who declares,
"All the horns of the wicked will I cut off;
But the horns of the righteous shall be lifted up."

Ps. 95:7 ff.

כי־הוא אלהינו ואנחנו עם מרעיתו וצאן ידו
היום אם־בקלו תשמעו
אל־תקשו לבבכם כמריבה כיום מסה במדבר

For He is our God,
And we are the people of His pasture and the flock of His hand.
Today, if ye would but hearken to His voice,
As he says,
"Harden not your heart, as at Meribah,
As in the days of Massah in the wilderness;
When your fathers tried Me,
They tested me; though they had seen My work."

Ps. 22:27

יאכלו ענוים וישבעו יהללו ה׳ דרשיו יחי לבבכם לעד

Ps. 69:33

ראו ענוים ישמחו דרשי אלהים ויחי לבבכם

In both passages, the same phrase occurs in second person: יחי
לבבכם. It is easy to emend it to יחי לבבם[28], but its identical occurrence
in two similar contexts make one wary of this facile solution. It bears
all the earmarks of an idiomatic formula of blessing or congratulation,
or perhaps of a banquet-toast, like "skoal" or "to your health" or the
Hebrew "lehayyim" for "life." Hence, render these verses as follows:

"The humble will eat and be sated,
May those who seek Him praise the Lord,
As they proclaim, "May your hearts live eternally.[29]

The humble have seen it
Those who seek God rejoice[30]
And proclaim, "May your hearts live."

4. *The words of the people*

In the famous crux Hos. 4:4: אך איש אל ירב ואל יוכח איש ועמך
כמריבי כהן, the last stich is to be read: וְעַמְּךָ כִּמְרִיבֵי כֹּהֵן, the Kaph
being asseverative and כהן in the vocative. This is attested to by the
next verse, which employs the second person and refers to the
prophet: וכשלת היום וכשל גם נביא עמך לילה.

Stichs a and b in v. 4 are best taken as a quotation of the people's
stubborn refusal to accept instruction. The entire passage is to be
rendered:

> *Yet the people say*,
> "Let no man argue, and no man offer reproof!"[32]
> Thy people are surely My adversaries, O priest!
> Thou shalt stumble by day,[33]
> And the prophet shall stumble with thee by night.

The last two stichs refer to the ritual functioning of the priests by
day and to the nocturnal visions of the prophet.

In Isa. 28:9–12, a similar portrayal of the people's contumacy is
met with, their position and sentiments again being embodied in a
quotation:

> *For you say to me:*
> "Whom will he teach knowledge,
> And whom will he make to understand the message,
> Infants freshly weaned from the milk,
> Just removed from their mothers' breasts?
> For it is precept upon precept, precept upon precept;
> Line upon line, line upon line,
> Here a little, there a little."
>
> Indeed with foreign speech and a strange tongue
> Will it be spoken to this people;
> To whom God had said:
> "This is the secret of rest—give rest to the weary;
> And this means refreshment,—"
> But they would not hear.

IV

B. The use of quotations naturally leads to the *development of dialogue* with the particular speaker not specifically indicated, but left to be inferred by the reader.

Protagonists of the dramatic theory of the Song of Songs naturally postulate such procedure, but for substantial reasons, this theory has been steadily losing ground to the view that the book is an anthology of love and wedding songs.[34] Nonetheless, dialogue between the lovers or the singers and the chorus is widespread in the book.[35]

Moreover, the use of dialogue is common in the Prophets, who found it an effective technique for dramatizing their message.

Hosea offers several instances of a deeply moving dialogue between Israel and God.

Hos. 5:15—6:4

עד אשר־יאשמו ובקשו פני   אלך ואשובה אל־מקומי
בצר להם ישחרנני
לכו ונשובה אל־ה'

יך ויחבשנו   כי הוא טרף וירפאנו
ביום השלישי יקמנו   וחיינו מימים
ביום השלישי יקמנו   יחיינו מימים
ונחיה לפניו ונדעהו
כשחרנו כן נמצאהו   נרדפה לדעת את ה'
כמלקוש יורה ארץ   ויבוא כגשם לנו
מה אעשה־לך יהודה   מה אעשה־לך אפרים
וכטל משכים הלך   וחסדכם כענן־בקר

God says:
"I will go and return to My place,
Till they acknowledge their guilt and seek My face;
In their trouble they will seek Me earnestly:
Saying
'Come, and let us return unto the Lord;
For He hath torn, and He will heal us,
He hath smitten, and He will bind us up.
After two days will He revive us,
On the third day He will raise us up,

That that we may live in His presence and know Him.[36]
We will eagerly strive to know the Lord
And as we seek Him, we shall surely find Him.[37]
And He shall come to us as the rain,
As the latter rain that waters the earth.' "

But God answers,
"O Ephraim, what can I do with thee
What can do I with thee, O Judah,
Your goodness is like the morning cloud
And like the passing dew of the morn."[38]

An elaborate example of dialogue occurs in Hos. chap. 14. Here the Prophet calls upon the people to repent (2, 3a) and to proclaim their return to Him (beginning with אמרו אליו, 3b, 4). God responds in vv. 5–8. Then comes v. 9: אפרים מה־לי עוד לעצבים אני עניתי ואשורנו אני כברוש רענן ממני פריך נמצא.

Ephraim *shall say* "What have I to do any more with idols?"
And God will answer, "Then I shall respond and look after him."—
Ephraim shall say, "I am like a leafy cypress-tree,[39]
And God will answer, "From Me is thy fruit found."

The use of אפרים in v. 9 is particularly interesting. As many commentators have understood, it represents the *dramatis persona* and is therefore rendered: "Ephraim *shall say*." It has not been noted that, though rare, the usage is not without analogues. In Jer. 50:7 f., the Masoretic text reads:

וצריהם אמרו לא־נאשם	כל מצאיהם אכלום
נוה צדק ומקוה אבותיהם ה׳	תחת אשר חטאו לה׳
ומארץ כשדים יצאו (כתיב) וגו׳	נדו מתוך בבל

The final word יהוה in v. 7 is lacking in the LXX and is moreover superfluous in meaning and disturbing to the rhythm. Hence it is deleted by most exegetes. Actually the word is to be added to v. 8, where it introduces God's speech after the words of the enemy in v. 7:

All that found them have devoured them;
And their adversaries said: "We are not guilty,
Because they have sinned against the Lord,
The habitation of justice, and the hope of their fathers."

The Lord calls out:
"Flee out of the midst of Babylon,
And go forth out of the land of the Chaldeans."

Another example of the absence of the *verbum dicendi* occurs in
Eccl. 8:2: אני פי מלך שמר ועל דברת שבעת אלהים.

"I *say*, "keep the word of the king.""

Attention has been called elsewhere[40] to a similar usage in the Talmud
(B. Kid 44a): אנא לא רב אבין בר חייא ולא רב אבין בר כהנא אלא רב
אבין.

I *report this tradition*, not in the name of R. Abin ben Hiyya or R. Abin
bar Kahana, but simply in the name of R. Abin (without a patronymic).

In the difficult 12th chapter of Hosea, v. 5 would seem to be a
quotation of the words of God. The passage is as follows:

So he strove with an angel, and prevailed;
He wept, and made supplication unto him;
Saying, "At Beth-El he would find him, and there he would speak with him."

Similarly v. 7 appears to be a Divine call, where a verb of speaking
must be supplied.

The development of dialogue is most extensive in Hosea's spiritual
descendant, Jeremiah. Only a few illustrations will be cited here:

Jer. 2:25

מנעי רגלך מיחף   וגרונך (כתיב) מצמאה

ותאמרי נואש

לוא כי־אהבתי זרים   ואחריהם אלך

I said, "Withhold thy foot from being unshod,
And thy throat from thirst;"
But thou saidst: "There is no hope;
No, for I have loved strangers, and after them will I go."

Here the verb of speaking is lacking before stich a, but occurs in
stich c (ותאמרי).

Jer. 3:22 f.

שובו בנים שובבים ארפה משובותיכם
הננו אתנו לך כי אתה ה׳ אלהינו

God calls, "Return, ye backsliding children, I will heal your backslidings."
Say ye to Him, "Here we are, we are come unto Thee; For Thou art the
Lord our God."

In Jer. 6:4 f. we have a series of speeches spoken within the enemy
camp. In 4a the foes urge one another to begin the attack; in 4b they
lament that they have let the noon pass (when a siesta is taken and a
surprise attack is readily made); in v. 5 they decide on an assault by
night.[41]

קומו ונעלה בצהרים	קדשו עליה מלחמה
כי־ינטו צללי־ערב	אוי לנו כי־פנה היום
ונשחיתה ארמנותיה	קומו ונעלה בלילה

"Prepare war against her, arise and let us go up at noon."
"Woe unto us, for the day has declined and the shadows of
    evening stretch themselves out."
"Arise, let us go up even at night and destroy her palaces."

Jer. 12:1–6 contains the heartrending query of the prophet: "Why
does the way of the wicked prosper" (vv. 1–4) and the enigmatic
reply of God with its promise of new trials for Jeremiah (vv. 5–6).
  An elaborate dramatic form is met with in Jer. chap. 14. Vv. 2–6
describe the ravages of the drought; vv. 7–9 contain the people's
prayers for relief, both these speeches not being identified either by
a subject or a verb of speaking. Then follows (vv. 10–12) God's
rejection of the plea (כה אמר ה׳, ויאמר ה׳). The prophet then voices
his complaint against the false prophets who promise prosperity (v.
13 וָאֹמַר) which is succeeded by the Lord's emphatic repudiation of
their activity (vv. 15–18 לכן כה אמר ה׳).
  The passage Jer. 6:9 begins with God announcing the doom
(כה אמר ה׳ צבאות). The prophet then voices his helplessness before
the stubbornness of the people (vv. 10, 11), whereupon God proclaims the doom of exile (v. 12, cf. נאם ה׳, אטה). While God's words
are explicitly attributed to Him, the reader must understand vv. 10
and 11 as the speech of the prophet.
  An example of quotations within quotations occurs in Jer. 6:16 f.,
with the speaker to be understood at the beginning of v. 17:

Thus saith the Lord: "Stand ye in the ways and see,
And ask for the old paths, "Where is the good way,'
And walk therein, and ye shall find rest for your souls."

But they said: "We will not walk therein."
And God said: "I have set watchmen over you who say,
'Hearken to the sound of the horn',"
But they said: "We will not hearken."

In Ps. 4:7 f. we have a striking contrast between the hedonism of the masses and the spiritual striving of the Psalmist for God's presence:

רבים אמרים מי־יראנו טוב
נסה־עלינו אור פניך ה׳
נתת שמחה בלבי
מעת דגם ותירושם רבו

Many say, "Would that we could enjoy pleasure!"
But I say, "Lift upon us the light of thy countenance;
O Lord,[42] Thou hast placed a joy in my heart,
Greater than that of the time that their corn and wine increased."

It is noteworthy that in these dialogues, a verb of speaking occurs at one point (Jer. 2:25b; 3:5; 6:9, 12:6–16 f., Ps. 4:5, etc.) and thus serves as a clue to the remainder of the passage where it must be understood.

This absence of any external indication of the speakers in a dialogue, which must be understood by the reader, is not limited to Hebrew literature. A striking instance occurs in the Sumerian poem "Gilgameš, Enkidu and the Nether World," which is virtually a verbatim translation of the so-called "twelfth" tablet of the Babylonian "Gilgameš Epic." Here, the recognition of this use of quotations with no external sign is crucial to the understanding of the entire poem, as Kramer has pointed out.[43] At a given point in the poem, the *pukku* and *mikku* of Gilgameš, probably a drum and a drumstick, have fallen into the nether world. Gilgameš laments their loss.[44] Thereupon, his faithful companion Enkidu volunteers to go down to the nether world and restore them to him.[45] Then follows a passage containing a warning concerning a number of tabus which must be guarded against in the nether world.[46] In accordance with the universal motif of world literature, Enkidu disobeys this advice, with disastrous consequences.

In the Ur tablet U 9364 there is no indication as to the identity of the speaker of this message of warning, but *on the basis of the sense demanded by the context*, Kramer suggested the insertion of a line

"Gilgameš says to Enkidu." The correctness of this suggestion has been strikingly verified by duplicate tablets which actually include this line![47]

In interpreting the Babylonian "twelfth tablet," all the modern translators assumed that this admonition about the nether-world tabus were addressed by some unknown person or deity *to* Gilgameš, and that it was Gilgameš who violated the tabus. The Sumerian parallel makes it clear that the warnings were spoken *by* Gilgameš and that the violator was Enkidu. Both the Sumerian and the Babylonian reader, like his Hebrew counterpart, was expected to understand the identity of the speaker in the poem before him, even when there was no external indication.

Another instance of an unexpressed quotation in dialogue occurs in the Sumerian epic, "Gilgameš and the Land of the Living."[48] The hero Gilgameš, realizing that like all men, he must die, is determined to raise up an immortal name by going to "the Land of the Living," known also as a land of cedars, and (probably) bringing back cedars to Erech (ll. 1–2). He tells his loyal retainer Enkidu of his plan (ll. 3–8), who urges him to inform Utu, the sun-god, of his intention, since he has charge of the cedar-land (ll. 9–12). Gilgameš acts upon this advice (ll. 13–18). At first, Utu is skeptical (ll. 19–20), but Gilgameš renews his plea (ll. 21–34) and Utu has pity upon his tears and decides to help him.

The passage, with which we are concerned, is contained in ll. 16–21:

> He says to Utu of heaven:
>   "O Utu, I would enter the land, be thou my ally.
>   I would enter the cedar land, be thou my ally."
> Utu of heaven answers him,
>   ". . . . . verily thou art, but what art thou to the land?"
> *Gilgames answers him,*
>   "O Utu, a word would I speak to thee, to my word thy ear."[49]

The line in italics does not exist in the text; it has been supplied by the editor, who correctly remarks that "the restoration, which is crucial to the context, is quite certain."[50]

What is particularly noteworthy in this dialogue, is that exactly as in the Biblical instances cited above, the speaker is explicitly indicated in several instances and left to be understood in another.

Thus, 1.3: "He (i. e. Gilgameš) says to Enkidu"
1.8: "His servant Enkidu answers him."
1.16: "He says to Utu of heaven."
1.19: "Utu of heaven answers him."

Only after Utu's speech, must the additional line be supplied to indicate that Gilgameš is now pleading once more:

"Gilgameš answers him (i.e. Utu)."

V

C—*Direct quotations of the thoughts of the subject.* Hence a verb of *thinking* must be understood.

1—Expressing the *present thought or motive* of the *subject*, hence supply a verb of thinking.

Gen. 26:7 כי ירא לאמר אשתי פן־יהרגי אנשי המקום על־רבקה כי־טובת
מראה היא.

He feared to say: "She is my wife"; *thinking* "lest the men of the place should kill me for Rebekah, because she is fair to look upon."

Ps. 8:4 ff.

כי־אראה שמיך מעשה אצבעתיך
ירח וכוכבים אשר כוננתה
מה־אנוש כי־תזכרנו
ובן־אדם כי תפקדנו

"When I behold Thy heavens, the work of Thy fingers,
The moon and the stars, which Thou hast established;
I say: "What is man, that Thou art mindful of him?
And the son of man, that Thou thinkest of him?"

Ps. 10:4

רשע כגבה אפו בל־ידרוש
אין אלהים כל מזמותיו

The wicked, in his arrogance *says:*
"God will not requite,"
All his thoughts are: "There is no God."

That the words בל ידרש are a quotation of the sinner's thought is certain not only from the parallelism, but from the direct citation of the verse below in v. 13:

על־מה נאץ רשע אלהים אמר בלבו לא תדרש

> Why does the sinner despise God,
> And say in his heart "Thou dost not requite."

This citation in v. 13 also proves that the two closing words of v. 3 belong to v. 4, which is a tristich in 3.3 rhythm:

נאץ ה׳ רשע ‖ כגבה אפו בל־ידרש ‖ אין אלהים כל־מזמותיו

> The sinner despises the Lord,
> In his arrogance, he declares, "He does not requite,"
> "There is no God"—these are all his thoughts.

Ps. 59:8

הנה יביעון בפיהם חרבות בשפתותיהם כי־מי שמע

> Behold, they pour forth with their mouths; swords are
> in their lips, for *they think* "Who doth hear?"

Job 7:4

אם־שכבתי ואמרתי מתי אקום
ומדד־ערב ושבעתי נדדים עדי־נשף

Here the parallelism indicates that the closing clause is a quotation. The verse is to be rendered:

> When I lie down, I say:
> "When shall I arise?"
> And when the night is long, *I say,*
> "I have had my fill of tossings until daybreak."

Job 15:21

קול־פחדים באזניו בשלום שודד יבואנו

That the clause בשלום שודד יבואנו describes the psychological terror of the sinner during his ostensible prosperity and is not a picture of his actual doom, is clear from the preceding and the following verses, 20, 22 and 23. The entire passage is to be read as follows:

All the days of the wicked, he is atremble,
During the number of years stored up for the oppressor.

The sound of terrors is in his ears,
Even when he is at peace *he fears* that the despoiler will overtake him.
He does not hope to escape from the darkness,
But he looks forward to the sword.
He wanders about for bread, *asking,* "Where is it?"
He knows that the day of darkness is ready for him.[51]

Job 22:12–14

ור'אה ראש כוכבים כי־רמו	הלא־אלוה גבה שמים
הבעד ערפל ישפוט	ואמרת מה ידע אל
וחוג שמים יתהלך	עבים סתר־לו ולא יראה

In view of the attested usage of verbs of speaking used only in part
(note ואמרת in v. 13) there in no need to rearrange the verse order,
or delete v. 12 as a gloss.[52] V. 12 is a statement of Job's alleged
thoughts:[53]

You thought,
"Indeed God is in the lofty heavens,
and see the topmost stars, how high they are!"

So you said,
"What does God know?
Can He judge through the thick cloud?
Clouds cover Him, so that He cannot see,
as He strolls about the circuit of heaven."

2.—This usage occurs in *formulas of the naming of children:*

Gen. 41:51 f.

ויקרא יוסף את־שם הבכור מנשה כי־נשני אלהים את־כל־עמלי ואת כל־בית
אבי: ואת שם השני קרא אפרים כי הפרני אלהים בארץ עניי

Joseph called the name of the first-born Manasseh: *for he said,* "God hath
made me forget all my toil, and all my father's house."[54] And the name of
the second he called Ephraim, *saying,* "for God hath made me fruitful in
the land of my affliction."

Ex. 18:4

ושם האחד אליעזר כי־אלהי אבי בעזרי
ויצלני מחרב פרעה

And the name of the other Eliezer: *for he said,* "the God of my father was
my help, and delivered me from the sword of Pharaoh." Note אמר in the
parallel in v. 3.

I Sam. 1:20

ותקרא את שמו שמואל כי מה׳ שאלתיו

And it came to pass, when the time was come about, that Hannah conceived, and bore a son; and she called his name Samuel, *saying*, "because I have asked him of the Lord."

3. *Rabbinic literature* shows many examples of this direct kind of quotation, where a simple *verb of speaking or thinking* must be supplied:

Abot 2:4:

אל תאמר דבר שאי אפשר לשמוע שסופו להשמע

Do not say something which cannot be understood, *thinking* "it will ultimately be understood."[55]

Shab. 23a, b

בשביל ארבעה דברים אמרה תורה להניח פאה בסוף שדהו⋯ שלא יהו עניים יושבין ומשמרין עכשיו מניח בעל הבית פאה

For four reasons, the Torah commands that *Peah* be set aside at the end of the harvest season . . . so that the poor will not be compelled to sit and wait, *thinking* "Perchance the owner is going to set *Peah* aside now."

While a verb of speaking or thinking must be supplied here,[56] it is explicit in the sections that precede and follow it:

שלא יראה בעל הבית שעה שעה פנויה ויאמר לקרובו עני הרי זה פיאה⋯ שלא יהו עוברין ושבין אומרים תבוא מארה לאדם שלא הניח פאה בשדהו⋯

So that the owner may not see a free moment and say to his poor relative "This is *Peah* (and take it)" . . . and because of unjustified suspicion, so that passers-by (during the season) should not say "A curse on this man who did not set *Peah* aside."

B. Shab. 30a

אמר דוד לפני הקדוש ברוך הוא⋯ אמות בערב שבת אמר לו כי טוב יום בחצריך מאלף טוב לי יום אחד שאתה יושב ועוסק בתורה מאלף עולות שעתיד שלמה בנך להקריב לפני על גב המזבח

This passage is to be rendered:

David said to God: "Let me die on Friday."
God answered: "*Did you not say to me*, 'One day in Thy courts is better

than a thousand?' (Ps. 84:11)[57] Better one day that you spend on the Torah than a thousand burnt-offerings that your son Solomon is destined to offer up on the altar."

Here is a quotation from Ps. 84:11 cited without a formula, and then expanded by an interpretation, a usage that will be discussed below.

B. Taanit 23b

הוה שכיח (רב מני) קמיה דרבי יצחק בן אלישיב אמר ליה עתירי דבי חמי קא
מצערי לי אמר ליענו איענו קא דחקי לי ליעתרו איעתרו לא מקבלי אינשי ביתאי
עלאי מה שמה חנה תתיפה חנה נתיפתה חנה קא מגדרא עלי תחזור לשחרירותה
הדרה חנה לשחרירותה·

R. Mani used to attend the lectures of R. Isaac b. Eliashib. Once he complained before the latter that the rich members of his father-in-law's house annoyed him. Said R. Isaac: "May they become poor!" and they became poor. (R. Mani then complained) "They press me for support" (whereupon R. Isaac said): "May they become rich again!" and they became rich. (R. Mani then complained:) "I am not pleased with my wife." (Whereupon R. Isaac asked him): "What is her name?" "Hannah" (was the reply). "May Hannah become beautiful!" and Hannah became beautiful. "Now she lords it over me;" (whereupon R. Isaac said): "May Hannah become ugly again!" and Hannah became ugly again.[58]

VI

D—A related category is afforded by citations of *Prayers*. At times prayers for help in distress which had been previously offered are now quoted by the Psalmist in a mood of joyous thanksgiving.

Ps. 30:9–12

אליך ה' אקרא ואל אדני אתחנן
מה־בצע בדמי ברדתי אל שחת
היודך עפר היגיד אמתך
שמע־ה' וחנני ה' היה עזר לי
הפכת מספדי למחול לי פתחת שקי ותאזרני שמחה

Unto Thee, O Lord, did I call,
And unto the Lord I made supplication
Saying:
"What profit is there in my blood,

When I go down to the pit?
Shall the dust praise Thee?
Shall it declare Thy truth?
Hear, O Lord, and be gracious unto me;
Lord, be Thou my helper."
Thou didst turn for me my mourning into dancing;
Thou didst loose my sackcloth, and gird me with gladness.[59]

A prayer for salvation cited by the Psalmist in the name of all the righteous occurs in Ps. 32:6 f:

על־זאת יתפלל כל־חסיד אליך לעת מצוא
רק לשטף מים רבים אליו לא יגיעו
אתה סתר לי מצר תצרני רני פלט תסובבני סלה
אשכילך ואורך בדרך זו תלך איעצה עליך עיני

For this each pious one will pray to thee when Thou art near,
"May the flood of great waters not reach me.[60]
Thou art my shelter and wilt guard me from the foe,
With songs of deliverance Thou wilt surround me." (Selah)

Following this quotation, the words of God are cited, also without an introductory formula, explaining that the troubles of the righteous serve a disciplinary purpose:

And the Lord replies:
"I will instruct and teach thee the way thou shalt go,
"I will give counsel, Mine eye being upon thee."

Ps. 27 in the Masoretic Text contains a hymn of thanksgiving (vv. 1–6) and a prayer for help (vv. 7–13) ending with a colophon of hope (v. 14). The widespread view that regards these two sections as two independent Psalms may be right,[61] but it leaves unexplained why they were joined together by the editor. Perhaps he regarded vv. 7–14 as a quotation of the Psalmist's earlier plea for help, and this latter section should be prefaced by some such phrase "For I had cried out."[62] On the other hand the Psalm may indeed be a literary unit, and vv. 1–6 would represent a prayer of thanksgiving, which the Psalmist, now in distress, promises to offer when salvation comes. For even within the *fides triumphans* of the first section, the mood of *fides supplians* is strongly evident (vv. 2, 3, 5a, 6a).
In Psalm 22, the moving description of the poet's suffering (vv.

13–22) is followed by a joyous hymn of thanksgiving for the anticipated deliverance (vv. 23–32). Vv. 22–24 are as follows:

הושיעני מפי אריה ומקרני רמים עניתני
אספרה שמך לאחי בתוך קהל אהללך
יראי ה׳ הללוהו כל זרע יעקב כבדוהו וגורו ממנו כל־זרע ישראל

Save me from the lion's mouth;
Yea, from the horns of the wild-oxen do Thou answer me.
I will declare Thy name unto my brethren;
In the midst of the congregation will I praise Thee,
Saying:
"Ye that fear the Lord, praise Him;
All ye the seed of Jacob, glorify Him;
Stand in awe of Him, all ye the seed of Israel, etc."

In instances such as these, the cited portions may be quotations; that is to say, drawn from extant literature they may have been composed by the poet for the occasion.

VII

E. *Quotations embodying the previous standpoint of thought of the speaker, which he may now have surrendered.* They should therefore be introduced by a formula such as "for I thought."

The great Confession of Innocence in Job chap. 31 illustrates this usage. The speaker describes his standard of integrity and moral behavior toward all human beings, due to his vivid sense of the Presence of God, the embodiment of justice, by which he had been guided during his years of prosperity:

Job 31:1–4; 13–15

ברית כרתי לעיני   ומה אתבונן על־בתולה
ומה חלק אלוה ממעל   ונחלת שדי ממרומים
הלא־איד לעול   ונכר לפעלי און
הלא־הוא יראה דרכי   וכל צעדי יספור...
אם־אמאס משפט עבדי   ואמתי ברבם עמדי
ומה אעשה כי־יקום אל   וכי־יפקד מה אשיבנו
הלא־בבטן עשני עשהו   ויכוננו ברחם אחד

The introductory Vav in vv. 2 and 14 is worth noting. It indicates a break into the thought-processes of Job, from the description of his actions to his motivation.[63] These quoted passages express the same theme that is stated directly in v. 23:

כי־פחד אלי איד אל   ומשאתו לא אוכל

> For I always feared a calamity from God,
> And I could not have borne His destroying me.

The deletions and transpositions proposed by the commentators for the chapter are thus seen to be unnecessary, injuring the spirit of Job's impassioned words.[64] The passage is to be given:

> "I made a covenant with mine eyes;
> Nor did I look (lustfully) upon a maid,
> *For I thought*, "What will be the portion of God from above,
> And the heritage of the Almighty from on high?
> Indeed it is calamity to the unrighteous
> And disaster to the workers of iniquity!
> He surely sees my ways
> And counts all my steps!" . . .
> Did I despise the cause of my man-servant,
> Or of my maid-servant, when they contended with me?
> *For I thought*, "What then shall I do when God riseth up?
> And when He remembereth, what shall I answer Him?
> Indeed in the womb in which He made me He made him,
> And fashioned us in the same womb!"[65]

Another instance of this usage is afforded by Ps. 44:21 f.:

ונפרש כפינו לאל זר   אם־שכחנו שם אלהינו
כי הוא ידע תעלמות לב   הלא אלהים יחקר־זאת
נחשבנו כצאן טבחה   כי־עליך הרגנו כל־היום

These verses have usually been rendered:

> If we had forgotten the name of our God,
> Or spread forth our hands to a strange god;
> Would not God search this out?
> For He knoweth the secrets of the heart.
> Nay, but for Thy sake are we killed all the day,
> We are accounted as sheep for the slaughter.

This interpretation, however, does not commend itself. כי in v. 23
must then be given a negative meaning, which is unnatural, indeed
impossible here.[66] (Delitzsch, Ehrlich "nein," *JV*, "nay, but";
Moffatt, "But no"). Besides, the whole idea of v. 21, which in this
view contemplates the possibility of betraying God's cause, is an
anticlimax after the passionate affirmation of loyalty of v. 18 and 19
and is a weak prelude to v. 23.

The key to the passage is to be found in the usage just elucidated
in Job 31, where a rhetorical question expecting a negative answer
is followed by the *motivating thought* in the mind of the speaker. It
is noteworthy that both in Job and in the Psalms passage the rhetorical
question is introduced by אם (Ps. 44:21; Job 31:14, 16, 19, 24, 26, 33)
and the quotation of the thought by הלא (Ps. 44:22; Job 31:3, 4, 15;
also 22:12 above).

The passage is accordingly to be rendered:

> Have we forgotten the name of our God,
> Or spread our hands to a foreign god?
> *For we thought*, "Indeed God will search this out
> For he knows the secrets of the heart."
> Indeed,[67] for Thy sake have we been killed all the day
> We were accounted as sheep for the slaughter.

The recognition of this usage helps in the solution of the perplexing
problem of the restoration of the Third Cycle in Job.[68] It is clear that
in chap. 27, vv. 13–23 which describe the doom of the wicked in
conventional fashion, cannot belong to Job, and are best assigned to
Zophar as the remaining part of his Third Speech. It is equally clear
that 27:2–6 are a fragment of Job's address in which he avers his
innocence.[69]

The remaining section vv. 7–12 has proved a stumbling block to
the exegetes, aside from difficulties in detail. Vv. 7–10 express a conviction that the sinner is excluded from the favor of God, which is
surely not Job's standpoint in the Dialogue. Hence, these verses are
usually assigned either to Bildad or to Zophar.[70] But this procedure
does not commend itself, on several grounds.[71] In the first instance,
v. 8 is linked by כי to v. 7, which, for all its exegetical difficulty, can
only emanate from Job, as the first person sing. proves (איבי ומתקוממי).
Second, the use of the second person plural in direct address, in vv.
11–12 (אתכם, כלכם, תהבלו) proves that these closing verses also

belong to a Job speech, probably marking the conclusion, such attacks being characteristic of several of Job's perorations (6:26–29; 21:34).

The solution lies in recognizing that the entire section 27:7–12 is a unit and belongs to Job; it contains a description of Job's attitude during his previous state of happy innocence,[72] exactly like 31:2–4, 14 f., 23:

Job 27:5–12

לא־יחרף לבבי מימי	בצדקתי החזקתי ולא ארפה
ומתקוממי כעול	יהי כרשע איבי
כי ישל אלוה נפשו	כי מה־תקות חנף כי יבצע
כי תבוא עליו צרה	הצעקתו ישמע אל
יקרא אלוה בכל־עת	אם־על־שדי יתענג
אשר עם־שדי לא אכחד	אורה אתכם ביד־אל
ולמה־זה הבל תקבלו	הן אתם כלכם חזיתם

The passage is to be translated as follows:

My righteousness I held fast, and will not let it go;
My heart did not blaspheme as long as I have lived.
For I thought, "Let mine enemy be in the wrong,
And my adversary be the unrighteous one.
For what will be the hope of the godless, though he acquires gain,
When God will require his soul?
Will God hear his cry,
When trouble cometh upon him?
Will he be able to implore[73] the Almighty,
And call upon God at all times?"
I will teach you on behalf[74] of God;
And what is in the mind of the Almighty I will not conceal.
Behold, all ye yourselves have seen it;
Why then do ye speak vanities?

VIII

F.—Closely related is the citation of a *hypothetical* speech or thought, an idea that *might or should have* occurred to the subject. Here the *verbum dicendi* must not only be supplied, but must be made to reflect the required mood.

A striking illustration occurs in Eccl. 4:8—

יש אחד ואין שני גם בן ואח אין־לו ואין קץ לכל עמלו גם עיניו (ק׳) לא־תשבע
עשר ולמי אני עמל ומחסר את־נפשי מטובה גם־זה הבל וענין רע הוא׃

There is one that is alone, with no one besides him, neither son nor brother;
Yet is there no end to his toil, nor is his eye ever satisfied with his wealth.
He never asks himself[75] "For whom then am I labouring and depriving myself
of joy?" Yes, it is vanity, a bad business.

This usage is often to be met with in Rabbinic literature, particularly
in legal argumentation, where hypothetical considerations are frequently invoked.

M. Ketubot 13:3

בנכסים מועטים הבנות יזונו והבנים יחזרו על הפתחים אמר אדמון מפני שאני
זכר הפסדתי

"When an inheritance is small, the daughters are to be supported and the
sons go begging from door to door. Admon says "*A son might argue under
these circumstances*, 'Shall *I* suffer because I am a male?"

B. Kamma 56a

מהו דתימא אנא כסויי כסיתיה ניהלך

You might say, *he might argue* "I covered it for you."

The verb (לימא) which must here be understood is explicitly used
in the parallel passages above and below:[76]

מהו דתימא לימא מי הוה מי ידענא דאתיא רוח שאינה מצויה...

You might say "He might argue, 'Did I know that an exceptional
wind would arise?' "

מהו דתימא לימא דברי הרב ודברי התלמיד דברי מי שומעין

You might say, "He might argue, 'The Master's words take precedence over those of the pupil.' "

Baba Metziʿa 35a

וניהמניה לוה למלוה נמי בהא כמה הוה שוה לא קים ליה בגויה

Let the borrower believe the lender on this point too, as to what
the pledged object is worth. No, *the borrower could say*, "*The lender
is not familiar with its true value.*"[77]

The various categories discussed thus far reproduce sentiments and ideas which do not represent the present standpoint of the speaker and must be regarded as expressions of the view of other persons or times. They can only be understood by the addition of an introductory formula of speaking or thinking and quotation marks. They are not, however, quotations in the usual sense of the term, that is to say, these passages did not have an independent literary existence before they appeared in their present context.

Quotations of this latter type are also highly frequent. As one would expect, proverbs, brief, pithy and widely familiar, would naturally be widely utilized in this manner. The various types of usage of proverbs must now engage our attention.

IX

G—The straightforward use of *proverbial quotations*, cited to buttress an argument and therefore requiring no expansion or comment, because the writer accepts them as true. The parallelism and the meter are the hallmarks of the poetic *māšāl* in a prose context.

Ex. 23:8

ושחד לא תקח כי השחד יעור פקחים ויסלף דברי צדיקים

And thou shalt take no gift; for "a gift blindeth them that have sight, and perverteth the words of the righteous."

Deut. 16:19

לא־תטה משפט לא תכיר פנים ולא־תקח שחד כי השחד יעור עיני חכמים ויסלף
דברי צדיקים

Thou shalt not wrest judgment; thou shalt not respect persons; neither shalt thou take a gift; for "a gift doth blind the eyes of the wise, and pervert the words of the righteous."

Ps. 34:12–15

יראת ה' אלמדכם	לכו־בנים שמעו־לי
אוהב ימים לראות טוב	מי־האיש החפץ חיים
ושפתיך מדבר מרמה	נצר לשונך מרע
בקש שלום ורדפהו	סור מרע ועשה־טוב

Come, ye children, hearken unto me; I will teach you the fear of the Lord. "Who is the man that desireth life, and loveth days that he may see good therein?

Keep thy tongue from evil, and thy lips from speaking guile,
Depart from evil, and do good; seek peace, and pursue it."

Job 2:4 f.

ויען השטן את־ה׳ ויאמר עור בעד־עור וכל אשר לאיש יתן בעד נפשו· אולם
שלח־נא ידך וגע אל־עצמו ואל־בשרו אם־לא אל־פניך יברכך

And Satan answered the Lord and said, "Skin for skin, yea, all a man hath,
will he give for his life. But put forth thy hand and touch his bone and
flesh, surely he will blaspheme Thee to Thy face."

The first half of Satan's speech bears all the earmarks of a folk-
proverb. Note the parallelism of structure, the realistic character of
the generalization, and above all the idiomatic brevity of the first stich
(עור בעד עור) which creates the difficulties for the modern exegete.[78]
Only such stylistic criteria can help determine, with any degree of
assurance at all, whether the text is a folk-saying quoted by the author
or an apothegm composed by him.[79]

Job 17:5

ועיני בניו תכלינה   לחלק יגיד רעים

This highly difficult verse, which has been subjected to a great
variety of interpretations, is probably best taken as a folk-saying;

"He invites friends to share (his table), while his own children's eyes fail
(from starvation)."

Job argues that the friends are dispensing wisdom to him from an all
too slender stock of their own.[80]

This use of a quotation to support a point of view, with no external
sign of the borrowing, occurs in Rabbinic literature:

B. Erubin 54a

אמר ליה רב לרב המנונא בני אם יש לך היטב לך שאין בשאול תענוג ואין למות
התמהמה ואם תאמר אניח לבני חוק בשאול מי יגיד לך בני אדם דומין לעשבי
השדה הללו נוצצין והללו נובלין

While there is no formal indication, Rab begins this counsel to
Rab Hamnuna with a quotation from Ben Sira to which he appends
his own comments:

"My son, if you have the wherewithal,
Do good to yourself,
For there is no pleasure in the grave,
And no postponement of death."[80a]
And if you say, Let me leave a portion for my son,
Who can tell you in the grave (what will happen to it)?
Men are like the grass of the field,
These sprout and others decay.

The stichs in quotation marks are cited from Ben Sira 14:11–12;[81] the remainder is Rab's own, except for the last stich, which is a free paraphrase of Ben Sira 14:18b.

The same usage occurs in Egyptian literature. In the "Admonitions of a Prophet" which probably emanates from the end of the second millennium, we have a graphic description of the widespread destruction sweeping over the social order, with the lowly attaining to wealth and importance. In the "Second Poem," each stanza begins with the refrain, "Behold," a characteristic rhetorical device. Part of this section reads as follows:

Behold, he that had no bread now possesseth a barn; (but) that wherewith his storehouse is provided is the poverty of another.

Behold, the bald head that used no oil now possesseth jars of pleasant myrrh.

Behold, she that had no box now possesseth a coffer.
She that looked at her face in the water now possesseth a mirror.
     (A verse left incomplete.)

Behold, a man is happy when he eateth his food:
"Spend thy possessions in joy and without holding thee back! It is good for a man to eat his food, which God assigneth to him whom he praiseth . . ."

The last two sentences, as Erman notes, are "a quotation from an old book."[82] They have been introduced to buttress the argument. Actually they are not altogether appropriate. For while the author is describing the lot of a man formerly poor, who is now happy to have something to eat, the proverb urges the enjoyment of life. But the use of quotations only partly relevant to the context is characteristic of writers everywhere. An example occurs in Eccl. 5:1, 2, where only part of the proverb is relevant:

אל־תבהל על־פיך ולבך אל־ימהר להוציא דבר לפני האלהים כי האלהים
בשמים ואתה על־הארץ על־כן יהיו דבריך מעטים: כי בא החלום ברב ענין וקול
כסיל ברב דברים

Do not hasten to speak, nor let yourself be rushed into uttering words before God, for God is in heaven and you are on the earth—therefore, let your words be few. For "as dreams come with many worries, so the fool speaks with many words."[83]

Proverbial quotations may occur *without being part of a larger context*, the writer regarding them as sufficient to express his point of view.

This has often been overlooked in Ecclesiastes, who, for all his unconventional ideas, would by and large endorse the practical counsel given, for example, in the book of Proverbs.

Hence many of the proverbs in Ecclesiastes may be either sayings quoted from earlier literature which he approves or originally composed by Koheleth, doubtless in the course of his career as a Wisdom teacher. The most confirmed cynic will agree that

> By slothfulness the rafters sink in;
> And through idleness of the hands the house leaketh (10:18).

He might suggest that it is wise to diversify one's undertakings:

> Cast thy bread upon the waters,
> For thou shalt find it after many days (11:1).

The mishnic treatise Abot consists entirely of favorite sayings of Rabbinic teachers, generally introduced by the phrase: "he was wont to say, etc." In two instances, however, the sayings attributed to Rabbis are entirely quotations from extant literature, instead of being original maxims, yet they are introduced by the same formula. In Abot 4:4, R. Levitas cites Ben Sira 7:17[84] רבי לויטס איש יבנה אומר מאד מאד הוי שפל רוח שתקות אנוש רמה. In 4:24 Samuel Hakatan cites Prov. 24:17 f. שמואל הקטן אומר בנפל איבך אל תשמח ובכשלו אל יגל לבך פן יראה ה' ורע בעיניו והשיב מעליו אפו. Both passages should be rendered: "He was wont to say, '*It has been written*,' etc."

Another instance of this citation of a literary passage without any external mark of a quotation occurs in *B. Kethubot* 22b, as the Tosafists have noted.[85] The passage reads: משום דרב אסי דאמר הסר ממך עקשות פה ולזות שפתים הרחק ממך

This position is maintained because of R. Asi who used to say, "*It is written* (Prov. 4:24) 'Put away from thee a froward mouth, and perverse lips put far from thee.' "

It is noteworthy that these citations are all proverbial in character, being drawn from *Proverbs* and *Ben Sira*. The pithy character of the sayings lends itself to quotations and explains the frequency of this practice in the text of *Ecclesiastes*.

X

H—*The use of proverbial quotations as a text*, on which the author comments from his own viewpoint, is an outstanding stylistic characteristic of Koheleth.

Thus Eccl. 7:9–18 is a collection of seven *Hokmah* utterances, expressing conventional Wisdom teachings and linked together by the opening word *tōbh*. Each proverb is amplified by a comment bearing all the earmarks of Koheleth's style and viewpoint. A full discussion of this passage must be sought elsewhere.[86] One illustration may however be adduced here. Thus, a typically abstemious and moralizing doctrine is sounded in Eccl. 7:2a:

טוב ללכת אל־בית־אבל מלכת אל־בית־משתה

> It is better to go to the house of mourning
> Than to go to the house of feasting . . .

a proverb, warning against the revelry and immorality of the house of mirth.[87] But Koheleth gives it a darker undertone:—

באשר הוא סוף כל־האדם והחי יתן אל־לבו

> For that is the end of all men
> And the living will lay it to heart. (Eccl. 7:2)

Examples of this use of proverb as text with ironic comment are plentiful. Thus a proverb extols the virtues of cooperation. Koheleth approves the sentiment, but for reasons of his own:

Men say, "Two are better than one, because they have a reward in their labor." True, for if either falls, the other can lift his comrade, but woe to him who is alone when he falls, with no one else to lift him. Then also, if two sleep together, they will be warm, but how can one alone keep warm? Moreover, if some enemy attack either one, the two will stand against him, while a triple cord cannot quickly be severed. (Eccl. 4:9–12).[88]

The teachers of morality emphasized that love of money does not make for happiness. This idea is expanded by Koheleth through the characteristic reflection that strangers finally consume the substance of the owner, an idea to which he refers again and again (cf. 2:18 ff.; 4:7 ff.):

"He who loves money will never have enough of it and he who loves wealth will never attain it,"[89] this is indeed vanity. For as wealth increases, so do those who spend it, hence what value is there in the owner's superior ability, except that he has more to look upon? (Ecc. 5:9 f.)

The Book of Proverbs counsels submission to political authority:

Fear, my son, God and king, and meddle not with those who seek change. (Prov. 24:21)

Koheleth repeats this idea but with his tongue in his cheek:

I say: keep the king's command, because of the oath of loyalty.

Submit to the king because of your oath of fealty, but also, he adds as an afterthought:

> Since the king's word is law, who can say to him,
> "What are you doing?" (Eccl. 8:2–4)

because the king is powerful enough to crush you.

Similarly, to maintain oneself in an atmosphere of political tyranny and intrigue requires skill in choosing the proper occasion. That idea Koheleth appends as a comment to a perfectly moral utterance about the virtues of obedience:

"Whoever keeps the commandment shall know no evil," but a wise man's heart discerns the proper time. For every matter has its proper time, for man's evil is great upon him. (Eccl. 8:5–6)[90]

In addition to these examples which mirror the political conditions of Koheleth's time, several interesting instances of his use of conventional *Hokmah* material in the field of religion and philosophic speculation are apparently to be met with.

For example, Koheleth is not disposed to deny altogether that retribution overtakes the sinner. Yet, in many instances, the righteous and the wicked are treated alike. At other times, punishment is meted out to the sinner, but only after a long delay, which affords him the opportunity and the incentive to sin.

These two limitations on Divine justice are referred to in an interesting passage, 8:11–14, the center of which (vv. 12b, 13) is a quotation of the traditional view, from which Koheleth dissents. There is therefore no need to eliminate vv. 11–13 as a gloss.[91] Our rendering is as follows:

Because judgment upon an evil deed is not executed speedily, men's hearts are encouraged to do wrong, for a sinner commits a hundred crimes and God is patient with him, though I know the answer that "it will be well in the end with those who revere God and fear Him and it will be far from well with the sinner, who, like a shadow, will not long endure, because he does not fear God."

Here is a vanity that takes place on the earth—there are righteous men who receive the recompense due the wicked, and wicked men who receive the recompense due the righteous. I say, this is indeed vanity.

Koheleth would undoubtedly agree with the universal view that life on any terms is preferable to death. Yet his general intellectual conviction as to the futility of living impels him to a comment, which ostensibly justifies, but actually undermines, the entire proposition.

"He who is attached to the living still has hope, for a live dog is better than a dead lion!" The living know at least that they will die, but the dead know nothing, nor have they any reward, for their memory is forgotten. Their loves, their hates, their jealousies, all have perished—never again will they have a share in all that is done under the sun. (Eccl. 9:4–6)

This usage of a quotation cited by the author and then refuted, or at least discussed, occurs several times in the Babylonian "Complaint on the Injustice of the World," the so-called *Babylonian Koheleth*.[92] Thus the author explicitly cites two conventional proverbs on the well-being of the righteous, which he does not accept (11:69–71). On the basis of Ebeling's version, the passage reads as follows:

A saying I wish to discuss with you:
"They go on the road to fortune, who do not think of murder."
"More than a mere creature is the weak one who prays to God."
More than any other child of man, have I been troubled about God's plan.

Another quotation without an introductory formula occurs in ll. 215 ff. The poet laments the prosperity and success of the wicked. He cites the conventional proverbs which urge obedience to the god as the secret of well-being, which he then refutes by emphasizing the unpredictability and transitoriness of God's favor. In English, Ebeling's rendering reads:

Without God, the rogue possesses power,
For murder as his weapon accompanies him.
"You who do not seek the counsel of the God, what is your fortune?"
"He who bears the yoke of God, his bread is provided!"
No, seek rather a good wind of the gods.
What you have destroyed in a year, you restore in an instant,
Among men I have set offerings, changeable are the omens.

The lines in quotation marks are not indicated externally as such, but are evidently citations of accepted ideas, with which the melancholy poet is in disagreement. That ll. 69–71 and 217 f. are quotations is recognized by Ebeling who adds the comments "So sagen die Menschen" and "So sagen die Leute," the precise formula required in all the instances we have cited above, and adds the quotation marks.

XI

I—*Contrasting proverbs* offer another way of contradicting accepted doctrines. As is well known, proverbs frequently contradict one another, since they express the half-truths of empirical wisdom. "Fools rush in where angels fear to tread" is opposed by the saw "To hesitate is to be lost." The beautiful sentiment "Absence makes the heart grow fonder" is bluntly denied by the saying "Out of sight, out of mind."

The compiler of Proverbs was aware of this tendency when he quoted these two maxims in succession:

Answer not a fool according to his folly, lest thou also be like unto him.
Answer a fool according to his folly, lest he be wise in his own eyes.
    (Prov. 26:4, 5)

Job and Koheleth use the same device, but for their own purposes. They quote one proverb and then register their disagreement by citing another diametrically opposed thereto.

No theme was dearer to the hearts of the instructors of youth than that of the importance of hard work.[93] Koheleth expresses his doubts on the subject by quoting the conventional view and following it by another proverb of opposite intent:

> "The fool foldeth his hands together, and eateth his own flesh."
> "Better is a handful of quietness, than both hands full of labour and
>   striving after wind." (Eccl. 4:5, 6)

That Koheleth favors the second view is proved by its position as a
refutation after verse 5, by the characteristic phrase, "vanity and
chasing of wind," and by his oft-repeated view of the folly of toil in
a meaningless world.[94]

Like all the Wise Men, conventional or otherwise, Koheleth has a
prejudice in favor of wisdom as against folly. He himself tells how
the wisdom of one poor man proved more efficacious than a mighty
army. Yet he knows, too, how little wisdom is honored for its own
sake, and how one fool can destroy the efforts of many wise men.
These ideas seem to be expressed in some reflections, consisting of
brief proverbs contradicted by others.[95]

> *I thought* "Wisdom is better than prowess" but "the wisdom of the poor
>   man is despised and his words are not heard."
> "Wisdom is better than weapons of war." But "one fool destroys much
>   good." (Eccl. 9:16, 18)[96]

Here, the latter proverbs, in which Koheleth expresses his own
standpoint, are undoubtedly of his own composition. The former
proverbs, from which he dissents, may be quotations, or, as seems
more probable, original restatements by Koheleth of conventional
Hokmah doctrines.

The recognition of this device in Job (12:12 f.) helps to explain an
otherwise abrupt transition. Throughout the argument Job's friends
have insisted that they possess superior wisdom because of their
greater age:

> What knowest thou, that we know not?
> What understandest thou, which is not in us?
> With us are both the gray-headed and the very aged,
> Much older than thy father in days. (Job. 15:9, 10)

Job denies this principle, by citing it in one proverb and refuting
it by another. Here, too, the use of quotation marks and an introductory formula makes the connection clear:

> *You say* "With aged men is wisdom and length of days is understanding."
> *But I say* "With Him is wisdom and might; He hath counsel and under-
>   standing." (Job 12:12, 13).[97]

Per se, the second proverb merely asserts God's wisdom; but by being placed in juxtaposition to v. 11, it serves to undermine the doctrine of the superiority of the aged. The authenticity of both verses emerges from a careful noting of the terms employed.[98]

The relationship between these two verses is aptly illustrated by another passage of similar import from the Elihu speeches. Like Job, Elihu is impatient with the pretensions of the Elders to superior wisdom. He also quotes the accepted opinion as to the relation between age and wisdom and then proceeds to refute it. He does so, however, not by a proverb, but by a comment. Here the transition is clear because of the use of the introductory words: (v. 7, אמרתי; v. 8, אכן)

I thought "Days should speak, and many years should teach wisdom."
But it is the spirit in man and the breath of the Almighty, that gives
   understanding. (Job 32:7, 8)

XII

J. *Quotations are used in argumentation* in a different manner in the Dialogue in Job. In attacking the conventional views on reward and punishment, Job has no need to cite literary sources, for the doctrines are being expounded in his very presence by the Friends. Hence Job quotes the utterances of his adversaries, and even distorts them in some degree, as men have always done in controversy.

Job's closing speech in the Second Cycle (Chapter 21, vv. 19–34) supplies an excellent illustration. Here commentators have resorted to excision and emendation, in order to make the passage intelligible.[99] These expedients become unnecessary if we recognize that here, at the end of the Second Cycle of speeches, Job restates no fewer than four arguments of the Friends and refutes each in turn:

I. The Friends argue that the sins of the fathers will be visited upon the children (cf. Job 5:4; 18:12; 20:10, 26). This view, eminently satisfying in the old days of group solidarity, was becoming increasingly unattractive with the emergence of the individual personality in Hebrew thought. In 21:19a, Job quotes this view; in vv. 19b–21, he refutes it.

II. Another argument of the Friends is that God is too exalted for human comprehension and hence His Wisdom is beyond man's

criticism. This is a favorite theme of Eliphaz (4:17; 15:8, 14) and
Zophar (11:6 ff.). This view Job paraphrases in 21:22:

> Shall any one teach God knowledge,
> Seeing that He judges those on high?

Manifestly Job cannot deny the transcendence of God. He therefore proceeds to refute this conception of God's perfect dealings with
man, not directly but obliquely. He paints an unforgettable picture
of reality, emphasizing the contrast between the ease of the wicked
and the bitter lot of the just during their lifetime, while even in death
there is no just retribution, for they both meet the same end (vv.
23–26).

III. The Friends have delighted to point out that while the sinner
may seem to be well entrenched in his prosperity, calamity suddenly
comes upon him, destroying his habitation and leaving nothing to
mark the site of his former glory. This position has been emphasized
by Eliphaz (in 5:3 ff.; 15:32 ff.), Bildad (8:22; 18:5–21), and Zophar
(11:20; 20:26).

Job quotes this favorite doctrine of the Friends in the form of a
rhetorical question addressed to him (v. 28):

"Where is the house of the prince, or where the tent of dwelling of the
    wicked?"

Then, taking the rhetorical question at face value, he proceeds to
reply sarcastically that any passer-by can point out the mansion of
the oppressor standing unharmed in all its glory (v. 29).

IV. The Friends insist that punishment ultimately overtakes the
sinner, no matter how long the delay. Koheleth had already pointed
out that this delay in punishment encourages men to commit crime
(Eccl. 8:11 ff.). Job, however, is concerned with the injustice involved.
He quotes the opinion of the Friends (v. 30) but insists that justice
demands an immediate punishment of the sinner. Instead, Job says,
the transgressor lives a life of ease, and to cap it all is buried with
pomp and ceremony at the end (vv. 30–34).[100]

The entire passage understood in this light is a striking example
of effective argument, marked by passion, irony and logic:[101]

19. A. *You say* "God stores up his iniquity for his children."
       Let Him recompense *him*, that *he* may know it!

20.　　Let his own eyes see his destruction,
　　　　And let *him* drink of the Almighty's wrath.

21.　　For what concern has he in his house after him,
　　　　When the number of his months is cut off?

22. B.　*You say* "Shall anyone teach God knowledge,
　　　　Seeing He judges those on high?" . . .[102]

23.　　One dies in his full strength,
　　　　Being wholly at ease and secure.

24.　　His pails are full of milk,
　　　　And the marrow of his bones is moistened.

25.　　And another dies in bitterness of soul,
　　　　And has never tasted any joy.

26.　　Together they lie down in the dust,
　　　　And the worm covers them over.

27.　　Behold, I know your thoughts.
　　　　And the devices by which you do me violence.

28. C.　If you say: "Where is the house of the prince
　　　　And where is the tent of dwelling of the wicked?"

29.　　Haven't you asked the passers-by,
　　　　You cannot deny their tokens!

30. D.　*You say* "Indeed the sinner is saved for the day of calamity,
　　　　And will be led forth to the day of wrath."

31.　　But who shall declare his way at once,
　　　　And for what *he* has done—who will requite him?

32.　　For he is borne to the grave,
　　　　And men keep watch over his tomb.

33.　　The clods of the valley are sweet unto him,
　　　　And all men draw after him,
　　　　And before him an innumerable host.

34.　　How then do you comfort me with vanity?
　　　　And your answers remain only a betrayal. (Job 21:19–34)

It is noteworthy that three times, no *verbum dicendi* occurs (vv. 19, 22, 30), while once (v. 28) a verb does occur, a phenomenon we have observed frequently above.

K—Another form of quotation in Job may be described as *oblique restatement*. At times, Job cites the opinion of the Friends, not literally but ironically, in a form bordering on parody. Failure to recognize this fact has vitiated many attempts to interpret chapter 12, one of the most striking utterances of Job, as has been noted above.

A clue to the understanding of the chapter is to be found in vv. 7, 8:

ואולם שאל נא בהמות ותרך   ועוף השמים ויגד לך
או שיח לארץ ותרך   ויספרו לך דגי הים

It is obvious by the singular verbs and suffixes (וְתֹרֶךָ, שָׁאַל, שִׂיחַ, לָךְ,) that Job cannot be talking to his Friends, whom he always addresses in the plural (cf. 6:21 ff.; 16:2 ff.; 19:1 ff.).

The passage 12:7–8 is actually a *restatement by Job of the Friends' admonition to him*. In 12:5, he has declared that the secure can afford to look with contempt on the sufferings of their fellow-men. Then follows his recapitulation of the Friends' position as he sees it. They have had to admit the prosperity of the wicked (v. 6) but have sought, in effect, to deflect his attention elsewhere, by calling on Job to admire God's perfection as reflected in the natural order (vv. 7 f.; cf. 5:9 ff.; 11:7 ff.):

> He sets the lowly on high,
> and the afflicted are raised to safety. (Job 5:11)

Job meets this attempt to sidetrack the argument by replying that there is nothing new in the idea of the power and greatness of God (vv. 9–10); in fact, he can and does portray God's might far more effectively than the Friends (vv. 11–25). All this, he repeats, he knows as well as they (13:1, 2). Yet he still adheres to his desire to argue with the Almighty (13:3).

The entire passage (12:11–25) cannot be excised as simply as is sometimes taken for granted. This passage differs significantly from conventional descriptions of the greatness of God, like those to be met with in the words of the Friends (5:9 ff.; 25:2–6; 26:6–14). While the Friends stress the beneficent and creative functioning of the Almighty as revealed in the gift of rain (5:10), the discomfiture of the wicked (5:12 ff.), the glories of the heavens (26:2 f.) and creation (26:5 ff.), the tenor of Job's description of the power of God, both in our passage, as well as in 9:4 ff., is quite different.[103] Job emphasizes the negative and destructive manifestations. God moves the mountains, makes the earth tremble and shuts up the sun and stars that they give no light (9:5 ff.). God destroys beyond rebuilding, and imprisons men so that they cannot escape. He withholds water to cause drought and pours it forth to cause inundations. Nations are exalted only to be destroyed (vv. 14, 15, 23). Judges are made fools, the power of kings is broken, and priests are stripped naked; the mighty are overthrown, the elders robbed of understanding and the princes put to shame (vv. 16–21.). Incidentally, the fact that the poet regards the overthrow of the dominant political and spiritual leadership on a par with the calamities of nature as illustrative of the *destructive* powers of God, sheds important light on the basic upper-class social origins of Wisdom literature.[104]

A translation of the salient sections of this passage will demonstrate its unity and power and clarify the process of thought:

> 4. A mockery have I become to His Friend,
>   Who calls to God and is answered, a mockery to the perfect saint!
> 5. For calamity there is contempt, in the mind of the secure,
>   Prepared for those whose feet stumble.
>
> 6. *You admit:*
>   The tents of the robbers are at peace,
>   The dwellings of those who anger God,
>   Of those who have deceived God.
> 7. "But," *you say,* "ask the cattle to teach you, and the fowl of the
>   heaven to tell you.
> 8. Or speak to the earth that it instruct you and let the fish of the
>   sea declare to you."
> 9. Who knows not in all this, "that the hand of the Lord has made it!"[105]
> 10. In whose hand is the soul of every living thing and the spirit of
>   all human flesh.
> 11. Indeed the ear tests words as the palate tastes its food.
> 12. *You say:* "Wisdom is with the aged and understanding with length
>   of days."
> 13. *But I say:* "With *Him* is wisdom and strength, *His* are counsel and
>   understanding."
> 14. Behold He destroys and it cannot be rebuilt.
>   He imprisons a man and he is not released.
> 15. He shuts up the waters and they dry up or He sends them forth
>   and they overturn the earth, etc.
>
> 13. 1. Behold all this my eye has seen, my ear has heard and understood,
>   2. What you know, I know also; I am not inferior to you.
>   3. But I will dispute with the Almighty and desire to argue with God.

It is noteworthy that this oblique restatement by Job of the position of the Friends occurs in chap. 12, in the closing speech of the First Cycle, exactly as the detailed refutation of the Friends' standpoint is in ch. 21, Job's concluding speech of the Second Cycle. The imperfect preservation of the Third Cycle makes it impossible to know whether

Job used this method again at its close, especially since he ends, as he began (Chap. 3), with a non-argumentative soliloquy. This cycle contains Chapter 24, the content of which is particularly difficult. Hence, commentators have subjected it to radical deletion, dissection and transposition. These radical procedures become unnecessary if it be recognized that vv. 18-24 are Job's quotation of the Friends' standpoint. That most of his response has been lost is not astonishing in view of the extreme dislocation in this Cycle.

Finally, Job uses the device of quotations once more after the other side has spoken. In his final Reconciliation with God, he again repeats what has been said, but this time with no distortions or exaggerations. The Lord, speaking out of the whirlwind, began:

> "Who is this that darkens counsel
> By words without knowledge?
> Gird up your loins like a man;
> For I will ask you and you tell Me." (38:2 f.)

After the magnificent portrayal of the power of God and the beauty of His world, Job is overwhelmed and concedes his submission (42: 2–6). He cites these utterances of God, with no outward mark of the quotation, and adds his humble submissive comment:

> Then Job answered the Lord,
> I know that You can do all things
> and that no purpose of Yours can be thwarted.
> You have said,
> "Who is this that hides My plan without knowledge?"
> Indeed, I have spoken without understanding,
> of things too wonderful for me which I did not grasp.

> *You have said,*
> "Hear, and I will speak;
> I will ask you, and do you inform Me."
> I have heard of You by hearsay,
> but now my eyes have seen You.
> Therefore I abase myself
> and repent in dust and ashes.[106]

That this use of quotations occurs not once, but three times in Job, and each time in the protagonist's final reply is scarcely a coincidence. On the contrary, it adds considerable weight to the view that this rhetorical use is characteristic of the author, and incidentally strengthens the view that the "Dialogue with the Friends" and the "God-speeches" emanate from the same pen.

The evidence here adduced demonstrates, we believe, that the use of quotations is an authentic element of Biblical and extra-Biblical literature. When this usage is ignored, it leads to unnecessary and unwarranted excisions, transpositions and emendations and to a failure to grasp the spirit of the literature as a whole. When properly reckoned with, however, this use of quotations reveals the free play of varying emotions and the lively conflict of ideas, which characterized the ancients no less than their modern descendants.

NOTES

1. The history of the interpretation of Ecclesiastes until the middle of the 19th century is exhaustively treated in C. D. Ginsburg, *Coheleth* (London, 1861) pp. 27–223. The more recent trends are surveyed in G. A. Barton *ICC on Ecclesiastes* (New York, 1908) pp. 18–31; W. H. Hertzberg, *Der Prediger* (Leipzig, 1932) pp. 54–67 and R. H. Pfeiffer, *Introduction to the O. T.* (New York, 1941) p. 875 who gives a conspectus of the literature.

2. So Döderlein, Tyler. Cf. Barton *op. cit.* p. XXI.

3. Barton, *op. cit.*; Jastrow, *The Gentle Cynic* (Philadelphia, 1919), pp. 245–55; Volz, "Hiob und Weisheit" (*in die Schriften des A. T.*, Göttingen, 1921), p. 235; Eissfeldt, *Einleitung in das A. T.* (Tübingen, 1934), p. 558.

4. Duhm, *Das Buch Hiob erklärt* (Freiburg, 1897) passim. Driver-Gray *ICC on Job* (2 vol. New York, 1921) more conservatively, eliminate about 30 verses in the first 23 chapters of Job (Vol. 1, p. xxxvii, n. 1, and pp. xlix f.). Torczyner (*Das Buch Hiob*, Vienna, 1920), whose procedure is highly individual, emphasizes that he does not excise any passage from the book; he merely rearranges several hundreds of them (Preface, p. viii). This method is carried further in his Hebrew Commentary (1941, 1954). For a criticism of Torczyner's method, see Prof. Kemper Fullerton, "Job, Chap. 9 and 10" in *AJSL*, Vol. LV (July 1938) pp. 263–7). Cf. also David Yellin, *Hiqre Miqra'-Iyyob* (Jerusalem, 1927) who rearranges Chap. 7, 19 and 20 completely.

5. Siegfried omits 12:4–13:1; Grill (*Zur Kritik der Komposition des Buches Hiob*) omits 12:4–13:2. Driver-Gray delete 12:4–12 (*op. cit.*, vol. 1, p. 111). Volz leaves only five verses in Job's speech (12:2, 3, 11, 12; 13:2), and transfers the remainder (12:4–10, 13–25; 13:1) to Zophar in chap. 11 (*op. cit.*, p. 39 f.). Jastrow (*op. cit.*) omits vv. 4c, 5 in part, 6c, 10, 12, 13, 17–19, 22, 23, and 25. Ball removes vv. 4c, 6, 10 (doubtfully), and 13. Budde, on the other hand, argues forcefully against Grill and Siegfried's procedure (*Das Buch Hiob*, *ad loc.*; also *ThLZ*, 1891, no. 2). Dhorme places vv. 11–12 before v. 9.

6. The variety of views may be studied in Driver-Gray, Budde, Ball and Dhorme. A few examples may be noted here. Thus vv. 21b, 22–26 are eliminated by Volz. Dhorme reads v. 19a as a question, "Does God save his sin for his children?" Ball emends v. 22a to read: הֲלֹא אֵל יְלַמֶּד דָּעַת "Shall not El teach knowledge?" He understands this (p. 293) to mean that Job argues, "Should we not rather observe what God actually does rather than assert a priori notions of what he ought to do?" This interpretation seems far-fetched. Driver-Gray and Torczyner eliminate v. 22 as a gloss. Since v. 30 is obviously out of harmony with Job's views, scholars have generally accepted the emendations of לְיוֹם into בְּיוֹם and יוּבְלוּ into יִצֵּל (Siegfried, Beer, Steuernagel, Budde, Volz,) or יַבְלִג "will rejoice" (Dhorme), reading the verse:

כִּי בְיוֹם אֵיד יֵחָשֶׂךְ רָע בְּיוֹם עֲבָרוֹת יִצֵּל

"In the day of calamity the sinner is spared,
In the day of wrath he is saved. "(or, happy)."

Ball objects that these changes are graphically too extreme and reads:

כִּי מַאֵיד יֵחָשֶׂךְ רָע וּבְיוֹם עֶבְרָה יִפָּלֵט

"That the bad man is kept from calamity
And in the day of wrath he escapes."

Aside from the linguistic difficulties involved in these renderings, the problem of why these changes were introduced is entirely overlooked. A solution to this question is presented in the text.

7. For a recognition of the basic unity and integrity of Qoheleth, from varying points of view, cf. Ludwig Levy, *Das Buch Qoheleth* (Leipzig 1912) pp. 57–9; D. B. MacDonald, *The Hebrew Philosophic Genius* (Princeton, 1936); H. W. Hertzberg, *Der Prediger* (Leipzig, 1932); M. Haller and K. Galling, *Die Fünf Megilloth* (Tübingen, 1940); R. Gordis, *The Wisdom of Ecclesiastes* (New York, 1945); J. J. Weber, *L'Ecclésiaste* (Paris, 1947) and note 9 below.

8. Cf. his *Introduction to the O. T.*, vol. 1 (Copenhagen, 1948, p. 13).

9. Cf. "The Heptad as an Element of Biblical and Rabbinic Style" and "The Social Background of Wisdom Literature," both of which are included in the present volume, as well as a full-length study of Ecclesiastes, *Koheleth—The Man and His World*, 3rd ed. (New York, 1955, 1968) = *KMW*. We may now add a more recent work, *The Book of God and Man : A Study of Job* (Chicago, 1965) = *BGM*, chap. XII, "The Use of Quotations in Job," pp. 169–89, which contains the results of additional research on this subject.

10. On the LXX of Ecclesiastes, cf. S. Euringer, *Der Masorahtext des Qoheleth* (Leipzig, 1890); H. Graetz, *Koheleth* (Leipzig, 1871) pp. 173–79. Dillmann, in *Sitzungsberichte der Kgl. Akad. der Wissenschaften zu Berlin*, 1892, vol. 1, pp. 3–16; MacNeile *Intr. to Ecclesiastes* (Cambridge, 1904) pp. 115–34; Barton, *op. cit.*, pp. 8–11; Hertzberg, *op. cit.*, pp. 4–6; Kamenetzky in *ZATW*, 1904, pp. 181-239. The extreme literalism of the translation and the rendering of אֶת by συν (in 32 out of 72 cases) naturally recall Aquila, to whom Graetz attributed the version. However, since the LXX text differs from the Origenic fragments in Field, McNeile suggested that our present LXX text represents

the *editio prima* of Aquila, and the fragments, the *editio secunda*. Jerome refers to a second edition of Aquila, "quam Hebraei κάτα ἀκρίβεια nominant"(*Comm. in Ezech., ed.* Migne, PL, vol. 25, p. 39). To be sure, Jerome mentions this second edition of Aquila only for Jeremiah, Ezekiel and Daniel, but that may be purely accidental. There is no reason for assuming that only these three books were revised. (ag. Podechard, Hertzberg). This explanation is far more reasonable than Dillmann's theory that the LXX was revised "in the spirit of Aquila" and more plausible than Podechard's unsubstantiated view (which Hertz accepts) that the literalistic technique of translation was not limited to Aquila. After all, we find no evidence of this method in any other Greek version of any other biblical book. On the other hand a parallel to this Aquilan version "usurping" the place of the LXX exists in Daniel, where Theodotion has pre-empted the place of LXX and in the Aramaic Targum of Proverbs, which is strongly influenced by the Peshita, if it is not an actual recension. Barton's judgment that LXX "at all events was made from a text which differed a good deal from our present Hebrew" (p. 10) is not validated by a fresh study of the evidence. In KMW, Chap. XVI, we have demonstrated that the changes are minor and validate MT at nearly all points, the conclusion to which Euringer was led in his study. The Aquilan fragments collected by Montfauçon and Field are even closer to M T. If as Pod. believes, our present LXX is an originally non-Aquilan version revised along Aquilan lines, it would be even older than the 2nd century C. E., the date given in the text above.

11. The situation with regard to the LXX of Job is more complex. Our present LXX text contains additions from Aquila, Symmachus and principally Theodotion. These additions were supplied because the original LXX was doubtless a briefer recension of the book. This shorter translation was probably induced both by the difficulties of the Hebrew text and by what appeared as redundancies to Greek readers, unaccustomed to parallelism and other aspects of Semitic rhetoric. The Sahidic version probably testifies to the pre-Origenic text of Job (Ciasca, aganst Burkitt). Nonetheless, "in the main the Hebrew, as far as the extent is concerned, represents an earlier text than the Greek." (Driver-Gray, *ICC on Job* vol. 1, p. LXXVI, cf. pp. XLIX, LXXI ff.) It is noteworthy that LXX omits only 2 verses and 3 stichs in ch. 12 (8b, 9, 18b, 21a, 23). In ch. 21:19–34, LXX omits vv. 19b, 23, 28–33 and in many of these cases "the removal of the passages in the Greek destroys the poetical structure" (Driver-Gray, p. LXXV). All in all the evidence is clear that in contending with a difficult text like Job, the translator contracted his original and thus simplified his task. It should also be recalled that the Elihu speeches (ch. 32–33) the authenticity of which has been generally denied, are translated in LXX, and were included in the Greek version by 100 B. C. E., as evidenced by the passages extracted by Eusebius (*Praeparatio Evangelii* IX 25) from Alexander Polyhistor (80–40 B. C. E.) who cites Aristeas' referring to Elihu as a character in the book.

12. Cf. the radically different order in *Jeremiah*, where aside from other interruptions and changes, the section 25:15–45:5 in the Masoretic Text has changed places with 46:1–51:64 in the Greek. See H. B. Swete *Int. to O. T. in Greek* (Cambridge, 1914) p. 241 f.

13. Cf. the epoch-making study by C. Cornill, *Ezechiel*, Prolegomena; also G. A. Cooke *ICC on Ezekiel* (New York, 1937) vol. 1, pp. XC ff.

14. Cf. F. Buhl, *Canon and Text of the O. T.* (Edinburgh, 1892) pp. 3–32. H. E. Ryle, *Canon of the O. T.* (2 ed., London, 1909); M. L. Margolis, *The Hebrew Scriptures in the Making* (Phila. 1922) pp. 88–96; S. Zeitlin, *An Historical Study of the Canonization of Hebrew Scriptures* in *Proc. of Am. Acad. Jew. Research*, 1932, vol. 3, pp. 121–8; R. Gordis in *HUCA, op. cit.* p. 119, note 85.

15. On the date of the LXX of Job cf. Driver-Gray, *op. cit.*, vol. 1, p. LXV note p. LXXI; Swete, *op. cit.*, p. 25; on the date of the Greek of Ecclesiastes cf. Barton *op. cit.* p. 8 ff.; Swete, *op. cit.*, p. 26. This late date for Ecclesiastes assumes that our present LXX version is the work of Aquila. If it be authentically Septuagintal, its date would be earlier and the argument in the text even stronger. On the character of this version, see note 8 above.

16. The rendering of this clause "and I also knew" (JPSV) is incorrect because that would have been expressed by וגם אני ידעתי, besides being meaningless here. The clause means "But *I* know." On the adversative use of גם, an earmark of Koheleth's style (4:8, 14; 6:7; 8:17), cf. Jer. 6:15; 8:12; Ez. 16:28; 20:15, 23; Ps. 23:4; 95:9; 129:2; Neh. 5:8 and see *BDB* s.v. גם sec. 5, 6 and the parallel use of אף s. v. sec. 1, end. In this passage, Siegfried omits vv. 13, 14a, while Barton retains them. Levy regards v. 14a as a conventional proverb but not v. 13, which is a possible view.

17. On the relationship of the two schools, see "The Social Background of Wisdom Literature" in this volume, as well as *KMW*, pp. 22–38.

18. Cf. A. Erman, *Literature of the Ancient Egyptians* (tr. Blackman) London, 1927, p. 54; J. Fichtner, *Die Altorientalische Weisheit in Ihrer israelitisch-juedischen Auspraegung* (Giessen 1933) p. 3.

19. Cf. Fichtner, *op. cit.*, p. 6 "Wir treffen auch hier zwei Gattungen : *Lehrschriften und Klageschriften*. Anders als in Aegypten haben wir im Zweistromland auch Sammlungen von Volkssprichwörtern."

20. Cf. "Quotations in Wisdom Literature" in *JQR*, vol. 30, 1939, pp. 123–147.

21. So Delitzsch, who recognizes two quotations here and takes גֹּל as the imperative (so Briggs, Dr.) Cf. Ps. 37:5; Pr. 16:3, cf. Ps. 55:23. In view of the clear parallels, this view is preferable to regarding גל as the perfect = גַּל (LXX, cf. Mat. 27:43, Ew. Bi, Duhm, Buttenwieser) or the infinitive absolute (Rashi, Hitzig, Boettcher) or the participle (Kimhi, Ibn Ezra), all taken to mean lit. "He who casts his all (i. e. trusts,) in the Lord. He will save him, etc." In spite of variations in interpretation, all commentators recognize a quotation here.

22. Reading, with all the moderns, מֵחֲמָאוֹת, the comparative being attested by the parallelism מִשֶּׁמֶן.

22a. On the basis of the parallelism and the meaning of the root פלל "judge" (cf. I Sam. 2:25; פָּלִיל "judge" Deut. 32:31; Job 31:11; פְּלִילָה "office of judge" and פְּלִילִי Job 31:28; Isa. 28:17) this stich may perhaps be rendered: "And may his trial serve for his guilt (or, condemnation)."

23. In a study of this passage H. L. Creager, (*JNES*, 1947, pp.121-3) suggests that v. 20 be emended on the basis of *Pešita* (הנו עבדא דאילין דסקרין למריא) "The work of those who hate the Lord)" to read זאת פְּעֻלַת שֹׁטְנֵי ה׳ and rendered: "This is the reward of the enemies of God." However, this requires assuming the late insertion in MT of מאת which LXX validates, παρὰ κυρίου, cf. Vulgate *apud Dominum*, Targum מן יי. The varied readings of Pešita and MT are both derived from an original זאת פעלת שטנימאת "This is the work of those who hate the Lord," which MT divided שטני מאת ה׳ and P, שטנים את ה׳.

24. In this entire passage only vv. 15-18 offer some difficulty, since v. 15 is couched in religious terms and vv. 16–18 charge the object of the curses with being heartless and cruel to the poor, and therefore do not seem appropriate in the mouth of the Psalmist's enemies. V. 15a is however merely the biblical mode of praying for an evil fate for one's foe : the verse refers to the extinction of his memory (reading *zikro* with mss. LXX and Jerome) or that of his ancestors. V. 16 is suspicious on metrical grounds, disrupting as it does the tristich rhythm of the passage. It may, however, well be authentic, containing the charges that his enemies have sanctimoniously uttered against him. Note that in v. 20 b, the Psalmist describes his enemies as slandering him (הדברים רע על נפשי). On the other hand, vv. 16–19 may be out of place here, belonging after v. 29, in which case they would constitute the Psalmist's words. The singular verbs and suffixes in these verses would then require modification to the plural. The changes would have arisen from a scribe who "corrected" the forms to the singular, to agree with the context in v. 6 ff., when the passage was erroneously transferred to the present position. See also the following note.

25. Cf. JPSV, which places the entire passage, vv. 6–19 in quotation marks, and the commentaries of A. Cohen, Freehof and Creager, *loc. cit.*, who cogently defend this interpretation.

26. So Kimhi (who refers it to Doeg the Edomite), Delitzsch.

27. M. Buttenwieser, *The Psalms* (Chicago 1938) p. 747. Briggs regards it as a separate poem of imprecation against a wicked ruler, with harmonizing glosses (vv. 2a, 3b–5a, 19–20, 25, 28–29) and a liturgical ending (v. 30–31). Aside from the complications involved, there is no reference in the text to the object of these curses being a ruler.

28. So LXX, Kittel, *BH* on 22:27; Ehr. on 22:27. In 69:33 they are compelled to change the verbs to imperatives רְאוּ and וְשִׂמְחוּ to harmonize with the second person.

29. So Delitzsch (1st passage); Briggs (both passages), Ehr.

30. The pausal form יִשְׂמָחוּ is to be vocalized יִשְׂמְחוּ and construed with דֹּרְשֵׁי אֱלֹהִים as its subject thus producing a far smoother construction, besides giving the verse three stichs of two beats each. דרשי אלהים corresponding to ענוים receives only one beat, cf. קדוש ישראל parallel to ה׳ in Isa. 1:4; מלך מואב parallel to בלק in Num. 23:7; חטאת נפשי parallel to בכורי in Micah 6:7. This 2:2:2 rhythm occurs in the preceding verse as well: ותיטב לה׳ משור פר מקרן

מפריס "It will be more acceptable to the Lord than an ox, than the horn of a cloven-footed beast" (Read מַפְרִיס מַקְרֶן).

31. Cf. the writer's study "The Asseverative Kaph in Hebrew and Ugaritic," in *JAOS* 1943, vol. 63, pp. 176 ff.

32. Cf. Rashi and Kimhi *ad loc.*

33. Read, by a different division of the words, וְכָשַׁלְתָּה יוֹם to correspond to לַיְלָה, "by day" and "by night."

34. Cf. H. H. Rowley "The Interpretation of the Song of Songs" in *JThS*, vol. 58, 1937, pp. 357 ff. See the study "The Song of Songs" in this volume.

35. Cf. e.g. M. Jastrow, *The Song of Songs* (Phila. 1921) who notes the singers in each lyric.

36. Read with most moderns וְנֵדְעֵהוּ for וְנֵדְעָה and attach to v. 2, thus giving both vv. 2 and 3a a tristich rhythm and avoiding the difficult repetition of *yāda'* in 3a of the MT.

37. Read כְּשַׁחֲרֻנוּ כֵן נִמְצָאֵהוּ with Giesebrecht, based on LXX.

38. מַשְׁכִּים parallel to בֹּקֶר is a noun meaning "morning, lit. the rising time." It occurs in Mishnic Hebrew, cf. M. Bikkurim 3.2 למשכים היה הממונה אומר "At rising time, the official would say," and the *Book of the Damascene Sect*, 10.19 (ed. Schechter). Hence revocalize כְּטַל מַשְׁכִּים.

39. On the difficulties of this stich and the various proposals made, see Harper, *ICC on Hosea, ad loc.*

40. Cf. *Louis Ginzberg Jubilee Volume*, English volume (New York 1945), p. 198.

41. Cf. S. R. Driver *The Book of the Prophet Jeremiah* 2nd ed. (London, 1908) pp. 33 f. On the military tactics involved, cf. Jer. 15:8; 20:16; Zeph. 2:4; and Isa. 15:1.

42. The rhythm indicates that ה' is attached to v. 8, thus creating a 4:4 meter in both vv. 7 and 8.

43. Cf. the fundamental study of S. N. Kramer, "The Epic of Gilgameš and its Sumerian Sources" in *JAOS*, 1944, vol. 64, pp. 7–23, especially pp. 20–23 and notes 104 and 113. I am grateful to Prof. Kramer for citing this corroborative evidence from Sumerian, when the present paper was read (in part) at the December 1948 meeting of the Society of Biblical Literature in New York.

44. Lines 42–49 of the Ur Tablet 9364 published by Gadd.

45. Lines 50–52.

46. Lines 54–73, end of the same tablet.

47. Cf. CBS 10400, 15150 and UM 29–13–438. See Kramer *op. cit.*, n. 104 cited above.

48. Published by S. N. Kramer in *Journal of Cuneiform Studies*, 1947, vol. 1, pp. 3–46.

49. *Op. cit.*, pp. 8–9.

50. *Op. cit.*, p. 32.

51. On בְּיַד as a phonetic equivalent of בְּעַד, cf. I Sam. 21:14; Ez. 37:19; Isa. 64:6; Job 8:4; 27:11 and *Tel-el Amarna Letters* no. 245 line 35 (*ba-di-u* =

ba-ya-di-hu), as well as the Ugaritic texts where *be-yad* is spelled *bd*. Cf. H. Torczyner in *Samuel Krauss Jubilee Volume* (Jerusalem 5697) pp. 1 ff.; Gordis "A Note on Yad" in *JBL*, 1943, vol. 62, p. 341 ff. and the literature there cited.

52. Duhm and Hoelscher delete the verse; Driver-Gray, vol. 1, p. 195 are unable to reach a satisfactory conclusion.

53. Ehrlich and Dhorme recognize that v. 12 is essential to the text as the basis of Job's alleged standpoint in v. 13, thus approximating the point of view expressed above, but they do not concern themselves with the technical form of v. 12. The latter cites as a parallel Isa. 40:26–27, which would be a striking illustration of the same connection of ideas, if it were certain that those verses belong together and not to two different passages, as indicated by the Masoretic division. Here, as is so often the case, the medieval Jewish commentators, unaccountably neglected by modern students, intuitively grasped the intent of the passage. Rashi interprets v. 12 as a quotation (לאמר); Ibn Ezra has the quotation begin with v. 11 (חשבת) "You thought." On הלא as introducing a quotation, see p. 128.

54. The phrase את כל עמלי ואת כל בית אבי is best regarded as hendiadys and therefore to be rendered "all the toil of my father's house i. e. "all the trouble I sustained in Canaan." Note the parallel phrase in the contrasting formula: כי הפרני אלהים בארץ עניי.

55. So Bertinoro, Maimonides, *ad loc*. Though this seems to be the original reading, the text of the *Mahzor Vitry* differs from it. Cf. C. Taylor, *Sayings of the Jewish Fathers* (1st edition, Cambridge 1877), p. 44, and R. T. Herford *Pirke Aboth* (New York 1930) for a summary of the various interpretations advanced.

56. The passage occurs with several variations in Tos. Peah 1:6 (ed. Zuckermandl, p. 18) and in *Sifra, Kedoshim* chap. 1 (ed. Weiss, p. 87c). Here the verb אומרים is inserted after יושבין ומשמרין. That the usage without the verb is comprehensible is clear from the fact that the text in *Shabbat* is left uncorrected by the commentators.

57. Cf. Rashi *ad loc*.: כלומר כבר אמרת לפני טוב יום שאתה עומד בחצרי.

58. Cf. H. Malter, *The Treatise Taanit of the Babylonian Talmud* (Phila. 1928) p. 176, n. 334 : "All the words in parentheses to the end of the paragraph are added for clearness' sake, the Talmud usually omitting the connecting phrases."

59. Cf. the commentaries *ad loc*., and H. L. Ginsberg in *Louis Ginzberg Jubilee Volumes* (English section) p. 165, n. 14 end.

60. Instead of an indirect quotation in 6b continuing as a direct one in v. 7, אֵלָיו should be changed to אֵלַי. Even if MT is not emended, v. 7 represents the words of the Hasid, and vv. 8 f. is God's response. On indirect quotations, see n. 108 below.

61. Cf. Delitzsch, Briggs, Kittel, and most moderns, but not Ehrlich or Buttenwieser, *op. cit.*, pp. 495 ff., who argues forcefully for the literary unity of the Psalm.

62. On the use of quotations to describe a previous state of mind, see below.

63. On the use of the Vav in circumstantial clauses, indicating the concomitant conditions, modal, causal or temporal, of the main action, cf. S. R. Driver, *Hebrew Tenses* (Oxford, 1892) sec. 156–160; BDB, *Lexicon*, s. v. Vav, sec. 1, k, p. 253 a, b, and the analogous Arabic *Waw álḥāli*, Wright, *Arabic Grammar*, vol. 2, sec. 183; C. P. Caspari, *Arabische Grammatik* (Halle, 1876) see p. 548.

64. The use of אם in Job 31 has occasioned much difficulty. Efforts to excise verses or to rearrange the chapter have not met with any general assent. See Driver-Gray, Vol. 1, p. 261 f., who summarize these attempts and correctly caution : "It would be a great mistake to reduce all this variety to the monotonous repetition of a single scheme." But the implications of this just observation have not been kept in mind. There is no need for assuming that אם throughout the chapter must mean only "if" (15 or 16 times without and 4 times with the imprecatory clause). The repetition of the same word in the Hebrew gives the passage great power; the variety in meaning avoids monotony. Cf. Gen. 44:16 מה נאמר··· מה נדבר ומה נצטדק "*What* shall we say to my lord ? *What* shall we speak. *Or how* shall we clear ourselves ?" (AV), and Lam. 2:13: מה אעודך מה אדמה לך ··· מה אשוה לך ואנחמך "*How* shall I fortify you, *what* shall I liken unto you, O daughter of Jerusalem, *What* shall I compare unto you, and comfort you, O virgin daughter of Zion ?" On this passage cf. *JThS*, vol. 24, 1933, pp. 162 f. Similarly in this long chapter 31, two uses of אם occur: 1) = "if"; in a protasis with the apodosis expressed (vv. 7-8, 9-10, 21-22, 38-40). 2) = האם = *num*, the sign of a question expecting a negative reply, and hence without an apodosis (vv. 5, 13, 16, 19, 24, 25, 26, 33). אם לא is equivalent to הלא *nonne*, the sign of a question expecting an affirmative answer. (vv. 20, 31 ?) The accumulated force of the repeated particle is largely lost in the English. Dhorme (p. 411) recognizes both uses of אם, rendering it as the interrogative in vv. 5, 13, 16, 24, 25, 26, 33 and as "if" in vv. 7, 9, 19, 31, 38. Similarly Hoelscher renders it as the interrogative in vv. 5, 13, 16, 19, 24, 25, 26, 33 and as "if" in vv. 2, 9, 21, 38.

65. Reading with Targum in stich a and LXX in b, and most moderns: הֲלֹא בַבֶּטֶן עֹשֵׂנִי עָשָׂהוּ וַיְכֻנֶנּוּ בְּרֶחֶם אֶחָד. Hoelscher deletes this great affirmation of human equality—perhaps the tribute virtue is forced to pay to vice—his commentary was published in Tuebingen under the Nazis in 1937!

66. כי means "nay, but" only after a negative. Cf. Gen. 17:15; 24:3 f.; Ex. 16:8; Dt. 21:12; 1 Sam. 6:3; Isa. 10:7; Ps. 44:8; 118:17 and elsewhere. Cf. Brown-Driver-Briggs Lexicon s.v. כי, 3e p. 474a. Briggs *ICC on Psalms*, vol. 1, p. 381, places v. 23 after v. 20 and renders "Yea, for thy sake," adding that כי is difficult in context and is probably a dittography (p. 382).

67. On the asseverative *ki* (and *k*) already noted by the medieval Jewish commentators, and now attested in Ugaritic, cf. H. L. Ginsberg, "Notes on the

Birth of the Beautiful gods" *JRAS*, 1935, p. 56; Gordis, "The Asseverative Kaph in Hebrew and Ugaritic," *JAOS*, vol. 63, 1943, pp. 176 ff.

68. For the various efforts at reconstruction, cf. Driver-Gray, ICC on Job, vol. 1, pp. XXXVIII-XL and the succinct summary of Pfeiffer, *Int. to O.T.* (New York, 1941) p. 671. Our own view of the Third Cycle is as follows : *Bildad*: chap. 25; 26:5–14; *Job*: 26:1–4; 27:2–11; *Zophar*: 27:13–23; Job chap. 29–31. Zophar's speech is definitely fragmentary and Bildad's probably so. Chap. 28 is an independent poem, reflecting the same standpoint as the God speeches, and hence anti-climactic as part of the Dialogue, yet probably emanating from the same author or from his school as a separate literary composition. It may have been an earlier and less ambitious treatment of the theme later elaborated in the book of Job, like the early *Faust Gedichte* of Goethe. For a full discussion of these issues, see *BGM*, chap. VIII.

69. Both these conclusions are accepted by virtually all critics, as in the reconstructions of Kennicott, Stuhlmann, Reuss, Hoffmann, Bickell, Duhm, Barton, Dhorme, in spite of other divergences. A few critics like Siegfried, Laue and Buttenwiesser accept only the second conclusion, and solve the first problem in other ways.

70. So Driver-Gray (doubtfully); Hoffmann, Bickell, Duhm, Barton.

71. Thus Kennicott, Stuhlmann, Reuss, Dhorme, attribute these verses to Job.

72. Somewhat similar views of the passage were proposed by Hengstenberg in part; Budde, in *ZATW*, 1882, pp. 205–210 and in his *Commentary*. See S. R. Driver, *Int. Lit. O.T.* (New York, 1906), 9th ed., p. 422. That it was not more generally accepted may be attributed to the absence of evidence for this usage elsewhere, such as is adduced in this paper.

73. We hope to demonstrate elsewhere that on the basis of Semitic cognates *'anag* in the Hithpael means "to implore, plead" in Isa. 57:4; Ps. 37:4; Job 22:26 and probably in Isa. 58:14.

74. On this meaning of *b'ad*, see note 51 above.

75. So AV: "neither saith he." Moffat adds the formula and rephrases it in indirect discourse; "he never asks for whose sake he is toiling." The JV places the clause in quotation marks, "for whom then do I labor, etc." Or the hypothetical speech may be phrased positively. "*He might ask himself*, 'For whom, etc.' " See the next example of this usage given in the text.

76. The absence of לימא in our original passage cannot be explained as an error due to haplography, since it is not missing in both parallel clauses. Cf. Rabbinovicz, *Dikduke Sopherim, ad loc.*

77. Cf. Rashi *ad loc.*, who supplies the formula of quotation: מימר אמר לוה לא קים למלוה בגויה דמשכן.

78. בְּעַד cannot mean "in place of," which would be expressed by תַּחַת (Ex. 21:23 f.; Lev. 24:18, 20) or by the *Beth pretii* (Deut. 19:2). It must be interpreted "on behalf of" (e. g. Isa. 8:19) with יִתֵּן understood, "(a man will give one) skin on behalf of (another) skin." (So nearly all—Driver-Gray, Dhorme, Hoelscher, etc.) That it means "upon, about" hence "one skin lies upon another skin"

(Schultens, Merx, Budde) is less likely, since this meaning of בְּעַד is restricted (even in Jon. 2:7; Ps. 3:4; 139: 11) to verbs or nouns implying shutting off or protecting (cf. Judg. 9:51; Job 7:7 and often). Torczyner's ingenious suggestion in his Hebrew commentary that בְּעַד is the Arabism بعد "after, under," and hence is equal to תַּחַת, should also be mentioned, even if it does not carry conviction. Much more acceptable is his suggestion in his earlier German work (*Das Buch Hiob* 1920), p. 2, that the verse read originally: עור בעד עור יתן איש וכל אשר לו יתן בעד ביתו, though the change is not absolutely required.

79. Cf. the learned and stimulating work of Archer Taylor, *The Proverb* (Cambridge 1931), especially his illuminating observations on page 6: "We shall never know for example, which of the Exeter Gnomes in Old English poetry are proverbial and which are the collector's moralizing in the same pattern. . . . . In a dead language the means which are available are various, but not always effective or easily applied. A passage, when it varies grammatically or syntactically from ordinary usage or from the usage of the context, can be safely declared to be proverbial." See also his discussion of "Proverbs and individual authors" in which he cites countless examples of the difficulty in distinguishing folk sayings and the work of individuals (pp. 34–43), and his remark (p. 34): "Of course an individual creates a proverb and sets it in circulation. The inventor's title to his property may be recognized by all who use it or his title may be so obscured by the passage of time that only investigation will determine the source of the saying." His discussion of biblical proverbs (pp. 52–61) is also extremely interesting. Pertinent to our theme is his statement (p. 59): "Biblical proverbs, and among them perhaps even those which we have discussed, may have been proverbs before their incorporation into Holy Writ."

80. So Budde, Peake. Cf. Driver-Gray *ad loc.*

80a. These lines are egregiously mistranslated by Box and Oesterley in their edition of Sirach in R. H. Charles, *Apocrypha and Pseudepigrapha of the O. T.* (Oxford 1913) vol. 1, p. 367. They render: ואם תאמר אניח לבני חוק בשאול מי יגיד לך "If thou say, I will give rest to my sons, the decree of (lit. in) Sheol who will declare it unto thee?"

81. On the verbal variations between the talmudic citation and the Genizah text, cf. Israel Lévi, R. Smend, R. H. Charles *ad loc.* Talmudic quotations of Scripture were generally made from memory or were derived from uncollated vulgar, non-Masoretic codices. Cf. V. Aptowitzer, *Das Schriftwort in der rabbinischen Literatur* (5 Hefte, Wien-Leipzig, 1906-15) and Gordis, *BTM.*

82. A. Erman, *The Literature of the Ancient Egyptians* (London, 1927) p. 102. He is at a loss to explain the quotation and asks "But what is it doing here?"

83. The entire section 4:17–5:6 is excised as the work of the Hasid glossator by McNeile, while vv. 5:1–2 are regarded as the product of K5 by Siegfried. Haupt however regards 4:17, 5:1 as genuine, but eliminates 5:2. Barton accepts the entire section except 5:2, 6a. Volz eliminates vv. 1–2 as an "unimportant proverb." Actually, terms like כסיל, ענין, חפץ, and, above all, the general viewpoint expressed, are completely in accord with what we should expect of Koheleth, and there is no convincing reason for doubting the genuineness of the

passage. Levy does not recognize 5:2 as a proverb, which is clear by its parallel structure. So also Hertzberg.

84. On the text of Ben Sira, see note 81 above.

85. Cf. Tosafot *ad loc.*: פסוק הוא אלא רב אסי רגיל להביא. See also Barukh Epstein, *Mekor Barukh* (Vilna 1930), vol. 1, p. 70, note 1: והיה לגמרא לומר כדכתיב "The Gemara should have said, as it is written."

86. Cf. "The Heptad As An Element of Biblical and Rabbinic Style" in this volume and *KMW ad loc.*

87. Levy takes the entire verse as a quotation of an ascetic, but is unable to explain why, if Koheleth is opposed by its theme, he quotes it at all. Levy overlooks the fact that Koheleth's counsel of joy as the highest good flows from a profoundly tragic conception of life. Hertzberg remarks aptly (p. 120) "*Die Grundgestimmtheit macht hier den fundamentalen Unterschied.*"

88. While Siegfried, McNeile and Haupt eliminate these verses as glosses, Barton justly remarks, "It is an open question whether Koheleth himself may not have introduced them" (*op. cit.*, p. 110). Hertzberg and Levy see no quotations here at all, but retain the passage as authentic. The closing formula, however, suits a cited aphorism better.

89. לֹא תְבוּאָה is generally rendered, "he will have no increase," but aside from the difficult syntax, תְּבוּאָה means "grain," not "increase." Hence, vocalize לֹא תְבֹאֶהָ = לֹא תְבוֹאֶהוּ "lit. it will not reach him, i. e., he will not attain it," a perfect parallel to לֹא ישבע כסף. הָמוֹן is feminine in Job 31:34; on the meaning "wealth" cf. Ps. 37:16, also Isa. 60:5.

90. These verses are excluded as the work of the Hasid glossator by McNeile, Barton, Volz and Eissfeldt (*loc. cit.*). Levy, on the other hand, takes the entire passage, vv. 2-8, as a quotation of a pious sentiment, with a loss, it seems to us, in the piquancy of the passage. Hertzberg recognizes that מִצְוָה is not a religious commandment, but the command of the king.

91. These verses, 11–13 inclusive, are attributed to the Hasid glossator and deleted by Siegfried, Haupt, McNeile and Barton, largely because of v. 12, while Volz and Eissfeldt eliminate vv. 12, 13. Practically all translations and commentators seek to connect 12a and 12b, in accordance with the Masoretic punctuation, which places a full stop at the end of v. 11, and a secondary pause (*Athnah*) at the middle of v. 12 (לֹו). They therefore follow the Vulgate *attamen* and render the opening אֲשֶׁר in v. 12a as "although." This, in spite of the fact that the opening אֲשֶׁר in v. 11 is given correctly as "because." They therefore render "Although a sinner does evil exceedingly, and prolongs his days, nevertheless I know that it shall be well with those who fear God," etc. (so Barton, Hertzberg). Actually the opening אֲשֶׁר in v. 12, like אֲשֶׁר in v. 11, is to be given as "because," and v. 12a continues the idea expressed in v. 11, while v. 12b introduces the contrary and conventional view as a quotation. It may be added that the usual interpretation suffers from several linguistic difficulties. There is no warrant for אֲשֶׁר meaning "although" and Hitzig, Delitzsch and Wright correctly render it as "because." Moreover, on the accepted view, כִּי גַם is made to introduce the principal clause of the sentence and the principal idea. However, its usage else-

where (cf. Eccl. 4:14) as well as that of the equivalent conjunction, גַּם כִּי is invariably that of a subordinating conjunction = "although" (Isa. 1:15; Hos. 8:10; 9:16; Ps. 23:4; cf. also Prov. 22:6; Lam. 3:8). In our rendering, it introduces a genuine subordinate clause (vv. 12b, 13), subordinate logically as well as grammatically. It may be noted that our rendering agrees with that of Ludwig Levy.

92. See E. Ebeling, *Altorientalische Texte zum A. T.* 2nd ed. (Berlin-Leipzig, 1926) pp. 287-292 for a German version of the text and annotations, as well as a brief bibliography.

93. For the conventional view, cf. among other passages, Prov. 6:6–11; 10:4; 12:24, 27; 13:4; 19:24; 24:33. Koheleth's attitude is expressed in 2:18 ff.; 4:4 ff.; 5:12 ff.; 6:1 ff.

94. Vulgate, Ibn Ezra, and Levy supply "saying" after v. 5, thus making v. 6 the opinion of the fool, who prefers indolence to labor. This solves the contradiction of vv. 5 and 6, to be sure, but places Koheleth in the position of urging hard work, which is highly unlikely. See note 93 above. Barton's elimination of 4:5, as the gloss of the *Hokmah* interpolator, deprives the passage of the unique flavor of its author's personality.

95. So Levy. Barton, following Siegfried and Haupt, considers 9:17–10:3 a *Hokmah* interpolation. Volz eliminates 9:17, 18a as "unimportant proverbs." Such a procedure fails to reckon with the fact that Koheleth was himself a member of the *Hokmah* school. Verse 9:17, regarding the value of quiet speech, though a conventional utterance, is completely in accord with the unimpassioned spirit of Koheleth's own reflections, and there is no good reason for doubting its authenticity. Hertzberg recognizes in 16a and 17 the accepted opinion which Koheleth refutes.

96. The root חטא, as Barton (*op. cit.*, p. 165) notes, means "to miss, make an error" and refers here to intellectual slips, so that to Koheleth it is virtually identical with כסיל. So, too, חֲטָאִים in 10:4 refers to errors committed by a courtier before a ruler, and not to sin in the moral or religious sense. A study of the concepts "sin" and "folly" in Wisdom literature generally and in Koheleth in particular is a desideratum.

97. Driver-Gray, ICC *Commentary on Job*, vol. 1, p. 116 f., quote this interpretation, but do not accept it "because the antithesis is formally unexpressed." Instead they delete both vss. as unauthentic. The evidence adduced in this paper of the frequent absence of such formal signs should be sufficient to modify this judgment. Siegfried and Duhm omit these verses — an easy escape from the difficulty which solves nothing. Some scholars take v. 12 interrogatively, "Have the aged men wisdom, and length of days understanding?" (Volz, Ball). Others interpolate הֲכִי before the verse (Hoelscher) or prefix לֹא "The aged have not wisdom," etc. (Beer, Jastrow), thus deriving from the verse a denial of the wisdom of the old. On the other hand, Dhorme places vv. 11 and 12 after v. 9, retaining the affirmation of the wisdom of the aged. Budde stands alone in recognizing that v. 12 is a quotation of the traditional view, refuted in v. 13.

98. In v. 12a the aged are credited with חכמה, in 12b with בינה. That v. 13 follows directly upon it as a refutation is clear from the fact that 13a attributes

the same חכמה to God, and 13b, the identical בינה, but adds גבורה and עצה respectively. These four qualities are identical with the attributes of "the spirit of the Lord" given in Isa. 11:2: ונחה עליו רוח ה׳ רוח חכמה ובינה רוח עצה וגבורה רוח דעת ויראת ה׳. Job. chap. 12 offers other evidence of the familiarity of its author with the book of Isaiah. Thus 12:9 is a citation of Isa. 41:20c. Cf. the table of parallels with Isa. ch. 40–66 in Driver-Gray, *op. cit.*, I, p. LXVIII and our note below. Thus Job gives an earlier terminus *non post quem* for the uniting of the prophecies of Isaiah ben Amoz and Deutero-Isaiah than the reference in Ben Sira 48:24 f. to Isaiah, "With the spirit of might, he foresaw the future and comforted the mourners of Zion. For all time he proclaimed what was to be, and hidden events before their coming."

99. See Note 6 above for details.

100. The unconventional Wisdom teachers were greatly exercised over the fact that successful malefactors often attained to a mantle of respectability which enveloped them to their last moment and beyond, so that they have elaborate funerals with fulsome eulogies extolling their non-existent virtues. On the importance of these last rites cf. Eccl. 6:3 (read וְגַם קְבוּרָה לֹא הָיְתָה לּוֹ) "even if he have a large funeral" and 8:10 ff. (read וְיִשְׁתַּבְּחוּ = they are praised"). A reference to elaborate obsequies for a king apparently occurs in 4:16; on these passages cf. *KMW ad loc.*

101. The use of quotations in chap. 21 has been partially recognized. Thus, v. 19a is taken as a quotation by Budde and by Driver-Gray, who follow the English version and prefix "Ye say," and apparently by Ball (*Book of Job*, 1922). Verse 22 is similarly treated by Hitzig. The satiric intent of vv. 28 f. has been overlooked, and v. 30 proved another stumbling-block. See Driver-Gray, *op. cit.*, for an excellent conspectus of the interpretation of these passages. On the other hand, Yellin, *op. cit.*, p. 52, renders vv. 19, 22 and 30 as quotations but takes v. 28 differently.

102. Verse 22b may possibly be rendered differently, as follows :

"Shall any one teach God knowledge
And shall he judge the All high ?"

i. e., can any human being presume either to instruct or to judge God ? This rendering has the advantage of giving a better parallelism to the verse. For רָמִים as an epithet of God, compare the biblical and Canaanite use of עֶלְיוֹן (Num. 24:16; Deut. 32:8; II Sam. 22:14; Isa. 14:14; Lam. 3:35, 38; and very frequently in the Psalms, 91:1, 9; 92:2 and often). Cf. also the very common title גָּבוֹהַ "The All-High" in rabbinic literature, probably a development from the usage in Ps. 138:6. Note also the use of רָם וְנִשָּׂא in Isa. 57:15. The plural of רָמִים would be analogous to similar epithets, as קְדוֹשִׁים when applied to God (see Ehrlich, *Randglossen*, on Hosea 12:1; Prov. 9:10. So too Job 5:1, which is to be rendered: "Call out; is there one to answer thee, and to whom rather than to God can you call ?"

103. The distinction is clearly recognized by Driver-Gray, *op. cit.*, vol. 1, pp. 84 f.

104. Cf. "The Social Background of Wisdom Literature" in this volume. J. W. Gaspar, *Social Ideas in the Wisdom Literature of the Old Testament* (Washington, 1947) fails completely to reckon with this and other indications of a specific social milieu and orientation in Wisdom literature.

105. This verse has occasioned great difficulty because it contains the only use of the Tetragrammaton in the Dialogue. (אֲדֹנָי occurs in 28:28, the "Hymn to Wisdom" which is an independent poem, and the Tetragrammaton in 38:1 and 40:1, but these verses constitute the superscription rather than part of the poem itself, probably emanating from an editor.) To delete 9b as a gloss leaves 9a an isolated stich and requires the deletion of v. 10, with injury to the entire context. Actually the use of the Tetragrammaton is due to the fact that the poet is citing a familiar, quasi-proverbial phrase from Isa. 41:20c, which employs the national name of the God of Israel.

106. For a discussion of this difficult chapter and the procedures proposed for dealing with it see the commentaries and BGM, pp. 96, 271-4, and esp. p. 329, note 6.

107. The minor variations are natural in recapitulating an argument. In 42:3 מעלים עצה for מחשיך עצה in 38:2; שמע נא ואנכי אדבר in 42:4a replaces אזר נא כגבר חלציך as an introductory challenge. Were these verses in ch. 42 interpolated from ch. 38, they would be exactly repeated. That these verses are cited by Job is recognized by Driver-Gray 1, p. 372.

108. The various categories of quotations here analyzed are all direct. Subsequent research has disclosed the existence of indirect quotations as well, likewise used without a *verbum dicendi* in Job, where it is the key to the exegesis of the crux 13:14, 15 as well as 35:2,3; cf. 19:28, 29a. See BGM pp. 188f. On Ps. 32:6, see the text and note 60 above.

6. THE SOCIAL BACKGROUND OF WISDOM LITERATURE

One of the distinctive traits of modern scholarship has been the recognition of the importance of social, economic and political factors for the cultural and religious history of Israel.[1] To be sure, these material conditions do not *determine* intellectual developments but they affect and *condition* them and therefore cannot be ignored. We have therefore been led to re-examine Wisdom Literature as a whole in terms of its social background.[2] This investigation discloses an organic relationship among all the Wisdom writers, in spite of deep-seated individual divergences. Their doctrines and ideas, their points of agreement and difference alike, are, we believe, to be traced to their common social background.

I

It is today being increasingly recognized that the extant Wisdom Literature goes back to two schools, or more accurately, to one school with a group of dissidents on the fringe. The main school, whose major documents are Proverbs and Ben Sira, was conventional in its methods and goals. It was concerned with the practical problem of training men, and particularly the youth, how to live in a hard-headed, imperfect world, rich in pitfalls and temptations for the unwary . . . These teachers upheld morality because they were convinced that it was a more effective road to success than sin. They preached adherence to religion because of the same pragmatic viewpoint—it served to make men good, and, by that token, happy. In no invidious sense, this school may be described as the lower or practical Wisdom.

It is true that the human impulse to pierce the veil of reality and grapple with the abiding mysteries of life could not be crushed even among these teachers of the tangible. At times they yielded to the metaphysical urge and saw the Wisdom they taught as an imperfect human reflection of the Divine Wisdom, the plan of the universe, by which God had created the world:

> The Lord by Wisdom founded the earth;
> By Understanding He established the heavens. (Prov. 3:19)

Generally, they preferred not to inquire too closely into the details of the Divine plan, knowing the perils that lurked on the frontier where human reason met the unknown. Their standpoint was expressed by Ben Sira in words later teachers of religion have repeated countless times:

> What is too wonderful for thee, do not seek,
> And what is hidden from thee, do not search,
> Understand that which is permitted thee,
> And have no concern with mysteries. (3:20 f.)

This theme is the burden, too, of the Hymn to Wisdom incorporated in the Book of Job (Chap. 28). With matchless skill, the poet pictures the exertions men undergo until at last they unearth precious stones in the bowels of the earth. But his refrain is: "Where is Wisdom (*Haḥokmah*) to be found, and what is the place of Understanding?" Its value is above pearls, and its hiding place is not known to the deep, to the birds of the air, or to any living thing. Only God knows the place of Wisdom, for He created it together with his universe. The poet concludes:

> But to men, He has said, the fear of God is wisdom,[3]
> and abstaining from evil is understanding. (28:28)

Faith and morality are all man can hope to attain. The propagation of these ideals is the purpose of the conventional Wisdom writers.

For a few bolder spirits within the schools of Wisdom, these goals were not enough. They had been trained to apply observation and reasoning to the practical problems of daily life. They would use the same instruments to solve the more fundamental issues that intrigued them, the purpose of life, man's destiny after death, the basis of morality, the problem of evil. When they weighed the religious and moral ideas of their time by these standards, they found some things they could accept, but much that they felt impelled to reject as either untrue or unproved. Hence the higher or speculative Wisdom books, particularly Job, Ecclesiastes and perhaps Agur Ben Yakeh (Prov.

30), are basically heterodox, skeptical works, at variance with the products of the practical Wisdom School.

But the relationship between the main school and the dissidents is far from being merely that of antagonism. The writers of Job and Koheleth undoubtedly were trained in the Wisdom academies, and perhaps taught there themselves. That conditioning would affect their style and thought-processes ever after. Thus they would naturally utilize the conventional religious vocabulary of the schools, the only one they knew, to express their unconventional ideas.[4] Frequently, they would draw upon the proverbs and gnomes of the schools, either because they agreed with them, particularly in practical matters, or because they wished to modify or oppose them. Hence these books cannot be properly understood until the use of quotations is recognized.[5]

There is, however, another factor, perhaps even more basic, to explain why conventional and unconventional teachers of Wisdom spoke the same language—they emanated from the same social stratum. While this conclusion was arrived at inductively, by a detailed study of the literature, it is best set forth deductively, especially since a good deal of the evidence is cumulative and corroborative in character.

It is the thesis of this paper that Wisdom Literature, which reached its apogee during the earlier centuries of the Second Temple, roughly between the sixth and the first half of the second centuries, B.C.E., was fundamentally the product of the upper classes in society, who lived principally in the capital, Jerusalem. Some were engaged in large-scale foreign trade, or were taxfarmers, like the Tobiades.[6] Most of them were supported by the income of their country estates, which were tilled either by slaves, or by tenant farmers, who might have once owned the very fields they now worked as tenants.[7] This patrician group was allied by marriage with the high-priestly families and the higher government officials, who represented the foreign suzerain, Persian, Ptolemaic or Seleucid.

Obviously, this group had little in common with the poorer peasants clinging desperately to their holdings, or with the petty tradesmen and the artisans in the cities, who suffered their own discontents and were evolving new values in their religious tradition, that would ultimately flower in Pharisaism, Essenism and Judeo-Christianity.

As is to be expected, the upper classes were conservative in their outlook, basically satisfied with the status quo and opposed to change.

Their conservatism extended to every sphere of life and permeated their religious ideas as well as their social, economic and political attitudes. What is most striking is that this *basic conservatism is to be found among the unconventional Wisdom teachers as well*. Though they were independent spirits who found themselves unable to accept the convenient assumptions of their class that all was right with the world, they reflect even in their revolt the social stratum from which they had sprung, or with which they had identified themselves.

It is, of course, quite possible that these Wisdom teachers personally were themselves of lower-class origin. That might account for their greater awareness of social and moral ills. It is a common phenomenon for dominant groups in society to draw their intellectual leadership from gifted members of the lower classes. The opposite process is equally frequent, where the submerged groups draw their leadership from the aristocracy, Moses and the Gracchi being cases in point. On the other hand, the heterodox Wisdom writers may have differed from their more conventional colleagues merely in their more sensitive temperament. Whatever their personal origin, their writings reflect upper-class viewpoints. This conclusion seems to us to be valid, not only for Proverbs and Ben Sira, but also for Job, Koheleth and Agur ben Yakeh.[8]

II

Some general considerations in favor of this view may now be adduced. It is generally recognized that Wisdom was taught in special schools for young men. The extant Hebrew text of Ben Sira offers the first extant use of the well-known technical term *bet hamidraš* "house of study," in his plea "Turn aside to me, ye fools and lodge in my house of study." (51:23) The word *beni*, "my son," which occurs twenty-two times in Proverbs implies the same pedagogic approach.[9] The constant emphasis upon sexual morality in Proverbs and Ben Sira, which will be discussed below, implies that the students were not children but young men. By and large, the only youths who could afford to spend their days in school in ancient times would be the scions of the wealthy classes. The sons of the poor lacked the leisure as well as the means.

In favor of this contention is a striking parallel from another great culture, that of classical Greece, which reached its highest development roughly in the same period, during the Age of Pericles (c. 463–429 B.C.E.), and the following century.

The existence of a common name for the Greek and the Hebrew doctrine and teachers (*Sophia, Hokmah, Sophistai, Hakamim*) is itself significant, but the resemblances go much further. It is not being argued that the two movements influenced each other. The principle being invoked is that similar material conditions in different societies will produce similar spiritual and intellectual tendencies, *mutatis mutandis*. It is noteworthy that the same technique, of drawing an analogy from Greek to Hebrew religion, is employed in another connection by one of the most acute contemporary students of Wisdom literature, O. S. Rankin.[10]

The differences between these two culture-areas are fundamental. Hebrew life was permeated by a profound religious consciousness, a preoccupation with moral issues that even the most secular-minded groups could not escape. Greek life, on the other hand, especially in its higher manifestations, was predominantly humanistic, with the trend strongly secular. This was true, even when the ritual was observed, as by Socrates before his death.

The sophists were polymaths, teaching all the arts and sciences known in their day, and this basic aspect of their activity has no parallel in the post-exilic Jewish community. However, these differences should not obscure the resemblances existing between the *ḥakamim* and the sophists in technique and in goal. In the Platonic dialogue that bears his name, Protagoras, the sophist, declares that his goal is to teach his pupils prudence in public and private affairs, the orderly management of family and home, the art of rhetoric and the ability to understand and direct the affairs of state.[11] With the exception of the forensic art, these are the avowed purposes of Hokmah, as such passages as Prov. 1:4, 5; 6:24; 8:15 ff. and indeed every line of the literature amply attest,—the training of the upper class for administration and leadership:

> To give prudence to the simple,
> To the young man knowledge and discretion. (Prov. 1:4)

> By me kings reign,
> And princes decree justice. (Prov. 8:15)

> By me princes rule,
> And nobles, even all the judges of the earth. (Prov. 8:16)

In the case of the sophists a good deal is known about the economic arrangements that governed their activities, so that there is no need of *a priori* reasoning to establish the fact that their clients were the youth of the upper classes. Protagoras and Gorgias demanded ten thousand drachmas for the education of a single pupil; Prodicus, more moderate in his fees, asked from one to fifty drachmas for admission to his courses.[12] Evenus of Paros was praised for demanding only five hundred drachmas for instruction in "human and political virtue." No such rates could possibly have been demanded in Palestine, but whatever fees were required could only have been met by youths of means and leisure.[13]

Finally, and most significantly, the sophists and the hakamim exhibit the same process of intellectual development. In the case of some members of the group, at least, the sophists progress from the teaching of the conduct of practical affairs toward speculative thought in a skeptical spirit. Protagoras, who declared that "man is the measure of all things" and "with regard to the gods, I know not whether they exist or not," Gorgias of Leontini, whose chief philosophical tenet was that nothing exists, or at least that nothing is knowable, Thrasymachus of Chalcedon who identified might with right, and remarked that the success of villains cast doubt upon the existence of the gods, and above all Socrates, who subjected all ideas and ideals to his skeptical analysis, all these,[14] for all the vast differences of the Greek and the Hebrew ethos, are brothers of the spirit to Koheleth, who maintained that God had made the truth forever unknowable to man, and to Job, who doubted that justice operated in the world.

It is noteworthy that in developing skeptical tendencies, the Greek sophists continued to function in their more conventional and more lucrative role as teachers of the practical virtues. In precisely the same manner, the heterodox Wisdom books of Job, Koheleth and Agur contain much typical Wisdom material of the same kind as we meet in Proverbs. Hence attempts to excise this material as interpolations or to atomize the text by assigning it to many hypothetical authors must be stigmatized as unnecessary and therefore unsound. A more sympathetic insight into the personality of these Sages will spare us the necessity of resorting to such violent and subjective procedures.

In sum, Greek *sophia* and Hebrew *hokmah* are strikingly parallel in their concern with the education of the youth for practical life and in their culmination in philosophical skepticism. These analogies strengthen the view that the latter, like the former, arose in the upper strata of society, which alone had need of that type of training and could afford to pay for it.

These wisdom academies must be distinguished from the schools conducted by the Pharisees and their predecessors, the Sopherim. Here the students were largely the children of the poor. Unfortunately, little or nothing is known of these schools in pre-Maccabean days, but our fuller knowledge of the Mishnic period would imply that the teachers, as well as the pupils, earned their living as workers. The Talmudic teachers include blacksmiths, cobblers, tailors, bakers, potters and builders among others.[15] Hillel's daily earnings have been estimated at fourteen American cents. It therefore follows that the studies in the Pharisaic schools, except for the "professional" schools intended to train experts in the Law, must have been conducted largely on the Sabbaths and Festivals.[16]

Moreover, Pharisaism regarded the teaching of Torah as a commandment for which no payment might be accepted. The Rabbis depicted Moses as saying: "As I was taught freely, so teach ye freely."[17] This is closely akin to Jesus' injunction to his disciples: "Freely have ye received, freely give."[18] Professor Louis Ginzberg has called attention to the fact that this attitude is not merely haggadic, but actually occurs in the *Halachah*. In the Mishnah, Nedarim, 4:3, a man who has taken a vow not to receive any material benefit from his neighbor may nevertheless continue to teach him all except the most elementary branches of Torah (*mikra'*, Bible text), because no tuition fee is involved. Even the tuition for this elementary teaching, it was felt, required justification, and so legal casuistry was resorted to in the Talmud and the Codes.[19]

The difference in the points of view of the upper-class Wisdom teachers and the Pharisaic Sopherim may be graphically illustrated by contrasting the dictum on labor of the early Pharisaic teacher, Abtalion, of the first century B.C.E., the teacher of Hillel,[20] with that of Ben Sira. Abtalion is the author of the statement, "Love labor and abhor authority" (Aboth 1:11). Ben Sira, on the contrary, declares:

> How can he become wise that holdeth the goad,
> And glorieth in brandishing the lance,
> Likewise the maker of carving and cunning devices . . . .
> So also the smith that sitteth by the furnace,
> Likewise the potter who sitteth at the wheel . . .

Without them a city cannot be inhabited,
But they shall not be inquired of for public counsel,
And law and justice they understand not. (38:25 ff.)

To revert to the main theme, the existence of Wisdom academies presupposes the youth of the leisure class. Moreover, such schools could be maintained only in large centers of population, such as Jerusalem.

There are other general considerations that reenforce this view. It was observed long ago that Wisdom is the most secular branch of ancient Hebrew literature, being concerned with broadly human rather than with specifically Jewish problems.[21] Job actually treats the problem of human suffering through a gallery of non-Israelitish characters.[22]

The use of the Divine names in the Wisdom books is also highly instructive, being parallel to the development in Babylonian and Egyptian Wisdom, where the individual names of the gods do not disappear, but yield increasingly to general descriptions of "God" or "The Gods." The individual names tend to appear in traditional apothegms or in contexts concerned with the attributes of a specific god.[23]

The use of Divine names in Hebrew Wisdom is entirely similar. The oldest collections in Proverbs (10:1–22:16; chap. 25-29) which are probably pre-exilic, use JHVH, the national name of the Deity, exclusively. Yet even here, when JHVH does occur, it is often in stock phrases like "the fear of JHVH," "The blessing of JHVH," "the abomination of JHVH," "the knowledge of JHVH."[24] The later collections in Proverbs use JHVH much less consistently. A factor which may help explain the retention of the name JHVH is the gnomic character of the book, which would subject it to considerable quotation, in which the most popular name of the Deity would tend to be used. In Ben Sira, the general term is used in half the cases. The use of JHVH in the other half is apparently to be attributed to the identification of the God of Israel with the world creator, so that the specific national name has become divested of any particularistic character. The higher Wisdom writers avoid JHVH almost entirely, in favor of the general names, *'el*, *'eloah*, *'elohim*, *šaddai*. JHVH is virtually lacking in the poetry of Job, and *elohim* is the exclusive designation of the Deity in Koheleth.[25]

It is noteworthy that Umberto Cassuto explicitly recognizes the connection between this preference for "appellative" Divine names, characteristic of Wisdom literature, and the upper-class outlook, influenced by foreign contacts, encountered in Sadduceeism. He thus explains the Pharisaic enactment that the Divine name be used in greeting one's friend: והתקינו שיהא אדם שואל בשלום חבירו בשם (Berakhot 9:5) as reflecting the popular use of the national name of God, as opposed to the more universal terms popular among the upper-class Sadducees,[26] whose thinking was moulded by the international outlook characteristic of Wisdom. Similarly, the Damascus Scroll, which is part of the literary remains of the Essenes of Qumran, replaces JHVH with *El* even in Biblical citations.

Recent investigations have disclosed the Egyptian and Mesopotamian sources which have influenced much of Hebrew gnomic literature, notably the Sayings of Amenemope, which may be a direct source for Proverbs.[27] Today it is clear that Hebrew Wisdom is part of Oriental Wisdom generally, as Johann Fichtner's excellent study, *Die Alt-orientalische Weisheit in ihrer israelitisch-juedischen Auspraegung*[28] amply demonstrates.

This cosmopolitan character of Wisdom is likewise most naturally explained in terms of its upper-class origin. Foreign contacts, opportunities for travel and trade,[29] and a fondness for the culture and fashions of other lands, have always characterized the aristocracy. Ben Sira speaks of himself as having made many journeys, accompanied by danger (34:11 f.) and includes travel as an element in the life of the ideal scribe (39:4). Koheleth speaks of amassing "the treasures of kings and provinces" (2:8). On the other hand, the peasant, the petty merchant and the craftsman have neither the opportunity nor the penchant for such contacts.

Moreover, Oriental Wisdom is explicitly intended for the training of the ruler-class, for young princes, and the lords and scribes destined to be their servants at court. Professor Albright's succinct description of the gnomic and didactic works of the Old and Middle Egyptian Empires may be applied virtually unchanged to Hebrew Wisdom:

The Maxims of Ptah-hotep and another nearly contemporary work are characteristic in diction and attitude of the late Old Empire, where stability was traditional and where shrewd aphorisms and wise counsels were in constant demand on the part of persons ambitious for preferment. These aphorisms are often noble and always worldly: doing right and acting justly are necessary to success and will bring prosperity if combined with prudence.[30]

Fichtner supplies ample details to corroborate this truth.[31] We shall have occasion to point out that practically all the virtues inculcated by Hebrew Wisdom are applicable to the upper classes and their servants.

Nearly all of Oriental Wisdom is attributed to kings. Amenemket I is the author of the teaching intended for Sesostris I. The teaching for Merikare is composed by a royal father for his son and successor. The Insinger Papyrus calls itself the "Book of Kings." It is a striking fact that no other branch of Hebrew literature is ascribed so consistently to royal authors. Three of the collections in the Book of Proverbs are ascribed to Solomon, the last named also being associated with Hezekiah. Lemuel is a king (Prov. 31:1), as is Koheleth (1:1, 12).

The environment reflected in Wisdom is that of the wealthy classes. The striking emphasis upon abstaining from sexual liaisons outside the marriage bond is a case in point.[32] These women against whom the preceptor of youth warns are not the street walkers, who ply their trade among the poor, but the kept women, often married, whose homes are decked with tapestry woven of Egyptian linen and whose couch is richly perfumed. (Prov. 7:16 ff.) It has not been hitherto observed how commonly precious stones are used as an object of comparison and value in Proverbs.[33] The moralist warns against quarrelsome households, having meat to eat (*zibḥe ribh*, 17:1), a diet rarely if ever enjoyed by the poor. He repeatedly exhorts against the dangers of wine-bibbing and gluttony,[34] vices from which the poor are usually free, often through no will or merit of their own. The pupil is pictured as one in position to distribute largesse at will:

Say not unto thy neighbor: 'Go, and come again,
And tomorrow I will give'; when thou hast it by thee. (Prov. 3:28)

III

These general considerations constitute only part of the evidence for the upper-class orientation of Wisdom literature.

The morality inculcated in Proverbs and Ben Sira is utilitarian, from the standpoint of the possessing classes. The reader is perpetually

urged to display diligence and the perils of laziness are reiterated.[35]
The reward of virtue is characteristic:

> Seest thou a man diligent in his business?
> He shall stand before kings;
> He shall not stand before mean men. (Prov. 22:29)

Prudence, the capacity to foretell the consequences of one's actions
and diligence at one's tasks are emphasized as the cornerstones of
success.

Keeping one's own counsel and refraining from overmuch intimacy
with one's superiors are repeatedly insisted upon:

> When thou sittest to eat with a ruler,
> Consider well him that is before thee. (Prov. 23:1; cf. B.S. 13:2–20)

In common with Egyptian Wisdom and the Ahikar romance, the
Hebrew sages urge the attributes of zeal and reliability in the messenger.[36] Basic to these qualities are loyalty to the king and submis-
siveness to authority, which will be discussed at greater length
below.[37]

> The King's favour is toward a servant that dealeth wisely;
> But his wrath striketh him that dealeth shamefully. (Prov. 14:35)

The social virtues that are inculcated are approached from the
standpoint of the powerful groups toward the weaker:

> Do not rob the poor because he is poor, and do not crush the needy in the
> gate. (Prov. 22:22)

Job's great Confession of innocence (ch. 31) likewise reflects the
morality of a patriarch possessing wealth and influence, who refrains
from using his power to injure the weaker groups, his slaves, the poor,
the orphan and the widow, and does not yield to the temptation of
trusting in riches.[38]

Most striking of all, because it is so utterly at variance with the entire
tenor of Biblical thought, is the attitude of the Wisdom teachers on
going surety for one's neighbor. Here we find none of the humanitarian emphasis of the Deuteronomic Code on the "open hand" or
the Pentateuchal insistence on lending without interest.[39] On the
contrary there is a constant reiteration of the dangers of the practice:[40]

> He that is surety for a stranger shall smart for it;
> But he who hates those that strike hands is secure. (Prov. 11:15)

Ben Sira adopts the same attitude, and gives a perspicacious analysis of the perils of lending money. (8:12; 29:1 ff.) Yet he urges the practice and offers an interesting reason:

Help a poor man for the commandment's sake. and grieve not for its loss,
Lose money for the sake of a friend,
And let it not rust under a stone or a wall. (B.S. 20:9, 10)

It may be added that the Hebrew idiom for "going surety" *taka‘ kaph*, literally, "clasping the hand", implies a well-developed commercial usage among groups possessing assets that could be taken in pledge.

A revealing sidelight on the class origins of Wisdom is shed by the Wisdom Psalm 37.[41] The poet, wishing to contrast the wicked and the righteous, selects as an instance of the former a *borrower*, who does not repay a loan, and of the latter, the generous *lender*—types diametrically opposed to those the Prophets or the *'anavim* Psalmists would have chosen:

The wicked borrows, but does not pay,
But the righteous deals graciously and gives. (Ps. 37:21)

This social background alone can explain the sweeping assertion of the same Psalmist that the righteous never suffer want, a statement without parallel anywhere else in the Bible:

I have been young and now am old,
But I have not seen the righteous forsaken,
And his offspring begging bread. (37:24)

A passage, the rare pungency of which has been overlooked, because of the failure to reckon with its social background, is Proverbs 28:3. The Masoretic text reads:

גֶּבֶר רָשׁ וְעֹשֵׁק דַּלִּים מָטָר סֹחֵף וְאֵין לָחֶם

Because the idea of a poor man oppressing the poor is not met with elsewhere in the Bible, most moderns have emended *raš* "poor" to *roš* "chief ruler", *raša‘* "wicked", or *'ašir* "rich man."[42]

All these emendations create at best a platitudinous clause in stich a, and the comparison in stich b is meaningless.

Actually, no change is required, if the second clause is properly understood.[43] Rain generally serves to produce crops, but a beating downpour inundates the earth with no beneficial results. So too, a rich man who oppresses the poor reaps the benefit of his act by amassing wealth. But what an irony to see a poor man making life miserable for his fellows and gaining nothing thereby! The observation comes with especial aptness from a perspicacious son of the upper classes, who was tired perhaps of the perpetual accusations levelled against wealthy malefactors by prophets, lawgivers and sages. For irony and insight the saying is unsurpassed:

> A *poor* man who oppresses the poor
> Is like a sweeping rain that produces no food!

Utilitarian morality possessed lower elements, and these are not altogether lacking in Wisdom teaching. Thus kindness to an enemy is defended on the score that it is like pouring hot coals on his head, besides winning God's favor (Prov. 25:21). Rejoicing over the discomfiture of one's foe may arouse God's displeasure and lead Him to avert his wrath (24:17).

Generally speaking, the Hebrew sages, like all Oriental Wisdom teachers, extol impartiality in judgment and condemn bribery.[44] Yet this does not prevent them from stressing the practical utility of bribery in making one's way:

A gift in secret pacifieth anger,
And a present in the bosom strong wrath. (Prov. 21:14; cf. also 17:8; 19:6)

This may be the meaning of *marpe'*, "healing" in the following passage:

> If the spirit of the ruler rise up against thee,
> Leave not thy place;
> For healing allayeth great offences. (Ecc. 10:4)

Ben Sira actually uses the Pentateuchal statement, "Bribery blinds the eyes", in order to justify its use:

Presents and gifts blind the eyes of the wise, and as a muzzle on the mouth turn away reproofs. (B.S. 20:29)

As the *summum bonum* in life and the reward of moral conduct, the Wisdom writers universally set up practical success, in which economic prosperity is central. Wealth is uniformly regarded as a great good and poverty as an evil. The penalty for disobeying instruction is "poverty and shame" (Prov. 13:18), while adherence to Wisdom brings "riches and honor" (Prov. 3:16).

The Proverbist points out that the wealth of the rich is a mighty city while the undoing of the poor is their poverty (Prov. 10:15). Ben Sira also remarks on the difference in the treatment of rich and poor (13:21 ff.). While he declares that even a poor man may be honored for his sagacity, he adds:

"He that is honored in his poverty—how much more in his wealth!" (10:31). Koheleth goes further and insists that "Wisdom is good with an inheritance" (7:11), and "the wisdom of the poor man is despised" (9:16).[45]

Doubtless Koheleth's description of his wealth in Chapter Two is idealized, but there is no adequate reason for denying that it reflects his general condition.[46] On the contrary, there is decisive evidence at hand that he belonged to the upper classes. Again and again, he refers to the tragedy involved in a man's dying and leaving his wealth to another, to "a stranger", as Koheleth calls him.[47] This is surely not one of the problems of the poor. Even his disillusion with riches argues the surfeit of a man who has experienced the boredom of perpetual satiety, rather than the hunger of the destitute. No Hebrew prophet ever sought to console the downtrodden with the thought that wealth is not synonymous with happiness. The preoccupation of the Torah and the Prophets with social problems is one of their salient features, for which no detailed documentation is necessary.

It need not be labored that the high valuation placed by the Wisdom teachers upon economic prosperity does not betoken a surrender of moral values. The strong moral emphasis in Judaism is evident in Wisdom as well. All theft and wrongly acquired wealth are opposed.[48] In particular, the removal of landmarks, the besetting sin of the landowner, and false measures, the failing of the merchant, are described as abominations.[49] Above all, the practice of charity is constantly urged by the Wisdom teachers.[50]

Another virtue, appropriate to the well-to-do, is moderation in food and drink. Here the stress is laid on the physical and economic consequences of excess.[51] The same restraint is urged in the seeking of riches:

Weary not thyself to grow rich, cease from thine own wisdom. (Prov. 23:4)

This attitude is motivated not by the idea that riches are an unworthy or inadequate goal for human existence, but by the thought that wealth is fleeting[52] and the further consideration that chance plays a great part in its acquisition. This is naturally expressed in Biblical terms:

> The blessing of the Lord it is that gives wealth,
> And toil adds nothing to it. (Prov. 10:22)
>
> For riches certainly make themselves wings,
> Like an eagle that flieth toward heaven. (Prov. 23:5)

The virtue of contentment is preached in such passages as:

A little with the fear of God is better than a great treasure with turmoil. (Prov. 15:16)

These and similar statements[53] have been plausibly attributed to the plebeian Hasid glossator in Proverbs by some scholars.[54] On the other hand, it is not ruled out that a moralistic teacher of upper-class youth would feel called upon to counteract, in part at least, the prevalent apotheosis of wealth. Thus the teaching of Amenemope, which is indubitably upper class in origin and orientation, preaches contentment, restraint in the search for wealth and general moderation, virtues one would expect to find in the moral instruction of the youth of the aristocracy.[55] A few instances taken from Budge's translation will suffice:

Commit not an act of avariciousness so that thou mayest find (i. e., obtain) additional wealth. (l. 110)

Better is the beggar who is in the hand of the God than the rich who are safely housed in a comfortable dwelling. (ll. 158, 159)

Fashion not thy heart in such wise that it hankers after things of wealth (i.e., luxurious foods and apparel). (l. 163)

Form not the habit of ordering thyself to seek for more than thou hast,
When thy own goods and possessions are in thy safe keeping. (l. 167, 168)

Make not thyself to take pleasure in rich treasures that have been obtained by robbery. (l. 179)

In general, contentment is a doctrine more honored in the preaching than in the observance, the poor being exhorted to it by the rich, who testify from their own experience that riches are not synonymous with happiness!

It has long been noted that the Hebrew Bible, as a whole, is lacking in any ascetic glorification of poverty.[56] The Wisdom writers, in particular, regard the enjoyment of life as important:

> Ointment and perfume rejoice the heart, . . . (Prov. 27:9)

> Give and take, yea, indulge thy soul,
> For in Sheol there is no delight. (B.S. 14:15)

(Cf. B.S. 14:11 ff.; 30:21–25) The triad of wine, women and song appears in Ben Sira:

Wine and song rejoice the heart, but better than both is love. (40:20)

In Koheleth, the physical enjoyment of life becomes the only sensible goal left to man:[57]

There is no greater good for man than eating and drinking and giving himself joy in his labor. Indeed, I have seen that this is from the hand of God. (Ecc. 2:24)

Money is the means to this end:

Men make a feast for pleasure, and wine cheers the living, and it is money that provides it all! (Ecc. 10:19)

IV

The religious ideas of the Wisdom literature reflect the same upper-class orientation. Basic to its world-view is the idea that virtue leads to well-being and vice leads to poverty and disaster. Wealth is a blessing of the Lord bestowed upon the upright (Prov. 10:22) and removed from the wicked (12:22; 10:2, 16; 11:28). In its origin, this view was not the possession of a single group, but the standpoint of the entire nation, it being a corollary of the traditional Hebrew faith in the moral government of the world. During the days of the First Temple, when clan solidarity was all-powerful and reward and punishment were referred to the nation as a whole,[58] its truth was rarely questioned. With Jeremiah and Ezekiel, however, the individual begins to emerge as an independent personality demanding happiness for itself, as distinct from the fate of the family, clan or nation.[59] Throughout the Second Temple period, the problem of the individual's fate is the central problem of Jewish theology. That individual success is the seal of virtue and individual suffering the proof of sin, could continue to be maintained only by the successful groups.

The lower classes, ground by poverty and oppression, were tormented by the problem of the prosperity of the wicked and the suffering of the righteous. Holding resolutely to their faith in God and divine justice, they were nevertheless unable to make their peace with the world about them. The solution they ultimately reached was the doctrine of another world where the inequalities of the present order would be rectified. Thus the idea of a future life became an integral feature of Pharisaic Judaism and Christianity.[60]

The teachers of Wisdom, on the other hand, being representative of the affluent groups, felt no compulsion to adopt these new views. The sages of the conventional school maintain unchanged the old view of retribution here and now and make it, as has been noted, the cornerstone of their teaching of the youth.

So too, they retain the old doctrine of collective retribution, where the sins or virtues of the fathers determine the destiny of the children.[61] The idea of a future life, on the other hand, is not so much as mentioned in Proverbs, probably because the material is comparatively early. By the time Ben Sira wrote, in the second century B.C.E., the doctrine of an after-life had achieved wide currency and could no longer be passed over in silence. He therefore negates the belief explicitly:

When a man dies, he inherits worms, maggots, lice and creeping things. (10:11)[62]

A particularly interesting passage is to be found in 7:17. Ben Sira declares:

Humble thy pride greatly, for the expectation of man is worms.

His grandson and Greek translator, two generations later, gives it a Pharisaic interpretation:

Humble thy soul greatly, for the punishment of the ungodly is fire and worms.

The unconventional sages, the authors of Job and Koheleth, on the other hand, part company with their conventional colleagues on this very issue of reward and punishment. Though they are members of the same class, they are too clear-sighted and too sensitive to overlook the manifest instances of undeserved suffering or prosperity in the world. Yet neither writer accepts the Pharisaic solution of a life after death, though they are both familiar with it. Job toys with the idea but regretfully dismisses it at last:

> As water vanishes from a lake,
> and a river is parched and dries up,
> so man lies down and rises not again;
> till the heavens are no more he will not awake,
> nor will he be roused from his sleep . . .
>
> If a man die, can he live again?
> all the days of my service I would wait,
> till my hour of release should come. . . .
>
> As waters wear away stones
> and a torrent[63] washes away the earth's soil,
> so do You destroy man's hope. (14:11, 12, 14, 19)

It is noteworthy that even the Friends, for all their attempts to justify God's ways to Job, do not have recourse to this doctrine. Koheleth rejects the theory with a characteristic shrug of the shoulders:

All go to one place; all come from the dust and return to the dust. Who knows whether the spirit of man goes upward, and the spirit of the beast goes downward to the earth? (Ecc. 3:20 f.; cf. 9:10, 12)

It is in their reaction to the agonizing problem of evil that the social background of Job and Koheleth is most clearly revealed. It has long been evident that their predominant temper is that of skepticism, an incapacity to accept conventional ideas, merely because of the pressure of the mass. But it has not been noted that there is another element in the constitution of a skeptic—a psychological inability to act so as to modify conditions. In other words, skepticism is a state of mind possible only for those who observe and dislike evil, but are not its direct victims. Those who are direct sufferers are impelled either to change the conditions or to seek escape from them, through one or another avenue of action. Thus the Hebrew prophets, oppressed by the social iniquity of their day, utilized elements of the folk religion to create the exalted conception of the "End-time," when the kingdom of God would be ushered in on earth and a just order established for

men and nations. The teachers of Pharisaic Judaism and early Christianity offered the hope of another world after death where justice
would be vindicated. The mystics of all religions, faced by the same
problem, have chosen another way out by taking refuge in a realm of
the spirit, while their physical existence on the earth still continues. On
the other hand, reformers and revolutionaries in all ages have striven
to transform society in their own life-time through legislation or
radical reconstruction.

The teachers of Wisdom adopted none of these alternatives. Their
failure to do so was due to the fact that they personally found life
tolerable even under the conditions they deprecated, not being victims
of social injustice themselves. When these two elements of skepticism
are taken into account—an awareness of evil and an absence of compulsion to modify conditions—it becomes clear why skepticism is
usually to be found among the more intelligent groups of upper-class
society, rather than among the masses of the people.

Professor G. F. Moore's comment on the social origins of Buddhism
may be applied to the teachers of unconventional Hebrew Wisdom as
well:

It is a common observation that it is not the people whose life seems to
us most intolerable that are most discontented with life; despair is a child
of the imagination and pessimism has always been a disease of the well-to-do,
or at least the comfortably well-off.[64]

That all the Wisdom writers do not accept the nascent ideas of life
after death has, of course, long been noted, but it has usually been
attributed to their general conservatism and fondness for the older
ideas. But this explanation is inadequate, for we should then have
expected to find in Wisdom an adherence to the older doctrines of
the "day of JHVH", as expounded by Amos, Isaiah and Jeremiah,[65] or
the conception of the "End-time", as developed by Isaiah, Jeremiah
and Ezekiel.[66] *Actually the Wisdom writers, whether conventional or not,
accept neither the older nor the newer views that run counter to their
group associations.* The Messianic hope on earth and the faith in an
after-life alike find no echo in their thought. Nowhere in the entire
literature do we find the faith of the prophets in a dynamic world. The
Wisdom teachers are pre-eminently guides to the status quo, in which
they contemplate no alteration. Whether they accept their contemporary society as fundamentally just, or whether they have their

doubts, their basic attitude is that it is worth preserving without serious change.

Hence the clear-cut social conservatism in Koheleth, which is not due to interpolators but is integral to his outlook, as will be indicated below in Section V. Hence, too, the inability of Job to find any solution at all to the problem of suffering, if the JHVH speeches (chap. 38-41) be regarded as later additions. If, on the other hand, they are authentic, as we believe, the only answer the author finds lies in the mystery of the cosmos and in the thought that the harmony of the natural world, though incomprehensible to man, must have its counterpart in the moral world as well.

Koheleth lacks even this positive hope. He sees justice as nonexistent and truth as unattainable and therefore declares that joy is the only legitimate purpose of human life. That goal itself, it should be noted, is feasible only for those possessing the means of gratifying their desires. It can therefore be directed only to the upper strata of society. His advice would be a bitter mockery to those living on the fringe of starvation:

Go your way, eat your bread with joy, and drink your wine with a merry
    heart, for God has already accepted your actions,
Let your garments always be white, and oil on your head not be lacking . . .
Enjoy life with a woman you love all the days of your brief life . . .[67]
Whatever your hand can do, do with all your might, for there is no work,
    nor reckoning, nor knowledge, nor wisdom in Sheol, whither you are
    going. (Ecc. 9:7, 8, 9a, 10)

It may be added that when the author of Job wished to set the stage for the discussion of suffering, he selected the tale of a prosperous patriarch, who loses his wealth and position. It is undeniable that such a plot has greater dramatic power than the story of the suffering of a righteous man who had always been poor. Nevertheless, it is noteworthy that the book of Job raises the problem of evil in the form most likely to confront a member of the upper classes.

The enigmatic fragment of the Wisdom of Agur ben Yakeh (Prov. 30) is perhaps best discussed here. Though its spirit is not easy to grasp because of its brevity, it seems to voice the two basic themes of the higher skeptical Wisdom, which meet us in Koheleth, the unknowability of the world and the recognition of injustice suffered by the weak. The former is expressed in vv. 2-4:

Surely I am brutish, unlike a man . . .
I have learned no Wisdom, and do not know the knowledge of the Holy One,[68]
Who has ascended to heaven and descended,
Who has gathered the wind in his fists . . .
What is his name and his son's name, if you know it?

The latter theme occurs in vv. 12–14:

> There is a generation that are pure in their own eyes,
> and yet are not washed from their filthiness.
> There is a generation whose teeth are as swords,
> and their great teeth as knives,
> to devour the poor of the land,
> and the needy of the earth.

In spite of these sentiments, the class position of Agur emerges clearly from vv. 21–25, in which he declares that the earth quakes at the spectacle of a slave enthroned or a maid inheriting her mistress. This is an exact parallel to Koheleth's lament at the sight of "slaves riding on horses and lords walking on the earth like slaves" (Ecc. 10:7). So too, Agur's warning against slandering a slave to his master (v. 10) seems addressed to members of the slave-owning class. It is entirely of a piece with Koheleth's advice not to eavesdrop, lest one overhear oneself being slandered by one's own slave (Ecc. 7:21).

The remaining apothegms in the Agur fragment are not decisive for his social background. His prayer to be spared the extremes of poverty and wealth (vv. 7–9) could have been penned by any sound student of human nature. The sayings on diligence (vv. 24–28), strife (v. 32 f.) and the animal gnomes (vv. 29 f.) are conventional statements of accepted truths, such as are to be found in Koheleth, side by side with his more striking aperçus. They testify to the writer's origin within the official Wisdom schools.

The attitude toward free-will in Wisdom is also significant. In discussing the Jewish sects of his day, Josephus describes the Sadducees as believing in absolute free-will, while the Pharisees held that all things are from God.[69] Obviously, the idea that man is a moral free-acting agent cannot be dispensed with by any religious system, and Pharisaism also accepted the doctrine of free-will.[70] By and large, Rabbinic Judaism met the problem of the paradox of free-will versus predestination by grasping both horns of the dilemma, as in Akiba's famous formulation, "Everything is foreseen and free will is given."[71]

What is striking about the Sadducean position is its acceptance of free-will *without modification.* Doctor Finkelstein has ably demonstrated how natural this position would be for the more fortunate groups in society.[72] They were impelled to adopt this standpoint, not by the theological difficulty involved in justifying reward and punishment if men's actions are determined, but by the psychological need to validate their superior social and economic status. Poverty and riches are the result of man's own doing; their prosperity was due to their own ability and diligence. It was the doctrine which the Torah summarizes as: "My own power and the might of my hand have gotten me this wealth."[73] That the argument has considerable elements of truth is beside our present point. The Sadducees had the philosophy of "the self-made man."

The Wisdom writers reflect a proto-Sadduceeism in this as in so many other respects. Ben Sira insists on free-will:

Say not, 'from God is my transgression,' for what He hates, he did not make.
   (15:11)

Poured out before thee are fire and water,
Stretch out thy hand to what thou desirest. (15:16)

Though man has an evil nature (*yeṣer hara*) (37:3), he that keeps the Law, controls his "natural tendency" (21:11). The other Wisdom books do not react explicitly to the doctrine of free-will, though, as we have seen, their moral code is based upon this presupposition.

Another doctrine which becomes increasingly important in Pharisaic Judaism and Christianity, both of which represent the "plebeian" tradition, is the concept of Satan as an almost independent adversary of God.[74] Here too, Wisdom reflects the opposite tendency. It is true that in the Prologue to Job, Satan appears, but he is merely one, though the most distinctive, member of the heavenly court, entirely subservient to God's will. The use of the definite article with his name, *hassatan*, unlike the later use in I Chronicles 21:1 without the article, *satan*, indicates that in Job he is not yet a full-fledged personality. Even more significant is the fact that Satan appears only in the Prologue, which is a *Volksbuch*, slightly retouched, if at all, by the poet. In the Dialogue, which is original with the author, Satan is not even alluded to, though it would have been easy to refer the evil in the world to his agency.

In Proverbs and Koheleth, Satan is not specifically mentioned. Yet a passage like Ecc. 3:11 makes it not unlikely that Koheleth was familiar with the idea of evil existing independently of God in the world. This view he opposes by the theory that all things, whether or not they appear evil by human standards, have their proper place in the inscrutable scheme of things. This may be the intent of the difficult passage (3:11):

Everything He has made proper in its due time, and He has also placed the love of the world[75] in men's hearts, except that they may not discover the work God has done from beginning to end.

The famous Catalogue of Seasons in 3:1 ff., "For everything there is a time and season," is also to be understood in this manner and so integrated into Koheleth's thought.

This theory of evil seems also to be echoed in Ben Sira (39:16):

> The works of God are all good
> And supply every need in its season.
> None may say 'This is worse than that'
> For everything availeth in its season.

The concept of Satan, however, continued to win acceptance, as the passage in Chronicles proves. Ben Sira therefore feels it incumbent upon him to polemize openly against the doctrine:

When the fool curses his adversary (Satan) he curses himself. (21:27)

Thus the Wisdom writers fought against all efforts to limit the play of free-will in human affairs.

Their attitude toward the Temple cult is likewise in keeping with the later Sadduceean viewpoint—a conviction of the need to maintain the accepted ritual, coupled with little fervor or enthusiasm for religious exercises. Koheleth declares:

Watch your step when you go to the house of God, for it is better to understand than to offer sacrifice like the fools, who do not even know how to do evil! Do not hasten to speak, nor let yourself be rushed into uttering words before God, for God is in heaven and you are on the earth—therefore, let your words be few. (Ecc. 4:17 ff.; cf. 9:2)

In Proverbs, there are six references to sacrifices, one urging the payment of dues (3:9), a note struck by Koheleth as well (5:3 f.), three stressing the importance of righteousness above sacrifice (15:8; 21:3, 7) and two purely incidental (7:14; 17:1). A particularly interesting example of how ritual may become divorced from morality is afforded by 7:14, where the adulteress seeks to entice the youth by telling him that she has duly offered up her sacrifice and so has a supply of meat for the lovers' feast.

In Ben Sira, the Temple cult arouses a warmer emotion, perhaps as a reaction to the widespread assimilation in the upper classes due to Hellenistic influences. Righteous and unrighteous sacrifices are clearly differentiated (34:18–35:11). Essentially, however, it is the priestly caste that is glorified in Ben Sira, especially in the lengthy panegyric on Simon the High Priest (49:15–50:24) and it is the priestly dues that are defended (7:29–31; 38:11).

In the Prologue, Job offers sacrifices (1:5), but in his great Confession of Innocence (chap. 31), ritual plays no part, except for the avoidance of idolatry (vv. 26–28). Job, of course, is pictured as a non-Jew, so that in isolation this fact would not be significant. It is, however, worthy of notice, that in Proverbs and Ben Sira, all the other elements of Jewish ritual, aside from the Temple sacrifices, such as the Sabbath, the Festivals and the dietary laws, are not urged upon the reader. This is not to infer that the Sages did not observe these rituals, only that they did not regard them as central to their outlook. Egyptian Wisdom likewise shows practically no interest in ritual and Babylonian scarcely more.[76] Especially significant, in view of the stress on family morality by the Wisdom writers, is their silence on the subject of intermarriage which was a burning issue in Second Temple days, as Nehemiah, Malachi, Ruth and the history of the Tobiades amply attest.[77]

v

The social ideas expressed in this literature illustrate the same social background even more clearly. The attitude toward woman is characteristic. For the authors of Proverbs, there are three types of women: the temptress (5:7 ff.; 6:24 ff.; 7:5 ff.; 23:27 f.), the quarrelsome wife (21:9, 19; 27:15) and finally, the ideal wife, or woman of valor (chap. 31). Yet even in the latter case, the relationship has little of the personal. Her husband praises her for her industry and farsightedness, but the emotion of love is noticeably lacking in the entire poem. It undoubtedly presents an idealized picture of the rich, emancipated women of the upper classes who managed large estates and engaged in overseas trade. In Ben Sira, woman is regarded exactly as in Proverbs. She may be an ever-present temptation (26:5 ff., 19 ff.) or a source of well-being to her husband (26:1–4), her principal virtues being beauty and silence (26:13–18). Finally, she may be a perpetual burden, when she is "wicked" (25:15–26; 26:5–12). Ben Sira, however, goes considerably further than any Biblical writer in making woman the cause of evil and death in the world:

From a woman did sin originate, and because of her we must all die. (25:24)

In Job, too, the wife is, in Augustine's phrase, the *diaboli adiutrix* and Cheyne pointed out long ago that among the plagues visited upon Job is the fact that his wife was *not* taken! In Koheleth, woman is regarded as a snare from which only those God favors can hope to escape. The right kind of man is hard enough to find; the right kind of woman does not exist (7:26–28). All the more striking is Koheleth's injunction to "enjoy life with a woman thou lovest" (9:9), the sole reference in Wisdom literature to a more personal relationship between the sexes, though, as has been noted, it is highly doubtful whether a wife is here referred to.

The sages teach the avoidance of debauchery because of the unhappy consequences of such conduct, particularly poverty and physical debility:

He that keeps company with harlots wastes his substance. (Prov. 29:3b)
Be not a slave to thy passions, lest they consume thy strength like a bull.
   (B.S. 6:2)[78]

One characteristic of Hebrew Wisdom, lacking in Oriental Wisdom generally, is the stress upon piety as a womanly virtue (Prov. 31:30; B.S. 26:23). The joy of a good wife is regarded as a blessing from the Lord.[79] But other religious and ethical considerations, such as mutual trust, love and respect for the personality of the loved one, or the sanctity of the marriage bond, are lacking, or, at least, remain unexpressed. For motives of this kind, the Biblical reader must turn elsewhere, to the tale of Jacob and Rachel in Genesis, the tragedy of Hosea and his faithless wife Gomer, the narrative of Ruth, the lyrics of the Song of Songs and Malachi's attack upon divorce as treachery to one's "comrade and the wife of one's covenant". (2:14 f.) Equally eloquent of the more personal relationship between the sexes in ancient Israel are certain incidental phrases, such as David's lament over Jonathan, whose love was "more wonderful than the love of women" (II Sam. 1:26) or Ezekiel's touching allusion to his wife as "the delight of his eyes" (24:16).

The attitude toward labor and trade is likewise characteristic of the leisure class, who remain country gentlemen at heart, even when they move to the cities and become absentee landlords. It has been noted above how Ben Sira concedes that artisans are needed but denies to them either wisdom or authority. Merchants are summarily dismissed as swindlers (B.S. 26:29–27:2). On the other hand, the tilling of the soil is deemed the ideal occupation:

He that tills his own soil shall have plenty of bread,
But he that follows vain things is void of understanding. (Prov. 12:11; 28:19;
    cf. also 27:23–27)

That may also be the intent of a difficult passage in Koheleth:

> The advantage of land is paramount,
> even a king is subject to the soil. (Ecc. 5:8)

It is decisive for the social background of Wisdom literature that even the unconventional writers, acutely sensitive though they are to injustice, are at one with the dominant school in their opposition to social change. Even for Koheleth, who has few illusions left about human nature, "the fool" and "the rich" are contrasts:

> Foolishness is set in the high places,
> But the rich sit in low estate. (Ecc. 10:6)

The opposition to social change is also indicated, indirectly but unmistakably, in Job. As is well-known, the book contains several extended descriptions of God's power, which are placed in the mouths of the Friends (5:9 ff.; 25:2–6; 26:6–14).[80] In responding to them, Job also gives us elaborate pictures of the Divine power, but with a significant difference. The Friends always stress the beneficent and creative functioning of the Almighty as revealed in the gift of rain (5:10), the discomfiture of the wicked (5:12 ff.) the glories of the heavens (26:2 f.) and creation (26:5 ff.). Job, on the other hand, emphasizes the negative and destructive manifestations.[81] God moves the mountains, makes the earth tremble and shuts up the sun and stars that they give no light (9:5 ff). Similarly in ch. 12, God destroys beyond rebuilding, and imprisons men so that they cannot escape. He withholds water to cause drought and pours it forth to cause inundations. Nations are exalted only to be destroyed (vv. 14, 15, 23).[82] It is in this spirit that we must understand Job's description of how judges are made fools, the power of kings is broken, the priests are stripped naked, the mighty are overthrown, the elders robbed of understanding and the princes put to shame (vv. 16–21). For Job, and for the author, whose sympathies are obviously with Job throughout the book, the overthrow of the social and political order is a *calamity*, evidence of God's destructive power like the drought or the flood!

The Bible abounds in descriptions of God's power to transform conditions, so that the proud are abased and the humble exalted, but these are intended as paeans of praise:

> Those who were full, have hired themselves out for bread,
> And the hungry have ceased (to starve),
> While the barren woman has borne seven,
> And the mother of many has languished.
> The Lord makes poor and makes rich,
> He casts down and raises up. (I Sam. 2:5, 7)

> He raises the poor from the dust,
> And the needy from the dung-hill,
> To seat him among the princes,
> The princes of his people. (Ps. 113:7 f.)

But Job's description has nothing in common with such pictures of social change. The salient difference lies in the fact that the psalmists who praise God's greatness depict *both* aspects of the change, the fall of the mighty and the rise of the lowly. Similarly Eliphaz, who extols God's power:

> So that He sets the lowly on high,
> And those who mourn are exalted to safety. (5:11)

Job, however, includes only one-half of the picture, the decline of the powerful, because he is arraigning his Maker as a destructive force.

Nor is Job's attitude similar to that of the Prophets, who saw in the collapse of these elements of society condign punishment (Am. 6:1 ff.;

7:7 ff.; Isa. 3; Mic. 3, and elsewhere) or a necessary prelude to a reconstructed social order (Isa. 1:24–28; 5:8–17 and often). For the author of Job, as for all the Wisdom writers, a transformation of the social and political status quo is a catastrophe.

There will naturally be temperamental differences among men in the treatment of slaves and this is reflected in Wisdom. Thus Job takes pride in the fair treatment of his servants (31:13–15), while Ben Sira who demands considerate treatment of a good slave (7:20 f.), nevertheless urges that they be kept hard at work (B.S. 30:13–15). The ethical note in the treatment of slaves finds no parallel in any other branch of Oriental Wisdom, except the Babylonian.[83] But the implicit recognition of the right of all men to be free from physical and economic bondage, which is basic to the Pentateuchal legislation and the Prophetic attitude, is completely lacking.[84]

So, too the conservative political ideas of Wisdom stand in the sharpest possible contrast with the rest of the Bible. Here we find no denunciation of monarchy as in Samuel, no attack upon the crimes of royalty, as in Nathan and Elijah, no arraignment of the political status quo as in Amos, Isaiah, Micah, Jeremiah and Ezekiel. On the contrary, the most conservative passage in the Bible, unparallelled elsewhere, occurs in Proverbs (24:21):

> My son, fear the Lord and the king,
> And do not become involved with those who seek change.

This naive identification of God and the political status quo is not for Koheleth. But even he counsels submission to authority:

I counsel thee: keep the king's command, and that because of the oath of God (pledging loyalty to him).

But he then adds an after-thought:

For the king's word is all-powerful, and who can say to him, 'What are you doing?' (8:2, 4)

VI

We may now restate the conclusion that emerges from our survey of Proverbs, Agur ben Yakeh, Ben Sira, Job and Koheleth. Their political and social view-points, like their religious and moral conceptions, reflect an upper-class orientation. There are important individual differences among the various products of the Wisdom schools, but underlying them all is the outlook which later crystallized as Sadduceeism. This explains the absence of some of the most characteristic insights of Biblical thought, such as the concept of God in history, the passion for justice in society, the union of national loyalty with the ideal of international peace, the recognition of freedom as an inalienable human right, the unceasing dissatisfaction with the world as it is, because of the vision of what it can be.

Yet the contributions of Wisdom literature to human thought are equally notable. Proverbs and Ben Sira are distinguished by an exalted yet workable morality, a sagacious understanding of human nature, and an unabashed interest in the happiness of the individual here and now. Job and Koheleth belong to the chosen masterpieces of the race, not only because of their superb literary form, but also because of their fearless use of reason in grappling with the most fundamental issues, their unwillingness to pretend to certainty where none is to be had and their passionate quest for the truth at all costs.

It should be obvious that the recognition that Wisdom literature arises in a given social milieu does not detract from its inherent worth, for while it has its roots in one class, its fruits belong to mankind. On the abiding issues of life, no one is granted more than fleeting and partial glimpses of the truth, and every insight is therefore precious. When we recall that Pharisaic Judaism recognized the heterodox tendencies of Wisdom literature,[85] and fought energetically to eradicate the influence of Sadduceeism from the national life, we must be eternally grateful to the Librarian of the Synagogue who included these works in the Biblical canon. For it is to his tolerance and catholicity of taste that we owe the preservation of these monuments of man's striving after the good life.

NOTES

1. Cf. the researches of Ginzberg, Lauterbach, Baron, Tchernowitz, Zeitlin, Finkelstein, and many of their colleagues and students.

2. On the extent of Hebrew and Jewish Wisdom, see O. S. Rankin, *Israel's Wisdom Literature* (Edinburgh, 1936), p. 1 f. and Johannes Fichtner, *Die altorientalische Weisheit in ihrer israelitisch-juedischen Auspraegung* (Giessen, 1933), pp. 7–13. The literature cited by Fichtner and Rankin is, however, not homogeneous in character and origin, in spite of its preoccupation with "Wis-

dom." Treating it as a unit overlooks the fact that it arose in a special milieu, and only afterwards did *Ḥokmah* become a slogan and an ideal of all groups in post-exilic Judaism. It was identified with the Torah by Pharisaism and was equated with Greek philosophical ideas in Hellenistic circles, as in Alexandria.

We may therefore distinguish three main types of Hokmah literature, that may be somewhat summarily described as (proto-) Sadduceean, (proto-) Pharisaic, and Hellenistic. This paper is concerned only with the first group. It may be noted that only the works of this group found their way into the canon, in spite of the Rabbinic opposition to Sadduceeism: Proverbs, Job and Koheleth; Ben Sira, which was not admitted, probably because of its clear-cut indication of a late date, was accorded high honor and is cited in Rabbinic literature with the formulas used in introducing Scriptural passages. See e. g. B. Baba Kamma 92b ומשולש בכתובים followed by a passage from Ben Sira.

It is important to indicate the relationship of all the various documents in Jewish Wisdom literature. Thus many of the so-called Wisdom *Psalms*, like chap. 1 (cf. v. 2 on the study of the Law), 19:8 ff. and 119 are hymns in praise of the Torah and may fairly be described as proto-Pharisaic. So too the *'anavim* spirit of identification with the submerged groups places Psalms 34:12–23, 73 (cf. vv. 17, 25–28, expressing a passionate absorption in God); 94:8 ff. (cf. vv. 12,21) in the same group. In the case of Psalms 127 and 133, their brevity and lyrical character make it impossible to determine their standpoint. The enigmatic Psalm 49 seems to be directed against wealth (v. 7), but it possesses certain marks characteristic of the unconventional Wisdom books. Such is the stress on the uselessness of wealth or wisdom in averting death (vv. 11, 18) as well as the note, particularly noticeable in Koheleth (see below) on the tragedy of leaving one's wealth to others, *'aḥerim*. Psalm 37 is a composite, as its complicated and imperfect acrostic structure proves. The *'anavim* spirit is clear in such verses as 2, 16 and elsewhere. On the other hand, vv. 21, 25 and 26 show striking upper-class sympathies, as is indicated in the body of this paper. Psalm 112 is likewise definitely upper-class in viewpoint (cf. vv. 2 f., 5, 9), and so, apparently, is Psalm 128. Psalm 110:10 is a quotation of a stock phrase of the Wisdom schools.

Tobit, generally dated about 200 B. C. E., contains gnomic material in 4:13 ff.; 12:6 ff.; 14:9 ff., which, apart from the elements drawn from Ahikar, is largely in the Pharisaic tradition. Note the strong objection to inter-marriage (4:12), an idea conspicuously absent from the basic Wisdom books (see below in section V), the negative version of the "Golden Rule" (4:15), identical in form with the saying of Hillel (B. Shab. 31a), the emphasis upon prayer (12:6; 14:9) and the stress upon alms-giving (4:7–11).

Completely distinct in origin and character are the Wisdom books of Hellenistic provenance. They are the *Wisdom of Solomon*, which, in part at least, seems to be a traditionalist answer to the skepticism of Koheleth, *Pseudo-Aristeas*, *IV Maccabees*, *Pseudo-Phocylides*, and, possibly, the debate of Darius' pages in *I Esdras* 3:1–4:41 (so P. Volz in *Encyclopedia Biblica*, vol. iv, col. 1493).

The Mishnah tractate *Aboth* is of course a Pharisaic classic of much later origin than the basic Wisdom books which are our concern here.

3. Not Wisdom par excellence, hence no definite article.

4. See "The Wisdom of Koheleth" in this volume and the full-length study and commentary, in Gordis, *Koheleth, the Man and His World* (New York, 1951, 1955, 1968) = KMW.

5. See our paper on this theme in the present volume.

6. On the Tobiades, cf. A. Buechler, *Die Tobiaden und die Oniaden* (Vienna, 1899); E. Schuerer, *Geschichte des juedischen Volkes im Zeitalter Jesu Christi*, 3rd and 4th ed. (Leipzig, 1901-11), vol. 1, pp. 195 f.; S. Zeitlin "The Tobias Family and the Hasmoneans," In *Proc. Amer. Acad. Jew. Research*, Vol. IV, 1933, pp. 169–223; Finkelstein, *op. cit.*, vol. 2, pp. 580–87. It is interesting to recall that Klausner suggested long ago that Joseph ben Tobias was the author of *Koheleth*; see his book, *Biyeme Bayyit Sheni* (Tel Aviv, 1930) pp. 160–75, in which the paper is reprinted.

7. Cf. Isa. 5:8 ff.; Micah 3:3; Jer. 34:8 ff. for the same process in First Temple days.

8. For purposes of comparison with our views, it may be convenient to summarize Professor Finkelstein's conclusions on the class origins of Wisdom literature as set forth in his important work *The Pharisees—The Sociological Background of Their Faith* (1st ed. Philadelphia, 1938):

Proverbs is a collection of upper-class moralistic teaching, which has been subjected to persistent plebeian interpolation. Thus 2:1–4 is patrician, vv. 5–8, plebeian; 3:1–4 is patrician, vv. 5–12, plebeian. This view seems to us eminently valid. In a book of short, gnomic utterances, anonymous in character, and widely popular, it is altogether likely that interpolations would enter the text. Naturally, individual passages cannot always be assigned to one or the other school with complete assurance. Thus 10:2 f., 22; 15:3; 16:1, which Dr. Finkelstein ascribes to the plebeian writer, are not inconceivable as examples of patrician morality. On the other hand, the plebeian origin of 16:8 is unmistakable. See his entire illuminating discussion, *op. cit.*, pp. 203-16.

Ben Sira is regarded as a compromise between plebeian and patrician teachings (p. 588). "He retains the piety, reverence for the Jewish past and loyalty to Jewish literature and life of the plebeian outlook, but specifically denies any faith in its theology" (ibid.). But these traits are not incompatible with upper-class origins, and the reasons that have led us to regard Ben Sira as thoroughly patrician are indicated in the body of this paper.

Job is taken to be the work of a plebeian writer, who denies both free-will and Providence (p. 231). As evidence for this view, Job's kindness to his slaves, his sense of equality and his protest against injustice are adduced. The patriarchal, nomadic setting of the narrative is a curtain for the Jerusalemite traders among whom the author lived (p. 232 ff.). It may be countered, however, that kindness to slaves is a patrician virtue, and that no class has a monopoly on resentment of suffering. It seems to us that Job's failure to accept the idea of an after-life, and other indications given in the body of our discussion, indicate an upper-class origin for the book of Job. On the prose tale, see BGM.

Agur ben Yakeh is held by Dr. Finkelstein to be altogether plebeian, because of its denial of association with the Wisdom teachers (Prov. 30:2, 3), its belief in angels (v. 4), its distaste for both poverty and riches (vv. 5–9), and its comments on social oppression (vv. 13 f.). The entire chapter, however, is fragmentary and its exegesis consequently unclear, so that several of the passages referred to above may be interpreted differently. Our view of this enigmatic Wisdom document is given in section IV of this paper.

Koheleth is ascribed to a plebeian cynic (p. 235 ff.). Dr. Finkelstein discounts as imaginative Koheleth's picture of himself as a rich man (chap. 2), and stresses his preoccupation with social justice. He attributes passages extolling diligence and wealth (4:5; 7:11; 10:18; 11:9) to a glossator. But if all references to the enjoyment of life as a goal are regarded as unauthentic, a much larger number of passages must be excised, as any modern commentary on the book makes clear. For our approach to Koheleth, which makes such violent procedures unnecessary, and which, we believe, makes him a more credible personality, see the references in notes 5 and 6. It may be added that social injustice does not bulk as large in Koheleth's consciousness as the unattainability of true wisdom and the vanity of labor. Only one passage, 4:1 ff., deals with social oppression; the latter themes run through the book.

9. "My son = my pupil," though references to the instruction of parents are common. So C. H. Toy, *ICC on Proverbs* (New York, 1902), pp. 8, 12. Professor Louis Ginzberg has kindly pointed out that *beni* was the accepted mode of address of a master to his disciple in Tannaitic and early Amoraic times; cf· e. g. B. Sanhedrin 11a שב בני שב and L. Ginzberg, *A Commentary on the Palestinian Talmud* (New York, 1940), vol. 1, pp. 238, 300.

10. He advances a theory to explain the late emergence of the ideal of an after-life in Hebrew thought. His conclusion apart, his technique interests us here. He says, "To demonstrate this (i. e. the theory advanced), the coming and growth of the belief in a future life, as this belief appears in Greece, offers the best means of comparison and proof." Rankin, *Israel's Wisdom Literature*, p. 178.

11. Plato, *Protagoras*, 1. 317 ff. (Loeb Classics, New York, 1924, Plato, Vol IV, p. 124).

12. *Cambridge Ancient History* (New York, 1927) Vol. V, pp. 24, 377.

13. Ben Sira 51:25b קנו לכם חכמה בלא כסף "Acquire Wisdom for yourselves without money" is a poetical statement of the idea that wisdom is easily attained. Cf. the following verse, "She is nigh unto them that seek her" and the well-known passage Isa. 55:1 f. upon which Ben Sira undoubtedly bases himself.

14. Cf. E. Zeller, *Pre-Socratic Philosophy* (London, 1881) Vol. 2, pp. 394–516. G. Grote's classic rehabilitation of the sophist movement is to be found in his *History of Greece* (London, 1851 and often reprinted), ch. 67. A more recent account is to be found in W. Durant, *The Life of Greece* (New York, 1939) pp. 358–66.

15. Cf. S. W. Baron, *Social and Religious History of the Jews* (New York, 1937), p. 195 f. Cf. also the well-known statement in the Talmud (Ned. 81a) הזהרו בבני עניים שמהם תצא תורה "Be careful of the sons of the poor for learning comes forth from them." Also the moving story of the encounter of the Patriarch Gamaliel of Jabneh with Joshua ben Hananiah, and the latter's retort, אוי לו לדור שאתה פרנסו שאי אתה יודע בצערן של תלמידי חכמים במה הם מתפרנסים

ובמה הם ניזונים "Alas for the generation whose leader you are, knowing nothing of the privations of scholars, how they are fed and sustained." (Ber. 28a). On handicrafts in the Talmudic period, see S. Krauss, *Talmudische Archaeologie* (Leipzig, 1911), vol. II, pp. 248–313.

16. This is the view of Professor Louis Ginzberg, as communicated in a private conversation. In the advanced schools, where experts in the law were trained, moderate fees were probably imposed, not to compensate the teacher, but to defray the cost of maintaining the school quarters, to avoid overcrowding, or for some reasons stated by the Shammaites, cf. L. Ginzberg, in *Jewish Encyclopedia*, Vol. 1, p. 136b. This is most likely the explanation of the famous tale, in which Hillel, unable to secure admittance to the academy of Abtalion, climbed to the roof and was buried under the snow. The Talmud quotes the fee as being a tropaikon and a half (Yoma 35b). It may be added that the story, apart from its obvious folk-character, cannot pretend even to authenticity of atmosphere. Snow in Jerusalem is extremely rare, and a snow-storm sufficient to bury a man beneath it is almost certainly ruled out.

17. Nedarim 37a.

18. Mat. 10:8.

19. The teacher was paid *sekhar šimmur*, "fee for taking care of the child" or *sekhar pissuk teamim*, "fee for teaching vocalization and accents" or *sekhar battalah*, "compensation for the teacher's being unable to engage in a gainful occupation." No reflection on the teaching vocation was intended! See Nedarim 36b, 37a; Maimonides, *Yad, Hilkhoth Talmud Torah*, 1, par. 7, and *Shulḥan Arukh, Yoreh Deah*, 246, 5 and Isserles *ad loc*.

20. He is generally identified with the scholar Pollio referred to by Josephus in Ant. xv, 1, 1; the Pollio mentioned in Ant. xv, 10, 4, is almost certainly another scholar, perhaps an error for Hillel.

21. Toy, *op. cit.*, p. xxxi, notes " the absence of characteristic national traits," and says, "If for the name JHVH we substitute 'God', there is not a sentence or a paragraph in the Proverbs which would not be as suitable for any other people as for Israel." Hermann Gunkel, in "Religion in Geschichte und Gegenwart," believes that "the Hebrew Proverb literature was in its beginning altogether secular . . . . . . .The religious motive was introduced later." (vol. III, p. 2361).

22. On the origin of the proper names in Job, cf. Driver-Gray, *ICC on Job* (New York, 1921), vol. 1, pp. xxxvii ff.; G. Hoelscher, *Das Buch Hiob* (Tuebingen, 1937), p. 2. The locales from which the names are drawn are Edom and Arabia.

23. Cf. Proverbs of Amenemope (Col. XXV, I. 496), "The strength of Ra is to him that is on the road" as an instance of popular saying.

24. Thus, taking chapter 16 at random, we find JHVH used ten times, of which at least four are in stock phrases (vv. 5, 6, 7?, 20). On divine Names in Wisdom, see Fichtner, p. 103 ff. Rankin, p. 39 note, and Cassuto cited in note 26 below.

25. JHVH and אדני occur in the poetry of Job a) in 12:9 which is either an interpolation or, more probably, a reminiscence of Is. 41:20c, a stock phrase, b) in 28:28, in what is again a typical phrase of the Wisdom schools (the entire

chapter is almost certainly an independent poem), and in 38:1; 40:1, in the superscriptions. In Koheleth even the Temple is called *bet 'elohim*, not *bet JHVH* (4:17).

26. Cf. Cassuto, *Torat Ha t'eudot ve-Sidduram šel Siphre Hatorah* (Jerusalem, 1942) p. 28; cf. also pp. 21, 23 ff. He says: "The *minim* (lit. "heretics"), that is to say the Sadducees, the scions of the aristocracy exposed to the influence of the international Wisdom of the time, and especially to "Greek wisdom," which was also accustomed to refer to divinity by its general name, tended to see in this approach a kind of progress as against the national tradition, which held fast to the specific name of God, JHVH" (p. 28).

27. Cf. W. O. E. Oesterley, *The Wisdom of Egypt and the O. T.* (London, 1927); Paul Humbert, *Recherches sur les sources Egyptiennes de la littérature sapientale d'Israel* (Neuchatel, 1929); G. A. Barton, *Archaeology and the Bible* (Phila., 1937), 7th ed., pp. 511–15, and the literature there cited.

28. Giessen, 1933.

29. Cf. Hoelscher's correct conclusion, *op. cit.*, p. 7, that the author of Job was a Palestinian who had travelled widely, hence his familiarity with Egyptian flora and fauna, the Sinai desert, and the hail, ice, and snow of the north, probably the Lebanon region.

30. W. F. Albright, *From the Stone Age to Christianity* (Baltimore, 1940), p. 135.

31. *Op. cit.*, pp. 13–24.

32. Prov. 2:16 ff.; 5:9, 15; 7:5 ff.; 22:14; 23:27; 30:20; B.S. 9:1 ff.; 19:2 f.; 25:2; 23:16; 36:30.

33. *Peninim* occurs four times in Proverbs (3:15; 8:11; 20:15; 31:10), once in Job (28:18), and only once more in the entire O. T. (Lam. 4:7).

34. Prov. 23:1 f., 20 f., 29 ff.; 30:8–10; Ecc. 7:16 f.; B.S. 18:30 ff.

35. Prov. 6:6–11; 10:4 f., 26; 12:11, 24; 13:4; 14:23; 15:19; 18:9; 24:30–34; 26:13 ff.; Ecc. 10:18; B.S. 4:29; 7:15; 10:26 f.; 11:11; 13:21; 22:1 f.; 31:3 f.

36. Prov. 10:26; 13:17; 25:13; 26:6. On the frequency of this theme in Oriental Wisdom, see Fichtner, *op. cit.*, pp. 15, 16, note 1.

37. Prov. 14:35; 16:14; 19:12; 20:2; 22:29; Ecc. 8:3; 10:4; B.S. 9:13. For parallels in Egyptian and Babylonian Wisdom, see Fichtner, *op. cit.*, p. 16.

38. Cf. Job 31:13, 16, 17, 19.

39. Cf. Deut. ch. 15 and Ex. 22:24 ff.; Lev. 25:36 f.; Deut. 23:20 ff.; 24:10 f.

40. Prov. 6:1–5; 11:15; 17:18; 22:26 f.; 20:16 = 27:13. It is curious that Oriental Wisdom has no references to lending or pledges, except for one passage lamenting lending on a pledge, which is quoted by Ebeling, *Reste akkadischer Weisheitsliteratur*, p. 22. Fichtner, *op. cit.*, p. 16, regards it as purely a matter of chance that no such passages have survived.

41. See note 2, paragraph 3, *supra*.

42. *Roš*—"head," adopted by Hitzig, Delitzsch, Toy (doubtfully), and may others, to read גבר ראש, creates impossible Hebrew, *Raša* "wicked" is based on the LXX: 'Ανδρεῖος ἐν ἀσεβείαις "a bold man by wickedness etc." (Toy, doubtfully). Kittel (*Biblia Hebraica*) also suggests *'ašir* with a query.

43. Cf. Rashi and especially Gersonides *ad loc.*, who says: ידמה למטר סוחף

שישחית התבואות בדרך שלא ימצא לחם ומחכמת זה המשל כי המטר מכוין
ראשונה לגדל הצמחים ויהיה בדרך זה כלי להשחתתם.

44. Prov. 15:27; 17:15, 23; Ecc. 7:7b; B.S. 7:6. On Oriental Wisdom teaching on this point, see Fichtner, *op. cit.*, p. 28 f.

45. On the structure of this passage, see our paper "Quotations in Biblical, Oriental, and Rabbinic Literature" in this volume and *KMW, ad loc.*

46. Cf. Finkelstein, *op. cit.*, vol. I, pp. 235 f.

47. Cf. 2:21 f.; 4:8; 5:12 ff.; 6:1 ff. Cf. also Ps. 49:11c and our note 2, par. 3, above.

48. Prov. 1:13; 6:30 f.; 21:6; 28:22; 29:24; B.S. 5:8; 13:24; 20:25; 40:13.

49. On the former offence, cf. Prov. 22:28; 23:10 f.; also Job 24:2a; 31:38 and Deut. 19:14; 27:12. On the latter, cf. Prov. 11:1; 16:11; 20:10, 23; B.S. 42:4; also Lev. 19:35 f.; Deut. 25:13 ff.

50. Cf. among other passages, Prov. 14:31; 19:17; B.S. 3:31; 12:1; 18:18; 22:23.

51. See note 34.

52. Prov. 20:21; 28:20.

53. As e. g. Prov. 11:28; 15:17; 17:1.

54. *Op. cit.*, p. 209 f.

55. It is noteworthy that Prov. 23:4, which is opposed to the striving after wealth, is almost universally regarded as based on Amenemope, col. IX, ll. 163–68. Cf. Fichtner, *op. cit.*, p. 16, note 8. So too, Rankin, *op. cit.*, p. 79, note 1, who associates this passage, as well as Prov. 15:16 f., which stresses the joys of contentment, with Amenemope, col. VI, l. 110.

Budge, from whose *Teaching of Amen-en-apt* (London, 1924) the translations in the text are derived, points out that Egyptian Wisdom was written either by kings or professional scribes and officials, and was intended for princes and for those who aspired to official posts (pp. XI ff., 100 f.). However, he considers the Teaching of Amenemope the exception, being adressed by an official, "to no son, whether prince or subject, but to all men." H. Gressmann (*Alt-orientalische Texte zum A.T.*, Erste Lieferung, 2nd ed. Berlin and Leipzig, 1926, p. 38), on the other hand, notes that the author was a high officer and that the work is addressed to his youngest son, who was priest in the Temple of Min at Panopolis in Upper Egypt. Budge, too, comments on the aristocratic lineage of Amenemope and the many priestly offices he held (p. 96 f.). He also recognizes that "many of his Precepts would no doubt be of more use to officials than to any other class of people" (p. x). At all events, the hieroglyphic script would itself limit the readers of the work to the upper classes. Granted that it is superior to the other products of Egyptian Wisdom, its affinities with them remain very close. Its exalted morality does not disprove its upper-class orientation, while its other features make it clear that no other background may be assumed for it. That is the thesis of this paper with regard to Hebrew Wisdom as a whole.

56. Cf. H. Bruppacher, *Die Beurteilung der Armut in A.T.* (Zurich, 1924), p. 81 ff. On the other hand, a necessary corrective of extreme views that deny ascetic tendencies in Hebrew religion altogether is supplied by J. A. Montgomery, "Ascetic Strains in Early Judaism" in *JBL*, Vol. LI, 1932, pp. 183–213.

57. Cf. 3:12 f.; 8:15 f.; 9:7 ff.

58. Cf. M. Lohr, *Sozialismus und Individualismus im A.T.* (Giessen, 1906); Oesterley and T. H. Robinson, *Hebrew Religion* (New York, 1930), pp. 219 f.; 251 ff.; Rankin, *op. cit.*, pp. 53-98; the study, "The Temptation of Job" in this volume and, *The Book of God and Man* (= BGM), chap. XI.

59. Cf. the classical passages Jer. 31:26 ff.; Ez. 18:1 ff.

60. Cf. Oesterley and Robinson, *op. cit.*, p. 223; Rankin, *op. cit.*, pp. 124-197.

61. Prov. 13:22; 14:26; 20:7; B.S. 44:10 f.

62. Cf. also B.S. 17:27; 41:14.

63. Reading, with most moderns, סחיפה "torrent," for ספיחיה in the Masoretic text, which is clearly impossible.

64. G. F. Moore, *History of Religions* (New York, 1913), Vol. 1, p. 286.

65. Am. 5:18 ff.; Isa. 2:12; Jer. 4:23.

66. Isa. 2:2; Mic. 4:1; Hos: 3:5; Jer. 23:20; 30:24; 48:47; 49:39; Ez. 38:8, 16.

67. There is no warrant for translating אשה in the verse, which occurs without the article, as "wife," as in the Jewish Publication Society Version. See G. A. Barton, *ICC on Ecclesiastes* (New York, 1908), p. 163, and *KMW*, p. 306.

68. דעת קדושים = דעת ה', the Divine Wisdom. Cf Prov. 9:10; Hos. 12:1 (see Ehrlich *ad loc.*). We hope to demonstrate this meaning also for Job 5:1.

69. *Antiquities*, xiii, 5, 9. Cf. also idem, xviii, 1, 3. *War* II, viii, 14.

70. G. F. Moore, *Judaism* (Cambridge, 1927), vol. 1, p. 456 f., very properly calls attention to the fact that Josephus has inevitably distorted the outlook of the Jewish sects, because he attempts to make of them Greek philosophical schools. His criticism however, is directed against Josephus' interpretation of the Pharisaic position, not that of the Sadducees. It may also be added that even Josephus' statement that the Pharisees hold that "to do right or not lies principally in man's power, but destiny also cooperates in every action" (*War*, II, viii, 14) is a fair restatement in Greek terms of the Rabbinic view that "A man is led (by God) in the way he wishes to go." (B. Makkot 10b), a position Moore himself illustrates by copious examples (*loc. cit.*).

71. Mishnah Abot 3:15; cf. C. Taylor, *Sayings of the Jewish Fathers* (Cambridge, 1877), p. 73.

72. Cf. especially *op. cit.*, pp. 202, 250-54.

73. Deut. 8:17.

74. Oesterley and Robinson, *op. cit.*, pp. 66, 280 f.; Leo Jung, *Fallen Angels in Jewish, Christian and Mohammedan Literature* (Phila., 1926).

75. On the enigmatic *ha'olam*, see the commentaries. On the grounds for our rendering, see *KMW*, pp. 231 ff.

76. See the quotations and full discussion in Fichtner, *op. cit.*, pp. 36–40.

77. Cf. Neh. 13:23 ff.; Ezra, Chap. 9 and 10; Mal. 2:11 ff. (which probably refers both to intermarriage and divorce, cf. vv. 14 f.); Ruth, passim. On the Tobiades, see note 6.

78. Cf. Prov. 5:9 ff.; 31:3; B.S. 9:1.

79. Prov. 5:18 ff.; 18:22; B.S. 13:21; 25:2; 26:1–4; 36:29 f.

80. While the last passage is attributed to Job in the Masoretic Text, it obviously belongs to one of the Friends, probably Bildad, to whom it is assigned

by Reuss, Duhm, Siegfried, Dhorme and Hölscher. On the problem of the Third Cycle, to which this passage belongs, see *BGM*, pp. 93–103.

81. This distinction is clearly recognized by Driver-Gray, *ICC on Job* (New York, 1921), pp. 85 f.

82. Failure to note this difference in attitude has led some scholars to delete considerable portions of ch. 12. Siegfried and Grill retain only vv. 1–3; Jastrow omits vv. 4c, 5 in part, 6c, 10, 12, 13, 17–19, 22, and 23. Volz transfers vv. 4–10, 13–25, 13:1 to Zophar in ch. 11. Budde argued strongly in favor of the authenticity of the passage a half-century ago. On this chapter, cf. *BGM*, pp. 51 ff., 81–83.

83. Cf. Fichtner, *op. cit.*, p. 20 f.

84. Cf. Ex. 21:5 f., 26 f.; Lev. 25:39 ff.; Deut. 15:12 ff., and especially Deut. 23:16 f.; Jer. 34:6 ff.; Neh. 5:1 ff.

85. On the canonization of the Wisdom books, see F. Buhl, *Canon and Text of the O. T.* (Edinburgh, 1892), pp. 3–32; H. E. Ryle, *Canon of the O. T.* 2nd ed. (London 1909); the suggestive treatments of Max L. Margolis, *The Hebrew Scriptures in the Making* (Phila., 1922), pp. 83–96 and S. Zeitlin, "An Historical Study of the Canonization of Hebrew Scriptures" in *Proceedings of the American Academy for Jewish Research*, Vol. III, 1932, pp. 121–58.

It is generally agreed that the Hebrew canon was fixed long before the historic session of the academy at Jamnia in 90 c. e. At these sessions (referred to in Talmudic literature as *bo bayom* "that very day"), the status of various Biblical books was discussed purely as an academic question, prior to the official ratification by the scholars of what was generally accepted (cf. Buhl, *op. cit.*, pp. 25–27; Margolis, *op. cit.*, p. 88). Many of the sources cited below use the phrase בקשו לגנוז, which has sometimes been taken to mean "sought to declare uncanonical." S. Zeitlin has argued convincingly against this interpretation and made the plausible suggestion that the phrase means "sought to store away from public reading, so as not to be studied and interpreted in the academies" (*op. cit.*, pp. 124 ff.). The Talmudic phrase for "uncanonical" is אינו מטמא את הידים "does not defile the hands." At all events, these discussions, sometimes recorded in Amoraic sources, indicate an awareness of the heterodox and secular tendency of these books, as well as the objections felt against others, like Ezekiel and the Song of Songs.

Whether *Proverbs* should be "stored away" or not is discussed, because it contains "contradictions" שדבריו סותרין זה את זה (B. Shab. 30b) and consists merely of "sayings," which are not part of Scriptures משלות ואינן מן הכתובים (Aboth de Rabbi Nathan, Chap. 1).

Ben Sira is declared to be uncanonical אינו מטמא את הידים, because he wrote after the period of inspiration was over מכאן ואילך (Tos. Yadaim 2:13, ed. Zuckermandel, p. 683; B. Sanh. 100b). Margolis, *op. cit.*, p. 94, adds that it could not be attributed to an earlier period. Besides, Ben Sira is indifferent to individual immortality (37:25).

Koheleth aroused many misgivings. It suffered from contradictions שדבריו סותרין זה את זה (B. Shab. 30a, b). It consisted of mere "sayings" and was therefore not to be regarded as Scriptures (Aboth de Rabbi Nathan, ch. 1). It was the wisdom of Solomon and not Divine מפני שהיא חכמתו של שלמה (Tos. Yadaim 2:14, ed. Zuckermandel p. 683; Meg. 7a). The most fundamental objection is that it contains matters leading to heresy מפני שמצאו בו דברים המטים לצד מינות (Midrash Koh. Rabbah 3:1). The controversy between the Hillelites and the Shammaites as to its canonicity מטמא את הידים, is recorded in the Mishnah in Eduyot 5:3 and Yadaim 3:5, the latter passage recording the decision in its favor.

Job, it is also suggested by Margolis (p. 89), "seems likewise to have been scrutinized, for 'in that day', the question was discussed whether Job served God from motives of love or motives of fear." The Mishnic source is Sotah 5.5: בו ביום דרש רבי יהושע בן הורקנוס לא עבד איוב את הקב"ה אלא מאהבה... א"ר יהושע מי יגלה עפר מעיניך רבן יוחנן בן זכאי שהיית דורש כל ימיך שלא עבד איוב את המקום אלא מיראה...However, no question was ever raised with regard to its canonicity. Several factors probably played their part. The Job of the Prose Tale was God-fearing and patient. It was "the patience of Job" (Epistle of James 5:11) that entered into the popular consciousness, not the linguistically difficult speeches of protest of the Dialogue. In addition, there were Chapters 38-41 which emanated directly from "The Lord speaking out of the whirlwind.'

Thus all the works of Hebrew Wisdom were the subject of discussion before their position in the canon was officially recognized by the Pharisaic authorities in the first cent. C. E.

7. THE KNOWLEDGE OF GOOD AND EVIL IN THE OLD TESTAMENT AND THE DEAD SEA SCROLLS

I

As additional material from the Qumran Caves comes to light, the importance of these texts continues to grow apace. An excellent illustration of this truth is afforded by the material published by Barthélemy and Milik,[1] part of which consists of two columns that Barthélemy calls *serekh ha'edah* (1QSa). The editor believes that this document is to be distinguished from the previously published and now familiar *serekh hayaḥad* "the Rule of the Community" and calls attention to several significant differences.[2] He suggests that the *serekh ha'edah* may reflect the standpoint of the Ḥasidim during the Maccabean wars, while the *serekh hayaḥad* represents a later stage in the history of the movement, possessing strong affinities for the Essenes.

That the monastic tendencies in the sect were implicit in the beginning and gained in power may be demonstrated from an interesting passage in the document, commented on by the learned editor and since discussed by G. W. Buchanan,[3] the full implications of which remain to be explored.

In describing the Essenes, both Philo and Pliny state that they renounced marriage on principle. Josephus, on the other hand, declares that the Essenes abstained from marriage on practical grounds and adds that one branch of the sect practiced matrimony because they regarded celibacy as threatening the preservation of the human race.[4]

The passage now published is of great significance both for the process of development in the sect and in suggesting a definitive solution to a long-standing biblical crux. It reads as follows:

Col. 1.9–11

He shall not come near to a woman,	ולוא י[קרב] אל אשה לדעתה
in order to have sexual relations with her,	למשכבי זכר
until his completing[5] twenty years,	כי אם לפי מולואת לו עש(רי)ם שנה
when he knows good and evil.	בדעתו [טוב] ורע

What is the meaning of the familiar phrase בדעתו טוב ורע ? Barthé-lemy interprets it as "the age of reason." Buchanan similarly takes it to mean "the age of maturity, when one has sufficient experience and knowledge to be able to make important decisions."[6] Because of the juxtaposition of clauses in our passage, he concludes that this age is twenty. This meaning he assigns to all the OT passages where it occurs, like Deut.1:39, and the Immanuel prophecy in Isaiah (7:14 ff.). He gives the same meaning to the phrase in the aged Barzillai's reply to King David (II Sam. 19:36) and in the crucial passages in the Paradise tale (Gen. 2:17; 3:5, 22), though he is conscious of the difficulties involved in interpreting the phrase in these last two passages in a chronological, intellectual, or moral sense.[7]

The Qumran text and the OT passages prove mutually revealing and now enable us to give a definitive answer to a problem which is as old as biblical study itself.

II

Two decades ago, the present writer argued on a variety of grounds that all the usual interpretations of "the tree of knowing good and evil" in Genesis were unsatisfactory.[8] The first and most obvious theory was to explain it as referring to "moral judgment, the capacity to distinguish right from wrong."[9] This view cannot be sustained for two principal reasons. Were the moral capacity lacking in Adam orig-inally, before he ate the forbidden fruit, he could not justly be held guilty of violating the divine will. Disobedience is a sin only if a sense of right and wrong is presupposed. Moreover, it is inconceivable that biblical thought, with its overpowering moral consciousness, could conceive of the Deity creating man without a moral sense, for that is the essence of his humanity.[10]

Nor can the "knowledge of good and evil" refer to all the secrets of nature, the entire gamut of knowledge,[11] or even the magical arts,[12] in short, a comprehension of "everything." This suggestion is effectively refuted by the biblical narrative itself, which describes how Adam gave names to every living creature (Gen. 2:19–20). It is a truism that in ancient thought, including the biblical world-view, knowing the name of any person or object is tantamount to comprehending its nature. In Biblical Hebrew, *šēm* means "essence." Witness too, the significance attaching to the divine Name in biblical and post-biblical thought.[13] Indeed, naming an object represents the knowledge that spells power, so that in the case of God or the gods it is equivalent to creation. Thus the Babylonian "Creation Epic," *enuma eliš* opens with the familiar lines: "When on high, the heaven had not been named, and firm ground below had not been called by name." Entirely similar is the usage in Isa. 40:26: "Raise your eyes on high, and see who created these. He brings forth their hosts in number, and calls them all by name." There is at least a suggestion here that Adam's transcendent wisdom endowed him in some degree with a little of God's creative power and made him, in a sense, "God's co-partner in the work of creation" (cf. *B. Shabbat* 119b). In sum, one cannot fairly explain away the clear inference that being able to name all living creatures meant that Adam possessed limitless wisdom *before he ate of the forbidden fruit*.[14]

This conception of Adam as a paragon of wisdom before the Fall is no late midrashic fancy—it is both ancient, and, be it noted, universal in biblical and extra-biblical sources. It has left it traces in several poetical passages in the OT as well, which, as is well known, often enshrine ancient mythological references, as has become clear from the Ugaritic epics. Thus Ezekiel in his prophecy against Tyre (28:12 ff.) compares the Phoenician king in his glory to Adam in the Garden of Eden, aptly described by Cooke as "a glorious being, blameless by nature, gifted with wisdom and beauty."[15] Other vestiges of ancient Semitic mythology are also included, but the conception of Adam's perfect wisdom is unmistakable:

> Son of man,
> Take up a lamentation for the king of Tyre,
> And say unto him:
> Thus saith the Lord God:
> Thou seal most accurate, full of wisdom, and perfect in beauty.
>
> Ezek. 28:12

Another reference to the perfection of Adam before the Fall occurs in Ps. 82:6 f., which is to be rendered:

> I said: Ye are godlike beings,
> And all of you sons of the Most High.
> Nevertheless ye shall die like Adam
> And fall like one of the angels.[16]

Here the poet, who is castigating the judges of his time, speaks first of his former high veneration for their wisdom and probity and then of his present disillusion with them. In alternate parallelism (a:b || a′:b′) the psalmist utilizes two of the most ancient traditions of Genesis (chaps. 3, 6), the fall of Adam (vss. 6a, 7a) and the sin of the angels (vss. 6b, 7b). Originally he thought of the judges as virtually divine; now they are like Adam and the fallen angels after their respective transgressions.

This conception of Adam is not limited to the OT. With many fanciful additions it is frequent in apocryphal, pseudepigraphical, rabbinic, and patristic sources, all of which picture Adam in his "innocence," not as an ignorant child, but on the contrary, as a paragon of perfection, endowed with transcendental wisdom, strength, and beauty.[17]

The biblical and post-biblical sources do not exhaust the evidence for this conception of primal man as the paragon of wisdom, for it goes back to the common heritage of all the Semitic peoples. In the Akkadian epic, Adapa, the son of Ea, whose name is equated with *A-da-ap* 'man,'[18] and who, like Adam, is tricked into losing the blessing of immortality, is described as follows:

> Wisdom . . .
> His command was indeed . . . like the command of Ea.
> Wide understanding he had perfected for him to disclose the designs
>   of the land.
> To him he had given wisdom; eternal life he had not given him.
>
> Tablet A, ll. 2 ff.[19]

The epic of Gilgamesh enshrines a rich storehouse of primitive mythology, from most of which Genesis has been purged. Yet here, too, the hero is pictured as superlatively wise and powerful:

> He should be our shepherd,
> Strong, stately and wise.
>
> Tablet A, col. E. 26, 27

> He is radiant with manhood, vigor he has,
> With ripeness, gorgeous is the whole of his body . . .
> Anu, Enlil and Ea have broadened his wisdom.
>
> Tablet I, col. 5, 15, 16, 22[20]

The quest of Gilgamesh for eternal life, both in the Assyrian and Babylonian versions, ends in failure because "the gods have decreed death for mankind, retaining life in their own hands."[21]

It is characteristic of the biblical world-view that Adam's loss of immortality is not ascribed, as here, to divine caprice or envy, but to man's own sin, a shortcoming that God would have wished him to overcome.

In sum, our sources, Semitic, biblical and post-biblical, are at one in conceiving of primal man as endowed with supreme wisdom and beauty before his misadventure. The theory that it was the fruit of the "tree of knowing good and evil" that conferred the knowledge of the world and intellectual maturity upon Adam is therefore decisively ruled out.

The same objections hold with regard to a variant of this view, that the tree of good and evil refers to "the enlargement of capacity and experience, and ripeness of judgment, which distinguishes an adult from a child."[22] Adam is not a child in the garden of Eden, or he could not be held responsible for his disobedience.[23]

In view of the difficulties of each of these views, some scholars have had recourse to the convenient assumption that the narrative in Genesis 2–3 represents a composite of two distinct accounts of the first sin.[24] Even protagonists of this approach recognize that the "evidence" for a double recension is only "more or less decisive" and even "precarious."[25] In addition, analysis of each alleged source makes it clear that the hypothesis creates more problems than it answers.[26] Finally, the assumption made a generation ago that the alleged biblical redactor operated mechanically with his sources and could not be expected to have had any intelligent view of the material he used is now rightly rejected by contemporary research. Even if "sources" were to be assumed, we still must come to grips with the conception underlying the "finished product" that we find in Genesis. It is recognized today that the architectonic structure of the pentateuchal narrative, and particularly of Genesis, cannot be the result of chance or of a "scissors-and-paste" method of compilation, but represents a religious and literary achievement of the highest order.[27]

III

In view of the inadequacies of all these views, one conclusion emerges: the only conception of the "tree of knowing good and evil" that is validated by the Genesis narrative itself, besides being supported by biblical usage elsewhere and by the evidence of comparative religion and mythology, is that the tree of knowledge represents "sexual consciousness."

This view, which had been previously advanced by several scholars,[28] did not win general acceptance, for a variety of reasons that need not be entered into here. By and large, the scholars who favored a sexual interpretation of the tree of knowledge failed to offer any substantial evidence in its favor, contenting themselves in the main with a casual phrase or two.

When this view is adopted, however, it becomes clear that the two trees in the garden represent two roads to eternal life: eating of the tree of life conferred personal immortality upon the eater, while partaking of the tree of knowledge afforded the eater the vicarious immortality which comes from the procreation of children.[29] That these are opposing patterns of life is recognized by modern psychological theory, in Freud's dichotomy between the instinct of ego-preservation and the drive for sexual experience. The contrast was, however, sensed by the ancient writers of the Gilgamesh epic. After Gilgamesh is denied personal immortality, the alewife offers him sage counsel, in a famous passage the full significance of which has not been noted:

> Thou, Gilgamesh, let full be thy belly,
> Make thou merry by day and by night,
> Of each day make thou a feast of rejoicing,
> Day and night dance thou and play!
> Let thy garments be sparkling fresh,
> Thy head be washed; bathe thou in water,
> Pay heed to the little one that holds on to thy hand,
> Let thy spouse delight in thy bosom!
> For this is the task of (mankind)!

> (Old Babylonian Version, Tablet X, col. 3.6–14[30])

This injunction is more than the counsel of *carpe diem*, as it is usually understood. He is being offered the consolation of an alternative, the admittedly less attractive road to eternal life through the medium of sexual experience and the procreation of children.

That the phrase itself "knowing good and evil" means "sexual knowledge and experience" can be validated on philological and exegetical grounds.[31] The verb 'to know' is a universal euphemism for sexual relations, cf. Hebrew ידע, Arabic *'arifa*, Akkadian *lamâdu (idû)*, Greek γιγνώσκειν, Latin *cognoscere, noscere, notitiam habere*. The phrase טוב ורע may be a merismus expressing the entire range of experience in this area, without any specific meaning attaching to the terms.[32]

On the other hand, we believe that the phrase may have originated in the two aspects of sexual experience, the normal (טוב) manifestations of the impulse and the abnormal (רע). The variety and frequency of variant sexual patterns are well attested in biblical narrative and law.[33] For the ancients, the line of demarcation between the normal and abnormal forms of sexual experience was by no means as distinct as it is in the modern world, at least in its official code.[34]

That the Qumran sect, which made personal purity, if not celibacy, a cardinal virtue, was well aware of these aberrant forms of sexual behavior, is clear from a passage in the "Scroll of the Wars of the Sons of Light with the Sons of Darkness" (sec. 7, ll. 3–5): וכול נער זעטוט ואשה לוא יבואו למחנותם בצאתם מירושלים ללכת למלחמה עד שובם 'And every young lad and woman shall not enter their camps when they go forth from Jerusalem to go war until their return.'[34a]

As the editor of these eschatological texts, Yigael Yadin notes, "the intention of the sect was to remove any possibility of the temporary defilement of the warriors because of normal forms of impurity (cf. Lev. 15:18 ff.) and to remove the cause of male cohabitation (Lev. 18:22; 20:13)." He also suggests that the limitation in the use for war of horses to the male of the species, סוסים זכרים (sec. 10, l. 11) may have been induced by the desire to avoid sodomy, though this is less certain.[34b]

In sum, it is clear that both for biblical and post-biblical Judaism, the full gamut of sexual awareness included both its natural and unnatural manifestations.

The specific connotation here proposed for טוב ורע 'natural and unnatural,' may be supported by two similar biblical passages. In the story of Lot's difficulties with the Sodomites and in the equally primitive tale of the Levite from Mt. Ephraim and his concubine, who are attacked by the inhabitants of Gibeah in Benjamin, the

townsmen demand that the male guest(s) be handed over to them
ונדעה אותם (Gen. 19:5); ונדענו (Judg. 19:22). In each case, the host
replies אל · · · תרעו and expresses his willingness to offer up instead a
woman to their lust. The latter phrase, as Ehrlich correctly noted,
cannot mean, "do not do wickedly," for violating the chastity of an
innocent woman is surely an evil. Ehrlich therefore renders rightly
"do not act unnaturally."[35] Now, if רע refers to the abnormal aspects,
טוב would refer to the normal, and the phrase "knowing good and
evil" becomes a stereotyped idiom encompassing the entire range of
sexual experience.[36]

This meaning alone is appropriate to all the biblical passages where
the phrase occurs.[37] It has long been noted that the only direct consequence of Adam and Eve's eating of the tree of knowledge is sexual
awareness, the consciousness of their nakedness, which is followed by
the sewing of girdles made of fig-leaves (2:25; 3:7).

In Gen. 3:5, 22, the eating of the fruit of the tree of knowledge is
described as making Adam "like God, knowing good and evil." So
long as Adam had access to the tree of life and could eat of the fruit,
he would remain immortal.[38] If now sexual awareness were added to
him, man would indeed resemble God, for the human procreation
of life is the counterpart of the divine attribute of creation. Moreover,
we may recall that early biblical thought conceived of the בני אלהים
as possessing the procreative faculty, hence their liaisons with the
daughters of men, described in Gen. 6:1, 4.[39] In primitive thought the
gods are always pictured as possessing immortality in their own
persons, as well as the sexual appetites and capacities of men.

A striking parallel, hitherto unrecognized, to the biblical usage is
afforded by a passage in the Gilgamesh epic that illumines both the use
of the term "knowledge" for sexual awareness and the description of
this attribute as making man "like God."

The mighty Enkidu, "born in the hills, who with the gazelles feeds
on grass and with the wild beasts drinks at the watering place," meets
a harlot, who arouses his ardor and with whom he spends six days and
seven nights. After he has had his fill of her charms, the animals who
were his companions before, desert him.

> But he now had wisdom, broader understanding . . .
> The harlot says to him, to Enkidu,
> Thou art wise, Enkidu, art become like a god.[40]
>
> (Tablet I, col. 4, 29, 39)

Obviously, the only change in Enkidu which has taken place is his sexual experience, on the basis of which he is now described as being "wise . . . having become like a god."

To revert to the biblical tale, when Adam and Eve had eaten of the tree of knowledge, their expulsion from the garden of Eden was inevitable, if the basic distinction between God and man, upon which biblical thought lays such stress, was not to be obliterated. The divine hostility to man, which some scholars have found in the Paradise narrative,[40a] has no real basis in the text, properly understood. On the contrary, every feature of the tale, the planting of the garden, fruitful and well-watered, the setting of Adam in its midst, God's solicitude in seeking a companion for him, the creation of Eve, and the permission granted Adam to eat of the tree of life, all reflect God's unsentimental love of man that we inadequately describe as divine justice. But instead of meeting these marks of God's favor with reverence and gratitude, Adam permitted himself to be seduced into the sin of disobedience, from which flowed the consequences of suffering and mortality.

In sum, the Paradise tale, seen in its setting, contains some of man's oldest thoughts on life, death, and immortality. Had Adam not sinned, he would have remained eternally alive in his own person. His violation of the divine command brought death into the world and left man only with the compensatory and vicarious immortality that comes through children.[41]

IV

The other biblical passages, where the phrase "knowing good and evil" occurs, all receive their most natural and unforced interpretation on this view. In Deut.1:39, Moses refers to the very young children (טף) and the somewhat older ones (בנים) who have not yet attained to sexual maturity, as being permitted to enter the Promised Land.

In II Sam.19:36, no other view of the phrase is possible. Barzillai is not discounting his powers of judgment because of his old age;[42] for he is not being invited to the royal court to serve as a counsellor. The old man is emphasizing that his advanced years have deprived him of the capacity to enjoy the luxuries of court which David has offered him as a reward for his loyalty. The entire passage must be read:

I am this day fourscore years old; can I discern between good and bad? can thy servant taste what I eat or what I drink? can I hear any more the voice of singing men and singing women? wherefore then should thy servant be yet a burden unto my lord and king?

No longer can he find delight in food, drink, and music. Surely the third member of the triad of wine, women and song, could not have been overlooked by Barzillai.[43]

In Isaiah's Immanuel prophecy, the recognition that the phrase under discussion has a sexual connotation produces a striking chronological sequence. Speaking in 734, the year of the Syro-Ephraimitic war, the prophet points to the pregnant young woman nearby and foretells that Judah's foes would be exiled before her unborn child "would know how to refuse evil and choose the good," that is, become sexually conscious. This stage is reached at the age of puberty, roughly thirteen years. Isaiah is announcing in 734 that before thirteen years have passed the doom will have descended upon both Israel and Syria. A similar chronological "sign" is offered by the prophet in Chap. 8, which is probably a little earlier than Chap. 7, since in the latter an alliance with Syria and Ephraim is still favorably contemplated (see 8:6), while in the former Ahaz has definitely aligned himself with Assyria against the Confederacy (7:5 f). The prophet announces that before his new-born son will be able to say "father" or "mother," that is to say within approximately two years, "the wealth of Damascus and the booty of Samaria will be carried off before the king of Assyria" (8:4). Samaria was destroyed in 722, twelve years after the Syro-Ephraimitic War, and Damascus was captured by the Assyrians two years after the rebellion, in 732—a striking congruence of dates with the two prophetic passages![44]

V

The signal importance of our passage in the *serekh ha'edah* for biblical interpretation lies in the fact that here the phrase "knowing good and evil" is explicitly linked up with sexual experience and marriage, a meaning which needed to be inferred in the OT passages where it occurs.

As for the Qumran Community itself, the negative form of the injunction is highly significant: "He shall not come near . . . except when he reach twenty years of age, etc." Pharisaic Judaism, which looked upon procreation and the companionship of husband and wife as a sacred duty,[45] favored early marriages, close to puberty.[46] On the other hand, the Qumran sect sought to postpone marriage as long as possible and permitted it only when it could not safely be postponed any longer—at the age of twenty, when the sexual impulse is at its strongest.

The meaning of our passage is illumined by a rabbinic passage which presents the diametrically opposed Pharisaic standpoint:

Rab Huna follows his opinion, for he said: "He who reaches the age of twenty and does not marry, spends all his days in sin." Do you actually mean 'sin'? At least, in the thought of sin! Raba said, "So the school of Rabbi Ishmael taught: until the age of twenty, the Holy One, blessed be He, sits and waits for a man to marry. When twenty is reached and he does not marry, God says, 'May his bones swell up!' "[47]	רב הונא לטעמיה דאמר בן עשרים שנה ולא נשא אשה כל ימיו בעבירה· בעבירה סלקא דעתך אלא אימא כל ימיו בהרהורי עבירה· אמר רבא וכן תנא דבי רבי ישמעאל עד עשרים שנה יושב הקדוש ברוך הוא ומצפה לאדם מתי ישא אשה· כיון שהגיע לעשרים ולא נשא אמר תיפח עצמותיו·

The impatience of the Rabbis with those who postponed marriage until twenty is in striking contrast to the ordinance of the Qumran community, which does not permit marriage until that age.

On the other hand, the standpoint of the Qumran "congregation" bears a marked resemblance to the views of Paul, who likewise preferred celibacy, but conceded the necessity for marriage:

Now concerning the matters about which you wrote, it is well for a man not to touch a woman. But because of the temptation to immorality, each man should have his own wife and each woman her own husband. . . . I say this by way of concession, not of command. I wish that all were as I myself am. But each has his own special gift from God, one of one kind and one of another. . . . But if they cannot exercise self-control, they should marry. For it is better to marry than to be aflame with passion. (I Cor. 7:1, 2, 6, 7, 9)

The ascetic spirit, which finds moderate expression here in the effort by the leaders of the *serekh ha'edah* to postpone marriage, continued to

grow in intensity, until marriages were completely avoided by devotees of most of these sects. Thus, in the *serekh hayahad*, we find no
references at all to family life,[48] a situation which is in harmony with
the information in our other sources regarding the Essenes.

It is perhaps worthy of note that both the Pharisees, who favored
early marriage and the Qumran sectarians, who opposed it, were
realistically aware of this major aspect of human nature, which poses a
problem that our complex civilization has thus far failed to solve.

NOTES

1. D. Barthélemy and J. T. Milik, *Qumran Cave I. Discoveries in the Judaean
Desert, I* (Oxford, 1955), "La Règle de la Congregation" (1QSa), pp. 108–18.

2. *Op. cit.*, p. 108. Thus the new document (1QSa), in contradistinction to the
old (1QS), is marked by a preference for the term *'ēdāh* as against *yahad*, calls its
leader the "chief warrior," נשיא כול העדה as against (מלאכת) האיש המבקר על,
הרבים is marked by a martial spirit as against an attitude of nonviolence, and
refers to women and children in the "congregation" as against the semi-monastic
structure of adults envisaged in *serekh hayahad*.

3. "The OT Meaning of the Knowledge of Good and Evil," *JBL*, LXXV
(1956), 114–20.

4. Cf. Pliny *Historia Naturalis* v. 17; Philo, *apud* Eusebius *Preparatio Evan-
gelica* viii.11; Josephus *Antiquities* XVIII.i.5; *Bellum Judaicum* ii.8, paragraphs 2
and 13. See the succinct discussion of the sources in Millar Burrows, *The Dead
Sea Scrolls* (New York, 1955), pp. 244 f., 290 f.

5. In passing, Barthélemy's suggestion that his emended reading מילואת
(for מולואת), be vocalized as a construct noun *millū'at*, from a noun *millū'āh*
(*op. cit.*, p. 113) does not commend itself. The latter noun in Exod. 28:17, etc.
means 'the setting of a jewel,' not 'completion.' The form מילואת is a *plene*
spelling for מְלַאת which occurs in the identical construction in the MT of
Jer 29:10. *Shewa mobile* is frequently represented by *yod* in post-biblical texts.

6. *Op. cit.*, p. 114.

7. *Ibid.*, p. 118.

8. R. Gordis, "The Significance of the Paradise Myth," *AJSL*, LII (1936),
86–94. Detailed bibliography on this problem may be found in M. D. Cassuto,
La Questione della Genesi (Florence, 1934) pp. 37 f., 151 f., 184 ff., 257 ff.;
Me'adam 'ad Noah (Jerusalem, 1944), pp. 51 f.; and B. Reicke in *Journal of
Semitic Studies*, I:3 (July, 1956), 193–94, n. 1.

9. Cf. Dillman, *ad loc.*; K. Budde, *Die biblische Paradiesgeschichte* (1932).
Cf. also Paul Heinisch, *Theology of the OT* (Collegeville, Minn., 1950) p. 166;
L. Koehler, *Theologie des AT* (Tübingen, 1953), p. 158.

10. Some have sought to save the popular concept of Adam's innocence before
the fall, by arguing that the possessed no serious moral sense at all and that he

was simply confronted by an absolute prohibition and a threat, as a child might be forbidden to perform a given act. This view ignores the clear implication of Adam's wisdom, which underlies his naming all living creatures, as well as the unanimous testimony of all biblical references and extra-biblical parallels, which, as we have noted, picture primal man as perfect in wisdom.

Besides, a childlike violation of a prohibition could not justly lead to the severe, permanent punishments visited upon the human pair by the Lord.

Moreover, the denial of a moral sense to Adam runs counter to the whole ethical spirit of biblical religion, which could not punish him and his descendants for an act for which he was not morally responsible. On this view, nothing would remain of the concept of man's sin, which is the basic theme of the Paradise narrative, whatever other implications may or may not be drawn from it.

11. So Wellhausen, *Prolegomena,* 6th ed., pp. 297 ff.

12. So Gressmann in *Archiv für Religionswissenschaft,* X, 351 f.

13. Cf. Brown-Driver-Briggs, *Lexicon* (New York, 1907), the references cited *s. v.*; Koehler-Baumgartner, *Lexicon in VT Libros* (Leiden, 1951), p. 984a: "In many cases, šem *JHVH* means not only the name but the full being and power of Yahveh." Cf. also P. Heinisch, *Das Wort im AT und im Alten Orient* (Münster, 1922); J. Z. Lauterbach, "The Belief in the Power of the Word," *HUCA,* XIV (1939), 287–302.

On the importance of šēm *JHVH* for Israelite belief and ritual, see James Muilenburg's illuminating paper on "Psalm 20 and 21" read before the 1956 Annual Meeting of the Society of Biblical Literature.

14. After this paper was completed and submitted for publication, a study entitled "The Knowledge Hidden in the Tree of Paradise" by Bo Reicke appeared in the *Journal of Semitic Studies,* I:3 (July 1956), 193–201. One is grateful to the learned author on several counts, such as the bibliography on the subject (*op. cit.,* note 1) which supplements Cassuto, his decisive rejection of the view which identifies the 'knowledge' with the knowledge of sin" (p. 201), and his emphasis upon the ancient suggestion that the tree of knowledge was a fig-tree. Particularly welcome is Reicke's adherence to the view that good and evil is "a euphemism for the secrets of sex" (p. 196), though he does not seek to explain the origin of the phrase.

However, Reicke insists that "the sexual element seems to be part of a wider context" (p. 197) which he identifies as "the arts of civilization" (p. 198) so that the fall is a "usurpation of culture (the Promethean topic)" (p. 200). To establish a nexus between the motif of sex and that of the arts of civilization, he adds: "An important presupposition is that human procreation is a principle of civilization" (p. 198). This contention is far from self-evident.

He does not, moreover, make it clear what aspects of civilization he regards as relevant here. If "the knowledge of good and evil" be agriculture, the most natural view, it is contradicted by the biblical narrative, which states that *ab initio* Adam was charged with tilling and guarding the garden (Gen. 2:15), and it is hardly comprehensive enough to be attributed to God (3:5, 22).

If, as Bo Reicke's reference to the Promethean theme suggests, "the knowledge of good and evil" is to be referred to all the technical arts of civilization, the difficulties are even more numerous. In the first instance, he is constrained to assume that Adam before the fall was totally lacking in wisdom. Following Cohon and other scholars, he maintains: 1) that "the rest of the OT has scarcely any references to the Paradise story" (p. 194), and 2) that "direct references to Adam as a holder of perfect knowledge are only met with in later Jewish-Gnostic speculation....But the Genesis story of Adam has not touched upon this" (p. 195). In the body of our paper, we have demonstrated the error of both contentions. Second, there is no indication of an accession of knowledge to Adam in these areas after his eating of the fruit, the only changes being associated with the domain of sex, the sense of shame, the sewing of girdles, and the procreation of children. Third, the discovery of the arts is specifically attributed in the Bible not to Adam but to the descendants of Cain: Jabal, "father" of the arts of tent-making and herding, Jubal "father" of music, and Tubal-cain, inventor of the use of metals (Gen. 4:20–22). These are the authentic elements of the "Prometheus-motif." Thus, according to Greek mythology, Athena taught the giant "architecture, astronomy, mathematics, navigation, metallurgy and other useful arts, which he passed on to mankind" (Robert Graves, *The Greek Myths* [Harmondsworth, 1955], I, 144). The omission of agriculture, which alone is directly related to procreation, is significant. In the most familiar form of the myth, it was fire that the Titan brought down to man, thus enabling him to make weapons and tools, to warm his dwellings, to introduce the arts and coin money. Cf., e. g., T. Bulfinch, *The Age of Fable* (Modern Library edition; New York, 1934), chap. ii, p. 16. Fourth, to describe these arts as "knowing how life is increased and mastered," as does Reicke (p. 201), appears to be a modern interpretation, too sophisticated for the ancients, who did associate the fertility of crops and animals with that of humans, but would hardly regard metallurgy or music as part of the knowledge contributing to the increase and mastering of life. Witness the dissociation of the two themes in Genesis, where seven generations separate Adam from the progenitors of the arts of civilization.

With all due appreciation of the insights in Reicke's treatment, we therefore cannot regard as convincing his view of "the knowledge of good and evil" as representing the arts of civilization, when the theory is viewed within the framework of the biblical text and the world-view it expresses.

15. Cf. G. A. Cooke, *The Book of Ezekiel* ("International Critical Commentary" [New York 1937]), II, 315 ff., who notes that "in Ezekiel the purifying process (of the old Semitic myths) has not gone so far (as in Genesis)"; cf. also Cassuto, *Me'adam 'ad Noaḥ*, pp. 47 ff.

16. It is inexplicable to us that modern interpreters have failed to recognize the proper noun in 'ādām in this Psalm. Similarly Hosea (6:7) refers to his contemporaries as violating God's covenant kᵉ'ādām 'as did Adam,' and Job (31:33) protests that he did not try to hide any of his transgressions kᵉ'ādām 'as did Adam.' In view of the vast interest in Adam in post-biblical thought, we cannot understand the endeavor to ignore such references to him in the OT, particularly since the rendering 'like men' in these passages is exegetically inferior.

On *sārîm* as 'angels,' cf. Dan 10:13, 20, 21; 12:1 and the frequent rabbinic usage as e. g., שר של אש (B. Pes. 118a) 'the angel of fire'; שר של ים (B. Baba Batra 74b) 'angel of the sea.' Cf. Jastrow, *Dictionary*, p. 1627a.

The mythological basis of this psalm has been exhaustively studied by J. Morgenstern, "The Mythological Background of Psalm 82," *HUCA*, XIV (1939), 29–126.

17. Cf. the vast amount of material in all these categories assembled by L. Ginzberg, *Legends of the Jews* (Philadelphia, 1913–38), I, 52–62, and V:5, notes 21, 22, 27, 29, 30.

18. In an unpublished syllabary cited by E. Ebeling, *Leben und Tod*, p. 27a.

19. The material is conveniently accessible in the indispensable collection edited by J. E. Pritchard, *Ancient Near Eastern Texts* (*ANET*; Princeton, 1950). Cf. E. A. Speiser, *ANET*, p. 101a. The arts referred to in the lines that follow in the epic are part of Oriental "Wisdom," on the scope of which cf. e. g. R. Gordis, *Koheleth—The Man and His World* (New York, 1951) pp. 16 f.

20. *ANET*, p. 73b.

21. *Ibid.*, p. 90a.

22. Cf. H. Gunkel, *Genesis*, 2nd ed. (1902), pp. 25 ff. There is no evidence in the Biblical text that Adam and Eve are "sexually immature" before eating of the fruit as a child might be; they lack sexual consciousness *in toto*.

23. Cf. Ibn Ezra (on Gen. 2:17) who correctly notes: "Adam (before the fall) was filled with knowledge ...and was a great sage."

24. Cf. J. Skinner, *Genesis* ("International Critical Commentary" [New York, 1925]), pp. 52 f. The assumption that the narrative has not retained its original form or order is still maintained by C. A. Simpson in his "Exegesis of Genesis," *The Interpreter's Bible* (New York-Nashville, 1952), I, 496 ff.

25. Skinner, *loc. cit.*

26. The details may be found in the paper cited in note 8 above.

27. This insight underlies the "synthetic" approach to the Pentateuch, which has made significant gains in the last decades. Thus, for example, it lies at the basis of Cassuto's important Hebrew commentaries on Genesis and Exodus (*Me'adam 'ad Noaḥ, Minnoaḥ 'ad Abraham, Perush 'al Sefer Shemot* (Jerusalem, 1944–52) as well as his *Torat Hateudot Vesiduram šel Sifre Hatorah* (*The Documentary Hypothesis and the Composition of the Pentateuch*; 2nd printing; Jerusalem, 1953). Cassuto demonstrates with a wealth of evidence that the Pentateuch reflects a unity of structure both in its details and its over-all form. Even if one does not accept Cassuto's contention that this structure disproves the existence of originally separate sources for the Pentateuch, one cannot fail to recognize the unity of the biblical text as it has reached us, nor avoid the duty of comprehending its meaning *in its present form*. For a briefer example of the synthetic approach, available in English, cf. M. Buber, "Abraham the Seer," *Judaism*, Vol. V (Fall, 1956).

28. A sexual connotation for "the knowledge of good and evil" is assigned by Ibn Ezra (on Gen 3:16 והאחד עץ הדעת והוא יוליד תאות המשגל); by Ludwig Levy ("Sexualsymbolik in der biblischen Paradiesgeschichte," *Imago*, V [1917], 163; his contention, however, that there was only one tree in the garden is

expressly refuted by 3:22, which distinguishes both trees, a passage he is constrained to delete for the sake of his theory); by A. B. Ehrlich (in his Hebrew and German commentaries, *ad loc.*, but without supporting evidence); by G. A. Barton (*Semitic Origins*, pp. 93 ff.), who maintains that the fruit was an aphrodisiac; and by Hans Schmidt (*Die Erzählung von Paradies und Sündenfall* [1931]).

29. Cf. J. G. Frazer, *Folk Lore in the Old Testament* (one vol. ed.) pp. 11–33, who recognizes that the two trees stand in contrast with each other. He therefore suggests that the original account told of a tree of life and a tree of death and that Adam was tricked into eating the fruit of the latter. This hypothesis makes a purely gratuitous assumption of a fundamental transformation of the tale, for which there is no evidence in the text. Moreover, it is noteworthy that while rivers, trees, and fruits of life are frequent in the folklore of the world (cf. A. Wünsche, *Die Sagen vom Lebensbaum und Lebenswasser*; Frazer, *op. cit.*; Skinner, *op. cit.*, pp. 58 f.), we find no tree of death anywhere; man loses immortality simply by failing to avail himself of the life-conferring substance. Finally, the whole tenor of the biblical narrative, with its underlying conception of a beneficent Deity, runs counter to the possibility of the garden of Eden containing a tree of death. The great merit of Frazer's view is his recognition of a contrast between the two trees in the garden. Our view likewise recognizes the organic relationship between them, without, however, doing violence to the received text or the spirit of biblical thought.

30. *ANET*, p. 90a.

31. It need not be emphasized that this proposed meaning for הדעת טוב ורע does not exclude the entire range of meanings that the substantives possess in Biblical Hebrew, such as of 'right and wrong,' 'truth and falsehood,' etc. It is noteworthy, however, that when the wise woman of Tekoa praises David for his wisdom, the verb is not ידע but שמע 'understand,' (לשמע הטוב והרע (II Sam. 14:17). Similarly in Solomon's prayer for wisdom, the verb is not ידע but בין 'distinguish,' (להבין בין טוב לרע (I Kings 3:9).

32. Cf. the comprehensive study of A. M. Honeyman, "Merismus in Biblical Hebrew," *JBL*, LXX (1952), 22 ff.

33. The prohibitions of abnormal forms of behavior, like sodomy and homosexuality, are found in Exod. 22:18; Lev. 18:22 ff., 20:15; Deut. 27:21. As a legal commentary on the Pentateuch, the Talmud naturally deals with these negative injunctions as well; e. g., the Mishnah, Sanh. 7:4 and Gemara, B. Sanh. 54a–58a; and see L. M. Epstein, *Sex Laws and Customs in Judaism* (New York, 1948), pp. 133–47. With regard to the relations between the sexes, rabbinic law recognizes the existence of a wide range of experience. Thus from the plural of the construct in משכבי אשה (Lev. 18:22), the Talmud (B. Sanh. 54a) infers that both the usual and unusual modes are permissible (*kᵉdarkāh, šelō kᵉdarkāh*); cf. B. Yebamot 34b and Tosafot *s. v. velō'*). Needless to add, these aberrations become highly infrequent in post-biblical days under the discipline of the Law. See Epstein, *loc. cit.* for details. On the other hand, it is highly doubtful that the temple קדשים (I Kings 14:24, 15:12, 22:47; II Kings 23:7) were sodomites, as is maintained by Epstein (*op. cit.*, pp. 135 f.).

34. Cf. the material assembled in E. Westermark, *The Origin and Development of the Moral Ideas* (London, 1906–8), chap. xlvi, and in Hans Licht, *Sexual Life of the Ancient Greeks* (New York, 1952), as well as the frequent references to homosexuality and other aberrations in classical writers.

34a. Cf. Y. Yadin, *Milḥemet B*ᵉ*nei Ha'or Bib*ᵉ*nei Haḥošekh* (Jerusalem, 1955), p. 300 for the text, p. 66 for the editor's comment.

34b. Cf. *op. cit.*, p. 269 for the text, p. 66, n. 23 for the comment.

35. Cf. A. B. Ehrlich, *Randglossen zur hebräischen Bibel*, Vols. I & III, *ad loc.* He also suggests the meaning 'natural' for טוב in Gen. 1:3 and 'unnatural' for רע in Isa. 1:4. We may add the same meaning for זרע מרעים in Isa. 14:20, in which the king of Babylonia is taunted as being 'unnatural,' in that his actions have succeeded in destroying his own land and people, rather than those of his enemies.

The connotation 'natural', unnatural' for טוב, רע, respectively, represents one more nuance of the broad constellation of meanings of these common Hebrew substantives, the full range of meaning of which, illustrated by abundant examples, may be studied in the lexicons. Thus Koehler-Baumgartner, *s.v.* טוב defines it as 'good in every variety of meaning, pleasant, useful, efficient, beautiful, kind, right, morally good.' *BDB* in its superbly organized article on טוב distinguishes a large variety of meanings: a) pleasant, agreeable to the senses (to the sight, taste, smell); b) pleasant to the higher nature (hence pleasing, prosperous); c) good, excellent of its kind, hence fruitful (of soil), choice (of vegetation), fat (of animals), pure (of minerals); d) rich, plentiful, valuable; e) appropriate, becoming; f) of man's sensuous nature, hence glad, happy, prosperous; g) of man's intellectual nature, hence good (of the understanding); h) of man's moral nature, hence good, kind, benign; i) ethically good, right. Ben Jehuda, *Thesaurus*, p. 1850, defines טוב in the most inclusive manner שהוא כמו שהוא צריך להיות 'that which is as it ought to be.' The idea expressed in our modern idiom by 'natural' obviously falls within the scope of this definition; indeed, it may be subsumed under category *e* of BDB, 'becoming, appropriate to man's nature.'

36. Yet the terms טוב and רע do not altogether lose their specific content, as Isa. 7:15, 16 "eschewing evil and choosing good" indicates. Hence the substantives are not *ab origine* a general phrase.

37. Cassuto raises two objections to this proposed interpretation of the tree of knowledge: a) at the time when Adam was commanded not to eat of its fruit, the woman had not yet been created; b) the "knowledge of good and evil" is attributed to God (Gen. 3:5, 22) and therefore cannot bear a sexual connotation. Neither objection is decisive.

With regard to the first, the biblical narrative proceeds, in the very next verse after the prohibition, to the choice of a companion that will serve as Adam's helpmeet (2:18). In the biblical account, the animals prove unsatisfactory, and so Eve is created for him. In the primitive sources upon which Genesis drew, the animals might well have sufficed as his companions, as is the case with Enkidu in the Gilgamesh epic, Tablet I, col. 4.2–5, cited in the text of our paper above. Cf. Speiser, *ANET*, p. 74a. Sexual awareness was accordingly possible to Adam even before Eve's creation. It was denied to him only because, possessing personal immortality, he had no need of the procreative faculty. Moreover, Eve's existence from the beginning is presupposed throughout the narrative.

Thus the prohibition of the fruit of the tree of knowledge is never addressed to Eve, yet she is aware of the injunction and feels herself bound by it (3:2–3). Some commentators accordingly transpose the command, 2:16, 17, after 2:23 (so Simpson, *op. cit.*, p. 496). This radical procedure is unnecessary; we have only to recognize that in the biblical narrative the prohibition of the fruit and the creation of Eve are simultaneous.

The prohibition of the fruit of the tree is mentioned before Eve's creation for reason of style — it is directly connected with the preceding passage: the tree was the last detail mentioned in 2:9; vss. 10–14 describe how the garden was watered, vs. 15 contains the command for Adam to guard and till it. Vss. 16 and 17 complete the instructions to Adam.

Cassuto's second objection, which goes back to Naḥmanides, is dealt with above in the text of our paper.

38. The problem as to why Adam did not eat of the tree of life and thus achieve immortality once and for all before his expulsion is resolved by comparative folklore. The fruit of the tree did not possess the quality of conferring unending life upon whosoever ate of its fruit once. Rather, one was immortal so long as one continued to eat of it. This seems to be a common characteristic of the "fruit of life." Thus, the Germanic myth of "the twilight of the gods" tells that while the golden apples were within reach of the gods, they were youthful and happy. But when the giants stole the apples, the gods began to grow old and shrivel up, until Loki succeeded in bringing back the apples, whereupon the gods revived and grew young again. The phrase in Gen. 3:22 פן ישלח ידו implies that the apples are within easy reach, but not that "a single partaking of the fruit would have conferred eternal life" (against Budde, quoted by Skinner, *op. cit.*, p. 88).

39. Whether the term is to be rendered in these passages as 'sons of God' or 'divine beings' cannot be determined, nor is it certain that for the writer a distinction between the two existed.

40. Cf. the Akkadian version, Tablet I, sec. 5. ll. 29 ff. It is conveniently accessible in E. A. Speiser, *ANET*, p. 74. Speiser, *ibid.*, n. 28, notes that "the general parallel to Gen. 3:7 is highly suggestive." We are able to go considerably further, in recognizing the specific character of the parallelism between the Akkadian and the biblical usage in two basic respects: the sexual connotation of "knowledge" and the description of this attribute as making man "like a god."

40a. R. H. Pfeiffer's indispensable *Introduction to the OT* (New York, 1941), p. 164.

41. Cf. Ibn Ezra on Gen. 4:1: "When Adam saw that he would not live in his own person eternally, it was necessary to propagate the race."

42. Cf. Buchanan, *op. cit.*, p. 118.

43. He is hardly emphasizing that he is too old for marriage and its responsibilities, as has been suggested in a private communication. The invitation does not contemplate a new marriage for the old man.

44. It is true that in 7:16 "the two kings" are referred to, but the emphasis upon exile obviously refers to Israel. Similarly, in 8:4 both Damascus and Samaria are mentioned, but it was Damascus that was pillaged by Assyria in 732, while Israel was punished by the loss of its Trans-Jordanian territories.

45. The biblical basis for these two functions of marriage is, of course, Gen. 1:18 and 2:18. Because companionship is an important purpose, rabbinic law urges the marriage even of aged, infirm, and sterile people. (Cf. Eben Haezer 23:5 and Isserles on 1, 3, and see R. Gordis, "The Jewish Conception of Marriage," in *Judaism* [1953], II, 225 ff., esp. 232); *idem, Sex and the Family in the Jewish Tradition* (New York, 1967).

46. Thus the Talmud (B. Yebamot 62b; B. Sanh. 76b) praises the man "who marries off his sons and daughters close to puberty": תנו רבנן ... והמדריך בניו ובנותיו בדרך ישרה והמשיאן סמוך לפירקן עליו הכתוב אומר וידעת כי שלום אהלך.

Even the passage in M. Abot 5:21, בן שמונה עשרה לחופה 'eighteen — for the marriage canopy,' is interpreted by Maimonides in his Code to mean immediately after his seventeenth birthday (*Mishneh Torah, Hilkhot Išūth*, chap. xv). The passage in Abot, for all its familiarity, did not become normative either in law or in life except as a suggested outermost limit. It is attributed, incidentally, to a little known, unimportant sage, Judah ben Tema. The official teaching of Rabbinic Judaism, based on the various talmudic passages, is codified in the Shulḥan Arukh, Eben Haezer (sec. 1, par. 2) as follows: "Every Israelite is commanded to marry by the age of eighteen and he who marries earlier, at thirteen years of age, has performed the commandment most excellently (מצוה מן המובחר). But before thirteen he should not marry, because it resembles immorality. Under no circumstance should he pass twenty years without a wife. If a man has passed twenty years and does not wish to marry, the court compels him to marry, in order to fulfil the commandment 'be fruitful and multiply.' " The practice of early marriages was widespread in the Jewish communities so long as the tradition retained unbroken authority, from talmudic times to the modern age, indeed, virtually to our own day in eastern Europe.

47. Babylonian Talmud, Kiddušin, 29b.

48. W. H. Brownlee's reading of ל[כול הקהל מטף עד נ]שים in the opening lines of the *Dead Sea Manual of Discipline* ("Bulletin of ASOR, Supplementary Studies," Nos. 11–12 [New Haven, 1951], pp. 6 f., 47 f.) is a purely conjectural restoration, which rests in part on his assumption of an identity between 1QS and 1QSa. This assumption is now rendered highly unlikely; see our note 2 above. Even before the new texts were published, De Vaux hesitated to accept Brownlee's restoration on stylistic grounds, while A. M. Haberman (*'Edah V'eduth* [Jerusalem, 1952], p. 57) basing himself on Sukenik restored ל[כבד אלוהים ואנ]שים.

8. THE COMPOSITION AND STRUCTURE OF AMOS

Though Amos stands at the beginning of literary prophecy, the book that bears his name shows evidence of clear-cut, careful organization:[1] (A) The great Judgment Speech against the nations (chapters 1 and 2); (B) Three addresses beginning with the phrase "Hear ye this word" (3:1–15; 4:1–13;[2] 5:1–6); (C) Three charges beginning with "Woe" (5:7–17;[3] 5:18–27;[4] 6:1–14); (D) Five visions, four beginning with "Thus the Lord showed me" (7:1, 4, 7; 8:1), one with "I saw" (9:1); and (E) An ending of consolation and hope (9:11–15).

On the other hand, the reader is impressed by several exceptions to this order. The most striking anomaly is the insertion of the historical record of Amos' encounter with the priest Amaziah at Beth-El, which is placed between the third and fourth visions (7:10–17). All critics are agreed that it is not in its proper place, but there is no unanimity as to its original position.[5]

Duhm and Baumann have assumed that it stood after chapter 6 before the visions, but Sellin has well noted that that would be a highly illogical order, since the visions were the cause of Amos' expulsion, and should therefore precede, not follow, the account. Budde assumed that the historical account originally stood at the beginning of the book and that what we have here is only a fragment, the beginning and end of which have been lost. This view, however, requires a series of unproved assumptions, and is to be accepted only as a last resort, as Sellin has stated. Marti suggested that the account came at the close of the book, that is to say, after 9:7, since he rejects 9:8–15 as unoriginal. Löhr does not state what its original position was, and Eissfeldt claims its source is an independent composition now lost.

Sellin, who accepts the closing section as genuine, places 7:10–17 after 9:10 and claims that 9:10–15 is the end of this historical account. He must then explain why this record (7:10–17; 9:11–15) was divided, one part being placed in chapter 7 and the rest retained in chapter 9.

He argues that the first half was placed in chapter 7 after the third vision because of resemblances in phraseology, "With the sword" (7:9, 11) and "In the midst of My people (the house of) Israel" (7:8, 10). The second half was kept at the end to give the book a consolatory close. Unfortunately, this brilliant hypothesis requires a drastic reorganization of the book, for which there is no evidence. Moreover, immediately upon his expulsion, it would be entirely natural for Amos to denounce his adversaries and pronounce a doom upon the people, as is indeed the case with 7:14-17. He was hardly likely under those circumstances to voice the theme of reconstruction and hope (9:11–15).

A somewhat less disturbing problem is the position of the entire section (8:4–14), which begins with "Hear ye," and which we should have therefore expected with chapters 5 and 6, together with other prophecies of the same general structure. Löhr, Sellin and Eissfeldt move the passage to chapter 4 or 5, but admit that the reasons for the transfer to its present place "can only be guessed at."[5a]

In addition, most scholars have assumed that the passages referring to Judah are later insertions, and that all, or at least some, of them should be deleted (2:4 ff.; 3:1b; 5:5c; 8:14c; 9:11 ff.). That this solution is not altogether satisfactory will become clear in the ensuing discussion.

The thesis we wish to submit is that these three major difficulties in the structure of the book flow from the acceptance of two principles that have become virtually axiomatic in the modern study of Amos, and that these problems are eliminated or considerably reduced if these assumptions are reexamined in the light of an objective study of the material.

It has long been taken for granted:

(A) That Amos, though a Judean, was exclusively concerned with Israel and hence could not be the author, either of the denunciations of Judah now extant in the book, or of the promise of the restoration of David's tabernacle at its close.[6]

(B) That Amos prophesied for a short period and that his public activities ended with his expulsion from Beth-El.[7]

Now even a cursory study of the passages referring to Judah raises grave doubts as to the cogency of the arguments for their elimination. On the contrary, the deletion of these verses or clauses appears to be either unnecessary or actually impossible.

2:4 f.—Here Judah is denounced for neglecting Jahveh's Torah and going after falsehoods. It is usually explained as the gloss of a later Judean reader who wished to relate Amos' activity to Judah.

This view does not commend itself, for these later glossators generally strike the note of national restoration rather than doom, in line with the dominant characteristic of later prophecy and Jewish thought.[8] Moreover, the existence of *torot* in the days of the early literary prophets is today no longer disputed, in the light of our better understanding of the genesis of the Hebrew law-codes and such passages as I Samuel 15:23; Hos. 4:6; 8:1, 12; Isaiah 5:24; 8:16, 20; 30:9. The "falsehoods" could very naturally refer to the entire ritual system practiced without regard to righteousness which Amos castigates in Israel (5:21 ff.).[9] Besides, Amos' extraordinary grasp of international affairs and his noble impartiality of judgment make it impossible to believe that he would be either ignorant of or indifferent to conditions in his native land.

Two additional considerations reenforce the view that this passage is genuine. The Great Arraignment in chapters 1 and 2 was undoubtedly delivered at a gathering in Israel. With consummate skill, Amos begins the judgment on Damascus, Israel's hereditary enemy, an announcement which was undoubtedly heard with relish. He then passes to the other neighbors of Israel—Philistia, Tyre,[10] Edom, Ammon and Moab. He could not have omitted Judah, Israel's nearest neighbor, who so often proved its enemy. Finally, while it has been observed that the present text contains seven nations, exclusive of Israel, the main burden of Amos' prophecy, it has not been noted that the number seven is particularly popular with Amos. It occurs twice more in this relatively small book. Thus, there are seven questions in the series in 3:3–7, through which Amos seeks to emphasize the Divine source of his prophetic activity,[11] and seven calamities are listed in 4:6–13.[12] On all these grounds, there is no adequate reason for denying the genuineness of this passage, as a growing number of scholars have recognized.

3:1b—The phrase "Unto all the family which I have brought up from the land of Egypt" is rejected by Löhr and Sellin as an explanatory gloss, to prevent the later Judean reader from imagining that it refers only to North Israel. This likewise seems an unnecessary excision. Granted that Amos was especially concerned with deflating the chauvinism of the inhabitants of the Northern Kingdom, he could still use this phrase, which serves to remind them that they were not the only recipients of God's favor, for Judah, too, could claim the identical distinction.[13] In 9:7 Amos carries this thought to far greater lengths, by equating the Exodus with the movements of other peoples.

5:5c—"You shall not pass over to Beersheba"—This reference to a Judean sanctuary has also been regarded with suspicion by some scholars as foreign to Amos' thought. Attention has been called to the fact that it is not referred to in the end of the verse, which deals with the destruction of Gilgal and Beth-El. But the evidence that this shrine was held in high repute in Israel is clear, not only from 8:14 but from Elijah's pilgrimage there (I Kings 19:3).[14] The verb "pass the boundary" is highly appropriate from the vantage-point of Israel.

6:1—"Woe to those at ease in Zion" has also proved a point of great difficulty. The word Bᵉṣion has frequently been deleted from the phrase, leaving a lacuna that most scholars have been unable to fill.[15] Sellin's suggested Ba'ir, "in the city," for Bᵉṣion is inept, and Riessler's Bᵉṣiun, "rock," while it does less violence to the text, is not appropriate to Samaria. The present text is the only one that satisfies the minimum requirements of structure and content.

We believe that there is additional proof for the genuineness of the Masoretic text to be found in v. 2.[16] Ever since Geiger, the closing section of v. 2 אִם רַב גְּבוּלָם מִגְּבוּלְכֶם has been emended to read אִם רַב גְּבוּלְכֶם מִגְּבוּלָם or אִם רַב מִגְּבוּלָם גְּבוּלְכֶם and אַתֶּם inserted after הַטּוֹבִים. The phrase is then rendered "Are you better than these kingdoms? Is your boundary greater than theirs?" Elsewhere,[17] we have sought to demonstrate that this emendation is unnecessary, since, in prophetic style, the interrogative particle ha may be used where an affirmative answer is expected, in other words as equivalent to halo'. In such instances, the force of the passage becomes clear only if a negative is inserted in the translation. Thus, I Kings 22:23 הַיְדַעְתֶּם כִּי לָנוּ רָמוֹת הַגִּלְעָד "Do you not know that Ramoth Gilead is ours?"; Jeremiah 31:20 הֲבֵן יַקִּיר לִי אֶפְרַיִם, "Is not Ephraim my beloved son?" Cf. also Genesis 16:13b; I Samuel 2:27; Job 20:4, 5a.

On the basis of this usage, the Masoretic text here gives excellent sense:[18] "Are they not better than these kingdoms? Is not their boundary greater than yours?" In this rendering, hammamlakhoth ha'eleh, "these kingdoms," can refer only to Israel and Judah, mentioned as Zion and Samaria in v. 1, and hence bᵉṣion is authentic. It may be added that *mamlakhah* is used for the kingdom of Israel by Amos in 9:8.

8:14c—*v^{e}hey derekh b^e'er šebha'*, "As the way to Beer-sheba liveth." On the authenticity of this second reference to the Judean sanctuary, see above on 5:5. The juxtaposition of Dan and Beersheba and the reference to the "road to Beersheba"[19] would seem to strengthen the view that the clause is genuine.

9:8b—"But I shall not completely destroy (*hašmed 'ašmid*) the house of Jacob," is eliminated by some scholars as the interpolation of a reader, who could not bear the thought of Israel's complete destruction, implied in the first half of the verse. Unlike the glossator of 2:4; 6:1, who insists on including Judah in the doom, this glossator is one of milder tendencies. As a matter of fact, however, the thought that a part of the nation will escape is implicit in the metaphor of the sieve in v.9.[20]

9:11 ff.—This section has been widely regarded as a later interpolation (Duhm, Wellhausen, Marti, Cornill, Harper, Volz and Löhr) because of many reasons, the chief of which is the reference to the restoration of the fallen hut of David and the picture of idyllic conditions.

On the other hand, König, Orelli and, more recently, Stärk, Gressmann, H. Schmidt, Köhler and Sellin have argued persuasively for the authenticity of the section, in whole or in part.

"The fallen hut of David" refers to the Davidic dynasty, which was relatively weak in Amos' day, holding sway over only a fraction of its former domains. The passage does not presuppose the exile of Judah. Sellin justly points out that there is no later eschatological vision in v. 12. A later writer would have undoubtedly included far more territory in his hopes for the future. As an example of the grandiose scope of later eschatology, we may note Zech. 14:17: "And it shall come to pass that whoso of the families of the earth goeth not up unto Jerusalem to worship the King, the Lord of hosts, upon them, there shall be no rain." Here the prophet merely pictures the restoration of the Davidic kingdom to its former dimensions. For the clause "The nations over which My name has been called" means "the subject peoples of Israel." The sway of a God was coterminous with the power of his people.[21] Krochmal demonstrated long ago that "God" is frequently used where moderns would speak of the national spirit.[22]

V^{e}šabhti 'eth š^{e}bhuth 'ammi is the idiom frequently used of the exile, but its basic meaning is: "I shall restore my people to its former estate," as in Zeph. 2:7, Ezek. 15:63 and Job 42:10.

Concerning vv. 13–15, decision is more difficult. They are obviously based upon the Paradise traditions and would thus belong to the oldest eschatological stratum in Israel's thought, as Gressmann has persuasively argued.[23] On the other hand, these last three verses may be a post-exilic addition, designed to give the book a vividly consolatory close (cf. Joel 4: 18 ff. and Micah 7:14 ff.).

The basic objection to the genuineness of this entire passage (9:8 ff.) has been formulated by Wellhausen with characteristic forthrightness. Amos' words, he declares, are always blood and iron, and here we find roses and lavender. In other words, Amos is everywhere the stern proclaimer of doom; here he is the announcer of hope. While this characterization of Amos is somewhat exaggerated, it cannot be denied that there is a striking contradiction between the attitude toward Judah in 2:4 and that expressed in 9:11. If the evidence points to the genuineness of both passages, we are face to face with a real difficulty.

We believe that the solution may be found in reconsidering the second principle of Amos criticism, namely, that he prophesied a short time and that his public activity as a prophet ended with his expulsion from Beth-El by Amaziah. Besides having no objective evidence to recommend it, this hypothesis seems psychologically untenable. A powerful nature, like that of Amos, who answers Amaziah with dignity and conviction, would not consent to be silenced. He might be driven out of Beth-El, perhaps out of Israel, but he could never forget that "the Lord Jahveh has spoken, who can but prophesy!" It is because of this theory that varied but unconvincing efforts have been made to remove the historical section 7:10–17 from its present place.

Both the problem of the apparent contradictions relative to Judah's destiny and the position of this historical section can be solved by one basic assumption: *The book of Amos contains two collectiones of prophecies,—the first (chapters 1–7:9) delivered before the encounter at Beth-El (A), the second, chapters 8 and 9, added later and consisting of oracles delivered after the encounter (B).*[23a] *The historical material (7:10–17) (H) was added to the first collection before the second was part of the book.* Hence the history of the composition may be summarized in the formula A + H + B.

In support of this theory, the following considerations may be adduced. It seems clear that in the editing of the prophetic books historical material was often placed after the prophecies, as a kind of supplement. When additional prophecies, assumed rightly or wrongly to belong to the same prophet, were discovered, they were placed after the supplementary material.

Thus in the case of Isaiah, the original collection (chapters 1–35)[24] was supplemented by historical traditions (chapters 36-39). The additional chapters 40–66, which were assumed to be Isaianic,[25] were not placed in their "proper" position among the prophecies (after chapter 35), but were added after the historical material (after chapter 39).

The same procedure meets us in Jeremiah. The prophecies (A) (chapters 1–25) are supplemented by the extensive historical material (H) embodied in chapters 26–45. Finally the oracles against the nations (B) are added to the preexistent collections (chapters 46–52).

If this view be adopted, the problems of structure outlined at the beginning of this paper disappear. The first collection (A) was systematically edited. It contains (a) the great judgment on the nations (chapters 1, 2), (b) three prophecies beginning with "Hear this word" (chapters 3, 4, 5:1–6), (c) three denunciations beginning with "Woe" (5:7; 5:18; 6:1) and (d) three visions, constituting a unit, beginning with "Thus, the Lord showed me" (7:1, 4, 7).[26]

The second collection of prophecies (B), delivered after the encounter with Amaziah, will naturally show the stylistic traits characteristic of Amos. Again we have a vision beginning with "Thus, the Lord showed me" (8:1), and a prophecy beginning with "Hear" (8:4), besides a vision beginning with "I saw" (9:1), as well as material introduced by the clauses "it shall come to pass on that day" (8:9) and "behold, days are coming" (8:11 and 9:13). There is, therefore, no need to rearrange any section of the book.

Aside from clarifying the actual structure of the book, this theory of two prophetic collections sheds light upon Amos' thought. It has been universally recognized that "the scene at Beth-El marks a turning-point in Amos' thought."[27] If this be true, we should expect a marked change of attitude before and after the turning-point, nor are we disappointed in this expectation. The development of Amos' ideas may now be reconstructed as follows:

When Amos received a call to go to Israel, he was not assured of

success, but he had some hope that his message might help to save at
least a remnant in Israel. Hence in collection A, Israel is warned of
destruction but a modicum of hope is held out. The mighty will be
destroyed (2:14 f.) and the rich will be struck down with their possessions (3:15; 4:1 ff.) or go into exile (4:2 f.; 6:7). The suffering and ruin
of the people will be widespread (7:1 ff.). But if Israel will learn to
hate evil and establish justice, it may be that the Lord of Hosts will
have pity upon the remnant of Joseph (5:14 f. cf. 5:4, 6) and forgive
Jacob since it is weak (7:1–6). The people have but to seek the Lord
in truth (5:4) by striving after goodness, and God will be with them
(5:14), for it is justice that He demands above all things (5:24). It is
noteworthy that Amos proclaims only the destruction of the cult and
the political status quo in 7:9.[28]

Judah, on the other hand, is of slight interest to the prophet
during this period, since he is preoccupied with the destiny of Israel.
He is, however, too fair and too observant to overlook the sins of
Judah and he denounces its religious and social transgressions in no
uncertain terms (2:4 f.; 5:5c; 6:1a).

Then comes his encounter with Amaziah. Not only has Amos failed
to make a salutary impression, but further prophetic activity is forbidden him. We may perhaps discern his very human resentment
against this refusal to hear God's word in 8:11, 12, where he announces the day when men will be needing Divine guidance and
not finding it.[29]

As a result of his expulsion, Amos comes to the tragic conviction that
there is not the slightest hope for Israel. Hence in collection B, Israel's
total destruction is pictured. The end has come for My people Israel
(8:2); its crimes will never be forgotten (8:7); the sinful kingdom will
be totally destroyed (9:8).

Amos, however, is not only a prophet of the Lord; he is also a son
of his people.[30] He cannot believe that the house of Jacob will be
utterly destroyed. This conviction is more than an expression of kinship and group solidarity. After all, only the people of Israel, for all
their unworthiness, were aware of JHVH and bound by covenant
to Him. The total destruction of the nation would mean the total
annihilation of God's cause. How emerge from this impasse?

Exactly as Isaiah after him, his stern sense of justice declares that
the sinful people must be punished, but his innate love for his nation
does not let him acquiesce in its complete extinction. A generation

later, Isaiah solves the contradiction by his doctrine of the Saving Remnant, a process of moral selection in which only the morally fittest survive. Amos, confronting the problem at an earlier stage, solves it more simply—Israel is doomed, but Judah will be saved. The whole house of Jacob will not be utterly wiped out (9:8b). On the contrary, the Davidic dynasty will be restored to full power and hold sway over the kingdom once ruled by David (9:12). A noble Israel, obedient to God's will, will experience the genuine prosperity which is the reward of righteousness (9:13 ff.).[31]

We may summarize the discussion by the following theses:

1. The book of Amos consists of two collections of prophecies, with a historical record as a supplement to the first.

2. In the first collection, Amos still has hopes for a national salvation of Israel. Judah does not concern him greatly, though he is aware of its sins, and announces its punishment.

3. In the second collection, written after his expulsion from Beth-El, he sees only the complete destruction of Israel. It is to a reconstituted Judah that he looks for the survival of his people.

If these suggestions be adopted, there is no need for any extensive transfer or elimination of material. Barring minor additions, the book is the authentic work of Amos.

No less significant is the insight gained into the development of his personality and ideas. No longer need we assume a short period of activity and a long silence thereafter. Amos takes his place among the prophets not only as a dauntless teacher of the truth, but as a very human figure, knowing resentment and despair, but experiencing too the buoyancy of hope of one who deeply loves his people.

NOTES

1. Cf. E. Sellin, *Zwölfprophetenbuch* (Leipzig, 1922), p. 152; O. Eissfeldt, *Einleitung in das A. T.* (Tübingen, 1934), p. 441.

2. The doxology in 4:13, like those in 5:8 f. and 8:5 f., constitutes a distinct problem.

3. It is generally recognized that הַהֹפְכִים should be read as הוֹי הַהֹפְכִים. הוֹי may have been written as הֹ. Cf. 4:15.

4. Vv. 26–27 offer grave difficulties. The ingenious solutions proposed by H. Schmidt and Sellin do not carry complete conviction.

5. Cf. W. R. Harper, *ICC on Amos and Hosea* (New York, 1905), p. 168,
E. Baumann, *Der Aufbau der Amosreden* (Giessen, 1903), p. 14, Budde, *Z.
Geschichte des Buches Amos in Wellhausenfestschrift* (1914), pp. 65 ff., Sellin,
op. cit., pp. 156 ff., M. Löhr, *Untersuchungen zum Buch Amos* (Giessen, 1901,
Beihefte, ZATW, No. IV), pp. 26 f., Eissfeldt, op. cit., p. 442.

5a. Löhr, p. 10; Sellin, p. 158; Eissfeldt, p. 442.

6. S. O. Seesemann, *Israel und Juda bei Amos und Hosea* (Leipzig, 1898),
pp. 16 f., Nowack, *Die kleinen Propheten* (Göttingen, 1897), p. 126. Duhm omits
2:4 f. and the doxologies; Wellhausen and Cheyne add 9:8–15. Löhr rejects
2:4 f.; 5:5c; 8:14; 6:1a; 9:8 ff. (p. 13 a, e). Harper (p. cxxxii) omits 2:4 f. doubtfully; 9:8-15; G. A. Smith suspects 2:4 f., and rejects 9:8-15 decidedly. Sellin
removes 2:4 (because it contradicts 9:11 f. which he regards as original), 3:1a;
and *bᵉṣion* in 6:1. Eissfeldt omits 2:4 f. and 9:8–15.

7. Cf. Wellhausen, *Israelitische und jüdische Geschichte* (1894), p. 70; Cornill,
Prophetismus, p. 40. Seesemann, op. cit., pp. 3 and 4 assigns chs. 3–6 to Samaria,
and chs. 7–9 to Beth-El, and assumes that 7:10–17 marks the end of Amos'
activity. Also Sellin, p. 154, who assumes that after the expulsion Amos returned
to Judah and there wrote down his prophecies. On the other hand, Harper,
p. cxxix, says that Amos "continues for a while the work which he came north
to perform," but does not indicate whether any prophecies postdate his
expulsion.

8. Compare Joel 4:18 ff., Micah 7:14 ff. and such passages as Isaiah 60:1–17;
61:5–9, which can easily be augmented. Löhr claims that 2:4 f., 6:1 were added
because of the ritual use of the book in the synagogue. Actually the whole trend
of Rabbinic thought, which flowered during the period of Jewish subjugation,
was to deprecate and oppose the prophetic denunciations of Israel. Thus they
object to Isaiah's characterization of Israel as "a people of unclean lips" (Isa. 6:5)
and declare his alleged martyrdom to have been the penalty for this sin. Cf.
Yebamot 49b, Sanh. 103b and L. Ginzberg, *Legends of the Jews*, Vol. IV, pp. 263,
267; Vol. VI, p. 374, n. 103.

9. *Kazabh* occurs in the singular in Hos. 12:2, Ps. 40:5, and in the plural in
Hos. 7:13. Note also the use of *šikkusim* as early as Hos. 9:10.

10. The sections on Philistia, Tyre and Edom have been frequently deleted
(Harper, p. cxxxi; Eissfeldt, p. 444 "probably"). Sellin (pp. 165 f.) discusses the
objections raised against their authenticity and concludes that there are no
decisive grounds, either in fact or content, for rejecting them. He then proceeds
to eliminate Tyre, Edom and Judah on metrical grounds, which are not at all
conclusive. He also argues from the fact that these sections lack the concluding
formula *'amar Yahveh* found in the other four. Actually the desire for variety in
style, even within a compact structure, would account for this change perfectly.
It may be added that in the present text the use of the closing formula, *'amar
Yahveh* follows a definite scheme: It is used twice (Damascus v. 5, Gaza v. 6),
then omitted twice (Tyre, v. 10, Edom, v. 12), then used twice again (Ammon
v. 15, Moab 2:3), then omitted twice again (Judah 2:5, Israel 2:5). Sellin's final
reason for rejecting the section on Judah is its contradiction of 9:11 f., with
which we shall deal below. W. R. Smith, Kuenen, H. Schmidt, Köhler and

others have maintained the integrity of this passage. Cf. Driver, *Introduction to the Literature of the O. T.*, 12 ed. (1906), p. 318.

11. The seven examples are (1) two men meeting, (2, 3) the lion, two instances, (4, 5) the bird in the trap, two instances, (6) the trumpet, (7) the prophet.

12. They are (1) hunger (v. 6), (2) drought for crops (v. 7), (3) thirst in the city (v. 7,8), (4) blasting and mildew (v. 9), (5) locust (v. 9), (6) the plague (v. 10), (7) earthquake (v. 11).

13. Seesemann, p. 5, and Harper, p. 65, argue for the authenticity of this clause on slightly different grounds.

14. So Driver against Harper, who is doubtful about this passage and 8:14c (op. cit., p. 111).

15. Cf. Seesemann, p. 3, Löhr, op. cit., p. 17.

16. This phrase is generally regarded as a gloss because the Assyrian conquest of Hamath (720), Calneh (738) and Gath (711) took place after Amos' day. It may be left open whether early signs of weakness in these city-states could not have been obvious earlier to the keen gaze of the prophet, especially since the Assyrian conquerors proceeded piece-meal with their victims. (Cf. Is. 8:23 for the analogous treatment of Israel.) At all events, the gloss would be an early one, dating from the end of the eighth century (Harper, op. cit., p. 146).

17. "A Rhetorical Use of Interrogative Sentences in Biblical Hebrew" *(AJSL)*, Vol. XLIX, No. 3 (Apr., 1933), pp. 212–17.

18. The pronoun *hem* is understood after *hatobhim*. Cf. Ewald, *Lehrbuch* (Göttingen, 1863), sec. 303, b. 1. He compares also Psalm 16:8(sc. *hu'*), II Sam. 14:4 (sc. *'anaḥnu*), II Chron. 17:27 (sc. *hu'*), II Chron. 18:3 (sc. *'ani*); II Chron. 19:6 (sc. *hu'*).

19. Winckler's brilliant emendation of *derekh* into *dodekh* based on the Septuagint ὁ θεός σου has been widely accepted. The word, however, occurs only in proper names in the Bible (cf. II Chron. 20:37), and on the Mesha Inscription line 12. On the other hand, an oath "by the road to Beersheba" is paralleled by the Islamic oath "by the pilgrimage to Mecca"; cf. Harper and Sellin ad loc. If the Masoretic text be retained, the reference to "the road to Beersheba," like 5:5, testifies to a North Israelite point of origin.

20. The metaphor may be interpreted in two ways. The ṣᵉror may mean the corn, which remains in the fine sieve, after the dust is eliminated, and would thus refer to the righteous who are to be saved. Or it may mean "the stone" (cf. II Sam. 17:13), which is left behind in the coarse sieve, and hence be a symbol of the wicked who cannot escape punishment. Cf. Wetzstein in *ZDPV* (1891), pp. 1–7. In either case, there is a process of selection and hence a partial salvation.

21. Ps. 60:8–12 is particularly illuminating for our passage.

22. Krochmal, *More Nebuke Hazeman* (Berlin, 1934), chap. 7.

23. *Der Ursprung der israelitisch—juedischen Eschatologie* (Göttingen, 1905), passim. Cf. especially pp. 151 f.; 238 ff. and on our passage pp. 141, 209, 231, 255.

23a. When this paper was read at the Annual Meeting of the Society of Biblical Literature in December, 1939, Professor R. H. Pfeiffer kindly called our attention to the problem as to *where* the prophecies of the second collection were delivered. There is no decisive evidence on this point, but Amos' preoccupation with Israel's doom in chs. 8–9 would imply that he continued his activity somewhere in Israel, perhaps in Samaria. Even Beth-El is not ruled out, for the record (7:10–17) does not state that Amos was actually driven out, and it is he who has the last and decisive word. At all events, Amaziah's interdict proved no more successful than the later attempts made to prevent Jeremiah's activity.

24. That this collection had its earlier independent history goes without saying, but does not affect the argument.

25. Cf. Ben Sira 48:24 "With the spirit of might he beheld the future (*'aḥarith*) and comforted the mourners for Zion."

26. The historical reference in the opening section (cf. 1:1) is clear. The dating "two years after the earthquake" refers to the first period of Amos' activity, the literary remains of which are included in chaps. 1–7.

27. Harper, op. cit., p. cxxix.

28. It is Amaziah who seeks to heighten the impression by quoting Amos as announcing the death of Jeroboam himself and not merely of his dynasty, as well as the exile of the people (7:11). It is only as Amos is being expelled that he takes up these words of Amaziah and makes them part of his own message (7:17).

29. It is interesting that Amos couples the fruitless search for God's word with the perishing of youth. This association of idealism with youth is characteristic of Amos, cf. 2:11–12. The earlier passage indicates the sin, the later one the penalty, for suppressing the natural idealistic impulses of youth. There is no need, therefore, to eliminate 8:11b, 12b with Sellin, who thus leaves only the reference to a physical hunger in the text.

30. Eissfeldt's judgment on Amos (p. 446), "Denn Gott ist ihm alles, Israel nichts," while perhaps appropriate for a German theologian, is an impossible attitude for a Hebrew prophet.

31. One problem raised by the assumption of two collections divided at 7:17 must be discussed. That the four visions in 7:1–9 and 8:1–3 constitute a unit has been often taken for granted (so Löhr, op. cit., pp. 26 f.) though not always (cf. Driver, *ILOT*, 12 ed., pp. 315 f.). In the first two, the prophet interposes a plea for mercy and thus prevents the locusts and the fire from completing their deadly work. In the last two, the refrain is *lo' 'osiph od 'abhor lo* (7:9 and 8:2) and no plea for mercy would avail. The destruction of the cult and of the state is announced in the third vision, and the end of the people in the fourth.

If the fourth vision is regarded as distinct from the other three, there is no problem in the assumption that the first three belong to the first period and the fourth to the second. If they be regarded as a unit, the problem of the position of the narrative becomes especially acute, for the historical section is then inserted in the middle of a single utterance.

It seems most likely, however, that 8:1–3 is a distinct vision and that 7:1–9 constitutes a striking and effective unit. First one peril is averted by the prophet's plea, then another. The third time, no pleas will serve, for the catastrophe is certain—the cult and the state are doomed. The fourth vision would be an anticlimax by its repetition of the theme of doom. At a later time, of course, the prophet could return to the style of these visions, and pen another emphasizing his new conviction of the complete destruction of Israel (8:1–3).

It may be added that the fourth vision is not as identical in form with the first three, as is usually believed. In the latter, Jahveh appears himself, "He creates the locusts" (7:1), "He calls to judgment by fire" (7:4), and "He stands beside a wall" (7:7). In the fourth, Jahveh is not part of the vision at all. Besides, the word-play of *kais* and *kes* has no parallel in the earlier visions.

9. HOSEA'S MARRIAGE AND MESSAGE

I

For centuries, Biblical readers and scholars have wrestled with what has rightly been called "the vexed question of Hosea's marriage."[1] It would seem that every possible theory has already been advanced, with regard both to the actual nature of the event and the two accounts of the incident, A (chap. 1–2) and B (chap. 3).[2] Yet new treatments of the problem continue to appear.[3] Where so many views have been proposed, one may be permitted to suggest an additional theory, which will take as its point of departure the evidence of the literary documents before us.

Several views as to the character of Hosea's marriage have been advanced:

The first, the *non-literal view*, was particularly popular among the older commentators. They regarded it as morally repugnant that the Prophet would be commanded by God to marry an adulterous woman, and hence they ruled it out as impossible. Instead they assumed that the incident was an allegory or a dream[4] without any basis in real life. This view has rightly been abandoned by nearly all modern scholars.[5] Many of the details given are too concrete and realistic to be allegorical, besides having no figurative significance. Such are the name "Gomer, daughter of Diblaim," the reference to the weaning of a child (1:8), and the birth of a daughter rather than of a son as the second child (1:6). Moreover, the non-literal view does not meet the moral difficulty. For an act which is ethically objectionable in reality does not become defensible as a command in a vision.[6] Modern psychology has demonstrated that a patient under hypnosis will not execute a command which he would find morally repugnant when awake.

A second view suggests that *Hosea's marital experience was the cause of his prophetic activity*. According to this theory, proposed by Ewald and Wellhausen,[7] Hosea is conceived of as originally an ordinary

230

Israelite, who marries a woman of normally decent character, who later proves unfaithful. In his wrath he drives her forth from his home (2:4 ff.). Ultimately his love triumphs over his indignation, and he "loves her again" (3:1 f.), and takes her back. As Hosea ponders his tragic experience, he realizes that God's love for Israel cannot be of a lower moral quality than his own. He sees in his experience of betrayal, wrath and reconciliation a parallel to God's relationship to His people. Thus he becomes a Prophet of the Lord. He therefore recapitulates the incident under the aspect of a direct command of God (1:2), and interprets it as a parable of God's attitude toward Israel (2:4–22).

The dramatic features of this reconstruction have made this theory highly attractive to many scholars, as well as to general readers. Yet the human appeal of this theory is unable to obscure the difficulties under which it labors. That Gomer is called an "adulterous woman" at the outset might perhaps be explained away as a retrospective judgment based on her later behavior. But the symbolic names, "Jezreel," "Lo-Ruhammah" and "Lo-Ammi," given to the children at birth (1:4, 6, 9) rule out the view that Hosea did not become a prophet until *after* Hosea's separation from and reconciliation with his wife. For the giving to children of symbolic names possessing national or religious import is a characteristic form of prophetic activity, for which Isaiah is notable, as in the case of "Shear Yashub" (7:3, cf. 10:21) "Immanuel" (7:14, cf. 8:8, 10) and "Maher-shalal-hash-baz" (8:3). Moreover, the use of *'išāh* without the article in 3:1 rules out the possibility that we have here a reference to "the woman" already mentioned in chap. 1. Finally the clause in 3:1 cannot mean "go, love again the woman,"[8] unless we abandon all evidence of Biblical syntactic usage, as will be indicated below. Chapter 3 is therefore not the happy conclusion of the tragic estrangement described in chapters 1–2.

A third view believes that Hosea's *unfortunate marital experience was the result of his prophetic activity*.[9] According to this view, Hosea is a prophet, who is commanded by the Lord to marry an adulterous woman, in order to dramatize his message concerning the unfaithfulness of Israel.

Such symbolic acts belong to the oldest devices of Hebrew prophecy, being practiced by the popular seers whom the Bible stigmatizes as the false prophets (cf. I Kings 22:11; Jer. 28:10). The great literary prophets continued to employ this technique. Thus Isaiah is commanded to procreate a son and to give him a name that will announce the doom of the state (8:1 ff.), and to walk without a girdle and barefoot for three years and thus forecast the captivity of Egypt and Ethiopia (20:2 ff.). Similarly, Jeremiah is directed to make ropes to symbolize the need for subjugation to Nebuchadnezzar (27:2), and later is told to purchase a field at Anathot during the siege of Jerusalem, in order to dramatize his faith in national restoration (32:6 ff.). Ezekiel, in particular, is commanded to perform a variety of symbolic acts. He is bidden to build a model of the city on a brick (4:1 ff.), to sleep on one side for long periods (4:4. ff.), to write down the day of his prophesying (24:2), and, much later, to join two pieces of wood, in order to symbolize the ultimate reunion of Judah and Ephraim (37:16 ff.). Even more pertinent to our case are the instances where Ezekiel is commanded to perform acts that are repugnant and painful to him, either on religious or personal grounds. Such are the commands to shave his hair (5:1, cf. Lev. 19:27; Ezek. 44:20), to eat dung (4:12), against which he protests (4:14), and to witness the death of his beloved wife, without being permitted to fulfill any of the customary rites of mourning (24:15 ff.).

The theory accordingly suggests that it is in line with this well-attested practice of a prophetic "sign" that the three opening chapters of Hosea are to be understood. In obedience to the Divine command, the prophet marries an adulterous wife, by whom he has three children, who are given names that carry his message to the sinful people. It is part of the prophetic drama that he is enacting that he drives her from his home and then readmits her, to symbolize both Israel's estrangement from God and the possibility of Divine forgiveness.

This hypothesis, to be sure, avoids the difficulties of the preceding ones, but it suffers from major drawbacks of its own. The analogies from the prophetic activity of Isaiah, Jeremiah and Ezekiel are not quite parallel. Acts of discomfort may be enjoined upon the prophet, but they are still a very far cry from the command to marry an adulteress and to beget children who are illegitimate. The ancient Hebrew horror of adultery[10] went beyond the guilty parties and forbade the husband to continue to live with his faithless wife.[11] The status of children born in adultery was one of isolation from the community. That all this could be divinely ordered is difficult to believe.

Moreover, another, more crucial objection to this approach still remains. If Hosea knew of Gomer's disreputable character at the outset, there is no basis for his later indignation and for evicting her from his home. For where there is no trust at the beginning, there can be no betrayal at the end. Hosea's wrath under these circumstances would be purely artificial and indeed unjustified.

That is not all. The whole point of the parable is completely blunted, for its essence lies in the fact that Israel's *original* relationship to God was conceived of as one of complete fidelity and trust. That this was the prophetic conception is clear from Hosea himself (2:16), from Amos (5:25) and from Hosea's spiritual descendant, Jeremiah (2:1–3). The Prophets regard the desert period in Israel's history as marking the ideal relationship between God and His people.[12]

To meet the problems confronting these various theories, we should therefore like to present another view. Hosea is a prophet at the outset of his career. He is commanded by God to marry Gomer and beget children, whose names will symbolize the message of doom for Israel. She is described not as a harlot (*'išāh zōnāh*) but as a "woman of harlotry" (*'ēšeth zᵉnūnim*). The implication of the term is indicated by the succeeding clause (1:2c), "for the land is committing great harlotry against the Lord." The meaning of the phrase is to be sought in an analogous usage, in Isa. 6:5. When the young prophet, seeing the vision of God, cries out, "Woe is me, for I am undone, for I a ma man of unclean lips (*'iš tᵉmē sᵉphātayīm*) and I dwell in the midst of a people of unclean lips (*'am tᵉmē sᵉphātayyim*)," he is not accusing himself of personal impurity but, in accordance with basic Semitic and Hebrew attitudes of group solidarity, declaring that he is involved in the uncleanness of his people. Similarly, Gomer is "a woman of harlotry" not because she has personally violated her marriage vow but because she is implicated in the sinfulness of the nation, "for the land is committing harlotry against the Lord." Thus Gomer serves as a symbol of the adultery of Israel, as do her children, who are given names to recall Israel's bloody sin in the Valley of Jezreel and God's consequent lack of love for His people.

It is noteworthy that, after the birth of the children, all references to Gomer cease and the subsequent acts in the family drama are not described. It has been suggested that only the oldest child is Hosea's, hence the pronoun *lō* "she bore him a son" (1:3) which is lacking in the case of the other two children.[13] Be this as it may, her subsequent fortunes are not explicitly set forth and must be implied from the succeeding section (2:4 ff.) and from the second account (chap. 3). The discovery of Gomer's adultery, her expulsion from Hosea's home and her restoration are left undescribed, because the ground now shifts to the relationship of God and His faithless people Israel, with regard to whom the denunciation and rehabilitation are traced (2:4–20; 1–3).

The modern, Western reader may find this shift from personal history to prophetic parable disconcerting. But the key lies in the Hebrew concept of "fluid personality," to which H. W. Robinson and O. Eissfeldt independently called attention in treating the problem of the identity of the Servant of the Lord in Deutero-Isaiah.[14] The Servant Songs have long proved difficult, since they contain certain features that obviously refer to the people collectively and others that mirror individual traits.[15] Hence neither the collective interpretation, which refers the poems to Israel, nor the various theories, which refer it to one individual[16] do justice to every detail in the Servant Songs. The point of departure is the Prophet's role as a teacher of the Exilic community, serving as the messenger of the God of Israel to his co-religionists. This position he identifies with the function which Israel is destined to play among the nations. Hence the descriptions of the Servant contain both individual and collective features, with now one and now the other predominating. Rowley concludes a brief discussion on the identity of the Servant with this sound judgment: "It seems wiser, therefore, to adopt no simple individual or collective view. It is probable that the Servant is in part the personification of the mission of Israel, and in part the delineation of one who should embody its mission in himself . . . . the servant is both the community and the individual who represents it."[17] In North's summary, "the ebb and flow of Deutero-Isaiah's thought was from Israel to his own prophetic consciousness and back to Israel."[18]

The concept of "fluid personality" is generally assumed to be based on the idea of primitive psychology propounded by Lévy-Brühl[19] and E. Durkheim.[20] Actually, the validity of the concept of "fluid personality" rests upon the evidence in the Old Testament itself, and it is by no means exhausted by the Servant of the Lord Songs in Deutero-Isaiah.

It may be suggested that the age-old problem of "I" in the Psalms finds its solution in the same psychological phenomenon. In countless Psalms, the poet seems to be describing his own personal lot in unmistakable terms and then imperceptibly the ground shifts to his group or to his people as a whole.[21]

The problem of interpretation in the Psalms has been met in several ways. Formerly, critics fell back upon the assumption of multiple authorship in order to explain the discrepancy. This atomistic approach is, however, no longer as popular as it was in the past. It is particularly inapplicable to the Psalms, where it would mean dividing short literary units into mere fragments. Commentators have therefore adopted one of two alternatives. One view, going back to antiquity, has maintained that the "I" in the Psalms is always to be understood collectively, since the Psalter is a congregational hymn-book[22] and has admitted only a few isolated exceptions to the rule. It is undeniable that this view overlooks strongly individualistic traits in many Psalms. The other theory has insisted vigorously that the "I Psalms are all to be understood individually."[23] Thus Balla, a leading protagonist of this position, argues that only Psalm 129 is collective in meaning. Pfeiffer agrees that "the Psalter is on the whole the handbook of personal religion," but in view of the fact that many of the Psalms reflect group-traits is constrained to admit that "in the last analysis the situation is not entirely clear."[24] The conflict between the individual and collective interpretation of the Psalter is actually reflected in variations between singular and plural, registered in the Biblical text itself.[25]

The dilemma posed by these two contradictory theories dissolves when it is recognized that the Psalms reflect the same concept of fluid or corporate personality. The impetus to the Psalmist's outpouring of soul lies in his own individual experience, his physical anguish or the taunts of his foes, his sense of sin or his feeling of faith triumphant and joyous thanksgiving. But his individuality blends with that of the group in society with which the poet is associated or with the entire people of Israel of which he is a part. Hence it is not possible at every point to determine whether it is the individual or the group whom the Psalmist has in mind—he himself might be unable to give a definite answer, for both coalesce in his consciousness. This concept is a significant clue to the understanding of the Psalms.[25a]

It is also significant in understanding the patriarchal history in Genesis. It has of course long been noted that, to quote Dougherty, "in this ancient literary genre, personal and tribal history shade off into each other."[26] Actually the phenomenon is more complex than this description indicates. Not only do the lives of the patriarchs in Genesis exhibit both unmistakable personal traits and equally clear eponymous characteristics, but the transition from one to the other and back again is made with complete disregard of the logical canons and literary sensibilities familiar to the modern reader. Nor is this all. Often the narrative blends both the personal and the tribal aspects simultaneously.[27] The key here too is to be found in the concept of fluid personality, in which the patriarchs are flesh-and-blood individuals and yet coalesce with the people who trace their descent from them.

It should be added that this approach is by no means limited to the ancient world. Medieval Hebrew poetry which is, to be sure, based upon Biblical models, reveals the same phenomenon. This is not a matter of borrowing, but of a basic pattern of thought congenial to any stage of civilization.[28] Modern psychoanalysis has suggested the source of the concept in the phenomenon of "identification." This is defined as "the self-definition of the Ego in terms of some other person, initially the father or the mother . . . Identification is the mechanism underlying grouping . . . Each member of the group identifies himself with the others, via the prior identification of himself with the leader, who thus replaces the parent of the family group."[29] One need by no means accept Freud's conception of God as nothing but a Father-image, in order to recognize that the Prophet's entire activity is an identification with his God, whose instrument he has become.

This process of "identification" is the key to the understanding of chapter 2 in Hosea. After beginning with his own marital experience (chap.1), the prophet goes over to the subject of God's unhappy relationship with Israel, which parallels the event in his own household.[30] Yet the transition between the two is not altogether abrupt (2:4 ff.). Verse 4 constitutes a bridge:

> Plead with your mother, plead;
> For she is not my wife, neither am I her husband;[30a]
> And let her put away her harlotries from her face,
> And her adulteries from between her breasts.

These words, as T. H. Robinson has acutely noted, are "a remarkable combination of the collectivistic and individualistic conception of the people, with *Israel being regarded as a single person and the members of the people as her children*" (*italics ours*).[31] However, Robinson has failed to ask a most pertinent question,—what purpose is served by this combination, which is logically self-contradictory, for the mother and the children both refer to the people of Israel? What gain, psychological or literary, is achieved by dissociating the mother and the children? The answer lies in the process of "identification" which here finds its transition-point. In this verse, Hosea undoubtedly has in mind his prophetic message of the Lord's betrayal by Israel, but he is operating with the human figures of his personal tragedy. *The children who are being called upon to reprove their mother are Hosea's actual children, and they are, naturally, personalities distinct from their mother.* In verse 5, it is still the human husband who promises dire vengeance upon his adulterous wife:

> Lest I strip her naked,
> And set her as in the day that she was born,
> And make her as a wilderness,
> And set her like a dry land.

Only in the very last clause of verse 5, "And I shall slay her with thirst" and in verse 6,

> And I will not have compassion upon her children;
> For they are the children of harlotry,

does the transition become complete and the human husband dissolve into the Divine.

This transition from parable to message, from man to God, finds a striking parallel in Isaiah's "Song of the Vineyard" (5:1 ff.). Here the parable of the human ministrel and his vineyard is sustained from the beginning through v. 5 and v. 6a:

> And now come, I will tell you
> What I will do to my vineyard:
> I will take away the hedge thereof,
> And it shall be eaten up;
> I will break down the fence thereof,
> And it shall be trodden down;
> And I will lay it waste:
> It shall not be pruned nor hoed,
> But there shall come up briers and thorns.

Thus far the human owner of the vineyard speaks. But then comes 6b:—

> I will also command the clouds
> That they rain no rain upon it!

It becomes resoundingly clear that it is God and not a human being who is speaking.

Once the transition has been effected in Hos. 2:5e and 6 from the human to the cosmic plane, the personal lot of Hosea's wife is no longer of interest and is not referred to again in the chapter. That there was a reawakening of conscience, a period of penance, and a restoration to favor for the erring wife is to be inferred from the parable, which is now developed by the prophet (2:6 ff.). These developments are also indicated, with significant changes that are still to be discussed below, in the independent parallel account in chapter 3.

The prophet now utilizes the parable to foretell the tragic consequences of Israel's career of infidelity and degradation. As troubles overwhelm her, she will discover that it was not her Baal-lovers who were the source of her well-being. Her remorse will grow with her suffering and privation. The Lord will visit upon her all the days of the Baalim that she had been wont to celebrate, probably exposing her to an equivalent period of want to atone for her period of wantonness, on the principle of *lex talionis* (2:15). Similarly, the generation of the desert had to expiate for forty years the sin of the faithless spies who had explored Canaan for forty days (Num. 14:34). After this period of suffering, God will lead her out to the Wilderness, far from the corrupting influence of Canaanite civilization, and gently persuade her to return to Him. The Lord, who is the true source of Israel's well-being, will restore her vineyards,[32] the very symbol and center of the Baal cult, as of yore.[33] Israel will again respond to God's call as in the days of her innocent youth following the Exodus from Egypt (v. 17) and never again sink into Baal worship (vv. 18, 19). The relentless struggle against nature and the war against human foes will cease (v. 20). The Lord will betroth Israel to Himself in an everlasting bond (vv. 21, 22). The name "Jezreel" will now symbolize not the sin of Israel's past but God's sowing in the land, and the portentous names of the other two children will be changed to "My People" and "Beloved" (v. 25). In the three concluding verses of the prophecy, which have been placed by error at the beginning of the chapter,[34] Israel will become as numerous as the sands of the sea, while Judah and Israel, once more united under one ruler, will dwell secure in God's favor and love (vv. 1–3).

Thus a tragic event in the life of the prophet Hosea is made to serve

as a *message of warning* and as a *call to repentance* for the sinful people
of Israel.

II

At least as complex as the nature of the events described in chapters
1–2 is the problem raised by the existence of chapter 3. This second,
much briefer account of Hosea's personal life, is written in the first
person. The narrative tells how the Lord spoke to the Prophet again
(*'ōdh*) and asked him to "love a woman who is beloved by her husband,[35] yet practices adultery, as the Lord loves the children of Israel,
but they turn to other gods."[36] Hosea takes the woman in marriage,
as is clear from the misunderstood verb *nākar*, which is used here of
purchase in marriage.[37] The price he pays for her is that of a slave.[38]
He then tells her that she is to dwell in his home as his wife,[39] but
with no relations either with her former lovers or with him. This
period of separation is obviously intended to serve her as a time of
penance and purification. So, too, the children of Israel will dwell a
long time without king or Lord, sacrifice or pillar, ephod or teraphim.
Afterwards, they will seek the Lord their God and David their king,
and "come trembling" to the Lord and His goodness.

How are these two accounts (chap. 1–2 and chap. 3), which are
strikingly similar without being identical, related to each other, and
how are they to be evaluated? Here, too, various views have been
propounded:

1. Chapter 3, though written in the first person, is not authentic.[40]

2. Chapter 1 is un-historical, while chapter 3 is authentic.[41]

It is unnecessary to enter upon any detailed refutation of these
opposing and equally unsatisfactory views. Those who entertain
them are completely arbitrary in deciding what is or is not authentic.
Nor does one solve a problem by pretending that its elements do not
exist.

3. The two accounts were originally one and were expanded by
interpolators. Thus Sellin regards as authentic only the passages
written in the first person. Accordingly, he reconstructs and rearranges the original narrative and claims that it consists only of 1:2b;
3:1a, 3, 4, 5a, δ; 1:3a; 3:2.

The highly subjective nature of Sellin's procedure need not be

labored. He creates a mosaic out of the three chapters, and reduces
the 34 verses of the Masoretic text to a narrative which contains only
three full verses and 3 fragments.

4. The two accounts represent two distinct incidents.[42] The first
incident dealt with a good woman named Gomer, whose description
as 'ēseth zᵉnūnim is purely figurative and means virtually "a woman of
poor surroundings."[43] The second incident refers to the purchase of
a street-walker, with whom the prophet never has any relations. In
favor of the view that there was a second incident, it is pointed out
that the phrase in 3:1a וַיֹּאמֶר ה׳ אֵלַי עוֹד לֵךְ אֱהַב־אִשָּׁה must mean, "The
Lord said to me again, 'Go love a woman, etc.',", not, as often given
"And the Lord said unto me, 'Go, yet, love a woman, etc.' " or, "Go
again, love a woman, etc."[44]

Now, it is true this view does justice to the syntax of the adverb
'ōdh ("said again") in 3:1, as against those who construe it with the
verbs "go and love," as will be noted below. But this virtue aside, the
theory of two distinct incidents in Hosea's life suffers from several
grave drawbacks. The basic similarity of the incidents in the two
accounts cannot be ignored. In both, the prophet is commanded by
God to marry a woman of low repute (1:2; 3:1). In both, there is a
temporary period of estrangement (2:4 ff.; 3:3). In both, the conclusion
of Hosea's personal experience is not given explicitly, but dissolves
into the parable of the reconciliation of God and Israel (2:16 ff.; 3:5).
In both, this Divine forgiveness parallels a reconciliation between the
figures in the human drama. The inference that there was such a
reconciliation between Hosea and his wife is certain, not only because
without it the whole point of the parable is lost, but also by the actual
language in the text. The passage 2:22 f. is surely the formula of a
human betrothal, while 2:25 and 2:3, which conclude the prophecy,
mention Hosea's children by name and thus specifically relate to
Hosea's family life. It is stretching the long bow of coincidence very
far to say that the Prophet underwent so unusual an experience not
once but twice.

Moreover, this theory, in its laudable zeal for the rehabilitation of
Gomer, gives the phrase 'ēseth zᵉnūnim a very forced meaning. Granted
that the phrase may be less condemnatory than zōnāh, "harlot," it
must nevertheless carry a negative connotation stronger than "a
woman of poor surroundings."

This theory encounters additional and even more striking difficulties in chapter 3, as already set forth in our summary of the narrative. That we are dealing here with a married woman and not a street-walker is abundantly clear from a) the verb *nā'aph* "commit adultery," b) the verb *nākar* "purchase, in marriage," c) the price indicated for the woman, which is a purchase price and too high for a harlot's wage (*'ethnān*) d) and the use of *tēshbhī lī*, which implies a wife's dwelling in her husband's house. Moreover, the command, "love (*'ehabh*) a woman" (3:1), implies that there was a period of intimate relationship before the separation. Finally, the phrase "many days shalt thou sit" (v. 3) definitely implies that the period of separation is not permanent but will be succeeded by a restoration.

5. By a process of elimination, there is the only remaining possi-bility—that we have two accounts of the same experience, a view which avoids the difficulties set forth above.[45] That some scholars have nevertheless preferred one of the other views is due to two problems which have not been satisfactorily solved by the proponents of this view. The first is the meaning of *'ōdh* in 3:1, and the second, the purpose and significance of the two accounts.

With regard to the syntax of 3:1, some have attempted to argue that the Masoretes construe *'ōdh* with *lēkh* by placing the disjunctive accent *rebhī'a* on *'ēlai*. Actually no conclusion may be drawn from the Masoretic accentuation, since *'ōdh* is also marked by a disjunctive accent *yethīb*, so that the adverb stands apart both from the preceding and the following word.[46] Evidently the Masoretes preferred to leave the problem of construing the adverb to the reader! What is of greater moment, there is no sound warrant for construing *'ōdh* with *lēkh* "go" which follows. In the meaning of "again," *'ōdh invariably* follows its verb.[47] An exact syntactic parallel to our passage occurs in Ex. 4:6:

$$\text{וַיֹּאמֶר ה' לוֹ עוֹד הָבֵא־נָא יָדְךָ בְּחֵיקֶךָ}$$

"The Lord said to him again, 'Place thy hand in thy bosom.' " The only sound procedure is to construe *'ōdh* with the preceding verb, "The Lord said to me again." But what is the meaning of this opening clause in 3:1 ? It has been suggested that the adverb was added by an editor who, having the other account before him, felt it incumbent to take note of this second call to Hosea by adding the adverb "again." On that basis, it has been deleted.[48] Getting rid of obstinate facts in favor of a theory can hardly be described as sound scientific method.

We believe that a solution to the problem is available which does not do violence to the phenomena. We suggest that *the two accounts represent two interpretations by the prophet of the same experience, but at different periods in his career and from varying viewpoints.* In other words, the two accounts are the records of two revelations to the prophet, and the opening clause in 3:1 refers to the second revelation: "The Lord spoke to me again" i.e. on the same theme.

The nub lies in the answer to the second question: What is the purpose of the two accounts? The many similarities in the two narratives which we have set forth above have of course been noted by scholars, and they demonstrate that one incident and not two are referred to. But attention has not been focussed on the differences in the two narratives (A, chap. 1–2; B, chap. 3) which are of basic significance:

Account A revolves about the children, whose names in their original form dramatize the prophet's denunciation of Israel, while their changed forms emphasize his hopes for the repentance of his people. Account B makes no mention of the children at all. Two decades after their birth, the significance of their naming would have faded completely, particularly in view of the drastically altered historical circumstances.

Account B stresses the period of separation which will serve as penance for Israel's sin, devoting two verses (3:3–4) out of five to this theme. Account A, on the other hand, speaks at length of Israel's discomfiture and punishment (2:5–15), but makes only a very brief reference to Israel's penance (2:15a). Nor is there any mention of a period of separation after Israel becomes conscious of her faithlessness.

While account A speaks of the reunion of Judah and Israel (2:2), the second account goes further and links the return to God with a return to the Davidic dynasty (3:5). To be sure, critics have deleted these and all other references to Judah in *Hosea*.[49] However, this is an arbitrary procedure which effaces a very significant element in Hosea's activity, indeed, in the outlook of all the Hebrew prophets, as will be indicated below.

The differences between the two accounts find a natural explanation in the chaotic conditions of the closing years of the Northern Kingdom, which coincided with Hosea's prophetic activity.

Account A may be dated with considerable certainty as emanating from the period before 743 B.C.E. The passage in 1:4, "I shall visit the blood of Jezreel on the house of Jehu," which foretells the doom of Jehu's dynasty, must precede the murder of Zechariah, the last scion of the dynasty, which took place in that year.[50] At that time, more than twenty years before the destruction of Samaria, the state is basking in apparent prosperity and well-being, the heritage of Jeroboam the Second's able and successful reign. Hosea, beginning his prophetic career, is imbued with the optimism of youth with regard to his calling. Like Amos, he is aware of the inner corruption and weakness beneath the façade of national self-confidence. But he has hopes that his words will lead the people to repent their betrayal of their God. Without that hope, his activity would be meaningless. He therefore castigates the people and warns them of the imminent destruction, by giving symbolic names to his children. But the headlong plunge to national catastrophe (II Kings 15:8 ff.) cannot be averted by the prophetic word. The regicide of Zechariah after six months is followed by that of Shallum within one month. The next king, Menahem (743–737 B.C.E.), is forced to pay a tribute of one thousand silver talents to Tiglat Pileser in 738. His son, Pekahiah, is murdered two years after he ascends the throne by Pekah, whose ill-fated effort to throw off the Assyrian yoke leads to the loss of Galilee and Gilead in 733, and to his murder by Hoshea, who is a vassal of Assyria. When he attempts to revolt, condign punishment is the result, and the destruction of Samaria takes place in 721.

In these calamitous last days, Hosea no longer feels that there is any chance of saving the state. Both during the final agonies of Samaria and the bleak, hopeless days following its destruction, Hosea develops a new facet of his activity. His concern is with the people of Israel, the bulk of whom remained in the land after the Assyrian victory.[51] Not destruction, but consolation now becomes the burden of his teaching.

It is a pattern which was to be repeated again and again by the prophets of Israel. Thus Isaiah, who had opposed Judah's resistance to the Assyrian overlord, and announced the doom of the country, changes his attitude in the critical hour when Sennacherib's hosts threaten the Holy City (Isa. 36–38). Similarly Jeremiah, who had urged submission to Babylonia and foretold the dire consequences of rebellion, becomes a messenger of hope and rebuilding when the blow descends (Jer. chap. 30; 32), and despair grips the people. His younger contemporary, Ezekiel, who had foretold the same catastrophe and had gone into exile himself, undergoes the same metamorphosis from despair to faith. When the exiles are convinced that "all hope is lost, we are utterly cut off" (37:11), he experiences the Vision of the Valley of Dry Bones. Like Jeremiah, he looks forward to the reunion of Judah and the survivors of the Kingdom of Israel (37:12–14, 15–28). We have suggested that Amos, Hosea's older contemporary, after his trying experience with Amaziah at Beth-El, transferred his hope and desire for the survival of his people from the Kingdom of Israel to that of Judah.[52]

A similar shift of emphasis takes place in Hosea's thought, after all outward signs seem to point to the death of hope. It is upon Israel's restoration that Account B places its accent. It does not refer to the children, whose birth had taken place two decades before, and whose names, with their message of warning, no longer have relevance to the life of a broken people. The story of his wife's infidelity, symbolic of Israel's attitude to its God, is summarized in a brief phrase. Instead, it emphasizes God's love for Israel. Its basic theme is that a period of penance must necessarily intervene before reconciliation can come. During this period, there will be no independent political life for the Kingdom of Israel and no practice of the accepted religious ritual, *to both of which Hosea is opposed*.[53] The existence of a separatist Northern state and the succession of royal assassinations are both repugnant to him, as are the idolatrous and syncretistic religious practices of the people.

The theme of 3:4, as Tur-Sinai has acutely noted, is very similar to the passage in II Chron. 15:3–4: "Now for long seasons Israel was without the true God and without a teaching priest and without law; but when, in their distress they turned unto the Lord, the God of Israel, and sought Him, He was found of them." The spirit of Hosea's utterance, however, is quite different. While the Chronicler anticipates the *restoration* of these absent features of the national life, which he favors, Hosea looks forward to their permanent *elimination*. The Baal worship will be replaced by a sincere return to the God of Israel and the Northern Kingdom be replaced by reunion of Israel with Judah under the Davidic dynasty. Verses 4 and 5 thus stand in direct contrast with each other, in a chiastic arrangement. The present status "without a king or lord" (v. 4b) is opposed by Israel's return to "David their king" (5c) and the absence of "sacrifice or pillar, ephod, or teraphim" (4c, d) is replaced by Israel's future loyalty to "the Lord their God" (5b), when "they will come in trembling to the Lord and His goodness in the end of days."

This emphasis upon a united Hebrew nation, as representing the Divinely ordained consummation of Israel's history, is a basic attitude of the Prophets, who helped forge a sense of national unity out of the clan loyalties of the nomadic period. Whether the division of the kingdom represented a true secession, as tradition maintains, or simply a dissolution of the dual monarchy, as some modern students have suggested, the standpoint of the Biblical historians, who wrote in the spirit of the Prophets, is clear—for them Jeroboam's act was a national crime and a heinous sin against God. Hence Jeroboam ben Nebat and his successors are invariably stigmatized in blackest colors in the Book of Kings (I Kings 14:8 ff., 16 and *passim*), while the literary prophets look forward to a reunited Hebrew nation.[54] For whether they were northerners or southerners in origin, all the prophets regarded themselves as sons of the people of Israel and became the authentic creators of Hebrew nationalism.[55]

To be sure, for the prophets, national patriotism was not the ultimate ideal but the gateway to the more universal loyalty to humanity. That development, however, for which Amos, Isaiah, and Deutero-Isaiah were principally responsible, never denied the worth of nationalism, which was to be cultural in content and moral in expression, recognizing the over-arching sovereignty of God. Before that level could be reached, the hatreds and suspicions of tribal and sectional divisions had to be conquered by a sense of loyalty to the undivided people of Israel. It was to this task that Hosea, like Jeremiah and Ezekiel after him, addressed himself.

This ideal of national unity, which the prophets had helped to fashion during the period of political independence, they succeeded in preserving after the destruction of the state. In a time of apparent prosperity and power, they announced the inevitable catastrophe. But when the blow had descended upon the wayward people that they loved, they again contradicted the obvious realities and sounded a message of hope and reconstruction.

Hosea stands in this tradition. He had undergone a soul-shattering personal experience. Twice he turned to it during his subsequent career and found in it appropriate guidance for his people. So long as there still was hope for the nation, he utilized his personal tragedy to dramatize the theme of Divine chastisement, Israel's repentance and God's forgiveness. Two decades later, when the national life of the people was all but destroyed, he discovered a new meaning in his personal suffering and moral triumph—and he used his dearly won insights to sound for his people the note of regeneration through unity and faith.

NOTES

1. Cf. H. H. Rowley in *Book List of Society of O. T. Study*, 1951, p. 46.

2. For a conspectus of the older views, cf. W. R. Harper, *ICC on Hosea-Amos* pp. 208–210. The later views are summarized and criticized in R. H. Pfeiffer, *Introduction to O.T.* (New York 1941) pp. 566–569.

3. Three recent treatments are to be found in Y. Kaufmann, *Toledot Ha'emunah Hayisreelith* (Tel Aviv, 1947), vol. 6, pp. 93–107; J. Coppens, *Les Douze petits prophètes* (Bruges, 1950); N. H. Tur-Sinai, *Halashon Vehasefer* (Jerusalem, 1950), vol. 2, pp. 304–323. Kaufmann ascribes the book to two prophets, Proto-Hosea (chap. 1–3) and Deutero-Hosea (chap. 4–14). The former was a Judean prophet who lived during the reign of Jehoram ben Ahab (853–842), a century before the second prophet. To bolster his theory, Kaufmann removes the reference to בֵּית יֵהוּא in 1:4 by reading בֵּית יְהוֹרָם (*op. cit.* p. 99). Not only in this procedure entirely arbitrary, but his view suffers from other drawbacks as well. He is led to the assumption of two Hoseas by his pressing of the argument *e silentio.* Thus he argues that the chap. 1–3 do not refer to ethical transgressions, as do chap. 4–12 (p. 94). Not only is this not quite accurate, for 1:4 deals with an ethical sin, that of murder, but Hosea's negative attitude toward the monarchy is expressed in both parts of his book (cf. 3:4; 8:4). See below. In general he stresses religious infidelity more than ethical failings everywhere in his book. Nor is it to be expected that every section will present all facets of his thought. See also note 5 below.

Tur-Sinai, in line with his general view that the prophetic and poetical books of the Old Testament were originally imbedded in a vast historical work (cf. *op. cit.* p. 312), regards the two accounts as two variants of the same incident, paralleling other Biblical dittographs. He tends to prefer the prose narrative of chap. 3 as closer to the facts than the poetic expansion of chap. 1–2. He reads an erotic symbolism into the name "Gomer, daughter of Diblaim" and maintains that Hosea is a Judean, not an Israelite, who welcomes the destruction of the Northern Kingdom as a prelude to the restoration of Judah. These views of a brilliant scholar are stimulating, but we do not find them convincing.

4. Ibn Ezra, Maimonides, David Kimhi, Hengstenberg, Keil, among others, treat it as an allegory; Rashi, DeWette, Hitzig, Bleek, Reuss, Koenig, among others, as a dream.

5. The theory has been recently revived in a modified form by Kaufmann who sees in chap. 1–3 not a literary allegory but a "prophetic-dramatic allegory" (p. 103). He interprets the phrase *'ēsheth zᵉnūnīm* (1:2) to mean "a woman acting the role (*tafkīd*) of a harlot" by wearing the garb characteristic of such women (p. 102 ff.). Chapter 3 he refers to another woman. We find the interpretation of 1:2 far-fetched and the assumption of two distinct incidents difficult (see below). Kaufmann's view is very close to that of Guthe, on which see below note 42.

6. For other cogent objections to this view, see Harper, *op. cit.* p. 208.

7. Accepted by W. R. Smith, Kuenen, G. A. Smith, Nowack, *inter alios*.

8. On this rendering of 3:1a see below.

9. So Sellin, following Volz and Gressmann.

10. Cf. the Decalogue (Ex. 20:14; Deut. 5:17) and Deut. 22:25.

11. Cf. the primitive ordeal of the suspected wife (Num. 5:11 ff.). Note particularly the phrase 5:31a — "the husband shall be free from sin." The strength and persistence of this attitude is clear in the Talmudic principle כשם שאסורה לבעל כך אסורה לבועל "As the adulterous woman is forbidden to her husband, so she is forbidden (ever after) to her paramour" (B. Sotah 28a); טמאה לבעל טמאה לבועל טמאה לתרומה. "She is unclean (and forbidden) with regard to her husband, her paramour and the heave-offering" *Sifre, Numbers* (ed. Friedmann) sect. 7, p. 4a; sect. 19, p. 6b. Cf. L. M. Epstein, *Sex Laws and Customs in Judaism* (New York 1948) p. 199: "The Biblical law of adultery... makes adultery a moral crime rather than an injury to the husband... The husband cannot forgive his wife and his forgiveness has no bearing on the crime of the adulterer." The silence of Biblical law on the subject of possible forgiveness by the husband is in striking contrast with the provisions in other Oriental codes. Thus the Code of Hammurabi (par. 129) permits the husband to forgive his adulterous wife and extends to the king the right to spare her adulterous partner. Similar provisions obtain in the Assyrian Code (Part I, par. 14–16) and the Hittite Code (par. 198). The documents are conveniently accessible in J. M. P. Smith, *Origin and History of Hebrew Law* (Chicago, 1931), in the translations of D. D. Luckenbill, pp. 181 ff. and A. Walther, pp. 181 ff., and G. R. Driver-J. C. Miles, *The Babylonian Laws* 2nd ed. (Oxford 1952). As Hosea's experience indicates, men undoubtedly did forgive their erring wives *post eventum* (cf. Ezek. 16:63), but that the Lord would command Hosea to marry such a woman *in advance* and beget children who would bear the ineradicable taint of illegitimacy forever after (cf. Deut. 23:2), is most unlikely.

12. Cf. K. Budde, "The Nomadic Ideal in the O.T.," in the *New World*, vol. IV, pp. 726–45; J. W. Flight, "Nomadic Idea and Ideal in the O.T." in *JBL*, vol. 42, pp. 158–226; R. Gordis, "The Bible—Its Origin, Growth, and Meaning," in this volume. S. W. Baron's strictures on Budde and Flight in *A Social and Religious History of the Jews* 2nd ed. (New York 1952, vol. 1, pp. 335 f.) are not convincing. That the nomadic age was not as idyllic as it was pictured in the folk-memory and the thinking of the prophets, may be true, but this does not justify the assumption that the nomadic ideal played a "relatively minor role" or that the prophets are harking back to "the golden age of Adam or Abraham." Adam is practically never referred to in the Prophets. (If Hos. 6:7 refers to Adam, it is his sin, not his perfection that is mentioned.) Abraham is named only a few times and then only in the later prophets (Isa. 41:8; 51:2; Ezek. 33:24; II Chron. 20:7). On the other hand, the "golden age" of the prophets is the wilderness period after the Exodus (cf. e. g. Amos 5:25; Jer. 2:1 ff.). Cf. also Ehrlich's interpretation of Isa. 4:6.

13. Cf. Harper, *op. cit.* p. 211; Sellin, *ad loc.*

14. Cf. H. W. Robinson, *The Cross of the Servant—A Study in Deutero-Isaiah*

(London 1926) and "The Hebrew Concept of Corporate Personality" in *Werden und Wesen des A.T.*, ed. J. Hempel, 1936, pp. 49 ff.; O. Eissfeldt, *Der Gottesknecht bei Deuterojesaia* (Halle, 1933); H. H. Rowley, *The Servant of the Lord and other Essays* (London 1952), esp. pp. 33 ff.; 38 f.

15. For an admirable survey of the entire subject, cf. C. R. North, *The Suffering Servant in Deutero-Isaiah* (Oxford, 1948) and Rowley, *op. cit.*, pp. 3–88.

16. Such as Zerubbabel, or some other scion of the Davidic house, Moses, Uzziah, Ezekiel, the martyr Eleazar of the Maccabean period, Cyrus, an anonymous contemporary of the prophet, whom he regarded as the Messiah, or the prophet himself.

17. Cf. his "Meaning of Sacrifice in O.T." in *Bulletin of John Rylands Library*, vol. 33, 1950, pp. 108 f.

18. *Op. cit.* pp. 215 f.

19. Cf. his *How Natives Think* (1926).

20. Cf. his *Elementary Forms of the Religious Life* (1915).

21. For the statement of the problem, cf. the Introductions to the standard commentaries of W. R. Harper, R. Kittel and Hans Schmidt.

22. This interpretation is to be met with in the LXX, the Church Fathers, and the medieval Jewish commentators, and was defended by R. Smend, in *ZATW*, vol. 8, 1888, pp. 49 f., and Th. Engert, *Der betende Gerechte der Psalmen* (Würzberg 1902).

23. E. Balla, *Das Ich der Psalmen* (Göttingen, 1912), who was preceded by G. Beer, G. Coblenz and H. Roy.

24. Cf. R. H. Pfeiffer, *Introduction to O.T.* (New York, 1941) p. 634.

25. Cf. Ps. 17:11 סבבוני Kethib, סבבונו Qere; 60.7 ועננו Kethib, וענני Qere; 71:20 הראיתנו, תחינו, תעלנו Kethib, הראיתני, תחיני, תעלני Qere; 108:7 וענני Kethib וענני Qere. Cf. R. Gordis, *The Biblical Text in the Making* (Phila. 1937) pp. 140 f. and the relevant notes for the evidence of the Versions.

25a. For an application of this approach to the exegesis of a specific Psalm, cf. Gordis, "Psalm 9–10: A Textual and Exegetical Study," in *JQR*, vol. 48, 1957, pp. 104–22.

26. Cf. his "The World of the Hebrew Patriarchs" in *Scripture*, vol.3, 1948, p. 98.

27. Note the rivalry of the brothers, the birthright, and the blessing, which exhibit both individual and collective elements (Gen. 25:19–34; 26). The dream of Jacob at Beth-El is personal (28:10–22) as are his love and marital experiences (chap. 29), while the birth of the children by his wives and concubines (chap. 30) reflects tribal history. His escape from Laban (chap. 31), his encounter with Esau and the incident at Peniel (chap. 32, 33) are largely personal history, while the Dinah tragedy (chap. 34) is obviously tribal, as practically all scholars have recognized. The Joseph story is basically personal, but the role of Judah and Reuben as would-be saviors of the lad have tribal overtones and these become explicit in Jacob's adoption of Manassah and Ephraim. The Judah-Tamar incident (chap. 38) is patently tribal.

28. We may cite part of a poem by the medieval Todros Halevi Abulafia (1247–1307) הלוא כסלי ביה (in his divan, *Garden of Parables and Riddles*, ed.

D. Yellin, part 2, vol. 1, 1934, p. 104, no. 657). At times, the first person represents the poet, who addresses the Daughter of Israel in second person feminine singular, at others the first person is used by the Daughter of Israel herself. The transition is also abrupt by our standards. The translation is our own.

> Is not my trust in God, my Dweller on high,
> Why art thou downcast, my soul, and why dost thou moan?
> My faith is in His mercies and love,
> Why shouldst thou then fear men?
> O honored one, fear not time, the mocker;
> Place thy faith in thy Maker . . .
> If I have sinned to him, I shall repent,
> With my voice implore, until he forgives my sin . . .
> And praise His name for good and for evil,
> And sing to Him when I lie down and when I rise up.
> And if despoiling foes have come to my house,
> And stretched their hand against my son and my mother,
> I shall yet master them, by God's power.

The reference to "my son and my mother" by the Daughter of Israel is an illuminating example of this dual process of dissociation and identification that sheds light on Hos. 2:4 discussed later in the text.

29. *Encyclopedia of the Social Sciences* (New York, 1946), vol. 11, p. 584b.

30. That 2:1–3 are misplaced is widely recognized. Their place is after v. 20, so that vv. 2:1–3 complete the theme of restoration, with the name "Jezreel" being given a favorable connotation (2:20) instead of its originally unfavorable meaning (1:4) and the negative names "Lo-ruhammah" and "Lo-ammi" being changed to the positive (2:20, 1,3). So also Kaufmann.

30a. In a personal communication, Prof. C. H. Gordon suggested that v. 4b "for she is not my wife and I am not her husband" is a formula of divorce and that stripping the faithless wife naked (v. 5) constitutes the legal act of divorcement in such cases. In support of this view he cited the usage attested in *Ḥana* and *Nuzu* and referred to *ZATW*, vol. 11 (1934) pp. 102–109; vol. 13 (1936) pp. 237 ff.; vol. 14 (1937), p. 176; *Archiv Orientálni*, vol. 9 (1937) p. 93; *Orientalia* vol. 10 (1941) p. 358. From the last reference it is clear that the passage Hos. 2:3–6 was cited in the formula of exorcism of demonesses in Talmudic Babylonia.

Nonetheless, we are unable to accept this interesting view of our passage because of several considerations, both general and specific. It is precisely in the field of "faith and morals" that Israel parted company most decisively with their neighbors in the Fertile Crescent. Undoubtedly there are many parallels between Israel and her environment, but they must be buttressed by concrete evidence from Hebrew and Jewish sources, before they can be regarded as certain. No evidence of such a procedure in divorce is to our knowledge available in Biblical and Rabbinic sources, and this in spite of the copious material available on the subject in Talmudic and post-Talmudic literature, on which see A. H. Freiman, *Seder Kiddushin uNesuin* (Jerusalem 1945) and L. M. Epstein, *Marriage Laws in the Bible and the Talmud* (Cambridge 1942); *idem, Sex Laws and Customs in Judaism* (New York, 1948). Even more pertinent is the difficulty of context in Hosea. If v. 4b, c were the formula of divorce, it would not be *followed* by the plea "let her put her harlotries away from her face, etc." (4d,e); the order of the clauses would be reversed. So, too, if stripping her naked (v. 5) were the legal act of divorce, it would not be introduced by *pen* "lest," for it would be too late for threats. As for the use of the passage in formulae of exorcism, Biblical sources were often used for ritual ends not contemplated by their authors. Thus vv. 21, 22 in this very chapter are used to the present day in the ceremony of the donning of phylacteries.

The most natural view of the passage is to regard it as a figurative description not of a divorce but of the punishment of an adulteress. According to Biblical law, the adulteress was executed (Lev. 20:10; Deut. 22:22), but according to widespread custom, the wrath of her wronged husband found expression in stripping her naked and exposing her to public infamy (Nah. 3:5; Jer. 13:26; Ezek. 16:37; 23:27). Rabbinic law before the end of the Second Commonwealth likewise retained the old practice of stripping the condemned woman bare, but modified it out of considerations of pity and modesty (Mishnah, Sanhedrin 6:3; *Sifre Numbers*, ed. Friedmann p. 5a; cf. also Mat. 27:28, 35, and see Epstein, *Sex Laws*, p. 200, n. 39). Here is an illuminating instance of how the traditional mores of the ancient Orient developed differently in different cultures. In Ḥana and Nuzu, stripping the woman bare became a legal procedure in divorce. In Israel, it survived only as a punishment for crime, not as a procedure for divorce, and even this practice, post-Biblical law sought to modify. Hosea threatens his faithless wife with both the customary and the legal punishments for adultery (note 2:5e for the figurative death penalty).

31. Cf. Robinson-Horst, *Die Zwölf kleinen Propheten* (Tübingen 1938) p. 8. See note 28 above for a striking medieval parallel.

32. Robinson's emendation קִשּׁוּרֶיהָ "her bridal ornaments," which is graphically very distant from כְּרְמָהּ, vitiates the prophet's theme.

33. מִשָּׁם is temporal, not spatial = lit. "from then" cf. Arabic *thumma* "then," not *thamma* "there." Harper, *op. cit.*, p. 241, recognizes the temporal force of the word. The same temporal usage of the adverb probably occurs in Hos. 6:7; Ps. 14:5; 36:13, as well as in Isa. 65:20, where it is directed to the future. Tur-Sinai proposes to read כַּרְמִי הַמֻּשָּׁם "Carmi, destroyed (one)," in which he sees a reference to Achan ben Carmi in Jos. chap. 7. But the context then requires a far-fetched interpretation (*op. cit.* pp. 322 f.), as his discussion makes clear.

34. See note 30 above.

35. Following the lead of LXX and P, who render the phrase אֲהֻבַת רֵעַ actively, most moderns have interpreted "loving a paramour" (so already Ibn Ezra). Thus Michaelis, Oort, Harper, T. H. Robinson vocalize MT אֹהֶבֶת רֵעַ. Even if this meaning is desired, the change is unnecessary. On the active (or middle) use of the *kātūl* participle form, cf. זָכוּר (Ps. 103:14), נָחוּץ "pressing" I Sam. 21:9, אָחוּז "holding" (Cant. 3:8) *inter alia*, and such common Mishnic forms as עָסוּק "active," שָׁקוּד "diligent" etc., see the fundamental discussion of J. Barth,

Nominalbildung in den semitischen Sprachen (Leipzig 1889), pp. 175 ff. However, in spite of the widespread acceptance of the active sense for the phrase, we believe that the context is best served by rendering "beloved of a husband, yet practicing adultery." This is validated by the clause immediately following, which interprets the parable, "like the Lord's love for the children of Israel, while they turn to other gods," as Rashi, Kimhi and Karo recognized. רֵעַ is used of "paramour" in only one passage, Jer. 3:11, and then in the plural; in the singular it is used of the rightful husband in Jer. 3:20, a verse which is the oldest commentary on our passage:

אָכֵן בָּגְדָה אִשָּׁה מֵרֵעָהּ כֵּן בְּגַדְתֶּם בִּי בֵּית יִשְׂרָאֵל (read בְּרֵעָהּ, with LXX, P,T). "Indeed as a woman betrays her husband, so have you betrayed me, O house of Israel."

רֵעַ in the singular is also used of the true lover in Cant. 5:16 parallel to דּוֹד, a term applied to the Lord in Isa. 5:1. On *re'a* and *ra'yāh* as referring to the true love, cf. Gordis, *The Song of Songs* (New York, 1954), pp. 31 f.

36. That the difficult closing phrase of v. 1 וְאֹהֲבֵי אֲשִׁישֵׁי עֲנָבִים (3:1) "who love cakes of raisins," refers to some pagan rite was recognized by W. R. Smith, Volz, Martin, Haupt and Harper. The difficulties of content and syntax have led N. H. Tur-Sinai to propose the brilliant emendation וָאֹהַב אֵשֶׁת עֲגָבִים, "And so I loved a woman of lust" (cf. Ez. 33:31 f. etc.). He has since modified the suggestion to read וָאֹהַב אֲשִׁישֵׁי עֲגָבִים (which he interprets to mean, "I loved a woman of broad hips"), on the ground that it is graphically closer to MT (*op. cit.* pp. 313 f.). We believe that MT is entirely satisfactory if the final clause is interpreted as describing "the other gods" and the Vav is recognized as epexegetical (or is deleted). Hence, render: "They turn to other gods who love raisin cakes." The *'ašīšāh* was regarded as highly stimulating (Can.2:5) and was, therefore, used in fertility rites (cf.Isa. 16:7). The *kawwanim* (Jer. 7: 18; 44:19) were also used similarly. See W.R. Smith, The *Old Testament in the Jewish Church*, lecture 11, note 7.

37. This view of the meaning of the verb *vā'ekkrehā* was taken by Ibn Ezra and Kimhi, who interpret the verb to refer to a marriage price (Kimhi: קניתיה לי לאשה). Ibn Ezra also recognized that the root is *nākar*, not *kārāh*, hence the dagesh in the Kaph in MT. This intuitive grasp of the passage was rejected out of hand by most moderns (cf. Harper, *op. cit.* p. 219), a procedure that has happened more than once (cf. e. g. the present writer's "The Asseverative Kaph in Hebrew and Ugaritic" in *JAOS*, vol. 63, 1943, pp. 176 ff.). In 1938, C. H. Gordon proposed to read the verb *nkr* in the Ugaritic King Keret tablets and suggested that the word "was the technical term referring to the payment upon re-marriage" (cf. his "*Trh, TN* and *NKR* in the Ras Shamra Tablets," in *JBL*, 1938, vol. 57, pp. 407–10). He was later persuaded to surrender this view in favor of the interpretation of *nkr* as "stranger" (cf. e. g. H. L. Ginsberg, *Legend of King Keret*, New Haven 1946, p. 16). In response to a communication from the present writer, Gordon reaffirmed his original view of the root, connecting it with Hos. 3:1. It should be added that a) it is unlikely that a special technical term would exist for so rare a procedure as *re*-marriage, and b) that even if the

Keret legend requires the idea of re-marriage, Semitic usage would not require that the theme of repetition be expressed in the root; cf. the frequent use of Hebrew *bānāh* in the meaning "rebuild" (Jos. 6:26; I Kings 16:34; Isa. 58:12; Ps. 69:36, etc.). We are, of course, not dependent on the Ugaritic for the meaning of the Hebrew. The root *nkr per se* means "buy, as in marriage," in the Qal (here in Hos. 3:1) and "sell, hand over" in the *Piel* (in I Sam. 23:7: *nikkar 'ōthō elōhīm beyādī*, lit. "God has sold him into my hand"). Note the identical use of the more common *makhar* in Judg. 4:9. The Aramaic root *zbn*, which means "buy" in the *Peal* and "sell" in the *Pael* is an exact parallel. So too the Hiphil הקנה means "sell, transfer ownership" in Mishnic Hebrew. All the proposed emendations for the verb in Samuel, *makhar, sikkar, siggar* are unnecessary. LXX (πεπράκεν = "sold"), like the other Vss. (P *'ašlᵉmāh*, V *tradidit*, T מסר) followed the context correctly and read MT, not *makhar* (ag. BH). On "buy" as meaning "marry," cf. the ancient Mishnic usage in Kid. 1.1 האשה נקנית בשלש דרכים "A woman may be acquired in marriage in three ways"; *ibid.* וקונה את עצמה lit. "buys herself, i. e. becomes free of the marriage bond." The Talmud *ad loc.* interprets even the Biblical verb *lakaḥ* (Deut. 24:1), which is used of marriage as equivalent to purchase: גמר קיחה קיחה משדה עפרון "He derives the verb 'taking' to mean 'buying' from the field of Ephron (Gen. 23:13) where the verb for buying is 'taking'."

38. In addition to the fifteen shekels, he pays a *ḥōmer* (= *kor*, or 30 seah) and a *lethekh* (half a *ḥōmer*, or 15 seah) of barley. On *lethekh*, cf. the *Mishnah Shebuoth* 6:3, T. *Baba Batra* 7a and see K. Galling, *Biblisches Reallexikon* ('Tuebingen, 1937) column 367. From II Kings 7:1, 16 we learn that during a siege, 2 seah of barley sold for one shekel. Under more normal conditions (though not much more normal, see below for the circumstances) the price would be cheaper, probably 3 seah for a shekel. The 45 seah of barley that Hosea gave thus were worth 15 shekel, making a total of 30 shekels. The commentators have noted that this is the price of a slave (Ex. 21:32; Zech. 11:12) and also the redemption-fee for a woman (Lev. 27:4). The purchase of a slave-girl included marital rights, as is clear from the Book of the Covenant (Ex. 21:7 ff.).

39. *Yāšabh* has the nuance "dwell in the house of a husband" whether he be living (Lev. 12:4; Deut. 21:13) or dead (Gen. 38:11; Isa. 47:8). Cf. both senses of the verb in the Aramaic proverb cited in the Talmud, *Kid.* 7a: טב למיתב טנדו מלמיתב ארמלא "It is better to dwell in grief than to dwell as a widow." The Hiphil, הוֹשִׁיב "give a dwelling," therefore develops the meaning "marry" in late Hebrew (Ez. 10:2, 14, 17, 18; Neh. 13:23, 27; cf. also Ps. 113:9), a sense possessed by the Ethiopic cognate *'awsaba*.

40. So W. R. Smith, Volz, Marti, Haupt, R. E. Wolfe.

41. So Peiser.

42. So Hoelscher, Staerk, Arnold, Pfeiffer, and Kaufmann, who combines it with the allegorical theory. Guthe, troubled by the long arm of the coincidence, assumes that the first account is allegorical, while the second is a real incident.

43. Cf. Pfeiffer, *op. cit.* p. 567.

44. The first is the translation of the Jewish Publication Society, the second of the American Revised and Standard Revised Versions.

45. So Steuernagel, Kittel, Eissfeldt, T. H. Robinson, Tur-Sinai.

46. See W. Wickes, *A Treatise on the Accentuation of the Twenty-One So-called Prose Books of the O. T.* (Oxford 1887) pp. 10, 19, 106.

47. E. g. Gen. 4:25; 9:1; 18:29 and often. Cf. Brown-Driver-Briggs, *Lexicon*, s.v., section c, p. 729a. To be sure, BDB adduces seven instances where '*ōdh* precedes the verb (Hos. 12:10; Jer. 31:3, 4, 22; 31:15; 33:12–13). They are, however, all instances of prophecies where the verb is in the imperfect and *ōdh* has the meaning "yet," e. g. Jer. 31:3 עוֹד אֶבְנֵךְ וְנִבְנֵית "I will yet rebuild thee"; Jer. 33:12 עוֹד יִהְיֶה בַּמָּקוֹם הַזֶּה "there will yet be in this place." Oort in *Theologisch Tidjschrift* vol. 24, p. 355, does not adequately distinguish the various meanings and uses of the adverb.

48. This is the view of T. H. Robinson. Tur-Sinai offers two alternative explanations of '*ōdh*: 1) that we have here a fragment of an autobiography which contained orther prophecies, hence "The Lord spoke to me again" or 2) God had to urge him again and again to marry the woman (*op. cit.*, p. 311). The first suggestion creates a hypothesis of far-reaching scope for which no other evidence exists. As for the second, it is doubtful whether the clause carries the nuance proposed. Tur-Sinai's own doubts are, of course, indicated by his double suggestion.

49. Kaufmann (*op. cit.*, p. 100) and Tur-Sinai (*op. cit.*, p. 307) rightly protest against the wholesale excision of the references to Judah in the book. Actually, when each passage is studied independently, on the basis of relevance of context and literary form, the authenticity of most of the references to Judah becomes clear. That 2:2 and 3:5 are fundamental to Hosea's theme, will be shown below. In 4:15, יהודה is a conscious scribal change for יהוה (cf. R. Gordis, "Studies in the Relationship of Biblical and Rabbinic Hebrew" in *Louis Ginzberg Jubilee Volumes* (New York, 1945) English section, pp. 195 f. The reproof heaped upon Judah in 5:5 and 5:10 militates against the assumption of a later interpolator, who might be expected to exalt Judah, not to condemn it. This consideration in favor of the integrity of the text is re-enforced by the meter in 5:13; 5:14; 6:4 (note the plural חַסְדְּכֶם); 12:1, 3 and by the chiastic parallelism in 8:14. The meaning of 6:11a is unclear. On the other hand, 1:7 and 10:11 may be instances of interpolations.

50. Y. Kaufmann's emendation seeks to get rid of the text because it is the greatest obstacle to his theory, but there is no warrant for this entirely subjective procedure. See notes 3 and 53.

51. That this is the intent of II Kings 17:27 ff. is clear from many facts. Sargon II claims to have taken 27,290 Israelites into captivity. Undoubtedly exaggerated, as all Assyrian military claims are, it represents a fraction of the population. Judean prophets continue to consider Israel a living entity (cf. e. g. Jer. 31:19; Ezek. 37:15 f.). That the seventh-century Judean kings regarded Northern Israel as *terra irredenta* (see e. g. Albright in *JBL*, vol. 61, 1952, p. 252) argues for a substantial Israelite population in these areas after 721. Hezekiah actively seeks to win the religious loyalty of the North Israelites for the Jerusalem sanctuary after the destruction of Samaria, his efforts winning varied success (II Chron. chap. 30, cf. particularly vv. 6, 10, 11). The account in W. E. Oester-

ley and T. H. Robinson, *A History of Israel* (Oxford, 1932) vol. I, pp. 376 ff., which assumes a high degree of depopulation, is to be corrected accordingly.

52. Cf. "The Composition and Structure of Amos" in this volume. On the unity and integrity of *Amos*, which is there defended in terms of Amos' outlook on Judah and Israel, as well as other considerations, see now W. S. McCullough, "Some Suggestions About Amos" in *JBL*, vol. 72, 1953, pp. 247 ff.

53. On his attitude to public worship, see Hosea *passim*. On the institution of the kingship, cf. Hosea 8:4 and perhaps 7:5. This point of contact with chapter 3 is another refutation of Kaufmann's insistence that there are no resemblances between Hos. chap. 1–3 and 4–14.

54. Cf. S. W. Baron, *A Social and Religious History of the Jews* 2nd ed. (New York 1952) p. 94: "For (the Biblical historian) the people of Israel and Judah are an indivisible unity."

55. On the prophetic concept of nationalism cf. S. W. Baron, *op. cit.* pp. 96 ff.; *idem, Modern Nationalism and Religion* (New York 1947) pp. 213 f., esp. p. 214, and "Micah's Vision of the End-Time" in this volume.

10. ISAIAH—PROPHET, THINKER, WORLD STATESMAN

I

By common consent, Isaiah is recognized as the greatest figure after Moses in that unique group of religious teachers and thinkers who are known as the prophets of Israel. He is a supreme literary artist, though he was not concerned with the art of composition. He is one of the mightiest intellects in the history of mankind, yet he never had the benefit of training, either in science or logic, in philosophy or theology. He was a prophet whose basic ideas and conceptions have exerted a mighty influence upon civilization for twenty-five hundred years and more.

It is perhaps for this very reason that it is difficult for us to appreciate fully the originality and profundity of his thought. Because his ideas, even his language, have entered into the warp and woof of the Western world, the full extent of his contribution is not generally recognized. In an age which has abundantly validated Voltaire's taunt that the Bible is more celebrated than known, Isaiah's name is familiar to all educated people, but little more besides.

Nevertheless, few other figures of history have contributed so vitally to the past thought of the world and can give so much inspiration and guidance to our own confused and chaotic age.

Like all Hebrew worthies in the Bible, Isaiah tells us tantalizingly little about his personal life. From incidental references we learn that he was married and had several children. Apparently he came of a prominent family in Jerusalem, and perhaps was related to the royal line, for he speaks to the King of Judah with the easy familiarity of a relative, unless we attribute it to the audacity of a prophet. In his mature years, he had a circle of disciples to whom he transmitted his insights and who are probably responsible for the preservation of his words.

Isaiah's call to prophecy came in the year 740 B.C.E. It was the year of King Uzziah's death. The long reign of this Judean king, which coincided in large part with the rule of Jeroboam the Second in the Northern kingdom of Israel, was the high-water mark of the Hebrew monarchy. Between them, these two kings of the North and the South had restored the boundaries of the Solomonic kingdom. Their reigns were characterized by commercial expansion, political prestige, and military success. As a result, the first half of the eighth century, B.C.E., the days of Jeroboam the Second in Israel and of Uzziah (sometimes called Azariah) in Judah, were marked by a general sense of prosperity and national confidence.

Only after both kings died did it become apparent how flimsy were the foundations of the new-found prosperity and how temporary the illusion of national greatness. In the East the new Assyrian Empire had arisen, and its shadow grew ever more portentous for all the small states of the Middle East. Today in the perspective of history, we can discern clearly the inexorable march of Assyrian power, but at the time only the prophets saw the inevitable doom of the nation. Thus, the forty years of Isaiah's prophetic activity were a long period of deepening national crisis. They coincide with the decline of the Judean state and the final destruction of the Northern kingdom in 721 B.C.E. They thus reflect the ebb and flow in the tide of national disaster.

The first great national crisis in which Isaiah emerges is the Syro-Ephraimitic War in the year 734. Some of the smaller states in Western Asia plan a military alliance against Assyria. Because Ahaz, the King of Judah, has not joined their ranks, the allies, Syria and Israel, send an expedition to ravage the land and replace Ahaz by a puppet of their own choosing. Like all the great prophets, Isaiah is opposed to military adventures directed against the Assyrian overlord. He sees that these rebels, for all their loud threats and mighty protestations, are no flaming torches of liberty, but, rather, "smoking firebrands." He counsels the king to have courage and faith in God, to remain calm, and to wait for the storm to pass.

Ahaz, however, in his abject fear, hastens to invite the aid of Assyria, who would in any event have punished the rebels. As a result of the king's timidity and lack of faith, Judah becomes a vassal state. Ahaz is compelled to send a heavy bribe to the king of Assyria—all the gold and silver treasures stored in the Temple precincts. What the prophet surely regarded as worse, Ahaz now introduces pagan practices into the Temple of the Lord in Jerusalem. Thus the weak king opens his borders to alien cultural and religious influences, which undermine still further the morale and integrity of the people.

The second great crisis in Isaiah's life comes twelve years later, in 722. As he had repeatedly foretold, the Kingdom of Israel in the north finally pays the penalty for its fondness for military and diplomatic adventures. First it is dismembered province by province, and at last it is completely destroyed by Assyria. The leaders and many of the people are deported by the conquerors. Their place is taken by alien colonists. These intermarry with the remnants of the Israelite population and become the ancestors of the half-Jewish Samaritan sect of the Second Temple period, who have survived to the present day.

From various references it is clear that like Amos and Hosea before him, and Jeremiah and Ezekiel after him, Isaiah regarded the original division of the Jewish state as a sin and the destruction of the northern kingdom of Israel as a catastrophe. For him, as for all the great prophets, there was only one people of Israel, and he looked forward to its full restoration under God.

The final crisis in his career comes in 701 or 688. On the throne of Judah there now sits Hezekiah, whom it is tempting to describe as a disciple of the prophet Isaiah. Hezekiah has carried through a religious reformation that has swept away the pagan rites introduced by his father. He has encouraged literary and cultural activity by his support of scholars, scribes, and sages in their work. With an eye to practical needs as well, the king has constructed a tunnel to give Jerusalem an adequate water supply, has rebuilt the city walls, and has strengthened the military forces of his realm.

In the upsurge of national feeling the king and the people are chafing under the yoke of the Assyrians and they object to the payment of the annual tribute to the eastern empire. As a result, a large and influential party looks westward to Egypt for assistance and support. The wily Egyptian diplomats are only too eager to have a group of buffer states between them and Assyria and are generous with promises, at which the king eagerly grasps.

The prophet sees more deeply than the politicians. Isaiah is convinced that the only salvation for tiny Judah, lying between Assyria and Egypt, lies in abstention from entangling alliances. As he had opposed Ahaz' earlier capitulation to Assyria, he now opposes any dependence upon Egypt. Isaiah sets forth a doctrine of neutrality for the little country as the policy for his nation: "For thus says the Lord God, the Holy One of Israel: In peace and rest shall you be saved; in quietness and confidence shall be your strength" (30:15).

However, his advice is again ignored—and the penalty is swift. When the king stops paying the tribute, the Assyrian general sweeps down on Palestine and brings devastation and ruin to the countryside. The promises of Egypt prove to be as reliable as the solemn covenants of modern diplomats and Judah is left to its fate. Jerusalem is besieged by the enemy, who grimly awaits the dying agonies of the Jewish people.

In that hour Isaiah rises to his full stature. He has opposed the course that led to the tragedy, but now he forgets partisanship and even surrenders consistency. Zion is the seat of God's temple and no conqueror can violate its sanctity. In the face of the despair of the king and his advisers, and in sublime disregard of all the probabilities, Isaiah proudly replies to the Assyrian boast: "Whom have you taunted and blasphemed? Against whom have you raised your voice? Indeed, you have raised up your eyes on high against the Holy One of Israel!" (37:23).

The prophet's colossal faith is justified. A plague, which the Greek historian Herodotus tells us was brought on by field mice, breaks out in the army. Disease and demoralization play havoc with the Assyrian forces and Jerusalem is saved.

Byron has given a spirited description of the Assyrian coming down like a wolf on the fold and meeting sudden destruction:

> Like the leaves of the forest when summer is green,
> That host with their banners at sunset were seen.
> Like the leaves of the forest when autumn hath flown,
> That host on the morrow lay withered and strown.

That triumphant vindication of Isaiah's faith is the last time we meet him. According to an old rabbinic legend, not without credibility, the aged prophet was murdered by Hezekiah's son, Manasseh, in a wave of religious reaction.

It is obvious that Isaiah was intimately involved with the occurrences of his own age. Yet his profound understanding of the world and his deep insight into the processes of history make him not only a great statesman in his own day, but a mighty spiritual genius for ages yet unborn.

II

Isaiah's greatness is to be sought, not in the realm of politics, nor even in literature, but in the field of religion. In his own person he proved that religion at its highest and truest is not an opiate for men, but, on the contrary, a vital force, stimulating them to fearless thought and dynamic activity.

Central to the world outlook of Isaiah was his conception of God. For him, God was no petty anthropomorphic deity, but neither was he a metaphysical abstraction to be contemplated from an ivory tower. In his inaugural vision Isaiah had seen the Lord sitting on a throne, while the Seraphim, the heavenly hosts, were chanting their hymn of praise:

> Holy, holy, holy is the Lord of hosts,
> The whole earth is full of His glory. (6:3)

In the hour of his consecration the young prophet had experienced God in two of His cardinal attributes, His majesty and His holiness. Throughout all the succeeding years of his activity and discouragement, Isaiah never wavered in his faith in the limitless power and the ethical perfection of his Maker.

But if God is all-powerful and all-perfect, there is work to be done in the world, for a tragic abyss yawns between the Creator and His creation. Isaiah's God was therefore no easy comfort for tired spirits, but a spur to ceaseless, if not overhopeful, activity, an inspiration to remold the world nearer the pattern of God:

> The Lord of hosts is exalted through justice,
> God, the Holy One, is sanctified through righteousness. (5:16)

To demand the establishment of justice became Isaiah's mission to the world, and in particular to that small corner of it that was his native land:

> Zion shall be redeemed through justice,
> Her inhabitants through righteousness. (1:27)

Isaiah found in his God of holiness a touchstone for evaluating the world as it was, and the standard and goal for the world as it could be. Hence, the first aspect of his prophetic activity was as a fearless critic of society. We have already referred to his adherence to the unpopular doctrine of neutrality between Assyria and Egypt. In him it was a direct consequence of a true faith in God. But as events proved, it was good practical politics—of the kind, however, that few practical politicians would dream of adopting.

Not only the political maneuverings of the leadership aroused his displeasure; he had scarcely more use for the religious life of his countrymen, which expressed itself in an elaborate and costly ritual of sacrifice and song in the Temple:

> Who hath required this at your hand
> To trample My courts,

he calls out to the pious multitudes in the name of his God. But it is an error to assume that Isaiah is opposed to religious ritual *per se*. His inaugural vision of God came to him during a visit to the Temple. His conviction of the inviolability of Jerusalem is based on the sacredness of the house that stood on Zion's hill.

What Isaiah opposes is religious externalism without accompanying moral fervor. He fights against a concern with ritual as a substitute for righteousness, the great and pervasive danger to which institutional religion is always exposed. In words that will never die, Isaiah emphasizes that the essence of religion, to which all else must minister or be an abomination, is the practice of justice:

> Wash you, make yourselves clean.
> Put away the evil of your doings from before Mine eyes,
> Cease to do evil, learn to do right,
> Seek justice, relieve the oppressed,
> Judge the fatherless, plead for the widow. (1:16 ff.)

But his most searing indignation Isaiah reserves for the social and economic conditions of his day. Jerusalem is now a rich and populous city. It is the home of absentee landlords who spend their days and nights in revelry and carousal, while the peasant farmers, expropriated by monopoly, are becoming peons on large estates.

It is important to emphasize that Isaiah is opposed to the concentration of wealth not merely because of the impoverishment of the poor, but also because of the demoralization of the rich. He is no class

agitator, but a Hebrew prophet concerned with the soul as well as
the body, with the well-being of the oppressor and of the oppressed:

> Woe to those that join house to house
> That attach field to field,
> Till there be no room,
> So that you may live alone
> In the midst of the land.
> Woe to those that rise early in the morning,
> In pursuit of strong drink.
> That tarry late into the night
> Till wine inflame them. (5:8 ff.)

Like Amos before him, Isaiah is revolted at the luxury and disso-
luteness of the daughters of Zion, and he has painted their portrait
in vitriol for all time:

> The daughters of Zion are haughty,
> Holding their heads high as they walk,
> Ogling with their eyes,
> Walking with mincing steps,
> Their anklets jingling. (3:16)

In verses that follow these, Isaiah lists more than twenty articles of
finery worn by the gentler sex. From this catalogue of adornment it
is clear that the prophet has not permitted his indignation to interfere
with his observation.

When he contrasts the vain luxury of the rich and the abject
poverty of the poor, made possible through legalized fraud and violence, he cries out:

> Woe to those who enact wicked decrees,
> Who inscribe ordinances of evil,
> Robbing the weak of their rights,
> And defrauding the poor of their due,
> So that widows become their booty
> And the orphans they despoil. (10:1–2)

This far-flung criticism of contemporary society, with all its manifestations, still possesses a power to stir us profoundly. In an age
marked by the wholesale collapse of morality, both as an ideal
standard and as a code of practice, Isaiah's indictment is, if possible,
more telling than it was in his own day.

III

Isaiah's criticism remains vital for the modern world in a deeper
sense as well, not merely negatively, but positively. It was his faith
that stimulated the prophet to the enunciation of his two greatest
ideas. The contradiction between the ideal of an all-powerful God of
righteousness on the one hand, and the reality of a world reeking with
violence and injustice on the other, had to be resolved. Isaiah did this
by his profound contribution to the prophetic concept of God in
history, of which he was one of the principal architects.

Perhaps the most significant contribution of the Hebrew prophets
to human thought, as Morris Raphael Cohen pointed out, lay in their
formulating a philosophy of history. This was the achievement not of
the Greeks, but of the Hebrews. For the prophets of Israel, history
is not a meaningless succession of accidental events, but rather part of
a pattern, an unfolding plan, a cosmic drama in which men are the
actors and God is the director. Since the world has been created by a
God of righteousness, it follows that evil must inevitably be destroyed
and justice emerge triumphant.

Isaiah himself has expressed this faith, but he is too clearheaded to
use it as a smoke-screen to shut out reality. He sees that the swift
and remorseless rise to power of Israel's enemies, the Assyrians, can
hardly be explained in terms of justice. The Assyrians are surely no
knights in shining armor. How can he explain this triumph of evil in
a world created by a good God? Isaiah's answer is one of his most
brilliant insights, his doctrine of "the rod of God's anger." Unquestionably, Isaiah believes, Assyria is engaged in executing Divine
judgment upon the sinful and corrupt nations, but ultimately Assyria
itself will come under Divine judgment when its appointed task is
completed:

Woe to Ashur, rod of My anger,
Who is the staff of My wrath!
Against a sinful nation, I send him
And against the people with whom I am wroth, I command him,
To take booty, to capture loot
And to trample it underfoot like the clay of the open places.
But Ashur cannot imagine this,
And his mind does not think so,

For his lust is to destroy . . .
And to cut off nations not a few . . .
But it shall come to pass,
When the Lord has completed all His work
On Mount Zion and Jerusalem,
I shall visit punishment upon the fruit of the king of Ashur's arrogance
And his haughty insolence.
Can an axe lord it over him who hews with it?
Can a saw magnify itself over him who lifts it,
As though a rod could lift those who lift it,
Or a staff raise what is not made of wood. (10:5, 6, 12, 15)

Isaiah therefore sees all human history as being part of a process in which evil is used to destroy evil and usher in the good. It is a bold intuition, this conception of God in history, but again and again it seems to be vindicated in the real world. When the history of the twentieth century is finally written, it may perhaps become clear that the cruelty, chaos, and conflict of our day are part of a cosmic pattern in human history. The monstrous evils of totalitarianism in all its colors, the struggle everywhere engendered by economic want, the battle against colonialism in Asia and Africa, often willful and destructive, the worldwide racial strife taking the form of bloody revolt and blind reaction—all these phenomena of our day may ultimately stand revealed as part of the process of God in history, the painful yet irresistible march of mankind toward its divinely ordained heritage of justice and freedom. But we are no prophets. We can peer but darkly at the world as through a smoked glass. But Isaiah saw more clearly, as in the light of day.

Another great contradiction faced the prophets. How was one to reconcile God's justice, which demanded the destruction of the sinful people of Israel, with God's unquestioned love for the seed of Abraham? Isaiah's reason told him that because of its abundant sins Israel deserved to die, but Isaiah's love for his people forbade any such catastrophe.

The prophet's solution lay in the profound doctrine of the "Saving Remnant." In his inaugural vision he had seen Israel as an oak tree in the autumn, whose leaves fall away but whose trunk endures forever. Later he names one of his sons "A-remnant-shall-return" as a token of his faith that the history of his people was a continuous process of selection:

For though thy people, O Israel, be as the sand of the sea, a remnant shall
return. (10:2)

—a remnant precious in its moral quality, embodying the ideal
aspirations of the people of God.

This theory of the "Saving Remnant" may be described as a pre-
Darwinian theory of the survival of the fittest. Since, for the prophet,
this world is a moral universe, he sees human life as the survival of
the morally fittest. Who knows but that in the great synthesis of knowledge that we call reality, the prophet and the scientist will both be
seen to have expressed two aspects of one great truth.

At all events, Isaiah's theory of the "Saving Remnant" does not
exhaust the miracle and the mystery of Jewish survival. It is, however,
one of the most fruitful formulations in the philosophy of history,
borne out by thirty centuries of Jewish existence, suffering, and
achievement.

IV

Isaiah's criticism of society flowered into his two conceptions, that
of God in history and that of the Saving Remnant. This process of
moral selection would serve as a bridge between the world as it was
and the world as it would be, for Isaiah did not content himself with
excoriating the present. He sought to picture the future world under
the guidance of a leader upon whom there would rest "the spirit of
wisdom and understanding, the spirit of counsel and might, the spirit
of knowledge and the fear of the Lord." (11:2)

We possess no complete picture of Isaiah's dream of the future.
His life was too intimately bound up with the stirring events of his
own day for him to write a leisurely Utopia. But the partial descriptions that have reached us belong to the golden pages of the world's
literature. Woven of dream stuff, they are the fabric of a nobler world.

Isaiah gives us no hint of his solution for the economic ills of his
age. Perhaps the prophet counted upon institutions like the jubilee
and the sabbatical year, which are ordained in the Torah, to remove
the grosser forms of inequality and privilege, and upon the birth of a
new ethical sensitivity in men to usher in an era of plenty and security
for all.

One positive trait that emerges is his dream of a return to simple,

idyllic conditions. Like Theocritus the Greek, Rousseau the Frenchman, and countless others after him, Isaiah seems to have sought
escape from the degeneracy and tumult of urban civilization in the
peace and quiet of a rustic life:

> A hut shall be for shade in the daytime from the heat,
> And a refuge and a covert from storm and the rain. (4:6)

> Yet one day from the heights of heaven
> A spirit shall breathe into us
> Till the down grow like an orchard
> And the orchard like a forest.
> Justice fills the very downs—
> And honesty the orchards,
> And justice brings us peace and quiet,
> Honesty renders us secure.
> My people shall have homes of peace
> And rest in houses undisturbed.
> A happy folk, to sow land watered everywhere,
> And let your ass and ox range free. (32:15 ff.)

Whatever our uncertainty as to Isaiah's economic and social philosophy, we are in no doubt as to his views on international relations.
For him the goal is the establishment of universal peace. Here the
significance of the prophet's thought cannot be exaggerated. Centuries after his day, the noblest of the Greeks, the philosopher Plato,
pictures the ideal society of the future, The Republic, and he sees it
as being safeguarded by a standing army. For Plato war is the inevitable lot of mankind, even at the ultimate end of history. For the
Hebrew prophet, on the other hand, peace is the inescapable destiny
of the human race:

> Men shall break their swords into plowshares,
> And their spears into pruning hooks;
> Nation shall not lift up sword against nation;
> Neither shall men learn war any more. (2:1 ff.)

Merely to have enunciated the faith that a peaceful world was a
possibility would of itself have been enough to give Isaiah a unique
place among the moral teachers of mankind. But the prophet goes
much further. He dares not only to dream of peace, but to posit the
techniques for achieving it. The attainment of peace, the prophet

teaches us, is not dependent either upon the miraculous transformation of human nature, nor upon the cessation of conflicting interests among nations, nor even upon the disappearance of nations. Peace will come into being when the nations accept the sovereignty of the moral law as binding upon them all.

Let it therefore be clearly understood that the prophet does not look forward to the elimination of national loyalties in the End-time. He would reject the vacuous cosmopolitanism that masquerades as internationalism no less than the strident chauvinism that has made nationalism a by-word and a menace in our day. He is, in brief, a true *inter-nationalist*. He conceives the relation between peoples as based on cooperation, on a voluntary acceptance by all nations of the laws of justice and peace. Therein lies the function of Israel and the secret of its eternal life, for it is to Mount Zion that the nations will stream in order to receive God's law:

> And many peoples shall go and say:
> Come ye, and let us go up to the mountain of the Lord,
> To the house of the God of Jacob;
> And He will teach us of His ways,
> And we will walk in His paths.
> For out of Zion shall go forth the law,
> And the word of the Lord from Jerusalem. (2:3)

His theme is expounded further in a profound rabbinic utterance: "The world stands upon three things: upon truth, upon justice, and upon peace. When truth prevails and justice is done, peace results." (J. Taanit 4:5).

For countless ages men's dreams of a just world-order have been sustained by Isaiah's vision of nations living under the sovereignty of God, and by his beautiful picture of nature at peace:

> The wolf shall dwell with the lamb,
> And the leopard shall lie down with the kid,
> And the calf and the young lion, and the fatling together,
> And a little child shall lead them. (11:6)

Perhaps his noblest prophecy of peace, as it is the most concrete, is in his vision of a true United Nations, uttered twenty-seven hundred years ago. Here the great Jewish patriot rises to a height never surpassed before or since. He sees his country's implacable foes, cruel Assyria and treacherous Egypt, both receiving God's blessing:

In that day shall there be a highway out of Egypt to Assyria, and the Assyrians shall come into Egypt, and the Egyptians into Assyria, and the Egyptian shall worship with the Assyrian. In that day shall Israel be the third with Egypt and Assyria, a blessing in the midst of the earth, for the Lord of hosts has blessed him, saying: Blessed be Egypt, My people, Assyria, the work of My hands, and Israel, Mine inheritance. (19:21 ff.)

v

Isaiah is an outstanding figure because of his boundless love of country, his unrivaled literary gifts, and his political sagacity—but his uniqueness lies in his profound sense of God in the world. It was his religious insight that caused him to weigh society and find it wanting, and boldly to sketch the outlines of a regenerated world. His moral courage demonstrated the vitality of religion. His intellect plumbed the purposes and the goals of human history. His love for Israel led him to evaluate aright the spiritual capacities of his people. Thus he gave meaning to Israel's existence and direction to the course of human history.

Through his teaching he helped immeasurably to confer eternal life upon Israel. But his influence knows no boundaries of race or religion, for he has inspired men in every age to carry on the long and arduous task of molding civilization nearer the heart's desire, shaping society after the kingdom of the Almighty, which he described unforgettably (11:9) as the era when "men shall do no evil and work no destruction upon all My holy mountain, for the earth shall be filled with the knowledge of the law as the waters cover the sea."

11. MICAH'S VISION OF THE END-TIME

I

While ignorance of an important subject is deplorable, intimate knowledge often raises problems of its own. Thus, familiarity with the great classics of the past tends to blunt the impact of their message. In proportion as their words and ideas have become the accepted heritage of the race, later generations find them self-evident, if not downright platitudinous, like the old lady who was not impressed by her first visit to a performance of *Hamlet* because she found it "a string of old quotations." Time marches on, however, and human events take a new turn. Suddenly what seemed obvious and trite before discloses unsuspected revolutionary power and contemporary relevance.

A striking illustration of this tendency may be seen in the teaching of the Hebrew Prophets on nationalism. Few passages in the Bible are more familiar, and less understood, than the Vision of the End-time, which occurs in Micah (4:1–5) and, with some verbal changes, in the Book of Isaiah (2:1–5):[1]

> In the end of days it shall come to pass,
> That the mountain of the Lord's house shall be established on the
>   top of the mountains,
> And it shall be exalted above the hills.
> Peoples shall flow unto it,
> And many nations shall come and say,
> "Come, let us go up to the mountain of the Lord,
> To the house of the God of Jacob;
> So that He will teach us of His ways,
> And we will walk in His paths;
> For from Zion shall go forth the Law,
> And the word of the Lord from Jerusalem."
> And He shall judge among many peoples,
> And rebuke strong nations afar off;
> They shall beat their swords into plowshares

268

And their spears into pruning-hooks;
Nation shall not lift up sword against nation,
Neither shall they learn war any more.
They shall sit every man under his vine and under his fig-tree;
And none shall make them afraid;
For the mouth of the Lord of hosts hath spoken it.
For as all the peoples walk every one in the name of its god,
We will walk in the name of the Lord our God forever.

At the very outset, the true meaning of the opening phrase, 'aharith hayamim, "end of days," should be noted. The words do not refer to the last climactic act of the human drama before the dissolution of the natural order. That the idiom is very ancient is clear from the parallel in Akkadian (ina ahrat umi) and from its use in some of the oldest Biblical poems, like the "Blessing of Jacob" and the "Prophecies of Balaam." It is used relatively rather than absolutely of the future. As the distinguished Biblical scholar, S. R. Driver, put it, the phrase "end of days" refers to the final period within the speaker's perspective, whatever that may be.

Now, undoubtedly, the author of the Vision of the End-time was thinking of the future, even of the distant future. Yet it is significant that there is no indication that he believed that the new world-order could be ushered in only through a special, supernatural intervention taking the form of a great cataclysm in the natural world, a miraculous transformation of human nature. For the Prophet, the nations of the earth, constituted as at present, would surrender their present attitude of mutual hatred and lawlessness in favor of a new outlook.

Therein lies the basic difference between Hebrew prophecy at its highest and the Apocalyptists, "the Revealers of Hidden Things," who emerged after the Babylonian Exile. In the face of deteriorating world conditions, before which they felt themselves to be powerless, the post-Exilic writers despaired of the natural capacities of men to improve matters. Yet because they held fast to their faith in a God of justice, these latter-day seers created the conception of a supernatural catastrophe as the prelude to the salvation of Israel and the world.

Today, the same mood of despair over man's nature, evoked by the tragic world situation, has found expression in crisis-theology, which emphasizes man's sinfulness and inner corruption, and pins its faith entirely on God's grace, bestowed upon His unworthy creatures. Whatever one's attitude toward these spiritual currents of our own day may be, it is important to note that our Prophet did not share this attitude. For him, the End-time would come to pass without any dramatic catastrophe, but rather as a result of the free conviction of men, voluntarily accepting the law of God as the norm for conduct. He does not look forward to a Utopia into which men will have been driven by an upheaval of natural forces or by the compulsions of human power, which have scarcely been gentler, whatever the formula, be it the *Pax Romana*, "Rule, Britannia," *Deutschland Über Alles*, the "American Century," or "the dictatorship of the proletariat." The Prophet's vision rests on faith in man's capacity to achieve the ideal by means of the free exercise of his reason and will.

This End-time will be strikingly distinguished from the reality of the present order by the existence of universal peace, and it is in this connection that the passage is generally cited. Here, too, an excess of familiarity with its phrases has dulled men's perception of the novelty and originality of its ideas. Even today, insistent and influential leaders of nations, races, and classes loudly deny that peace is either a practical means for achieving progress or the inevitable end and goal of human history. In the ancient world, universal peace was beyond the ken even of a Plato, as we have seen. For him, mankind was forever divided into Greek and barbarian, with the sword as the arbiter of human destiny.

In direct contradiction is the statement in the Midrash (*Sifra Kedoshim*) that the fundamental principle in the Torah is expressed in the Biblical verse, "This is the book of the generations of Man" (Gen. 5:1), a passage which emphasizes the common descent and therefore the brotherhood of all humanity. The Hebrew Prophet may have lacked the dialectic skill of the Greek sage, but it was he who enunciated the ideal of peace which entered the mainstream of Jewish thought and which, through the Scriptures, sacred to Christianity as well, became part of the world view of western man.

The extent to which this ideal has penetrated the soul of mankind is illustrated by one observation. Men today often develop a sense of bitterness and frustration at the failure of world organizations to achieve lasting peace. Yet rarely, if ever, is the feeling general that the goal itself had best be abandoned as chimerical. On the contrary, peace is today regarded as an inalienable human right, the rightful heritage of the race, and those who, rightly or wrongly, are considered as depriving men of this boon are stigmatized as the archvillains of our day.

II

The contribution of the Vision of Isaiah and Micah to the formulation of human rights is not exhausted by its enunciation of the ideal of peace, nor even by its faith in the destined attainment of this goal. The Prophet goes further and points out that the road to peace, through the creation of a binding international law, must be centered in a recognized authority. He does not depend on good will or on love to guard the peace, nor does he expect that all differences of outlook and all conflicts of interest will miraculously disappear in the End-time. Before peace can be a reality, there must be a law which shall go forth from Zion, which will be accepted as binding among the nations and will be enforced among the peoples. The Prophet would have denied the doctrine of national sovereignty, when defined in terms of "My country, may she always be in the right, but my country, right or wrong." If government means an agency capable of imposing its will upon its members, the Prophet emphatically believed in world government under God and His law.

It is noteworthy that he speaks of judging between nations. Judgment means the enforcement of justice. For the Prophet, this Law emanated from the God of Jacob, who, as all the Prophets taught, is the one God of humanity. But irrespective of its source, the character of this international covenant is not legalistic, but moral, rooted in justice and truth and therefore capable of supporting the structure of peace. A Talmudic utterance makes this idea explicit: "Upon three things the world rests—upon justice, upon truth, and upon peace. And the three are one, for when justice is done, truth prevails and peace is established" (Jerusalem Talmud, Taanith 4:2; Megillah 3:5).

Unquestionably, however, the most significant contribution for our age to be found in the Prophet's vision of the End-time is one which has been generally overlooked: his conception of nationalism. Within five short verses, the words for "people" and "nation" occur no less than seven times—striking testimony to his belief that national groups will remain as permanent features of human society even in its ideal phase. The bearing of his thought on our age is obvious. For today, nationalism has reached the acme of its power and the nadir of its degradation. It is the basic ill of our age, aside from the economic strife, to which, indeed, it has largely contributed. No greater peril threatens the survival of man than nationalism, men's total absorption in the view that all law emanates from one's own ethnic or political group, that there is no morality beyond it, and that its interests at all costs are the highest good.

It is sufficient to recall the intimate bond between nationalism and Nazi German and Italian fascist dictatorship. But communism, too, which began with the slogan of internationalism and the world proletariat, has adopted with mounting fervor the gospel of the "communist fatherland," whose "rights" to expansion and to buffer states are indistinguishable from the "legitimate interests" of the Czarist Russia of more than fifty years ago, except that they are pursued with greater efficiency and ruthlessness. World War II was the result of unbridled national ambition, which wiped out every vestige of fair play and pity in the hearts of otherwise normal men. Should World War III eventuate, it would be another colossal and horrible burnt-offering on the altar of exclusive national loyalty.

What is the remedy? Some have proposed the ideal of cosmopolitanism, the merging and disappearance of all national groupings. Instead of being Frenchmen, Germans, or Americans, men would become citizens of a world state. One nationality, one language, one culture, and, if religion is to survive at all, one faith—this would constitute the common heritage of mankind.

At first blush, such an ideal has an undeniable grandeur and nobility as the concrete embodiment of the ideal of the unity of mankind. Upon sober examination, however, it becomes clear that if current versions of nationalism are a nightmare, this type of internationalism would prove an impractical dream.

The history of mankind, both recent and remote, discloses no signs that nations are disappearing, or are seeking to sink their differences in a common world patriotism. On the contrary, the past half century has seen the creation of scores of new nations, which struggle desperately for their place in the sun. World War I created many independent states in Central Europe. The last few decades have seen the emergence of nationalism as a dynamic factor in the Arab world, and in India, China, Burma, and Indonesia. Africa si now the home of a spate of new independent states, seething with new-found national consciousness. In sum, all signs point not to a diminution of nationalist loyalty, but to its intensification or at least to its retention for decades to come.

Nationalism will endure, not merely because of propaganda or the innate corruption of man, but because it draws upon deep roots in the soul of man. It is normal that a man should be attached to the soil where he was born, and where he spent the pleasant years of his childhood; that he should feel drawn to his own people, with whom he is most familiar. The songs one's own mother sang, the language she spoke, the festivals of one's childhood—these have an appeal beyond words and beyond reason, an appeal which no reasonable man will lightly dismiss.

The goal of a uniform mass of human beings seems, therefore, to fly in the face of reality. But aside from being impractical, this conception of internationalism would prove disastrous for the human spirit. National loyalty is the matrix in which all culture is formed. Every cultural achievement of which we have record is particularistic in origin, however universal its goal. Culture is always rooted in a given milieu, drawing its substance from a specific tradition, expressing itself in a given language, and deriving its power from a sense of kinship with a definite people. It is true that Hebrew prophecy, Greek art, Italian opera, German poetry, and English drama "belong to the world." But in every instance, they reflect their ethnic sources and their environmental influences, without which they are inconceivable. If, contrary to all indications, national loyalties were to dissolve, it would spell cultural anemia for the world. To borrow a distinction employed by some thinkers, *civilization*, the science and technology of the world, being impersonal, may be conceivable without nationalism, but not *culture*, which embraces the literature, art, music, and philosophy of the age.

That this recognition is growing even with regard to the more technical aspects of culture is clear from the words of two distinguished authorities on modern architecture, who write: "In so far as architecture is based on reason instead of sentiment, it is not concerned with frontiers. But countries also have their own different temperaments and ideals, and different climates, habits, and raw materials. They also have a past, and the national culture of which their modern architecture is part is not separable from its roots. So, as modern architecture matures, it tends to differentiate itself according to national characteristics—not on the basis of the racial exclusiveness of Nazism, and not so clearly and distinctly as would have been the case before steam, the airplane, the telephone, and the radio broke down once and for all many national barriers; but Americanness is a definable quality found in things American, as Frenchness is found in things French" (Mock and Richards, *Modern Architecture*, p. 96).

This process of "re-nationalization," as the authors call it, is not limited to any one art or technique, but is essential to most aspects of a healthy, rooted culture. The uniform pattern of a mechanical civilization which is spreading over the world is the result of the first flush of technological invention, to which men are still enslaved. Sooner or later, men will master the machine and then the deadening conformity of a mass production culture will give way once more to the quest for a living and creative culture of infinite variety, color, and form, rooted in the God-given uniqueness of each individual and group. Unless all signs fail, nationalism is here to stay.

Now if nationalism is, on the one hand, natural and even essential to the growth of culture, and if, on the other, it constitutes a potential menace to human survival, a tragic dilemma seems to face the human race: either stagnation or death. Must mankind be condemned to choose between the Scylla of a sterile, colorless cosmopolitanism and the Charybdis of a mad, bloodthirsty nationalism?

Merely to castigate nationalism as evil may offer some psychological relief, but as a practical program it is quixotic and doomed to failure. In this area of human conflict, as in others, another solution, at once more practical and more ideal, may be discovered in the Prophets of Israel. In the literal sense of the term, the Hebrew Prophets were the true internationalists, believers in the creation of proper relations among nations.

The author of the Vision of the End-time looked forward, not to the elimination but to the "moralization" of national loyalties. Since authority would be vested in the World Law, the nexus binding the members of each people together would not be force, but their common cultural heritage, the voluntary association of men and women for the preservation and cultivation of a cherished body of ideals, practices, and values. This ideal of nationalism as exclusively a cultural-ethnic loyalty has scarcely penetrated the thinking of most men, but it offers the only road to survival for mankind.

It is noteworthy that the only group which, however imperfectly, embodies this prophetic conception of nationalism is the Jewish people, a people united the world over by no central political allegiance, military power, or geographical contiguity. This unique group, best described by the Hebrew term 'am, or people, possessing an unbroken history of approximately thirty-five centuries, feels itself bound by a sense of kinship with the past, and claims Abraham, Isaac, and Jacob as its ancestors, while welcoming those who voluntarily seek to join its ranks from without. Its members share a common religio-cultural tradition in the present, which they feel free to interpret in accordance with their own attitudes and insights. Finally, they look forward to a common destiny in the future, however much their status may differ under varying political, social, and economic conditions across the globe.

The preservation of Jewish group loyalty, which has been so signally advanced in our day by the creation of the state of Israel, does not represent a retrogression from the prophetic ideal, as is sometimes erroneously supposed. The state of Israel makes possible a full national life for those members of the Jewish people who accept Israeli citizenship and take up residence within its borders. For the majority of Jews, who continue to live throughout the world, cherishing their political and civic allegiance to their native lands, the cultural and spiritual influence of the land of Israel is already proving to be a regenerative force of incalculable value.

For the author of the Vision, as for all the Hebrew Prophets, the presence of the people of Israel in its homeland was a necessary prelude to the redemption of the world, for the future of humanity was inconceivable without the survival of Israel as a recognizable entity. It is to "the house of the God of Jacob" on Mount Zion that the world would turn for guidance and for government.

As the frequent repetition of the terms "nation" and "people" indicates, however, not only Israel must survive in the End-time. The future has room for other national groups on the same terms, *a national loyalty cultural in essence and moral in function.* In Santayana's words, "A man's feet must be firmly planted in his own country, but his eyes must survey the world." The Prophets went further; their hearts embraced the world.

The Vision of the End-time is a far-sighted interpretation of nationalism, in which love of one's own people and loyalty to humanity represent two concentric circles. The bugbear of dual allegiance, which exercises little minds to the present day, would never have troubled them, because for them all loyalties, national as well as international, were peaceful in expression and subject to the moral law. Hence every

Hebrew prophet, from Amos and Hosea to Deutero-Isaiah and Malachi, exemplifies both nationalism and internationalism. A theologian may find a contradiction between particularism and universalism. The Prophet sees them both as organically related to each other and therefore both indispensable to the full flowering of the human spirit.

Modern thinkers, who deplore nationalism or at best seek to ignore it or dismiss it as irrelevant to their conception of the good life of society, would do well to be instructed by the Prophets of Israel. For their lives and careers are grounded on the conviction that nationalism is not necessarily evil and, what is more, can prove a source of spiritual enrichment in the life of man.

Our unknown prophet would have agreed completely with Amos, who may indeed have been his contemporary, in demanding the same high standard of righteousness from Judah as from Moab, from Israel as from Aram. The conception of an ethical nationalism, implicit in this Vision of the End-time, found its noblest and most concrete expression in Isaiah. Although he saw his people being ground to death in the world war fought between Egypt and Assyria, he foresaw the day when Israel would be "the third with Egypt and with Assyria, a blessing in the midst of the earth; for the Lord of hosts hath blessed him, saying: 'Blessed be Egypt My people, and Assyria the work of My hands, and Israel Mine inheritance' " (Isa. 19:24–25).

It has been said that those who are born before their time are punished by being forgotten. No such cruel fate overtook the Prophets of Israel, for though far in the vanguard of the human race, they possessed too much vitality to be ignored. In the ancient Vision of the End-time, an anonymous prophet revealed his faith in man's capacity to build a world worthy of its Maker, through the use of his innate intelligence and will. He proclaimed his faith in peace as the attainable, indeed the inevitable, goal of human history. He pointed the way to its realization through the establishment of a sovereign law binding upon all nations.

Yet with it all he remained firmly grounded in the world of reality. He looked forward to the preservation of national loyalty, which would ultimately prove a blessing and not a curse to the world, because it would be cultural in form, peaceful in expression, and obedient to the divine law of morality, which would be embodied in world government. The Prophet was able to attain to this exalted plane of vision, because his own heart revealed to him that love of humanity was not

merely compatible with love for one's people but actually its fulfillment, and that true peace implies not merely safety for the body of
man, but also freedom for his spirit. Thus, early in the history of the
race, the Prophets indicated the goal of human history. It may yet be
given to their descendants to lead men forward toward its realization.

NOTES

1. Four principal views regarding the authorship of the prophecy have been
maintained: a) that Isaiah is the author (Duhm); b) that Micah is the original
(Gesenius, Ryssel); c) that the author is a prophet older than either Micah or
Isaiah (Koppe, Hitzig, Ewald, Delitzsch, Dillmann, and Box); d) that the passage is post-exilic in origin, either in the sixth century, roughly contemporaneous
with Deutero-Isaiah and Ezekiel, or possibly as late as the Greek age (Stade,
Wellhausen, Nowack, Cheyne, Toy and Gray). Cf. *International Critical Commentary on Isaiah*, I–XXXIX, by George Buchanan Gray, Charles Scribner's
Sons, New York, 1912, p. 44.

Basically the argument in favor of a post-exilic date rests upon a low valuation
of pre-exilic biblical thought and upon the conception of a rectilinear religious
development in Israel from primitivism to universalism. These attitudes are,
however, becoming increasingly untenable, as archeology, buttressing historical
and literary research, reveals the complex and highly developed character of
ancient Oriental thought, which served both as the framework and the foil of
Israel's religion.

Thus on p. 45 f. Gray asks: "Did the prophets of the eighth century attach
worldwide significance to the Temple mount?" A dogmatic answer is impossible, but surely Amos attached world sovereignty to the God of Israel, when he
pronounced God's punishment upon Aram, the Philistines, the Phoenicians,
Edom, Ammon, and Moab, as well as upon Judah and Israel. This passage
(Amos 1:3–2:16) is preceded by a verse (1:2) which sets the stage for the Great
Judgment, and which surely attributes worldwide significance to the Temple
mount in Jerusalem:

> The Lord will roar from Zion,
> and utter His voice from Jerusalem.
> The habitations of the shepherds shall mourn,
> and the top of Carmel shall wither.

There is no substantial reason for denying the authenticity of this verse to
Amos. Similarly, Isaiah speaks of the nations sending gifts to the sanctuary in
Jerusalem (16:1; 18:7). That he conceived of Zion and its Temple as the seat of
the One God Whose glory fills the entire world (6:3) is clear from his Inaugural
Vision (6), which took place in the Temple precincts. It is this holiness of the
universal God which assures the inviolability of Zion at the hands of the
Assyrian conqueror (37:22 ff.).

Nor is universalism in pre-exilic Israel limited to the prophetic books. The narratives in Genesis, notably the stories of Adam, Noah, and the Tower of Babel, all attribute the knowledge of the one living God to the entire human race. Elijah is commanded by the God of Israel to anoint Hazael, King of Aram (I Ki. 19:15). Elisha, one of the most nationalistic of the prophets, conceives of the God of Israel as governing the affairs of Aram, even when the events work to the detriment of his own people (II Ki. 8:11 ff.), and going so far as to be accessible to the prayers of a heathen general, Naaman (II Ki. 5:10). Amos is merely carrying this universalism farther when he maintains that Israel is on a par with the Ethiopians in the eyes of God and that His hand is to be found in the migrations of the Philistines and the Arameans, no less than in Israel's Exodus from Egypt (9:7). Thus there is no reason for denying that the author of our Vision, who attached worldwide significance to the Temple mount in Jerusalem, may have lived in the pre-exilic period.

Another argument advanced against the early authorship of Micah 4:1–5 and in favor of the assumption that it is a late interpolation, is that the passage is at variance with Micah, ch. 3. But this contention is also untenable. The prophetic books were compiled by joining together brief and sometimes fragmentary oracles, the connection being often an external resemblance of phrase or superficial similarity of theme (cf. Isa. 19:16, 18, 19, 23, 25 *bayyōm hahū*, "on this day": Micah 4:8 *ve'atta*, "and thou" v. 9, *'attah*, "now," v. 11 *ve'attah*; v. 14 *'attah*; v. 5:1 *ve'attah*). Hence extreme transitions of thought and standpoint are thoroughly explicable, since these utterances are each independent and vary with mood and circumstance. Practically all the prophets foretold doom and yet held out the hope of restoration. Micah is a short book and prophecies of consolation are few, yet verses like 2:13, 4:6 f., 8:11 f., 5:1 ff., 5:6, 7:14 ff., stand side by side with condemnatory passages. It is, therefore, entirely conceivable that Micah or his disciples would include a vision of the End-Time in his book, especially in view of Micah's exalted conception of religion expressed in 6:1–8. As for the compatibility of the Vision with Isaiah's thought, cf. such Isaianic passages as 9:5 ff., 11:1 ff., 18:7, 19:16–25.

Aside from the weakness of the evidence advanced for a post-exilic date, several positive considerations for an early date may be noted. The occurrence in Joel 4:10 of the phrasing of v. 3 b in reverse, in a description of an outbreak of war, manifestly presupposes our passage. Though this is not conclusive, in view of the uncertainty of the date of Joel, a pre-exilic date for Micah 4:1–5, rather than a post-exilic one, is more plausible in allowing time for the parodying of the passage in Joel.

So, too, the fact that the prophet pictures the nations as coming to Zion and not the Jews as going to the nations, would also imply the pre-exilic period, as G. A. Smith has acutely noted. (G. A. Smith, *The Book of the Twelve Prophets*, A. C. Armstrong & Sons, New York, 1900, p. 401.)

V. 5 is regarded as an addition to the original prophecy by a long catena of scholars (Cornill, G. A. Smith, J. M. P. Smith, Nowack, Marti). Its absence from the parallel passage in Isaiah reinforces this view. The crucial issue is the date of the verse. If the main body of the prophecy be regarded, as is here maintained, as older than Micah or Isaiah, then this verse (which differs in both books) constitutes the comment of Micah and of Isaiah, who cite this vision of the End-Time, in order to use it to strengthen Judah's loyalty to its God. The verse in Micah is clear:

> For as all the peoples walk each one in the name of its god,
> We will walk in the name of the Lord our God for ever and ever.

In Isaiah the v. 2:5 has the same meaning, as is clear from the context: "O house of Jacob, come let us walk by the light of the Lord. For you have forsaken your national character (Hebrew 'ammekha, lit. your people) O house of Jacob, for they are filled from the East, with magicians like the Philistines."

This interpretive addition, which varies in Isaiah and Micah, coupled with the absence of evidence in favor of either one as the author, and the unacceptability of the post-exilic date, as indicated above, lead, by a process of elimination, to the acceptance of Koppe's view. The prophecy of the End-Time, which was utilized by two great pre-exilic prophets, is older than either. It is thus a product of the same age which made of an obscure sheep-hand named Amos, the first true citizen of the world.

12. ALL MEN'S BOOK—THE BOOK OF JOB

"A noble Book; all men's Book! It is our first, oldest statement of the never-ending Problem,—man's destiny, and God's ways with him here in this earth. And all in such free flowing outlines; grand in its sincerity, in its simplicity; in its epic melody, and repose of reconcilement. There is the seeing eye, the mildly understanding heart... Sublime sorrow, sublime reconciliation; oldest choral melody as of the heart of mankind,—so soft, and great; as the summer midnight, as the world with its seas and stars! There is nothing written, I think, in the Bible or out of it, of equal literary merit."[1] Thus ran Carlyle's sweeping tribute to the Book of Job.

Similarly, a distinguished Oriental scholar of our century, Morris Jastrow, declared that just as every actor, however humble, nurses a secret hope to play Hamlet, so every Biblical scholar has the ambition to write on Job.

But interest in the Book is by no means limited to specialists. The narrative of God's wager with Satan in the opening chapters was utilized by Goethe for the Prologue to *Faust*. William Blake found scope for his unique artistic genius in his strangely moving "Illustrations for the Book of Job." After the First World War, H. G. Wells used the framework of the dialogue of Job as a model for his treatment of the same basic problem in his novel, *The Undying Fire*. Archibald MacLeish's drama *J.B.* has attracted wide and continuing attention in the post-war era. Indeed, the influence of Job on the literature and art of the Western world can be documented at very great length. Its very phrases and idioms have entered the warp and woof of the English language—even into its colloquialisms, as in the phrase "by the skin of his teeth."

Job is, however, much more than a work of literary imagination. Its basic significance lies in its undying contribution to man's ceaseless effort to penetrate the riddle of existence. It addresses itself to the most agonizing mystery in the world—the problem of evil and human suffering.

On its literary form, which is without parallel elsewhere, only a word need be said.[2] Within the framework of a prose narrative we have a long dialogue in which logic and passion, emotion and thought are fused by the hand of a master genius. This dialogue cannot be described as lyric poetry, for it contains the conflicting utterances of varied protagonists. Yet, unlike the *Dialogues* of Plato, it contains no deeply reasoned, close-knit arguments expressed in prose. Nor does it qualify as a drama, even as a Greek drama;[3] there is neither incident described nor character developed within the body of the book. It is as unique in form as it is profound in content.

I. BACKGROUND OF THE BOOK

In spite of its universal significance, the *Book of Job* can be understood only against the background of the time and culture from which it rose.

Composed in the early years of the Second Commonwealth— roughly between the sixth and fourth centuries, before the Christian era[4]—it represented the culmination of a long, many-sided and fruitful intellectual activity in ancient Israel. The prophets Jeremiah and Ezekiel, who first foretold and then were fated to witness the destruction of the Temple and the loss of the Jewish State (586 B.C.E.), both make reference to the three basic strands of spiritual life in ancient Israel.[5] Jeremiah speaks of "the instruction of the priest, the counsel of the wise, and the word of the prophet." Ezekiel declares that, in the day of doom, men "shall seek a vision of the prophet, and instruction shall perish from the priest, and counsel from the elders."[6]

The first and most central type of spiritual leadership in ancient Israel was *Torah* (instruction or law), supplied by the priest (*kohen*), the custodian of *Torah*. Fundamentally, as the expert in ritual, the priest officiated at the Temple sacrifices. But he did much more. He acted as judge, medical expert and diviner. The authority of the priest derived from the divine revelation at Sinai under Moses, when the Torah was given to Israel.[7] After the Babylonian Exile and the building of the Second Temple (516 B.C.E.) the priest—as we have seen— continued to be the officiant at the ritual but lost his post of primacy as the authority on the *Torah*. His place was taken by a democratic, non-hierarchical leadership of *Sopherim*, generally but inadequately rendered "scribes," a term meaning "Masters of the Book (of the Law)." These *Sopherim*, spiritual progenitors of the Rabbis of the Mishna and the Talmud, became the expounders of the Law which, under their interpretation, grew and developed to keep pace with the needs and insights of a new age.[8]

The second kind of spiritual activity in pre-exilic Israel was supplied by the prophet, who proclaimed the Vision (*hazon*), or the Word (*dabar*) of the Lord. Lacking both the station and the emoluments of the priesthood, the prophet was supported by voluntary gifts from those who saw in him a direct communicant with the Deity. For the prophet declared that his utterances were not his own but his God's; they were stamped by the formula, "Thus saith the Lord."

The book of Jeremiah, for example, contains many deeply moving passages in which the prophet rebels against his tragic lot as a man of strife and contention to all the earth, but finds that he cannot be silent because God's word is "as a fire pent up in my bones, that cannot be contained."[9]

The Babylonian exile, which led to the transfer of authority from the priest to the scholar, had a far-reaching effect on the institution of prophecy. After the Return from Babylonia, prophecy declined and ultimately ceased, having performed its historic mission. But its greatest themes and expressions were preserved in what the entire people now recognized as sacred Scripture. Only in a derivative and debased form did one current of prophecy remain creative, producing the mystic "Apocalyptic" literature.

The third strand of intellectual activity in ancient Israel was *Hokmah*, cultivated by the sage (*hakam*) or elder (*zaken*). It was far more inclusive than the honorific and abstract term "wisdom" would indicate. Basically, Wisdom was concerned with all the practical arts and skills of ancient life: not only the conduct of government and such crafts as architecture, tapestry weaving and sailing the sea, but also the composition and rendering of poetry and music, and even the interpretation of dreams and the practice of magic.

Beyond these techniques, Wisdom was an intellectual discipline, concerned above all with the education of upper-class youth. The *hakam* was a teacher who sought to inculcate in his pupils the virtues of hard work, zeal, prudence, sexual moderation, sobriety, loyalty to authority and religious conformity—all the elements of a morality making for worldly success. In brief, Wisdom represented a hard-headed, matter-of-fact, "safe-and-sane" approach to the problems of living.

While, as before noted, the Babylonian Exile and the Return witnessed the decline and disappearance of prophecy, and ushered in a new phase of oral interpretation of the Torah, it was in this period that Wisdom reached its Golden Age. The exalted hopes of a Restoration had been realized on a very disappointing scale in the tiny Second Commonwealth. The Jewish community in Palestine suffered under a succession of foreign masters, Persian, Greek, Egyptian and Syrian; and fared even worse under the native Jewish rulers of the Hasmonean dynasty, who paved the way for the Roman conquest and the ultimate destruction of national independence.

It was the decline of faith in the fortunes of the nation, coupled with the growth of interest in the individual and his destiny, that stimulated the development of Wisdom. Wisdom was concerned not with the group but with the individual; with the actual present rather than a longed-for future. Wisdom's eminently practical goals for success in the here and now appealed, above all, to those groups in society who were least dissatisfied with the *status quo*—the government officials, the rich merchants, the great landowners whose soil was tilled by tenant farmers. These groups, even the high-priestly families among them, whose prestige and income derived from their position in the hierarchy of the Temple, were concerned less with the will of God than with the way of the world. Their goal in education was the training of their youth for successful careers. Their needs were admirably met by the Wisdom teachers who arose, principally if not exclusively, in Jerusalem, the capital city. From these teachers of a workable morality emanated the short maxims of the books of Proverbs and the longer essays in Ben Sira, who makes explicit reference to the *bet hamidrash*, or "academy."

Among them, however, were some whose restless minds refused to be satisfied with these practical goals of what may be termed the lower Wisdom. They sought to penetrate to the great abiding issues: the meaning of life, the purpose of creation, the nature of death, the mystery of evil. Several of these devotees of the higher or speculative Wisdom were able to transmute the frustration and pain of their quest into some of the world's greatest masterpieces, notably Job and Koheleth.

Koheleth, or Ecclesiastes, the skeptical observer of life and man's pretensions, was keenly aware of the problem of injustice in society, and reacted far more strongly against it than one might have imagined.[10] Primarily, however, his malaise is intellectual in origin. He is troubled by man's inability to discover the ultimate truth—the real meaning of life and the purposes of creation.

On the other hand, the author of Job, possessing perhaps a greater fund of feeling, was roused to indignation, not by man's intellectual limitations in a world he had not made, but rather by man's suffering in a world in which he had not asked to be born. A work of grand proportions, which may well have occupied his lifetime, was the notable result.[11] Therein he attempted to grapple with the central problem of religious faith, with which psalmist and prophet and poet alike had wrestled for centuries. Why do the wicked prosper and the righteous suffer? Why is there evil in a world created by a good God?

II. The Traditional Tale of Job

Like the great Greek dramatists, like Shakespeare, Milton and Goethe, the author of Job did not invent his own plot. He chose instead, to serve his purpose, the familiar tale of a righteous man named Job.[12] *A priori*, one would expect the traditional story of Job to have undergone a long development. But only recently has it become possible to reconstruct with some assurance the stages in the evolution of the tale before its final form in our book.

The sixth-century prophet Ezekiel, in one of his stern calls to repentance, warns his generation its iniquity is so great that, were the three righteous men Noah, Daniel and Job then alive, their righteousness would avail to save them personally but not their children from the general catastrophe. "Though these three men, Noah, Daniel, and Job, were in it, they should deliver but their own souls by their righteousness, saith the Lord God. . . . As I live, saith the Lord God, they shall deliver neither sons nor daughters; they only shall be delivered, but the land shall be desolate."[13]

The reference to Noah was, of course, always clear. Noah was a "righteous man in his generation" whose virtue avails to save not only his life but his wife's and children's when the Flood descends.[14]

But the reference to Daniel in Ezekiel always proved troublesome to the commentators. For in the Biblical book bearing his name,

Daniel is a wise interpreter of dreams, and there is no suggestion anywhere about his saving his children.[15] The key to the puzzle was unlocked only recently. In Ras-es-Shamra, a village in Syria, there were discovered the remains of an extensive literature going back to the middle of the second millennium B.C.E. It was written in Ugaritic, a North-West Semitic dialect akin to Hebrew; and in this literature is the epic of Aqhat, first published in 1936.[16]

The assembling of the narrative from scattered tablets, with unfortunate breaks at several crucial points, has been a major enterprise of Oriental scholarship in the last decades. Now the outlines of the story are tolerably clear. It tells the tale of a king of Hermon named *Dan'el* who rules an elaborate court with his wife *Dnty*. Virtuous and hospitable as they are, they are sad because they have no son. The poem begins with Dan'el's prayers and rituals of supplication. Finally their prayers are answered, and a male child is born to them who is named Aqhat. The boy receives a gift of a bow from the god Ktr, the craftsman-god of Ugarit. The bow, however, arouses the envy of the war goddess 'Anat, who offers to pay for it, either in precious ore or through the gift of immortality. When all these offers are rejected, the wrathful goddess has the lad slain by an assassin, Ytpn. This murder may perhaps have been avenged; but Dan'el, the father, is heartbroken. Carefully and lovingly he inters his son's remains. This, and other indications, would seem to imply that Aqhat is finally recalled to life and restored to his family.

In spite of its fragmentary character, the Ugaritic epic holds the key to the passage in Ezekiel. For it is now clear that Dan'el, not the Biblical Daniel, belongs in the company of Noah, as one who was able to save his son from death.

On the basis of the Ezekiel passage, thus illuminated by the Ugaritic parallel, we may now reconstruct the oldest form of the Job narrative, though only in its broadest outlines. As it was familiar to Ezekiel's contemporaries of the sixth century B.C.E., the tale doubtless told how the patriarch Job, because of his piety, had been able to save his children from death like Noah, or, failing that, had brought them back from the nether world like Dan'el. In this stage of the story Satan could have played no part, since the figure of the prosecuting attorney in the heavenly court, who later became the Adversary, did not enter Jewish thought until later. The Satan episode must belong to the

Persian period, when Jews came into contact with the Zoroastrian dualistic doctrine of Ahriman, the god of darkness and evil, and Ahura-Mazda, the god of light and goodness.

The next phase in the development of the story is more familiar to us, because it is imbedded in the prose chapters of Job, the so-called Prologue and Epilogue.[17] The tale opens on earth. Job is a patriarch whose life is marked by integrity and piety, enjoying prosperity and universal respect and the companionship of his entire family. The scene shifts to heaven. Satan, the prosecuting angel, standing in the presence of God, charges that Job's piety is dictated entirely by his prosperity. God enters into a wager to test the depth and sincerity of Job's piety by giving Satan permission to bring heavy calamities upon Job. The scene shifts back to earth. A series of disasters, alternately natural and man-made, come upon Job's family and possessions; his flocks are carried off and his children destroyed. But Job does not complain against his Maker. The fourth scene is again in heaven. God questions Satan on the results of the experiment, and Satan proves a hardy adversary. Still unprepared to concede the disinterested character of Job's virtue, he cites a familiar proverb: "Skin for skin, everything a man has he will give to save his life." Only if Job's own person suffer will the test be complete. God gives Satan permission to inflict disease on Job. The fifth and concluding scene again takes place on earth. Job has been smitten with leprosy, and only his wife remains at his side. Unable to bear the sight of his agony, she urges Job to curse God and die; but Job reproves her rather curtly: "Thou speakest like one of the impious women. Shall we receive only good from God's hand and not accept the evil?" And Job permits no sinful words to cross his lips.

It was a little less than kind of St. Augustine to describe Job's wife as *adiutrix diaboli*, the assistant of Satan. Actually, as the Midrash recognizes, her reaction is dictated out of her love and loyalty to her husband, a theme touchingly elaborated in the apocryphal Testament of Job, which relates that she sells her hair to support her husband. Thus far the story in the Prologue.

What other incidents, if any, followed in the original story we cannot tell, but Job's restoration is not too long delayed. In the Epilogue, his kinsmen and friends assemble to comfort him and bring him gifts of money and golden ornaments. God blesses Job, who is restored to double his previous prosperity and is blessed with seven[18] sons and three daughters famous for their beauty. Job is privileged to see four generations of his family, dying at the ripe old age of 140.

This folk tale, with its well-wrought delineation of character, its subtle touches of irony, its five scenes alternating between heaven and earth, and the vigor of the narrative, is a masterpiece of storytelling art. Here is no naive unsophisticated folk tale. It is rather the work of a literary craftsman of the first order, who has retold a familiar tale in his own way. Probably he is identical with the author of the poetic Dialogue, who saw in this tale an excellent framework for the great theme with which he was concerned. As is characteristic of Oriental literature, he was not overly concerned with harmonizing all the details of the familiar folk tale with his own poetical work, and so various differences of style and content remain which testify to the independent origins of the prose and the Dialogue.[19]

Having decided to use the familiar folk tale for his purpose, the poet finds it necessary to effect a transition from the prose Prologue to the poetic Dialogue and from the Dialogue to the prose Epilogue once more. This he achieves by adding two brief jointures.[20] In the first section, he introduces the protagonists of the discussion. While Job is sitting among the ashes, he is visited by three friends who begin to comfort him and end by infuriating him. Following the poetic Dialogue, the author has added the second jointure. That this section does not belong to the original folk tale but originates with the poet is clear from the fact that the Lord upbraids the friends: "The Lord said to Eliphaz the Temanite: 'My wrath is kindled against thee, and against thy two friends; for ye have not spoken of Me the thing that is right, as My servant Job hath'" (42:7). This phrase, which is repeated in verse 8—"for ye have not spoken of Me the thing that is right, as My servant Job hath"—can emanate only from one whose sympathies are with Job, rather than with the friends who have tried to defend God, but have done so inadequately, unconvincingly. For this poet, as for countless other sensitive seekers of the truth, "there lives more faith in honest doubt than in half the creeds."[21]

With the prose tale as the background the poet now turns to his theme—the problem of evil in a world governed by a good God. Nothing but the briefest survey can here be attempted of the basic ideas of the Dialogue. Only the text itself can communicate the mounting passion and emotional drive of the speeches, the growing bitterness and heartbreak of Job as he sees himself misunderstood and alone, confronted by the ever more blatant hostility of the friends. All their conventional theories of sin and punishment founder on the rock of Job's unwavering insistence on his innocence. Here is no cold analysis of logical propositions. Here rather is a dramatic interplay of human emotions. Faith and unbelief, hope, despair and hope resurgent—all battle in Job's breast for mastery; while the friends, beginning with a few conventional expressions of sympathy for Job's lot, prove more and more ineffectual in comforting Job or convincing him of their views.

The author's own sympathies are clearly with Job; it is he whose speeches are not only the longest but the most eloquent. The literary conscience and skill of the poet, however, compel him to do justice to the friends' standpoint as well. The regnant views of traditional theology have never been more effectively expressed than in the speeches of Eliphaz, Bildad and Zophar. Similarly, in *The Merchant of Venice*, Shakespeare's conscious sympathies lay with Antonio, but he could not help putting into Shylock's mouth words that penetrate to the bitter soul of the persecuted and despised Jew.

III. THE DIALOGUE OF JOB AND HIS FRIENDS .

The poetic section of the Book of Job begins with a deeply moving soliloquy by Job himself.[22] His friends are gathered round him in silence. The much-tried patriarch breaks out in a lament, cursing the day of his birth. As yet he has uttered no complaint against his Maker, contenting himself with a description of the peace that would have waited for him in the grave.

In an effort to console him, Eliphaz, the oldest and most respected of the friends, begins a reply. With tact and consideration he reminds Job of the universally accepted doctrine that justice prevails in God's world, and therefore no innocent man is ever destroyed, while, on the contrary, the sowers of iniquity reap the fruit of their doings. Eliphaz makes a few significant additions to the conventional doctrine of reward and punishment. Often the sinner's just penalty is visited upon his children, a view highly congenial to the ancient concept of the solidarity of the family. Moreover, suffering often acts as a discipline and is therefore a mark of God's love. Finally, all men are sinful; in fact, sin is not God's creation, but man's doing. It therefore behooves

Job to be patient and wait for restoration. For all its urbanity, the address of Eliphaz contains nevertheless the implication that Job must be a sinner, since suffering is the result of sin.

Job has no theory to propose as a substitute, merely his consciousness that he is suffering without cause. He does not claim to be perfect, but insists he is not a willful sinner. Their conventional ideas he confronts with the testimony of his own experience, which he will not deny, whatever the consequences. But his attacks upon the disloyalty of his friends, his pathetic description of his physical pain and mental anguish, his indignant rejection of the theology of the friends, serve all the more to convince them that he is a sinner. For do not arrogance and the assumption of innocence by man, with the implied right and capacity to pass judgment on God, constitute the height of impiety?

Bildad paints a picture of the destruction of the wicked and the ultimate restoration of the righteous, and he hymns the power of God. Job does not deny God's power; it is His justice he calls into question.

Zophar, probably the youngest and least discreet of the friends, summons Job to repent of his secret sins. Then, with matchless irony, Job turns again upon his friends who, in their security and ease, can afford to indulge in artificial arguments far removed from the painful realities of life. In a passage long misunderstood,[23] he parodies their speeches on the greatness of God and concludes that their defense of God, dishonest and biased as it is, will not likely win His favor. Job flees from God to God, convinced that behind the God of reality is the God of the ideal. He appeals for God's mercy, a quick and painless death. For a moment he considers the idea of resurrection, which would perhaps justify suffering the pain of the present in the hope of a happy future; but sorrowfully he rejects the possibility. Death comes to all, knowledge and sentience die, and man's career of agony ends in nothingness.

Thus ends the First Cycle of speeches.

In the Second Cycle changes are rung on the same ideas, but with greater vehemence.[24] And a few additional ideas emerge. Eliphaz emphasizes that there is even more to the punishment of the wicked than his ultimate destruction, whether in his own person or in that of his offspring. During the very period of his ostensible prosperity he lives in trepidation, never knowing when the blow will fall. Job, on the other hand, insists that, though his unjustified suffering does arouse universal pity, righteous men will not be deflected from the good life because of his sad fate. Thus Job boldly cuts the nexus in utilitarian morality between virtue and prosperity, and makes righteousness its own justification. He calls upon the earth not to cover his blood or absorb his cry. In fact, he wants his words to be engraved permanently upon a monumental inscription to await his ultimate vindication, because he is convinced that God, his witness, is in the heavens and that his "Redeemer liveth, even though he be the last to arise upon earth."[25]

The Second Cycle is concluded by Job again with a powerful refutation of the friends' arguments. As against the comfortable doctrine that the wicked are destroyed, Job paints a picture of the actual case—well-being and honor enjoyed by the malefactors. He cites four of the friends' contentions and riddles them with logic.[26] That the sinner will ultimately be punished, or that his children will pay the penalty, is unsatisfactory and therefore unjust. He himself should be brought to book—and immediately. That God is beyond man's comprehension Job cannot deny; but still he insists on calling attention to the disparity between the lot of the righteous man, whose days are embittered by trouble, and the destiny of the sinner, who enjoys life to the full, while awaiting them both is the same silent death. As for the contention that the house of the wicked is suddenly destroyed, Job invites his friends to ask any passer-by to point out the proud mansions of the evil-doers. Far from coming to an ignominious end, the wealthy malefactor caps his career with an elaborate funeral!

The Third Cycle has been gravely disarranged, and a good deal of the original material has been lost.[27] Imbedded in this section is an independent lyrical poem, "The Hymn to Wisdom."[28] Its basic theme is the inaccessibility of Wisdom to the human understanding. Men may dig for precious stones in the remote corners of the earth, revealing many hidden things; but Wisdom *par excellence*, the secret of the universe, is with God alone. For man all that remains is reverence for God and the avoidance of evil.

There are good grounds for assuming that this hymn, though not part of Job, came from the author or his school.[29] Perhaps it was an early effort to deal with the theme that the author later expanded into the book of Job, like Goethe's *Faust Fragments* which preceded the drama.

To a large degree, though not without lacunae, the Third Cycle can be restored.[30] A few new notes are struck in the ever blunter argument. Now Eliphaz accuses Job of being an out-and-out sinner, who has taken refuge in God's distance from man and therefore expects to avoid retribution. Observe that the heretic in ancient Israel, like the Epicurean school in Greece, did not deny the existence of God but rather His interference in human affairs. Eliphaz relentlessly presses Job to repent, even promises his restoration to Divine favor, so that as of yore he will be able to intercede for other sinners.[31] Bildad somewhat academically reemphasizes the imperfection of all men. Job insists again upon his innocence, picturing the absolute faith in God's government by which he had formerly lived.[32] Zophar declares once more that the prosperity of the wicked is an illusion; it is but a process of garnering wealth for the enjoyment of the righteous.

This speech of Zophar's, Job does not dignify by a reply. The friends and their arguments fade from his consciousness. He ends as he began, with a soliloquy, his last great utterance. At the outset, Job recalls the high estate of dignity and honor he once occupied, and the universal esteem he once commanded. Then on to his magnificent climax—his "Confession of Integrity."[33] This classic statement may be described as the code of the Jewish gentleman. It is significant that, with the exception of a brief reference to the worship of heavenly bodies, the code is exclusively moral and not ritualistic in character. Job recounts his personal morality with regard to women, his fairdealing with slaves whose basic human equality he affirms, and his consideration for the poor, the widow and the orphan. He has never grown arrogant because of his wealth or rejoiced in the discomfiture of his foes, nor has he ever been ashamed to confess his errors because of the scorn of the mob.

The impact of this "Confession of Integrity" is heightened by the form in which it is couched—a series of rhetorical questions, in which Job denies wrong-doing, alternating with passionate oaths, in which Job calls down condign punishment upon himself if he has been guilty of a breach.[34]

Job's final words are a plea to God to answer him and at least thus compensate him for his agony. The grandeur of Job's opening lament is matched by the dignity of his closing affirmation.

IV. THE SPEECHES OF ELIHU

Ended are Job's words, and the friends are left without a reply. But a young man named Elihu ben Barakhel breaks into the august silence. Aware of his effrontery in invading the discussions of his elders, he insists, with some braggadocio, that it is not the number of a man's years, but the spirit within him, that determines his wisdom and his right to speak. Elihu's complaint is directed at least as much against the friends as against Job himself, for with the brashness of youth he proclaims that their defense of God's ways has been inadequate. He presents his ideas in impassioned language, often obscure to us today.

Job has contended that God avoids answering him. Elihu declares that God does communicate with His creatures. Through dreams and illness He reminds men of His presence and thus saves them from falling into sin. That God persecutes Job is the rankest blasphemy—each man gets his just reward. As for the argument that righteousness and sin both meet the same fate, Elihu answers that, to be sure, God is not affected by man's actions, but man is. Finally, he emphasizes that affliction is an instrument used by God to strengthen man's faith and recall him to virtue. And, as signs of an approaching storm appear in the north, Elihu emphasizes that God's power, which Job has conceded, is matched by God's justice. He is both "mighty in strength and great in righteousness."[35]

The authenticity of these Elihu chapters has been widely doubted by modern scholars. They have called attention, first, to striking variations in the style and vocabulary, which is particularly rich in Aramaisms. Moreover, there is the fact that neither in the Prologue nor in the Epilogue does Elihu appear. Lastly, it has been argued that Elihu contributes nothing new to the discussion.

On the other hand, it is possible to meet these objections and defend the authenticity of the chapters. Elihu's absence in the Prologue is not so strange, in view of his being confessedly an interloper and a stripling to boot. The stylistic variations can be attributed to the fact that Elihu represents a younger and less dignified generation.[36] It is also likely that the Elihu speeches were added by our author at a later period. Similarly, Goethe's *Urfaust* goes back to the poet's *Sturm und Drang* period, the third decade of his life; the First Part of *Faust* did not appear until more than thirty years later, in 1808; and the Second Part was completed shortly before his death in 1832; and in the long process the poet's conception of his theme underwent a profound transformation. Something like that may well have been the case with the author of Job.

As for the argument that Elihu contributes nothing new: if that were granted, it would raise the question why his speeches were introduced altogether. As a matter of fact, they do have their place in the architecture of the book.

For there is one idea which is emphasized in Elihu's words, which with a single brief exception[37] had not been previously referred to— the doctrine that suffering frequently comes upon man as a discipline, as a warning to prevent him from a sinking into sin. It is conceivable that the author of the book looked on this idea as true, though certainly not the whole truth regarding the problem of evil. Obviously the doctrine could not be placed in the mouth of Job, who denies that there is any justice in suffering. Nor would the author place it in the mouths of the friends, for their ideas he wishes to reject.[38] Finally, were this idea included in the subsequent God-speeches, it would weaken the force of the principal answer. By creating a character like Elihu, who opposes the attitude of the friends as well as that of Job, the author is able to express this secondary idea, giving it due place in his world-view.

V. The God-Speeches

After Elihu, the Lord answers Job out of the whirlwind.[39] These speeches of God belong to the supreme nature poetry of our literature. Can Job comprehend, let alone govern, the secrets of creation? Earth and sea, cloud and darkness and dawn, snow and hail, rain and thunder, snow and ice, and the stars above—all these wonders are beyond Job. Nor do these exhaust God's power. With a vividness born of deep love and careful observation, the poet pictures the beasts, remote from man, yet precious to their Maker, the mountain goat, the wild ass, the buffalo, the ostrich, the horse, the hawk, all testifying to the glory of God. For all their variety, these creatures have one element in common—they are not under the sway of man, or even intended for his use.

Job is overwhelmed and confesses his weakness. But God ignores

Job's surrender, and with torrential force continues to hurl His challenge at His human opponent.[40] Were Job able to destroy evil in the world, even God would be prepared to relinquish His throne to him—a moving acknowledgment by God that the world-order is not perfect! Then follow exultant descriptions of massive beasts—*behemot*, the hippopotamus, and *leviathan*, the crocodile. Far as they are from being conventionally beautiful, these ponderous creatures arouse the triumphant ecstasy of the poet. Their choice is not accidental. The author here rises above the anthropocentric point of view which, however natural for man, distorts his comprehension of the world. The monstrosities fashioned by God's hand constitute a revelation of the limitless range of God's creative thought.[41]

Job finally yields—overwhelmed, not by the mere might of God which he had conceded long ago, but by the majesty and order revealed in His power. With Job's surrender the Dialogue comes to an end.

VI. THE EPILOGUE

The first portion of the Epilogue (42:7–10), which connects the poetry and the prose, as has already been noted, emanates from the author of the poetic Dialogue, whose sympathies are with Job. After Job's confession, the Lord declares that He is wroth with the three friends because "they have not spoken the truth about Me." Only after Job intercedes for them are they forgiven, and Job himself is given double his possessions in the past.

The second section of the Epilogue (42:17 ff.) takes up the strand of the folk tale which has been interrupted at chapter 2, verse 10. Job's friends and relatives come to comfort him and contribute gifts to aid in his restoration. The Lord's blessing descends upon Job; and wealth, family, and long life are his portion.

VII. THE BOOK OF JOB AND THE PROBLEM OF SUFFERING

The motives of the author in writing his book should be clear from our discussion. He is opposed to the conventional theory of suffering, as taught by the religion of his day. Being, however, a gifted poet as well as an honest thinker, he does full justice to this traditional view in the eloquent speeches of the friends. Those addresses are far more than a foil to Job; they remain the classic statement of the conception of human suffering as maintained by traditional theism. Basically, the doctrine flows from the conception of a just God, Who is unlimited in power. In His world it must follow that righteousness leads to happiness, and sin brings its penalty.

This is the burden of the prophetic teaching. The prophets applied this view to the destiny of the nation as a whole. In Hosea's words, "They sow the wind, and shall reap the whirlwind"; or, as formulated by Isaiah, "Declare to the righteous that it is well with him. For men eat the fruit of their deeds. But woe to the wicked for it goes ill with him, for the recompense of his hands will be done to him."[42] This doctrine served as the foundation of the prophetic conception of history, underpinning the prophets' denunciation of the *status quo*, and later their message of hope and restoration after the destruction of the Temple and the State.

After the Return, however, interest shifted from the group to the individual personality. Not so much the prosperity of the nation as the well-being of the individual now occupied the forefront of attention. Traditional religion of the Second Commonwealth transferred the prophets' idea of reward and punishment to the individual—a process which, to be sure, had been initiated before the Exile by the prophets themselves. Jeremiah and Ezekiel, in their endeavors to rekindle hope in the despairing hearts of their people, had taught that each man's weal or woe depends upon his own virtues or vices.[43] But when matter-of-fact observers applied this doctrine to the actual life about them, they saw that experience contradicted it at every turn.

Tradition finds it much easier to supplement, modify and reinterpret older elements than to discard them when they prove inadequate. This characteristic is strikingly exemplified in the history of the doctrine of reward and punishment in normative Judaism, from the Biblical epoch down to the Hasidic age. Layer upon layer was added to older ideas, while little was surrendered.

Traditional Hebrew thought began with the older Semitic doctrine of family responsibility. When God visits the sins of the fathers upon the children, it may seem unjust to us from the standpoint of the individual affected; but *sub specie aeternitatis* it may well be just, since the individual is only a link in the chain of the family, which is judged as a unit. This doctrine of group responsibility operates not only "vertically," through time, but also "horizontally," across space. Each individual is linked not only with his ancestors and his descendants in the unit of a *family*, but also with his contemporaries with whom he constitutes the unit of a *generation*. Thus a righteous individual may sometimes be in position to save an evil generation.[44] By the same token, the innocent may sometimes suffer for the sins of his age.

Increasingly, however, the individual, with his personal hopes and fears, could not be denied. Nonetheless, the traditional doctrine was not abandoned. Instead, qualifications were introduced to explain "exceptions" to the law of retribution. Thus it came to be held that the prosperity of the wicked and the suffering of the righteous alike are only temporary; ultimately, justice is done and the balance redressed. Moreover, even during the period of his prosperity the wicked man is not free to enjoy his good fortune because, like the sword of Damocles, the threat of punishment is always suspended over him. In at least one important passage, the theme is stressed that man and not God is the source of sin, and therefore everyone must expect retribution for his actions. Hence, the conviction that suffering can be minimized by the practice of justice is a fundamental element of Biblical religion. A different nuance is expressed several times in Job: man, by his very nature, is imperfect; how then can he expect to avoid sin or its consequences?

These ideas form indeed the principal content of the friends' speeches in Job. As orthodox religion came to recognize that these answers did not suffice, it ultimately elaborated the concept of life after death with judgment beyond the grave. It is noteworthy that the friends make no reference to the idea. Job himself does refer to this new faith springing up in his day, but sorrowfully finds himself unable to accept it.[45]

Yet even when other-worldly conceptions of retribution became universal, the validity of older ideas of theodicy was retained. In John Donne's classic formulation:

. . . No man is an iland, intire of it selfe; every man is a peece of the Continent, a part of the maine; if a Clod be washed away by the Sea, Europe is the lesse, as well as if a promontorie were, as well as if a Mannor of thy friends or of thine owne were. Any man's death diminishes me, because I am involved in Mankinde; and therefore never send to know for whom the bell tolls; it tolls for thee. . . .

Though the author of Job presents the traditional point of view with all the eloquence and power at his command, he is deeply conscious of its inadequacy. His spokesman and hero, Job, attacks this accepted theodicy, not on the grounds of abstract logic, but in terms of personal experience, his unshakable consciousness of integrity. It is characteristic of Jewish thought that in spite of all the calamities that came upon him, Job does not yield to atheism. Job cannot deny the evidence of his senses—his bitter suffering is a challenge to the justice of God. But neither can he surrender the promptings of his heart —in his darkest hour he retains the faith that behind the tragic reality of a cruel God stands the ideal God who will ultimately vindicate him. More than once Job stands poised on the threshold of dualism; but the basic Jewish concept of the Divine Unity prevents him from making a dichotomy between the God of might and the God of justice.

If Job is essentially the critic who refutes the accepted pattern of religious thought, he makes one positive contribution as well. Impaled on the tragic dilemma of a righteous man's suffering in a world created by a righteous God, Job is nevertheless unwilling to surrender his ideal of rectitude. Though virtue has brought him no reward, "the righteous cleaves to his path and the innocent increases his strength" (17:9). The Mishna quite correctly concludes that Job served God not from "fear" but from "love."[46] The truly ethical life is motivated not by the desire for reward, but by its own inherent satisfactions.

The author's positive views on suffering, as already indicated, are stated in two sections of the book.

Elihu stresses the idea that suffering frequently serves as a source of moral discipline, and is thus a spur to higher ethical attainment.

The principal answer, however, is reserved for the climax, the speeches of "the Lord out of the whirlwind." Job cannot fathom the mystery of nature. How then can he hope to penetrate the secrets of man's fate?

That is not all. For the vivid and joyous description of nature in these chapters testifies that nature is more than a mystery; it is a cosmos, a thing of beauty. The implication is not lost upon Job. Just as there are order and harmony in the natural world, so there are order and meaning in the moral sphere. Man who cannot fathom the meaning of the natural order is yet made aware of its beauty and harmony. Similarly, if he cannot expect to comprehend the moral order, he yet must believe that there is rationality and justice within it. After all legitimate explanations of suffering are taken into account, a mystery still remains. The analogy of the natural order gives the believer in God the grounds for facing the mystery with a courage born of faith in the essential rightness of things.[47] What cannot be comprehended through reason must be embraced in love. As Kant pointed out, if it is arrogant to defend God, it is even more arrogant to assail Him.[48] For the author of Job, as for Judaism always, God is one and indivisible. As nature is instinct with morality, so the moral order is rooted in the universe.

One other significant contribution to religion emerges from the Book of Job. For the poet, the harmony of the universe is important not only as an idea but as an experience, not only logically but esthetically. When man steeps himself in the beauty of the world, his troubles grow petty and dissolve within the larger plan, like the tiny dabs of oil in a masterpiece of painting. The beauty of the world becomes an anodyne to man's suffering.

The author of Job is an artist to whom we may apply the words of Havelock Ellis:

Instead of imitating these philosophers who with analyses and syntheses worry over the goal of life and the justification of the world, and the meaning of the strange and painful phenomenon called Existence, the artist takes up some fragment of that existence, transfigures it, shows it: There! And therewith the spectator is filled with enthusiastic joy, and the transcendent Adventure of Existence is justified. . . . All the pain and the madness, even the ugliness and the commonplace of the world, he converts into shining jewels. By revealing the spectacular character of reality he restores the serenity of its innocence. We see the face of the world as of a lovely woman smiling through her tears.[49]

Artist and poet, the author of Job is no theologian with a neatly articulated, all-inclusive system. He does not pretend to have discovered the final solution to the problem of evil. He recognizes instead the residuum of the Unknown in the world. For this reason, and because of its literary greatness, the book will never grow out of date. It will be read, pondered and loved as long as men possess moral as well as intellectual integrity, and some men, at least, refuse to surrender either to self-deception or to immorality. It will always help men to face life with reverence before the mystery of the world and with joy at its beauty.

NOTES

1. Thomas Carlyle, *Heroes and Hero-Worship*—Lecture II: "The Hero as Prophet."

2. The so-called "Egyptian Job" and "Babylonian Job" are fragments of poems of lamentation bewailing personal misfortunes by men who were scrupulous in the observance of ritual obligations. They bear little resemblance to the Biblical Job either in content or in form. Cf. Driver-Gray, *International Critical Commentary on Job* (New York, 1921), vol. 1, pp. xxxi ff.

3. A view propounded by H. M. Kallen, *The Book of Job as a Greek Tragedy* (New York, 1918).

4. In the absence of clear-cut historical allusions, scholars differ as to the date of the book. It is assigned to the period before Deutero-Isaiah by Kuenen; to the 6th century B.C.E. by Kittel and G. Hoffman; to the 5th century by Moore, Driver-Gray, Dhorme, Buttenwieser, Budde; to the 4th by Eissfeldt, Finkelstein, Meinhold, Steuernagel, Volz; and to the 3rd by Cornill and Holzmann. For a careful discussion of the internal and external criteria for dating the book, cf. Driver-Gray, *ICC on Job*, vol. 1, pp. LXV ff., and other standard commentaries. Basically, the book reflects the attitudes of Wisdom literature, which reached its apogee in the first half of the Second Commonwealth period.

The *terminus a quo* is determined by these facts: (1) the book takes monotheism for granted without argument, thus post-dating Deutero-Isaiah; (2) it reflects an early stage in the development of the Satan idea (Satan in chapters 1, 2; Zec. 3:1, 2 occurs with the definite article as "the Adversary": he is not yet completely an independent personality, as in Satan without the article (I Chr. 21:1); (3) it is aware of the new ideas about life after death (14:14) but does not accept them; (4) it reflects city life and monogamy, characteristics of later periods.

The terminus *non post quem* is determined by the existence of a Greek translation, the Elihu chapters included, by the year 100 B.C.E., a reference to Elihu being found in a citation from Alexander Polyhistor (80-40 B.C.E.); and by an apparent reference to Job in Ben Sira 49:10, written about 190 B.C.E., though this is more doubtful.

5. On the three strands, cf. Max L. Margolis' *The Hebrew Scriptures in the Making* (Philadelphia, 1922). The stages of development of each type are discussed in the opening chapter in this volume.

6. Jeremiah 18:18; Ezekiel 7:26.

7. See the opening study in this volume, "The Bible—Its Origin, Growth, and Meaning", on the spiritual trends briefly summarized in the text above.

8. Cf. such histories of Jewish law as I. H. Weiss' classic *Dor Dor Vedorshav*,

5 vols. (1871–91), and the more recent work of Ch. Tschernowitz, *Toledot Hahalakah*, 3 vols. (New York, 1934); as well as briefer treatments like S. Zucrow, *The Adjustment of Jewish Law to Life* (New York, 1935), and the writer's "The Nature of Jewish Tradition" in *Judaism For the Modern Age* (New York, 1955), pp. 127–52.

9. Cf., e.g., Jer. 20:7–12, 14–18; 15:10, 11; 11:18–20; 12:4–6.

10. Cf., e.g., Eccl. 4:1 ff. An effort to reconstruct Koheleth's spiritual development may be found in *KMW*, chap. X.

11. On the length of time in composing the book, see below on the Elihu chapters.

12. That the locale of the book and of its protagonists is not Israelite is not strange. Literary works often choose a foreign scene. The Homeric epics arose not among the Achaeans, who are its heroes, but among the Ionians and the Aeolians. The Niebelung-cycle developed not among the Burgundians but among the Franks (cf. Kraeling, *The Book of the Ways of God*, p. 15). Pfeiffer's theory of the Edomite origin of Job and other parts of the Bible (Source S=Seir, cf. his Introduction pp. 159–67, 678–83) has not been generally accepted, since virtually nothing is known of Edomite religion or literature. Ibn Ezra's remark (in his *Commentary on Job* 2:11) that the work may be a translation of the Arabic is likewise unacceptable. On the theory that some Biblical books are translations of non-extant books written in languages other than Hebrew, see our comments in *Jewish Quarterly Review*, vol. 37, 1946, pp. 69 f. The author of Job was a man of broad general culture, widely traveled. Pfeiffer calls him the most erudite ancient before Plato. But such unconscious usages as "Jordan" for "river" in 40:23, the references to many Biblical laws, the thoroughgoing monotheism of outlook, and countless Biblical reminiscences (cf. Dhorme, *Le Livre de Job*, pp. cxvi ff.), as well as its congruity with the intellectual development of post-exilic Hebrew Wisdom, and the fact that it was admitted to the canon of Hebrew Scripture, all testify that it is not foreign in origin, but rather an authentic Jewish work of universal import.

13. Ezek. 14:14, 16; cf. also verses 18, 20.

14. Gen. 6:9, 18.

15. A number of perspicacious commentators, like the medieval David Kimhi (*ad loc.*), noted the difference in the orthography of the name Daniel. In the Biblical book of the same name, it is written with *Yodh, d-n-y'-l*; in Ezek., without it, *d-n-'l*. The significance has only now become apparent. Not even in the incident of Daniel in the den of lions is there a reference to children (Dan. 6).

16. Published by Ch. Virolleaud, *La Légende Phoenicienne de Danel* (Paris, 1936). Cf. S. Spiegel, "Noah, Dan'el and Job" in *Louis Ginzberg Jubilee Volume I*, p. 310, n. 1., whose reconstruction of the plot of the Dan'el epic is fundamental (pp. 310–18).

17. The Prologue consists of chapters 1 and 2; the Epilogue is to be found in chapter 42:7–17. However, the two passages 2:11–13 and 47:7–10 do not belong to this original stage of the tale, but were added by the poet himself. See below in the text for details.

18. Or "fourteen," depending on how the rare form of the numeral *shiv'anah*

is interpreted. The 140 years of Job's life and the four generations of his descendants that he beheld (42:16) represent double the normal and lend plausibility to the view that the numeral in question is a dual, equal to "twice-seven."

19. The principal differences are these: (a) In the prose, God is pictured in anthropomorphic terms, as a ruler on a throne; in the poetry, He is an exalted abstract Being. (b) In the prose, the Divine name used is JHVH, the national name of the God of Israel; in the poetry, the abstract names for the Deity used are exclusively *El, Eloah, Elohim* and *Shaddai*. There are only two exceptions where JHVH is used in the poetry. In 12:9 it is used in a common phrase borrowed from Isa. 41:20; and in the superscriptions in 38:1 and 40:1 it introduces "JHVH from the whirlwind," perhaps because of the ancient tradition of the theophanies of JHVH in a storm (Ex. 19; Deut. 33; Jud. 5; Habakkuk 3; etc.). In addition *Adonai*, "The Lord," occurs in the independent poem "Hymn to Wisdom" (28:28) in the common phrase "fear of the Lord." (c) In the prose, Job's suffering is due to the wager of God and Satan; in the poetry, Satan does not appear at all and the entire debate revolves around the mystery of Job's suffering. (d) In the prose, Job is bereaved of his entire family, except his wife, and sits in isolation on the dung-heap; in the poetry, Job pictures himself as the butt of scorn and hatred by his household and acquaintances, who are presented as all about him (cf. 16:9; 19:13–16; 30:1). (e) In the prose, Job is the epitome of patience and resignation; in the poetry, his is the voice of flaming revolt.

20. The first jointure is 2:11–13; the second, 47:7–10.

21. Various attempts have been made to reconstruct the pre-history of the Job tale. Macdonald, Duhm and Alt, followed by E. Kraeling, *op. cit.*, p. 169, have suggested that the prose is a folk tale in which originally the friends urged Job to blaspheme his Maker, hence the Lord's castigation of them as "not speaking what is right" (42:7, 8). Aside from the fact that there would be no need for the friends in the tale, since Job's wife performs the same function (2:9), the phrase cited as evidence actually disproves it. The word *nekhonah*, "right, correct, true" (cf. Gen. 41:32; Ps. 51:12; 57:8; 78:37; 108:2; especially Deut. 13:15; 17:14) is a synonym of *'emet*, "true." It could be used in the negative to describe an unsatisfactory defense of God, but is much too weak for blasphemy —for that the word is *nebhalah*, "disgrace, contumely" (Gen. 34:7; Deut. 22:21), the root of which is used of the denial of God in Job 2:9 and Ps. 14:1 = 53:1; 74:22.

Alt has suggested also that we have two prose tales, one in chapter 1 and 42:11–17; the other in chapter 2 and 42:7–10. This theory has several drawbacks. (1) It destroys the dramatic architecture of the five scenes of the tale in chapters 1–2. (2) It leaves the first account hanging in the air. (3) The story beginning with chapter 2 opens abruptly without introduction, so that it must be assumed that part of it is lost. (4) The role of the friends remains superfluous and God's description of their speeches, as we have noted, inappropriate. Alt's merit lies in having noted that 42:7–10 is quite distinct from 42:11–17.

All the facts are accounted for by the view here presented, which agrees in most essentials with R. H. Pfeiffer, *Introduction to the Old Testament* (New York, 1941), p. 669. The folk tale, reworked by the author of the Dialogue, consists of chapters 1, 2, and 42:11–17. To make it serve as the framework of the Dialogue, the poet added two connecting sections, one introducing the friends (2:11–13), the other passing judgment upon their conventional defense of God (42:7–10). As evidence that this material is interpolated, we may cite the striking resemblance in theme and language between 42:11, the original continuation of the tale ("*And all his brothers*, and all his sons and all his former acquaintances *came* and ate bread with him in his home and *they consoled him and comforted him*") and 2:11, the insertion of the poet ("*And Job's friends* heard of the trouble that had come upon him and they *came each man* from his place, Eliphaz the Temanite, Bildad the Shuhite and Zophar the Naamatite and they met together to *come to console him and comfort him*").

22. The First Cycle (3–14) begins with Job's soliloquy in chapter 3, followed by Eliphaz 4, 5; Job 6, 7; Bildad 8; Job 9, 10; Zophar 11; and concludes with Job's final, longest and most eloquent reply (12–14).

23. On the use of quotations, which is the key to chapters 12, 21, 27 and 42:1–6, and which obviates the need for wholesale deletion in these and many other passages, cf. "Quotations as a Literary Usage in Biblical, Oriental, and Rabbinic Literature," in this volume.

24. The Second Cycle (15–21) begins with Eliphaz 15; followed by Job 16, 17; Bildad 18; Job 19; Zophar 20; and ends with Job 21.

25. Job's defiance is expressed in 16:18, his faith in 19:23 ff.; his assertion of the good life as an end in itself is in 17:8–9.

26. The citations of the friends' arguments are to be found in chapter 21, verses 19a, 22, 28, and 30.

27. For a full discussion of the Third Cycle, now to be found in chapters 22–31, cf. Driver-Gray, *op. cit.*, vol. 1, pp. xxviii–xl. The principal evidence for the dislocation: (1) Bildad's speech (25) is too short; (2) Job's speech (26–31) is manifestly too long and, what is more, contains a great deal of material not appropriate to his point of view (as e. g., 26:5–14; 27:13–23); (3) Zophar's third speech is completely lacking.

28. That this poem, chapter 28 in our present book of Job, is an independent "Hymn to Wisdom, the Inaccessible" is clear from the following facts: (1) It is lyrical and not argumentative in character. (2) It contains a refrain, "Wisdom, where may it be found, and where is the place of understanding?" (28:12, 20). Its basic theme is that the ultimate Wisdom is beyond man, and what remains for man is religion and morality. In its present position this Hymn is not merely an interruption; it is actually an anti-climax anticipating the theme of the God-speeches.

29. On the basis of the presence of chapter 28 in the book, its finished literary form, the wide range of technical knowledge it displays and the similarity of its point of view to the God-speeches (38–41), the poem can plausibly be attributed to the author of Job or a disciple.

30. For a conspectus of the various efforts at restoration by different scholars see R. H. Pfeiffer, *op. cit.*, p. 671. Our own reconstruction, based on Graetz and Elzas, is admittedly tentative, as all such efforts must be, but requires a minimum of manipulation of the material in the Masoretic text. It is as follows:

Eliphaz 22; Job 23, 24; Bildad 25:1–6, 26:5–14; Job 25:1–4, 27:2–12; Zophar 23: 14–23, 13 (manifestly incomplete); Job 29–31.

31. This concept, expressed in 22:29 ff., may be described as "horizontal responsibility" binding the members of a single generation together as against the "vertical responsibility" of succeeding generations of a family.

32. On the proper interpretation of this passage, 27:2–12, which has suffered considerable excision at the hands of scholars, see the discussion on pp. 128-29, above.

33. The soliloquy is in chapter 29–31, the last chapter constituting the "Confession of Integrity."

34. It has often been assumed that the conjunction *'im* which occurs throughout the chapter must always introduce an oath couched in the form of a condition. This schematic approach necessitates considerable deletions and transpositions of material, since the alleged conclusion of the condition actually occurs only four or five times and is lacking ten times. Cf., e. g., Yellin, Duhm, Hoelscher, Torczyner. Actually, the conjunction is used in several ways: (a) to introduce an oath (verses 7, 9, 21, 38, 39); (b) as equivalent to *ha'im*, the mark of a question (verses 5, 13, 16, 24, 25, 26, 29, 31, 33); and (c) in its meaning of "if" in a conditional sentence (verse 19). The repetition of the vocable gives the chapter great power; the variation in its meaning avoids monotony.

35. The Elihu speeches are in chapters 32–37. The highlights of his arguments are to be found in chapters 33:14 ff.; 34:10 ff.; 35:9–13; 36:15–21; 37:23.

36. The variations are relative rather than absolute. Elihu uses divine names like *Shaddai* and *Eloah* less than the friends, and *El* more; the rarer forms of the preposition are less common in Elihu, Aramaisms more so. On the stylistic variations cf. Driver-Gray, *op. cit.*, vol. 1, pp. XL ff.

37. The exception is one verse in Eliphaz's first speech, 5:17: "Happy is the man whom the Lord chastises; the reproof of the Almighty do not despise."

38. Cf. 42:7, 8, the implications of which have been discussed above.

39. The first speech of the Lord consists of chapters 38 and 39 and verse 40:2. The correct chapter division within this speech should have come after 38:37, the first half dealing with inanimate nature, the second with living creatures.

40. Job's brief reply is in 40:3–5, God's second speech is in 40:6–41:28. Here, too, our present chapter division is wrong, since 41:1 ff. continues the description of *leviathan*, begun in 40:25. The second God-speech falls into the following sections: (a) the difficulty of establishing a just world order (40:6–11), description of (b) the hippopotamus (40:15–24), and (c) the crocodile (40:25–41:26).

41. This consideration (on which cf. E. Kraeling, *op. cit.*, p. 159) suffices to set aside the objections raised, partly on technical grounds, to the authenticity of several sections of the God-speeches: (a) the ostrich (39:13–18); (b) the hippopotamus (40:15–24); and (c) the crocodile (40:25–41:26). The first section is lacking in the Septuagint, and all three are not couched in the question-form of the First Speech. But the Septuagint on *Job* has been notoriously abridged, probably because of the difficulty of the text and the repetitious character of the poetry. Nor is there any real reason for assuming that the poet must monoto-

nously use the question-form for the length of all four chapters (38–41). The contrary is far more likely. Scholars are in disagreement on how many of these sections are to be deleted. Cf. Pfeiffer, *op. cit.*, pp. 673 and 674, Note 7; Dhorme, *ad loc.*, and *BGM*, chap. X for details. The ostrich section is the most doubtful, since, in addition to the grounds already mentioned above, its removal leaves seven creatures described in the first God speech. On the heptad as a principal of literary composition see Chapter 4 above.

42. Hos. 8:7; Isa. 3:10, 11.

43. Jer. 31:26–33; Ezek. 18.

44. Cf. Gen. 19; Job 22:29–30; Talmud Babli, Mo'ed Katan 16b: "Said the Holy One, Blessed be He, 'I rule over man, but who rules over me ? The saint; for when I issue a decree, he sets it aside.' " Cf. H. W. Robinson, "The Hebrew Conception of Corporate Responsibility," in *Beihefte ZATW*, vol. 6, 1936, pp. 49–62; A. R. Johnson, *The One and The Many in the Israelite Conception of God* (Cardiff, Wales, 1942), pp. 6–17; R. Gordis, "Corporate Personality in Job," *Journal of Near Eastern Studies*, vol. 4, 1945, pp. 54 f.

45. Cf. 14:7, 11, 14. On the other hand, it is an error to refer 19:26 to the doctrine of personal immortality.

46. *Sotah* 5:5. For a classic statement in traditional Judaism of this concept of disinterested virtue, see Maimonides' *Commentary on the Mishna Sanhedrin*, "Introduction to Helek," printed in all standard Talmud editions.

47. Cf. Midrash *Genesis Rabbah*, sec. 12, beginning: "If you cannot fathom the order of the thunderbolt (*ra' am*), how much more so, the order of the world ('*ōlām*)!" a comment on Job 26:14, cited also in *Yalkut Shimeoni* on Job, sec. 914 and *Ma'yan Gannim ad loc.*

48. In "On the Failure of All Philosophical Attempts in the Matter of Theodicy."

49. *The Dance of Life.*

13. THE TEMPTATION OF JOB

I

Ever since Matthew Arnold called attention to Hellas and Israel as
the two sources of Western civilization, it has been a widespread
practice to draw contrasts, eloquent or epigrammatic, between these
two creative cultures. Greece was the home of philosophy and science;
Palestine, of religion and morality. Hellas invented science, Israel
discovered conscience. The Greek ethos was predominantly intellectual and skeptical, its highest symbol being the philosopher; the
Hebrew ethos basically emotional and moral, rooted in faith, its noblest
exemplar being the prophet.

The fundamental unity of the human spirit should have made us
wary in advance of drawing such sharp distinctions between two
peoples. As modern scholarship has explored all the facets of life
in both centers, it has documented the similarities of the Greeks and
the Hebrews, as well as their differences. Notable progress has been
registered in the study of Greek religion, as expressed both in public
rites, which spoke for the group, and in the mystery cults, which
appealed to the individual. These investigations have served to reveal
the emotional, nonrational aspects of the Greek spirit. Conversely,
contemporary research into biblical Wisdom literature has indicated
a strong intellectual cast in Jewish religious thought. Divergences
undoubtedly exist between the Greek and the Hebrew spirit, but they
are largely differences in emphasis, significant, to be sure, but not
mutually exclusive.

Consider, for example, what may perhaps be described as the
supreme embodiment of the creative genius of the two peoples, the
Dialogues of Plato and the Book of Job. Here the distinctions between
the two cultures are most striking. The Dialogues are, of course, the
expression of an incisive intelligence, seeking to establish the proper
norms of human conduct through the exercise of reason. In Books I
and II of *The Republic* the effort is made to analyze the concept of
justice, discarding false notions and arriving at a true understanding.

It is the same theme that preoccupies the author of Job, but what a world of difference in temperament and method, in the mode of expression, and in the conclusions reached! Nowhere in Job is there an analysis of the nature of right and wrong. What the Greek philosopher sought to discover through the mind, the Hebrew poet knew through the heart. It is not merely Job's antagonists in the debate who do not doubt that right is right and wrong is wrong. He himself never differs with them on the nature of righteousness. To raise such questions is possible only for sinners who wish to confuse their fellows so that they may despoil them.

> Woe unto them that call evil good,
> And good evil;
> That change darkness into light,
> And light into darkness;
> That change bitter into sweet,
> And sweet into bitter! (Isa. 5:20)

For honorable men, however, the truth was clear: "It hath been told thee, O man, what is good and what the Lord thy God doth require of thee, to do justice, to love mercy, and to walk humbly with thy God" (Micah 6:8). Man knows the good because God has revealed it to him—and justice and mercy are recognizable by their presence or absence in human affairs.

The far-reaching difference between Plato and Job, in content and temper, is reflected in striking variation of form. The Greek Dialogues are prose, the Hebrew Dialogues exalted poetry. If we seek a parallel to Job in the Hellenic world, we must turn to Aeschylus, perhaps the most "Hebraic" of the Greeks.

Having noted the vast distinctions between Plato and Job, we should not ignore the affinities, recognizing that what is primary in the one is likely to be secondary in the other. It would be a grave error to underestimate the emotional drive underlying the ostensibly cool analysis of the Socratic dialogues. It was the poet in Plato that led him to banish poets from his Republic, for he knew the strength of the irrational, creative aspects of human nature, which brook no discipline and confound the neatest blueprints of the future. The entire structure of Platonic Ideas is a creation of the poetic faculty, a myth which seeks to interpret the nature of reality. To ignore the emotional underpinning of the Platonic dialogues is fatal to their understanding.

II

Equally disastrous is the failure to recognize the strong intellectual content of the Book of Job. It is not merely that the author of Job is, in Pfeiffer's words, the most learned ancient before Plato; indeed, he possesses a range of knowledge and perhaps of experience that recalls that of Shakespeare. The temptation of Job, the heart of the tragedy and the triumph, is, to be sure, expressed in passionately emotional terms, but it is intellectual as much as it is moral. Beyond the specific theme of the problem of suffering with which it is concerned, the book posits a problem as enduring as man himself, who remembers the past but lives in the present, and it points the way to an answer. This perennial issue is the conflict between the accepted tradition of the group and the personal experience of the individual. Though Job has suffered the full gamut of human misery, the accepted religious doctrine of his day has a ready answer: suffering is the result and consequently, the sign of sin. Heretofore, Job has never had cause to doubt the proposition, for it was a logical consequence of his faith in a world ruled by a just God. In fact, Job's prosperity and well-being were the best evidence of the truth of the conventional doctrine! Now he has been exposed to a rapid succession of calamities that have destroyed his wealth, decimated his family, and wracked his body with loathsome disease.

For his friends, the severity of Job's affliction serves only to demonstrate the gravity of his offenses. A few months before, Job himself would not have doubted the conclusion. Had it been reported to him during the period of his well-being that some individual had been visited by such devastating blows, the God-fearing Job would have reacted exactly as do his friends.

Hence the discussion does not begin as a debate at the outset. When the friends come to comfort Job in his affliction, they naturally take it for granted that his faith is unshaken. For even his tragic lament on the day of his birth (chap. 3) is couched in general terms; it is not yet directed against God. Eliphaz is certain that all that is required is to remind Job of the basic religious truth that has been momentarily darkened for him by his suffering:

If one tried a word with you, would you be offended? . . .
But now that it has come to you, you cannot bear it;

It touches you and you are dismayed. . . .
Think now, what innocent man was ever destroyed? (Job 4:2, 5, 7)

Soon enough, Eliphaz and his colleagues discover that it is a vastly changed Job that confronts them. Job has undergone a shattering personal experience, but he knows, with the knowledge that defies all logic, that he is innocent. He must now choose between tradition and experience, between the body of convictions and beliefs accumulated by the generations, on the one hand, and the testimony of his own senses and reactions, on the other. For the individual to set himself against the generality of mankind is both a tragic and a heroic enterprise. Its pathos in Job's case is heightened by the feeling, which he himself had always shared, that the body of religious truth which he now opposes is the very bedrock of morality. His adversaries can therefore accuse him in all sincerity of undermining the foundations of society. In Bildad's words:

> O you who tear yourself to shreds in your anger,
> Shall the earth be forsaken on your account,
> Or the rock be removed from its place? (Job 18:4)

The personal suffering involved is intense for all concerned, for Job, who now recognizes his loneliness in a world where once he was at home, and for his friends, who stand helplessly by as the chasm opens between them.

III

Job's tragedy, however, goes deeper, for he is compelled to challenge no superficial body of ideas, but the very heart and essence of biblical thought. The axis on which all of Hebrew religion turns is the tension between two poles, that of faith in God, the just Ruler of the universe, and that of the widespread phenomenon of human suffering. The profoundest spirits in Israel had labored to solve the tragic paradox of evil in God's world. In the process, an imposing body of thought had developed in which the lawgiver, the prophet, the historian, and the sage had each played a part, either in emphasizing one pole or the other, or in seeking to reconcile the contradiction through a theodicy justifying the ways of God to man.

At the very beginning of Israel's meeting with God, the process had begun, for the Decalogue proclaimed on Sinai rests on faith in the justice of God as an effective force in the universe. In that immortal Code, God has introduced Himself, as Judah Halevi had noted in another connection, not as the Creator of heaven and earth, but as the Author of liberty, who had brought Israel out of the house of bondage. The implication of the First Commandment, surely not apparent to all of Moses's contemporaries, was that God held universal sway and was no merely national deity, limited to his own territorial domain, like the gods of the Canaanites, the Ammonites, or the Moabites. The God of Israel, who had delivered the weak from slavery in a foreign land and had executed judgment upon their oppressors, was by that token both all-powerful and all-just.

From this basic conviction, the Pentateuchal doctrine of retribution followed naturally—righteousness would be rewarded and wickedness would receive its condign punishment. The doctrine was expressed in the famous Deuteronomic passage:

And it shall come to pass, if ye shall hearken diligently unto My commandments which I command you this day, to love the Lord your God, and to serve Him with all your heart and with all your soul, that I will give the rain of your land in its season . . . Take heed to yourselves, lest your heart be deceived, and ye turn aside, and serve other gods, and worship them; and the anger of the Lord be kindled against you, and He shut up the heaven, so that there shall be no rain, and the ground shall not yield her fruit; and ye perish quickly from off the good land which the Lord giveth you (Deut. 11:13, 14, 16, 17).

The principle was elaborated with graphic power in the Comminations, which set forth the rewards of righteousness and the penalty of sin for the nation (Lev., chap. 26, and Deut., chap. 28).

The doctrine of retribution could be held with total conviction, because it arose early in Hebrew history, when group-consciousness was all powerful and the individual was conceived of as little more than a cell in the larger organism, whose personal destiny had no existence apart from the clan and the nation to which he belonged.

The biblical historians, the authors of Joshua, Judges, Samuel, and Kings, made the doctrine of national retribution the cornerstone of their philosophy of history, explaining the ebb and flow of Hebrew prosperity and disaster in terms of the people's fluctuating obedience or resistance to the word of God:

And they forsook the Lord, the God of their fathers, who brought them

out of the land of Egypt, and followed other gods, of the gods of the peoples
that were round about them, and worshipped them; and they provoked the
Lord. . . . And the anger of the Lord was kindled against Israel, and He
delivered them into the hands of spoilers that spoiled them, and He gave
them over into the hands of their enemies round about, so that they could
not any longer stand before their enemies (Judg. 2:12, 14).

The Prophet Hosea emphasized that the law of consequence was
rooted in the universe, by expressing it in a metaphor drawn from
nature:

> For they sow the wind, and they shall reap the whirlwind; . . .
> Sow to yourselves in righteousness, reap in mercy,
> Break up the fallow ground,
> For it is time to seek the Lord,
> Till He come and teach you righteousness.
> Ye have plowed wickedness, you have reaped iniquity,
> Ye have eaten the fruit of lies—(Hos. 8:7; 10:12, 13).

Hosea's older contemporary, Amos, had applied the same principle
of justice as the law of history to contemporary world affairs, and
found in it the key to the destiny of all the neighboring nations and
not only of Israel (Amos, chaps. 1, 2).

Even in its collective form, the doctrine of retribution created im-
mense difficulties. In their effort to resolve these problems, the
Prophets deepened the content of Hebrew religion. If God is all-
righteous, it follows that a sinful people, even if it be Israel, deserves
to perish. The Prophets of Israel loved God, but they loved their
people, too, and could not make their peace with this logical but
devastating conclusion. Thus Amos, confronted by the iniquitous
Kingdom of Israel, which refused even to hear his message, let alone
reorder its national existence, foretold the annihilation of the northern
state. But the total disappearance of his people was an intolerable
prospect for the Hebrew Prophet, both because of his natural attachment to his kinsmen and his conviction that God's word needed a
spokesman in an idolatrous world. After his expulsion from the
Northern Kingdom Amos transferred his hopes for the future to the
smaller and weaker Kingdom of Judah (Amos 9:8 ff.).[1]

A generation later, his spiritual descendant, Isaiah of Jerusalem,
faced the same heartrending challenge of a righteous God judging His
sinful people. Incomparably the greatest intellect among the Prophets,

Isaiah refined still further Amos's faith that part of the Hebrew people would survive, by enunciating his doctrine of the Saving Remnant. Not all of Judah, but some of Judah, would be saved. History was a process of the survival of the spiritually fittest, directed by God, which would disclose those capable of regeneration and salvation.

Another challenge confronted Isaiah's faith in the God of hosts, Who is exalted in righteousness. The Assyrian conqueror, infinitely more arrogant and cruel than Israel had ever been, was treading all other nations, including Israel, under foot. How could that spectacle of evil triumphant be reconciled with a just and almighty God? This contradiction Isaiah resolved by another profound insight, the concept of "the rod of God's anger." Assyria, pitiful in its conceit, was merely an instrument in God's hand for rooting out the evil and ushering in the good. When its function would be accomplished, it would pay the penalty for its crime against God and man![2]

The same challenge in a far more agonizing form confronted Isaiah's anonymous namesake, Deutero-Isaiah, a century and a half later. The people of Judah were now in ignominious exile under the heel of the Babylonian empire. How explain the misery and degradation of Israel? It could not be justified in terms of Israel's sin, for, at its worst, Israel was better than its pagan conqueror. Unless these tormenting doubts were met, the people would be plunged into a despair that would be the prelude to dissolution. A message of hope and courage was needed, not only for Israel's sake, but for God's cause, for this people, weak and imperfect, remained "God's witnesses" (Isa. 43:10). A rabbinic comment spells out the implications of the Deutero-Isaianic metaphor: "Ye are My witnesses, saith the Lord. If ye are My witnesses, I am the Lord, but if ye are not My witnesses, I am not the Lord."[3] The great Prophet of the Exile accordingly evolved the doctrine of the Suffering Servant of the Lord.[4] Israel is not merely God's witness, but man's teacher, whose suffering at the hands of the nations is evidence of their moral immaturity. These tribulations are destined to end when the nations recognize Israel's true greatness:

Behold My servant, whom I uphold;
Mine elect, in whom My soul delighteth;
I have put My spirit upon him,
He shall make the right to go forth to the nations.
He shall not cry, nor lift up,

Nor cause his voice to be heard in the street.
A bruised reed shall he not break,
And the dimly burning wick shall he not quench;
He shall make the right to go forth according to the truth. . . .

Behold, My servant shall prosper,
He shall be exalted and lifted up, and shall be very high. . . .

Surely our diseases he did bear, and our pains he carried;
Whereas we did esteem him stricken,
Smitten of God, and afflicted.
But he was wounded because of our transgressions,
He was crushed because of our iniquities:
The chastisement of our welfare was upon him,
And with his stripes we were healed.

Therefore will I divide him a portion among the great,
And he shall divide the spoil with the mighty;
Because he bared his soul unto death,
And was numbered with the transgressors;
Yet he bore the sin of many,
And made intercession for the transgressors. (Isa. 42:1–3; 52:13; 53:4, 5, 12)

Thus for the first time the Prophet affirmed the possibility of national suffering that was not the consequence of sin, but, on the contrary, an integral element in the process of the moral education of the race. This insight of Deutero-Isaiah was not lost on the author of Job.

The tension between God's justice and the triumph of wickedness was also met in another way by the Prophets, who deepened an older folkbelief in the Day of the Lord. The people had long believed that the day would come when the Lord of Israel would give His people victory over its foes and establish its hegemony over all. This chauvinistic doctrine has its parallels in ancient and in modern times among all peoples. The Hebrew Prophets did not attack or denounce the doctrine—they moralized it. They agreed that the day would come when the Lord of Israel would arise and bring victory to His cause, but that did not mean Israel, only a *righteous* Israel. For several of the Prophets, notably, Isaiah and Micah, the instrument for God's purpose in the world would be the Messiah, the anointed scion of the house of David. The Messiah would restore the scales of justice to their true balance, by ushering in freedom and plenty for Israel and peace and brotherhood for the world. The Messianic age represents the triumph of the righteousness of God in an imperfect world. Justice would prevail—what was needed was patience in the present and faith in the future.

In sum, the contradiction between the doctrine of retribution and the spectacle of injustice in the world created some of the deepest insights of biblical religion.

IV

To wait patiently for the triumph of God's retribution was relatively easy, so long as the nation was the unit under consideration, for God has eternity at His command, and nations are longlived. This is particularly true of Israel. In Ben Sira's words:

> The life of man is but a few days,
> But the life of Jeshurun, days without number. (B.S. 37:25)

Yet from the beginning the individual played a part in the religious consciousness. His hopes and desires, his fears and frustrations, could not be submerged wholly in the destiny of the nation. The people might prosper and a man might be miserable; the status of society might be critical, yet the individual could find life tolerable. The Law of God demanded obedience from the individual; was it unfair to expect that righteousness or sinfulness would receive their reward or punishment in the life of the individual as well? Imperceptibly, the problem emerged in the days of the First Temple. Isaiah had taken the simplest course by reaffirming the traditional doctrine and applying it to the individual:

> Say ye of the righteous, that it shall be well with him;
> For they shall eat the fruit of their doings.
> Woe unto the wicked! It shall be ill with him;
> For the work of his hands shall be done to him. (Isa. 3:10, 11)

As inexorable doom began descending on the nation and the small Judean state saw its lifeblood ebbing away, the mere reiteration of conventional ideas was not enough. Now there was no comfort or compensation in collective retribution. Moreover, since the individual was now the unit and the scale of judgment, the counsel of long range patience was pathetically irrelevant, for man flowers but a brief instant. The Prophets Jeremiah and Ezekiel, whose tragic destiny was to foretell and to witness the destruction of the Temple and the Baby- lonion exile, agonized over the prosperity of the wicked and the suffering of the righteous:

> Because you are righteous, O Lord,
> I will contend with You,
> I will enter into controversy with You,
> Why does the way of the wicked prosper?
> Why are all the traitors secure? (Jer. 12:1)

Both prophets protested energetically against the popular doctrine enshrined in a folksaying:

> The fathers have eaten sour grapes,
> And the children's teeth are set on edge (Jer. 31:28; Ezek. 18:2).

Ezekiel in particular emphasized the doctrine of individual responsi- bility and individual retribution. He was content to bolster ethical living without formulating a complete theodicy. Other men of faith, psalmists and poets, urged obedience to God's will, buttressed by the faith that righteousness would soon triumph in the life of the indi- vidual:

> For His anger is but for a moment,
> His favour is for a life-time;
> Weeping may tarry for the night,
> But joy cometh in the morning. (Ps. 30:6)

> The Lord is good unto them that wait for Him,
> To the soul that seeketh Him.
> It is good that a man should quietly wait
> For the salvation of the Lord. (Lam. 3:25, 26).

Thus biblical religion, resting on the cornerstone of faith in a just and powerful God, met all challenges and held fast to its faith that justice prevails in God's world. Every generation in Israel had been nurtured upon this faith, drawing from it the motive for obedience to God's law, the strength to bear affliction, and the patience to await the hour of vindication.

V

Job, too, had always accepted this body of religious teaching as the truth. Then came the crisis, catastrophe following catastrophe, leaving the temple of his existence a mass of rubble. We know that Job's misery and degradation is a part of a cosmic experiment to discover whether man is capable of serving the ideal for its own sake, without the hope of reward. But Job has no such inkling—for him, *the accepted religious convictions of a lifetime are now contradicted by his personal experience*, by his unshakable knowledge that he is no sinner, certainly not sinful enough to deserve such a succession of blows upon his defenseless head.

Of Job's inner travail the friends are unaware. Eliphaz, the oldest and the wisest of the three, proceeds to remind Job of the truths by which he has lived. It is noteworthy that the author, whose sympathies are clearly on Job's side,[5] nevertheless gives the fullest and fairest presentation of the conventional theology. Divine justice does prevail in the world, the apparent contradictions in the world of reality notwithstanding. In the first instance, the process of retribution takes time and so Job must have patience. The righteous are never destroyed, while the wicked, or at least their children, are ultimately punished. Eliphaz then describes a vision from on high which discloses to him the truth that all men are imperfect, so that not even the righteous may justly complain if he suffers. God is not responsible for sin, for it is a human creation (vv. 6, 7). Moreover, suffering is a discipline—and hence a mark of God's love (v. 17). Ultimately, the righteous are saved and find peace and contentment.

In his later speeches, Eliphaz will emphasize the familiar doctrine of God's visiting the sins of the fathers upon the children, and will extend it, for by the side of this "vertical responsibility" linking all the generations through time, there is a "horizontal responsibility" in space, uniting all men in a given generation. Thus the entire people is visited by a plague because of King David's sin (II Sam. 24:11 ff.). On the other hand, it is this interdependence of mankind which makes it possible for the saint, by his presence, to redeem his sinful contemporaries, as when Abraham sought to save Sodom for the sake of a righteous minority. Accordingly, Eliphaz promises Job that if he repents and makes his peace with God, he will be able to intercede with Him for sinners and save them:

> Thou wilt then issue a decree, and it will be fulfilled for thee,
> And upon thy ways, light will shine.
>
> When men are brought low, thou wilt say, "Rise up!"
> And the humble will be saved.
> Even the guilty will escape punishment,
> Escaping through the cleanness of thy hands.[6] (Job 22:28–30).

Job has scarcely heard, let alone been persuaded, by Eliphaz's arguments or by the considerably more heated and less illuminating speeches of the other friends. He has no theory to propose as a substitute, merely his consciousness that he is suffering without cause. He does not claim to be perfect, but insists he is not a willful sinner. Against the conventional ideas he sets the testimony of his own experience, which he will not deny, whatever the consequences. As the round of debate continues, Job's fury mounts, as does the helpless wrath of his friends.

Bildad paints a picture of the destruction of the wicked and the ultimate restoration of the righteous, and he hymns the power of God, while Zophar summons Job to repent of his secret sins.

With bitter irony, Job parodies their speeches on the greatness of God and concludes that their defense of God, dishonest and biased as it is, is not likely to win His favor.[7]

As the first cycle ends, Job has been fortified in his conviction that he is right. What he experiences existentially cannot be refuted theoretically; it must be taken into account in any conception of reality.

Job is aware of the contention that morality depends upon faith in Divine justice. Denying the latter, how can he maintain the former? Job is driven to a desperate expedient, which is to prove one of the great liberating ideas in religion; he cuts the nexus between virtue and reward. Honest men will tremble at his undeserved suffering, but will not on that account be deterred from righteousness:

> Upright men are horrified at this,
> And the innocent will rise up against the godless.
> But the just will hold fast to his way,
> And he who has clean hands will increase his strength. (Job 17:8, 9)

The Mishnah (Sotah 5:5) quite correctly contends that Job served God from love and not from fear. God's ways still remain to be justified, but in the interim man's ways must be just.

In the succeeding cycles, Eliphaz adds a supplement to the traditional position. He emphasizes that there is more to the punishment of the wicked than his ultimate destruction, whether in his own person or in that of his offspring. During the very period of his ostensible prosperity he lives in trepidation, never knowing when the blow will fall. Otherwise, the same ideas are reiterated, but with greater vehemence. The conventional theodicy, maintained by the friends, has exhausted itself.

VI

The full meaning of Job's existential tragedy now begins to disclose itself. Increasingly, Job has become convinced, not merely that the friends have maligned him, but that they have traduced God. In the first cycle, Job has ventured a hope that some impartial arbiter might decide between him and God:

> For God is not a man like me, whom I could answer
> When we came to trial together.
> If only[8] there were an arbiter between us
> Who would lay his hand upon us both,
> Who would remove God's rod from me,
> So that my dread of Him would not terrify me.
> Then I would speak, and not fear Him,
> For He is far from just to me![9] (Job 9:32–35)

As the Friends proceed to attack Job's integrity with less and less restraint, the contact between Job and them all but disappears. Their conception of God is meaningless for him. He proceeds to discover a new faith, forged in the crucible of his undeserved suffering, as unshakable as his experience of his own innocence—behind the cruel reality of suffering, a just order must exist in the world. He can find no sympathy or understanding among his erstwhile friends; then there must be, there would be, a witness on his behalf later:

> O earth, cover not my blood;
> Let my cry have no resting-place.
> Behold, even now, my witness is in heaven,

> And he who vouches for me is on high.
> Are my friends my intercessors?
> No, to God my eye pours out its tears,
> That He judge between a man and God,
> As between one man and his fellow. (Job 16:18–21)

As the debate reaches a crescendo of fury, Job attains a crescendo of faith. The longing first expressed for an arbiter (*mōkhiah*) has become a conviction of a witness (*'edh*) ready to speak on his behalf. Now he reaches the peak of faith. In a moment of mystic ecstasy he sees his vindication through a Redeemer, Who will act to avenge his suffering. The term he uses, *gō'ēl*,[10] means a kinsman, a blood-avenger, who in earlier Hebrew law, was duty bound to see that justice was done to his aggrieved brother.

The inherent difficulties of communicating a mystic vision are aggravated by textual problems in the famous passage, which I believe should be rendered as follows:

> Oh that my words were now written;
> Oh that they were inscribed on a monument,
> That with an iron pen and lead
> They were hewn in the rock for ever!
> For I know that my Redeemer lives,
> Though He be the last to arise upon earth!
> Deep in my skin this has been marked,
> And in my very flesh do I see God.
> I myself behold Him,
> With my own eyes I see Him, not with another's—
> My heart is consumed with longing within me! (Job 19:23–27b)

But the momentary vision of God arising to redeem him fades; Job cannot hold the ecstasy—

> My heart is consumed with longing within me. (Job 19:23–27)[11]

Similarly, the modern saint, Rabbi Abraham Isaac Kuk, has sought to describe the ecstasy of the experience of "the nearness of God" which extends beyond "the walls of deed, logic, ethics, and laws." But exaltation is followed by depression, as the mystic sinks back "into the gray and tasteless world of conflict, contradiction, and doubt."[12]

Job, however, in spite of his experience, is no mystic, who can find

peace in the beatific vision. Even after the ecstasy has faded, he demands vindication. Only if God appears to him and answers, will he
know that his suffering is not meaningless, that it counts for something in the universe. In his last speech, which sets forth his code of
conduct, he closes with a plea:

> Oh that I had one to hear me!—
> Lo, this is my desire, that God answer me,
> And that I had the indictment my foe has written,
> I would surely carry it on my shoulder
> And bind it as a crown for myself!
> I would announce to Him the number of my steps,
> Like a prince would I confront Him! (Job 31:35–37)

Who is this Arbiter, this Witness, this Redeemer to whom Job
looks for salvation and comfort? Job's refuge is the God of righteousness, who lives and rules the world behind the sway of the God of
power. The dichotomy never becomes a dualism; for the Hebrew
author, as for his hero, these two aspects must be one. In the end, the
two aspects of the Divine emerge as one, when the God of reality not
only ignores the defenses of the friends in his speeches, but castigates
them, "for ye have not spoken the truth about Me as has my servant
Job" (42:7, 8), so that Job must intercede for them. God's power and
God's righteousness, the attribute of justice and the attribute of
mercy, are one in Him; it is only to man's limited and imperfect gaze
that they seem distinct, if not contradictory.

Centuries later, the medieval Hebrew poet, Solomon Ibn Gabirol,
in his *Royal Crown*, echoed the heartbeat of Job in his affliction, but
like him, retained his faith in the One Living God of the universe:

> Therefore though Thou shouldst slay me, yet I will trust in Thee.
> For if Thou shouldst pursue my iniquity,
> I will flee from Thee to Thyself,
> And I will shelter myself from Thy wrath in Thy shadow,
> And to the skirts of Thy mercies I will lay hold,
> Until Thou hast had mercy on me,
> And I will not let Thee go till Thou hast blessed me.[13]

The later poet, Immanuel of Rome, rephrased the same thought:

> I shall flee for help, from Thee to Thee,
> And cover myself with Thy wings in the day of trouble,
> And from Thy wrath flee to Thy shadow.[14]

Job's final speech is no longer addressed to his friends. Like his opening lament (chap. 3), his closing confession of innocence (chap. 31) is a soliloquy.

VII

There now appears a brash young character named Elihu, of whom, we are to assume, the dignified elders have previously taken no notice. He has overheard the debate and feels impelled to inject himself into the discussion. For a variety of reasons, many scholars regard the Elihu speeches (chap. 32–39) as a later interpolation, an easy method which solves little. What has been generally overlooked is the basic fact that in the architecture of the book, Elihu's speeches perform a vital function. Increasingly, the study of ancient literatures, like that of the Homeric epics, has been focusing attention upon the unity and meaning of the whole rather than upon the disparity of the parts. That the indiscriminate and even accidental lumping together of scattered literary fragments by an obtuse redactor, who often did not understand the material he was working with, will produce a masterpiece—that naive faith of nineteenth century literary critics is no longer widely shared today.[15]

The differences between the Elihu chapters and the rest of the book, which are fewer than is generally alleged, may perhaps be explained by the assumption that they were added by our author at a later period in his career. The creation of a masterpiece like Job might well have been a lifetime undertaking and Goethe's *Faust* is a case in point, having occupied the poet for six decades.

It is noteworthy that Elihu is at least as antagonistic to the friends as he is to Job. Actually he denies the truth of both positions. The friends have maintained that God is just and that therefore suffering is both the penalty and the proof of sin. Job has countered by insisting that his suffering is not the result of sin and therefore he charges God with injustice. Elihu denies the conclusion of both sides by injecting a virtually new idea, adumbrated in another form in Deutero-Isaiah and referred to in one verse by Eliphaz:[16] Elihu declares that God is just, and yet suffering may rightly come to the innocent, as a discipline and a warning. Job has contended that God avoids contact with man. On the contrary, Elihu insists, God does communicate with man through dreams and visions, and when these fail, through illness and suffering.

This recognition of the uses of pain is the kind of mature insight that would come to a man through years of experience: for life teaches at every hand how insufferable are those who have never suffered and that frustration and sorrow are men's passport to fellowship and sympathy with their brothers.

The author of Job would undoubtedly wish to express this observation. Yet suffering as a discipline is certainly not the whole truth regarding the problem of evil. How could the idea be given its proper weight? Obviously the doctrine could not be placed in the mouth of Job, who denies that there is any justice in suffering. Nor could it be presented by the friends, for the author wishes to negate their standpoint, as we have seen. Finally, were this idea included in the subsequent God speeches, it would weaken the force of the principal answer. By creating the character of Elihu, who opposes the attitude of the friends, as well as that of Job, the author is able to express this secondary idea, giving it due place in his world view.

VIII

Elihu's words end as a storm is seen rising in the east. The Lord Himself appears in the whirlwind and speaks to Job. The argumentation of the friends that Job must be a sinner is treated with the silence it deserves. Nowhere does God refer to Job's alleged misdoings. Instead, the entire problem is raised to another dimension. Can Job comprehend, let alone govern, the universe that he weighs and finds wanting? With a vividness born of deep love and careful observation, the poet pictures the beasts, remote from man, yet precious to their Maker. Even the ponderous hippopotamus and the fearsome crocodile, far from conventionally beautiful, reveal the creative power of God and His joy in the world. Moreover, God declares, were Job able to destroy evil in the world, even He would be prepared to relinquish His throne to him—a moving acknowledgment by God that the world order is not perfect!

Job is not overwhelmed, as is often alleged, by God's physical power. For that had failed to cow Job into silence during the earlier debate with the friends. It is the essential truth of God's position that impels Job to submit. His surrender, however, is still a victory, for his wish has been granted:

> I had heard of You by hearsay,
> But now my own eyes have seen You.
> Therefore I abase myself
> And repent in dust and ashes. (Job 42:5, 6)

Job's triumph lies in the fact that God speaks to him and does not ignore him. The confrontation of God is Job's vindication.

But that is not all. In rebelling against tradition because of his experience, Job has enriched tradition, for religious truth, like all truth, can grow only through the evidence derived from the experience of life. To use the language of the hour, Job's protest is existential, but it contributes to a deeper essential religion. It compels a reconsideration of the conventional theology, which the author incidentally does not reject out of hand; he merely regards it as inadequate. The author's positive ideas, one major, the other minor, are stated in the two closing sections of the book.

The minor thought is expressed by Elihu, who stresses that suffering frequently serves as a source of moral discipline and is thus a spur to high ethical attainment.

The principal idea is reserved for the God speeches, where the implications, in accordance with widespread Semitic usage, are at least as important as their explicit content.[17]

The vivid and joyous description of nature in these chapters testifies that nature is more than a mystery; it is a cosmos, a thing of beauty. Just as there is order and harmony in the natural world, so there is order and meaning in the moral sphere. Man cannot fathom the meaning of the natural order, yet he is aware of its beauty and harmony. Similarly, if he cannot expect to comprehend the moral order, he must believe that there are rationality and justice within it. After all legitimate explanations of suffering are taken into account, a mystery still remains. Any view of the universe that fully explains it is, on that very account, untrue. But what cannot be comprehended through reason must be embraced in love. For the author of Job, as for Judaism always, God is one and indivisible. As nature is instinct with morality, so the moral order is rooted in the natural world.

One other significant contribution to religion emerges from the Book of Job. For the poet, the harmony of the universe is important, not only as an idea but as an experience, not only logically but esthetically. When man steeps himself in the beauty of the world, his troubles grow petty, not because they are unreal, but because they dissolve within the larger plan, like the tiny dabs of oil in a masterpiece of painting. The beauty of the world becomes an anodyne to man's suffering.

The author of Job is not merely a great artist and poet. He is too deep a religious thinker to believe that any neatly articulated system of man can comprehend the beauty and the tragedy of existence. Yet he is too great an intellect to abdicate the use of reason and reflection in pondering on the mystery of evil and comprehending as much of it as we can. He would endorse the unemotional words of the third century sage, Jannai: "It is not in our power to understand the suffering of the righteous or the well-being of the wicked" (*Aboth* 4:15). There is a residuum of the Unknown in the world, but we have good grounds for holding fast to the faith that harmony and beauty pervade God's world. The mystery is also a miracle.

When Job found that the tradition of the past was contradicted by his personal experience, he resisted the temptation to submit to the platitudes of the past. Because of his unswerving allegiance to the truth, he refused to echo accepted truths, however respectable and ancient their source. His steadfastness and agony found their reward —for out of his suffering emerged a deeper vision of the Eternal and His ways.

NOTES

1. On the transformation of Amos's thought occasioned by his expulsion from Beth-El by the priest Amaziah, see "The Composition and Structure of Amos," in the present volume, and *cf.* W. S. McCullough, "Some Suggestions About Amos," *Journal of Biblical Literature*, vol. 72, 1953, pp. 247 ff.

2. Isa. chap. 10 and see "Isaiah—Prophet, Thinker and World Statesman" in this volume.

3. Cited in the name of the Tannaitic sage Simeon bar Yohai in *Sifre, Deut.* sec. 346; *cf.* also *Pesikta*, ed. Buber, p. 102b and *Yalkut Shimeoni, Isaiah*, sec. 455.

4. *Cf.* the careful study of the theme in C. R. North, *The Suffering Servant in Deutero-Isaiah*, Oxford, 1948, and the briefer survey of the various theories in H. H. Rowley, *The Servant of the Lord and other Essays*, London, 1952. The view adopted in the text, that the Servant is Israel in its ideal sense, is still the most acceptable position, particularly when the fruitful concept of "fluid personality" is taken into account. See H. W. Robinson, *The Cross of the Servant— A Study in Deutero-Isaiah*, London, 1928, and see my remarks in "Hosea's Marriage and Message," in this volume.

5. This is clear from the greater length and eloquence of the Job speeches and from the Divine judgment on the friends in Job 42:8. This verse is part of the "jointures" (12:11–13; 42:7–10), the links written by the poet to connect the prose tale, which he utilizes as prologue and epilogue, with the poetic dialogue. On the critical problems involved, see "All Men's Book—The Book of Job" in this volume.

6. *Cf.* my "Corporate Responsibility in Job," *Journal of Near Eastern Studies*, vol. 4, 1945, and the references cited there.

7. For this passage *cf.* "Quotations as a Literary Usage in Biblical, Rabbinic and Oriental Literature," in this volume.

8. Revocalizing *lō'* as *lū*, with many moderns.

9. Assuming a *tiqqūn sōpherīm* or euphemistic change by the scribes (*hu'* for *'anokhi*), with Yellin, "for He is not just with me."

10. *Cf.* Hastings, *Dictionary of the Bible*, vol. 2, pp. 222 ff., s. v. *Goel*.

11. On the exegesis of this crucial passage, see the exhaustive study of Julius Speer in *ZATW*, 1905, pp. 47–140, and Driver-Gray, *ICC on Job*, New York, 1921, vol. 1, pp. 170 ff.; vol. 2, pp. 126 ff.

12. *Cf.* the brief but illuminating summary of Rabbi Kuk's religious philosophy in J. B. Agus, *Guideposts of Modern Judaism*, New York, 1954, pp. 53 f.

13. *Cf.* I. Davidson, editor, *Selected Religious Poems of Solomon Ibn Gabirol*, Philadelphia, 1944, p. 118.

14. *Cf.* his *Mahbarot*, chapter 19.

15. *Cf.* the trenchant observations of H. D. F. Kitto, *The Greeks*, Harmondsworth, 1951, p. 63:

> The attribution (of the *Iliad* and the *Odyssey* to Homer) was accepted quite wholeheartedly until modern times, when closer investigation showed all sorts of discrepancies of fact, style and language, both between the two epics and between the various parts of each. The immediate result of this was the minute and confident division of the two poems, but especially the *Iliad*, into separate lays of different periods, appropriately called "strata" by critics, who imperfectly distinguished between artistic and geological composition. The study of the epic poetry of other races, and the methods used by poets by working in this traditional medium, has done a great deal to restore confidence in the substantial unity of each poem; that is to say, that what we have in each case is not a short poem by one original "Homer" to which later poets have added more or less indiscriminately, but a poem, conceived as a unity by a relatively later "Homer" who worked over and incorporated much traditional material—though the present *Iliad* certainly contains some passages which were not part of Homer's original design.

16. Eliphaz had briefly referred to the idea of suffering as a discipline in one verse (Job 5:16), but had not referred to it again or explored its implications. Deutero-Isaiah's doctrine of the Servant of the Lord describes the Servant's suffering as inflicted by other men, not as emanating directly from God. The affinities are, however, noteworthy.

17. For a detailed discussion of this literary phenomenon, see R. Gordis, *The Book of God and Man—A Study of Job* (= BGM), chap. XIV, "The Rhetoric of Allusion and Analogy."

14. THE WISDOM OF KOHELETH

A. THE ENIGMA

Not every century can boast a work that gives perfect utterance to a universal mood. No matter how radically the conditions of existence may change, such a work remains as the supreme expression of a basic, ever-recurring pattern in the life of the human spirit.

To this chosen group of masterpieces the Book of Koheleth, or "Ecclesiastes," belongs, aptly called the most modern book in the Bible. Suspected in days of orthodoxy, neglected in periods of optimism, treasured in days of frustration and disillusion, it has always drawn men, yet somehow eluded them. Since its composition, most of the significant history of the Western world has occurred. Classical civilization flowered and surrendered to decay; the Middle Ages laid their heavy hand on human life; the modern era of progress was ushered in—and is now battling desperately for its survival. Yet the enigmatic figure of the sage of Jerusalem still endures, the symbol of the ache of disillusion and of the peace that comes after. Whoever has dreamt great dreams in his youth and seen the vision flee, or has loved and lost, or has beaten barehanded at the fortress of injustice and come back bleeding and broken, has passed Koheleth's door, and tarried awhile beneath the shadow of his roof.

Men have paid willing tribute to the fascination of Koheleth as they wrestled with the enigma of his personality. They have been baffled by his place in the Biblical canon, wedged in among resplendent priests, ecstatic psalmists and implacable prophets. What was he doing in such company? Commentators were confused by the startling contradictions in which the book abounded, the cool skepticism of one passage, followed by unimpeachable orthodox sentiments in the next. Was he talking with his tongue in his cheek, or writing a Socratic dialogue? Or perhaps (that last resort of the troubled reader) there was no Koheleth, as there was no Homer: a dozen uninspired scribes had each written a few verses, and their pooled resources formed the book of Ecclesiastes. Centuries later a soul-brother of Koheleth unwittingly described the fate of the Hebrew sage at the hands of his readers and commentators:

> Myself when young did eagerly frequent
> Doctor and saint, and heard great argument
> About it and about—but evermore
> Came out by the same door where in I went.

As men wrote and argued and dissected, the elusive figure of Koheleth grew further away than ever. They succeeded merely in proving the truth of the words in the Epilogue to Koheleth:

> Of making many books there is no end,
> And much study wears one's strength away.

Koheleth himself would have seen in all the time and ingenuity spent on the interpretation of his tiny masterpiece one more example of the futility of human effort. For there is scarcely one aspect of the book, whether of date, authorship or interpretation, that has not been the subject of wide difference of opinion.

Its very title is an insoluble problem. The author effectively hid his identity under the strange name "Koheleth," apparently derived from the Hebrew word *kahal*, meaning "congregation" or "community." Very aptly the Greek translator utilized an equally obscure Greek term as an equivalent—"Ecclesiastes," a word which occurs only a few times in Greek literature and means "a member of the *ecclesia*, the citizens' assembly in Greece." In Christian times *ecclesia* became the regular designation for the Church. Basing themselves on both the Hebrew root and its Greek equivalent, some translators render "Koheleth" as "The Preacher." This has the advantage of being less ponderous than "Ecclesiastes"; but a less conventional preacher than our author would be hard to find!

Traditionally the authorship of the book is ascribed to Solomon because the opening sentence reads: "The words of Koheleth, the son of David, king in Jerusalem," and Solomon enjoyed a reputation for wisdom, perhaps not wholly unmerited. Yet the view that Solomon is the author has been generally abandoned today, with the growth of a truer recognition of the style, vocabulary, and world-outlook of Koheleth. Even with Solomon eliminated, the dates assigned to the book vary from the Persian period to the Greek age, while Graetz has placed it in the days of Herod. In other words, Koheleth may have lived anywhere between 500 B.C.E. and 100 C.E.—no less a span than six centuries.

While there may legitimately be differences of opinion regarding the date of a book where historical allusions are few and indefinite, it is striking that the very meaning and purpose of the work have been equally unclear. The earlier commentators, following the Jewish Midrashim and the Aramaic Targum, saw in it the penitent reflections of a Solomon, grown worldly-wise and sorrowful in the evening of life, an interpretation not without a poetic charm all its own. On the other hand, there were Church Fathers who found in the book definite teachings of the Trinity and the Atonement! Nor has this approach been completely surrendered even today. At least one commentator sees in Koheleth "a schoolmaster leading men to Christ" (Plumptre) because his book reveals how futile and vain life appears without Christian faith! One of the sanest of modern scholars (Cornill) sees in it the greatest triumph of Old Testament piety!

As a rule, modern students of Ecclesiastes have tended to regard it as basically heterodox, if not as downright heretical. At the same time, there is no unanimity as to whether Koheleth teaches natural enjoyment or Epicurean license as the norm of human life. Opinions differ as to whether he is a gentle cynic, or an embittered misanthrope, or whether, as Renan maintains, "Koheleth" is "the only charming book ever written by a Jew."

Most critical readers have been struck by the variations in mood and thought within the book. Some medieval commentators suggested that it was the unsystematic record of debates between men of varying temperaments—sensualists, refined worldlings, men of affairs, saints and sages.

Modern scholars have sought to explain the apparent incoherence in other ways. Thus Bickell has declared, with enviable omniscience, that the book was originally written on separate leaves, each containing precisely 525 letters. These leaves were disarranged and hence the book is incoherent and disorganized. His theory, it must be confessed, has won few adherents.

Other critics have preferred to assume composite authorship for the book, in line with similar tendencies in other branches of Biblical research. Tentatively advanced by Haupt, the theory of multiple sources was meticulously worked out by Siegfried, who divided the eleven score verses of the book among nine authors, at least one of whom represents an entire group. Less extreme and more widely accepted is the theory that the writings of Koheleth were fundamentally heterodox and unconventional, but that they were subjected to wide and persistent interpolation by conventional readers, in an effort to tone down—at least to dissent from—Koheleth's heresies. The difficulties involved in this view may be gauged by noting that Jastrow finds over 120 interpolations in a book of 222 verses. Barton, who is more conservative, claims that at least two hands were at work on the book, besides the original author, one, a *Hasid* or pietist, the other a *Hakam* or conventional Wisdom glossator. Between them, they are responsible for 45 important changes, besides many lesser ones.

Neither scholar seeks to explain why the book was deemed worthy of this effort to "legitimatize" it, when it could so easily have been suppressed. There were many other works written in this period, all attributed to ancient worthies, which were far less objectionable to the alleged orthodox sentiment of the time, with which no such pains were taken. Instead they were excluded from the biblical canon simply by being stored away in the *genizah* and thus consigned to destruction. Many, if not most, of these pseudepigraphical writings were lost altogether. Some managed to survive by accident, in Greek, Latin, Syriac, Ethiopic or Slavonic translations. That Koheleth did not meet this fate is surely significant.

Moreover, the theory of tendencious additions in Koheleth suffers from another crucial defect. It is difficult to believe that in the ancient Orient, where time moved slowly, and changes were few, so many steps in the process were consummated in a comparatively short time. The critical view must assume that the book was written, attained to popularity and sustained systematic interpolation at the hands of various schools of readers. Thereafter, these glosses were universally accepted as part of the original, the composite product was ascribed to Solomon and the book was admitted into the canon of Scripture. This complicated literary history must all be compressed into a period of three centuries at the most. For by the end of the first century of the Christian Era, its right to a place in the Biblical canon could still be theoretically discussed in the academies but was no longer open to dispute.

Other instances of radical divergences of interpretation are not lacking. The existence of Greek influence in Koheleth has been

affirmed by some commentators (Pfleiderer, Siegfried, Haupt, Plumptre, Tyler, Bickerman), and denied by others (McNiele, Delitzsch,
Nowak, Barton) while one scholar (Dillon) claims Buddhist influence.
Some authorities (Zapletal, Haupt) have applied elaborate metrical
theories to the book, in accordance with which they transpose and
excise at liberty. Hertzberg modifies the text to demonstrate its rhythmic structure, while others (Genung, Barton) are equally convinced of
its prose character.

Many of these theories about Koheleth have always seemed to us
questionable in method and psychologically unsound. If the book is
approached with an open mind and a grasp of the social and cultural
environment out of which it arose, it reveals itself as a literary unity, as
several recent students have realized. All that is needful is to forget
the learned authors, turn to Koheleth himself, and read him with
sympathy and imagination. Then the dry bones will take on flesh
and his spirit will live again.

B. The Man

As nearly as can be told, Koheleth, or Ecclesiastes, lived during the
dark and shadowy age in Jewish history that preceded the vivid
glory of the Maccabees, some time during the fourth or third century
before the Christian Era. It was an age well described by an older
contemporary as a "day of small things," with little to stir men's hearts
either to ecstasy or wrath. For the period of the Second Temple was
one when great dreams had turned into petty realities and the resplendent visions of the fathers had become the very real but colorless
background against which the children lived.

True enough, on the self-same site where Solomon had built his
Temple five centuries earlier, a replica now stood. But this was only
a modest imitation of the older structure, which continued to grow
ever more glorious in the national consciousness, as it receded further
into the past. That earlier Temple had been burnt in 586 B.C.E. by the
Babylonian conquerors, who exiled the most important classes of the
people. While many of the captives, no doubt, were absorbed by the
surrounding population in Mesopotamia and elsewhere, not all had
been assimilated by their foreign environment. There now arose
gifted leaders of deep spirituality, like Ezekiel and Deutero-Isaiah,

who sustained the courage of the Judean exiles and fortified their solidarity by painting glorious pictures of a Restoration to Zion.

That Restoration had indeed come, but on a scale far removed from the prophetic visions. A small band of settlers had been allowed to return to Palestine by the magnanimous and far-sighted Cyrus, founder of the Persian Empire. Instead of a mighty nation holding sway over distant lands, as the prophets had foretold, the Jewish people in its own homeland was a tiny island in a heathen sea. Centered in Jerusalem, the new community enjoyed at best a precarious autonomy in the religious and cultural spheres, while being completely subservient, politically and economically, to the Persian overlords. The Jewish settlement was also imperilled by internal discord. It had required the stern and heroic measures of an Ezra to stem the tide of intermarriage which was particularly prevalent among the priests and other leaders of the community. This tendency threatened to obliterate the Jewish identity completely within the space of a few generations. Moreover, there was the perpetual threat of enemies from without. Only the resourcefulness of the Jewish governor, Nehemiah, had succeeded in erecting a city wall around Jerusalem, in spite of the intrigues of the neighboring Ammonites, Samaritans and Arabs.

The next few centuries that followed Ezra and Nehemiah are among the most obscure in Jewish history. Only a few incidents are recorded by Josephus for the entire period, and these generally of the most disreputable kind. We hear of a high priest murdering his brother in the Temple precincts, and of the scion of an aristocratic family of Judea having an affair with a Greek dancer in Alexandria. Thus the upper classes were already showing signs of the moral disintegration that led them a little later into wholesale surrender to the blandishments of the Hellenistic world and the virtual abandonment of the Jewish way of life.

There were, to be sure, deeper spiritual currents among the people, which, inchoate and unrecognized until hundreds of years later, escaped the vigilant eyes of the chronicler. Due to the chastening influence of the Babylonian Exile and the Return, the long campaign of religious and ethical education waged by the prophets and legislators of the First Temple period was finally crowned with success. Scorned and vilified in their own day, the Prophets had now attained to wide authority, and were more truly alive centuries after their death than in their own lifetime.

Perhaps even more significant was the achievement of Ezra, who succeeded in establishing the Torah, or the Five Books of Moses, as the basic law of Judaism. At a great assembly, participated in by the heads of every family in the newly constituted community, it was publicly accepted as binding for all time. But the Torah, written in earlier days, could not become a living force in the new community without study and reinterpretation. This significant function was undertaken by the *Sopherim*, or Scribes, better rendered "the Masters of the Book." They expounded the letter of Scripture, amplified it where it was brief or unclear, and extended its provisions to meet new conditions as they arose. They not only preserved the Torah; they gave it new life.

The importance of their work can scarcely be over-estimated. Their activity made the Bible relevant to the needs of new generations and thus prepared it to serve as the eternal charter of humanity. Their discussions and decisions were incorporated into the Oral Law, constituting the oldest part of the Mishnah and the Talmud. Thus the Sopherim laid the foundations of Rabbinic Judaism. They gave to Jewish tradition some of its most noteworthy characteristics, its protean capacity for adjustment and its fusing of realistic understanding and idealistic aspiration. These nameless Scribes thus contributed in no small measure to the survival of the Jewish people. But their significance is not limited to the household of Israel. The Christian world, too, owes them a deep debt of gratitude, all too often left unacknowledged. As founders of Pharisaic Judaism, they helped create the background from which Christianity arose, and formulated many of the basic teachings that both religions share in common.

All this lay, however, within the lap of the unborn future. In their own day, the role of the Scribes and teachers of the Oral Law was unspectacular. Doubtless it attracted little attention, since they were drawn mainly from the lower and middle classes of society.

The upper classes also possessed a medium of intellectual activity which, like the dominant spirit of the age, was severely practical in purpose. These groups, even the high-priestly families among them, whose position and income derived from their service in the Temple, were concerned less with the will of God than with the way of the world. Their goal in education was the training of their youth for careers as merchant princes, landed gentry or government officials. To satisfy this need, a special type of preceptor arose, principally, if not exclusively, in Jerusalem, the capital. Like the Sophists in classical Hellas, who performed a similar function for the upper-class youth of Greek society, these Hebrew teachers taught what they termed "Wisdom" (Hebrew *Hokmah*, Greek *Sophia*).

This Hebrew Wisdom was a true Oriental product that had been cultivated for centuries throughout the lands of the Fertile Crescent —Egypt, Palestine, Syria and Babylonia—and for similar purposes, the preparation of youth for success in government, agriculture and commerce. Increasingly it is becoming clear that, even in Israel, the roots of Wisdom were very ancient, part of the cultural inheritance of the Orient, which the Hebrews shared with their neighbors and kinsmen. The tradition that King Solomon is the symbol of Wisdom is no longer airily dismissed by scholars as a figment of the folk imagination. It is seen to reflect the historical fact that the intensive cultivation of Wisdom goes back to his reign, when wide international contacts and internal prosperity contributed to the flowering of culture.

It was, however, during the first half of the Second Temple period that Hebrew Wisdom reached its apogee, for reasons that need not detain us here. Primarily, it was concerned with the arts and wiles of practical living. The Hebrew Wisdom teachers sought to inculcate the virtues of hard work, zeal, prudence, sexual moderation, sobriety, loyalty to authority and religious conformity—all the elements of a morality making for worldly success. What is more, they did not hesitate to urge less positive virtues on their youthful charges, such as holding one's tongue and distributing largesse, as aids in making one's way.

> Where words abound, sin is not wanting,
> But he that controls his tongue is a wise man. (Prov. 10:19)

> A man's gift makes room for him,
> It brings him before great men. (Prov. 18:16)

In brief, this practical Wisdom represented a hard-headed, matter-of-fact, "safe and sane" approach to the problems of living.

Not all the preceptors of Wisdom were of this type, however. There were some whose restless minds refused to be satisfied with these practical goals of what may be termed the lower Wisdom. They sought to penetrate to the great abiding issues: the meaning of life, the purpose of creation, the nature of death, the mystery of evil. In grappling with these ultimate problems they insisted on using the same instruments of observation and common sense they applied to daily concerns, rather than rely on tradition and conventional doctrines. Like so many rationalist minds since their day, however, they found the unaided human reason incapable of solving these issues. Some, no doubt, finally made their peace with the traditional religion of their day. But others, more tough-minded, refused to take on faith what their reason could not demonstrate. Hence their writings reveal various degrees and types of skepticism and heterodoxy. It is within this environment of economic well-being and intense intellectual activity that Koheleth arose and in terms of which he must be understood.

His brief book gives tantalizingly few hints about his personal life, and these have been seized upon and elaborated variously by his readers. Some have inferred from the detailed description of luxury in Chapter Two that he was a country gentleman, an aristocrat of the old school. In that passage, however, Koheleth is merely adopting the role of King Solomon as a literary device, in order to drive home his point on the futility of wealth and wisdom, for both of which the great King was renowned.

It seems much more likely that Koheleth was a teacher in one of the Wisdom academies in Jerusalem, which catered to the educational needs of upper-class youth. Not merely by vocation but probably also by birth, he was closely identified with this group. It seems clear that he never suffered poverty and want. Apparently he enjoyed the benefits of travel and other opportunities that were denied to the poor. While his range of knowledge may not have equalled that of the author of Job, who has been described as the most learned ancient before Plato, he was cultured and well-informed. He was able to draw upon history, contemporary affairs and the science of his day, in order to express his own world view. In strikingly independent fashion, he utilized some basic ideas of Greek philosophy, as well as the Torah and Prophetic literature of his own people as the medium for his own original ideas.

Only one other fact may be inferred about his personal history. Koheleth was a bachelor, or at least a man without children. For he is considerably exercised by the fact that when a man dies he must leave his wealth to "strangers," and he betrays no shred of sentiment for kith and kin.

If we must forego any other details about the external events of his life, we are fortunately in a better position to reconstruct his spiritual odyssey. From earliest youth his intellectual and emotional faculties were exceptionally keen and they determined the entire course of his development.

Fundamental in the boy and the man was a passionate love of life, the universal heritage of the healthy mind and the healthy body. He loved the tang of living. The sight of the sun, the breath of the wind, the good things of the world held him enthralled:

> Sweet is the light and it is good for the eyes to see the sun. (11:7)

The experience of life thrilled him to the core. Women he loved deeply, and knew well the world of sensation to which they beckoned.

> Enjoy life with the woman you love. (9:9)

Nor was he a stranger to other sources of material comfort and beauty. The cool spaciousness of gardens and orchards, the nobility of fine houses, the cheer of good food and fine wine, the charm of music and the grace of the dance, Koheleth savored them all. Even after his joy in life had been tempered by later experiences, he still felt that merely to be alive was a boon:

> For a living dog is better than a dead lion. (9:4)

Had Koheleth possessed no other elements in his spiritual constitution except his love of life, he would have been happy. Possessing the means of gratifying his desires, he might have spent his days in carousing and feasting or in the subtler forms of sensual enjoyment. He could have been a Philistine or an esthete, but in any event a happy man. That happiness eluded him was the result of other facets in his personality.

As a Jew, Koheleth was naturally reared in the rich religious and cultural tradition of his people. In his time, too, the three main strands of Hebrew thought were not mere ancient historical memories, but living and dynamic forces. As we have seen, the teachings of the Torah were being practiced in the Temple cult by the priests and being expounded in the academies by the scribes. The period of the Prophets was over, but their teachings were accepted as integral to Judaism. As for the third spiritual current, that of the *Hokmah*, or Wisdom, this was now at its height, richly creative and deeply influential.

All these were part of the educative influences brought to bear upon Koheleth. In particular, a spark of the prophetic spirit singed his soul, and he was never again the same carefree, lusty youth. The beauty of nature and the luxury of wealth could not blot out the marks of man's injustice to his fellows:

Furthermore, I saw under the sun, in the place of judgment, there was wickedness, and in the place of righteousness, wrong. (3:16)

Superimposed upon his innate love of life, there had come a second great motive power, the love of justice. But there was a cruel difference between the two. While the first could easily be gratified, he was doomed to failure in the second. As he grew older, and became aware of the tragic distance that yawned between the prophetic ideal and the real world, something snapped within him. The magnificent audacity of the Prophets, their unshakable faith in the ultimate triumph of the right, was not for him. He was too realistic, too sober, too narrow, if you will, for that. Too many years had elapsed since the Prophets had foretold the doom of evil and folly, and still the wicked prospered, and folly sat enthroned in the high places:

I have seen everything during my vain existence, a righteous man being destroyed for all his righteousness, and a sinner living long for all his wickedness. (7:15)

Folly is often enthroned on the great heights. I have seen slaves on horses, while lords must walk on foot like slaves. (10:6, 7)

Nor did Koheleth possess the spiritual energy to grow indignant and reprove his God, as did the author of Job. At the spectacle of injustice, the Prophets had thundered and pleaded and proclaimed the day of doom, but Koheleth merely smiled. Wrong and corruption were eternal, inherent in the scheme of things:

If you observe the despoiling of the poor and the perversion of justice and right in the state, do not be astonished at the fact, for each guardian of the law is higher than the next, and there are still higher ones above them! (5:7)

Yet Koheleth did not react with a cheap and easy cynicism to human suffering. On other themes he might be light or sarcastic, but here, as a rule, he was in deadly earnest, with a fervor almost prophetic in its intensity:

Again, I saw all the acts of oppression that are done under the sun. Here are the tears of the oppressed, with none to comfort them, and power in the hand of their oppressors with none to comfort them. So I praise the dead who already have died, more than the creatures who are still alive. (4:1, 2)

The happiness of a carefree and joyous existence was evermore beclouded for Koheleth by the vision of a world in agony. Koheleth became a cynic, not because he was callous to human suffering, but, on the contrary, because he was acutely sensitive to man's cruelty and folly.

But Koheleth had not yet plumbed the full depths of the despair that life was to breed in him. Stronger even than his love of justice was his love of truth. Possessing a keen mind and a lively curiosity, he eagerly sought after the profounder *Hokmah*, the fundamental insight into the world and its meaning. It was the Wisdom hymned by the Sage, after which Koheleth strove:

> The Lord by Wisdom founded the earth
> By Understanding He established the heavens. (Prov. 3:19)

Koheleth sought to probe these mysteries, which the more matter-of-fact Ben Sira had advised leaving alone, perhaps because he knew of the perils that lurked in the quest:

> What is too wonderful for you do not seek,
> Nor search after what is hidden from you,
> Seek to understand what is permitted you,
> And have no concern with mysteries. (Ecclus. 3:20, 21)

Job, too, had sought this Wisdom in vain:

> Where is Wisdom to be found?
> And where is the place of Understanding? (Job 28:20)

Yet in this very unknowability of the world, Job had found an anodyne for his suffering, a token that there was a rational and just world-order, though incomprehensible to man. For Job, the grandeur and harmony of the cosmos, created by Divine Wisdom, was an earnest of an equally pervasive moral universe, founded on Divine justice. But that faith was not for Koheleth. His fruitless search for justice in human life had grievously wounded his personal happiness. Now came the tragic realization that the all-inclusive Wisdom of the universe was also unattainable:

I saw that though a man sleep neither by day nor by night, he cannot discover the meaning of God's work which is done under the sun. Even if a man searches hard, he will not find it; and though a wise man may think he is about to learn it, he will be unable to find it. (8:17)

A deep woe now settled upon the youthful enthusiast, when the futility of his aspirations was borne in upon him. Justice he had sought, but it was nowhere; wisdom he had pursued, but the phantom had vanished. All life was meaningless and futile, and his judgment upon it was devastating:

> Vanity of vanities, says Koheleth,
> Vanity of vanities, all is vanity. (1:1; 12:8)

Hence I hated life, for all the work that is done beneath the sun seemed worthless to me, and everything, vanity and a chasing of wind. (2:17)

As the spectacle of human cruelty and suffering was revealed to him, he despaired of life:

More fortunate than both the living and the dead, is he who has not yet been born and so has never seen the deeds that are being done under the sun. (4:3)

Three great ideas had lighted his way in the world. The love of life was rich with promise of happiness, but the yearning for justice and wisdom had brought him only sorrow and disillusion.

For a space, one can live in a state of complete intellectual nihilism, without values or activities. Few men, however, and Koheleth was not among them, can abide that emptiness indefinitely. The quest for certainty is not abandoned merely because two of its roads have proved blind alleys. Koheleth *had* to discover some definite basis for belief, some rationale of action, if his life was to go on. It could not be wisdom or justice, for these had been weighed and found wanting. He had to retrace his steps to the first great principle of his life, the only law that had not brought him to grief. In the striving for happiness lay the only reasonable goal for human existence.

So Koheleth returns to his first love, but with a difference. The whole-hearted, instinctive gladness of youth is gone. His love of life is now the result of reflection, the irreducible minimum of his life's philosophy. He chants a hymn of joy, but there are overtones of tragedy, the sad music of the inevitability of old age, the echo of the cruelty and ignorance of mankind:

For if a man live many years, let him rejoice in them all, and remember that the days of darkness will be many, and that everything thereafter is nothingness. (11:8)

So I saw that there is nothing better for a man than to rejoice in his works, for that is his lot, and no one can permit him to see what shall be after him. (3:22)

Koheleth sets up the attainment of happiness as the goal of human striving, not merely because he loves life, but because he cannot have justice and wisdom. Joy is the only purpose that he can find in a monotonous and meaningless world, in which all human values, such as wealth, piety and ability, are vanity, where all men encounter the same fate and no progress is possible.

The modern reader might expect that Koheleth would be led by his views to deny the existence of God, but that was impossible to an ancient mind, and especially to a Jew. Even the Epicureans, who denied divine intervention in human affairs, and who sprang from a people to whom the gods never had the same burning reality as to the Hebrews, did not deny their being. Koheleth, a son of Israel, a pupil of the prophets and the sages, could not doubt the reality of God for an instant. For him, the existence of the world was tantamount to the existence of God.

It was on the question of God's relation to men that Koheleth parted company with the conventional teachers of his time. For all the barrage of platitudes of the sages, there was not a shred of proof that God wished to reveal the true Wisdom, the secret of life, to men. Similarly, there was tragic evidence to contradict the glib assertion of the moralists:

Say to the upright that it shall be well with him, for he shall eat the fruit of his doings. Woe to the wicked! It shall be ill with him, for the reward of his hands shall be given him. (Isa. 3:10, 11)

The Psalmist had sung:

I have been young, and now am old, yet I have never seen an upright man forsaken, and his offspring begging bread. (Ps. 37:25)

His words might be a prayer or a pious hope; they were scarcely the result of empirical observation!

All that is certain is that man has an innate desire for happiness. Since God has created man, He has also created this impulse. It thus becomes clear that God's fundamental purpose for mankind is the furthering of man's pleasure.

We may put it another way: Koheleth's morality recognizes the pursuit of happiness as the goal. His metaphysics postulates the existence of God. His religion is the combination of both. Koheleth recognizes God's creative power and His limitless sovereignty. His will He has revealed to his creatures in man's inborn desire for happiness. But beyond these attributes, Koheleth refuses to affirm anything about his God.

Accordingly, the basic note of the book is its insistence upon the enjoyment of life, of all the good things in the world. There is the love of woman—and the singular is noteworthy—

> Enjoy life with the woman whom you love,
> Through all the brief days of your life,
> That God has given you under the sun,
> For that is your life's reward,
> For your toil under the sun. (9:9)

With a moving sense of the transitoriness of life, he calls for the vigorous and full-blooded enjoyment of all it affords, food and drink, oil and fine clothes, beautiful homes and music:

Whatever you are able to do, do with all your might, for there is neither action nor thought nor knowledge nor wisdom in the grave toward which you are moving. (9:10)

In practice Koheleth advocates a moderate course, not very different from the attitude of the Rabbis of the Talmud:

Three things bring a sense of ease and contentment to a man: a beautiful home, an attractive wife, and fine clothes. (Berakot 57a)

What set his standpoint apart from theirs, was that his attitude stemmed not from a full-hearted acceptance of the world, as preached by religion, but from a sense of frustration and resignation, induced by his philosophy. Nothing really counts if truth and righteousness cannot be attained. Yet man lives and God rules, and God's manifest will is man's happiness, not that it matters overmuch, but this at least is certain.

This skeptical outlook with which Koheleth faced life needs to be analyzed a little more closely, both for the understanding of his personality and the evaluation of his message. Basically, his skepticism was rooted in his personality, to be sure, but it was nurtured by his upper-class origin and bias, as we have pointed out above. In essence, skepticism is an indisposition to accept conventional ideas merely because of the pressure of the mass. But there is also another element in the constitution of a skeptic—a state of mind possible only for those who, observing evil, are not its immediate victims.

Koheleth did not espouse the dynamic faith of the Prophets in the ultimate and inevitable emergence of a just world-order under "the Kingdom of God." Nor could he accept the nascent ideas of life after death and retribution beyond the grave, which were basic to normative Judaism and early Christianity. The mystic's flight to another world was totally uncongenial to Koheleth's temperament. Neither was he an apostle of "direct action" like the rebels, reformers and revolutionaries of all ages.

In part, Koheleth, like the other teachers of Wisdom, adopted none of these alternatives—because he personally found life tolerable even under the conditions he deprecated. His failure to respond actively to injustice is doubtless a crucial defect, so that our age cannot find in him the motive power toward the building of a better world that is so abundant in the Hebrew prophets. In the face of the towering evils of our own day, and the breath-taking vision of a better order for all men now for the first time within realization, Amos and Isaiah are incomparably more inspiring guides.

But this temperamental difference between Koheleth and the Prophets must not blind us to his enduring value in teaching men how to meet those ills that must be transcended because they cannot be transformed. It is true that nowhere does Koheleth preach the virtue of courage in so many words. For him courage is not a conscious ideal, nor even an idea—it is far more, an inborn, pervasive quality. Every line in his book is instinct with the spirit of clear-eyed, brave and joyous acceptance of life, for all its inevitable limitations.

And these limitations *are* inevitable, however unwilling a youthful and activistic generation may be to confess it. Though men be ever more successful in moulding the pattern of the world nearer hearts' desire, they will still meet pain and frustration in life, for which they will require dignity and courage and the saving grace of good humor. This need for resignation is independent of political and economic systems. It inheres in the character of the universe and man's nature. Man is a creature whose reach is always greater than his grasp, with a boundless imagination weaving hopes and desires far beyond the capacity of his brief, earth-bound existence to fulfill. As Koheleth observes, "All a man's toil is for his wants, but his desires are never satisfied." In teaching men to taste life's joys without self-deception and to face its sorrows without despair, Koheleth performs an everlastingly significant function.

To set forth these basic attitudes toward life, Koheleth writes his book in old age, recapitulating the stages of his spiritual history in the process. As he contemplates his past career, he has no complaint to make; life has been good to him. He has been spared the degradation of poverty and the terror of insecurity, nor has he ever had to taste the bitterness of personal tragedy. His charm, insight and skill have doubtless made him a successful teacher in the Wisdom academies and brought him tangible as well as intangible rewards. The competence he has acquired now makes it possible for him to enjoy the amenities of life—a fine house in Jerusalem, a sense of independence, and the blessing of unworried leisure. Thus he sits in the sunset hours of his life, a tiny island of ease and contemplation within the whirling currents of life in the capital city.

His is a comfortable old age, but there is a quiet loneliness about it. He has no wife to share either the simple happenings of ordinary existence or the rare moments of deeper experience. His home has never re-echoed with the voices of children at play. He has never been stirred to ecstasy by their laughter or driven to distraction by their tears. But perhaps, he muses, it is better so, as he recalls the fine brave rapture of youth and the febrile ambitions of maturity, all now revealed as emptiness and chasing of wind.

From time to time, his former pupils visit him, for Judaism declares it a duty to pay respect to one's former teachers by calling on them. He looks into the faces of these lads who have since gone forth to positions of prominence and dignity in the practical world. Some are important government officials, others are Temple dignitaries, while others have far-flung economic interests as merchant princes or landed gentry. As his wise, understanding eyes scan their faces, he notes that

they have paid a high price for success. The shining, carefree coun-
tenances of youth, the sparkling eyes brimful with mischief, are gone.
In their stead are worn faces, some drawn, others grown puffy with the
years, and tired, unhappy eyes sagging beneath the weight of responsibility. Time was when his pupils were young and he was old, but now
the tables are turned. True, Koheleth is a few paces before them in the
inexorable procession toward the grave. But in a deeper sense, he is
young and they are prematurely old. He knows what they have forgotten—that men's schemes and projects, their petty jealousies and
labors, their struggles and heartaches, all are vanity and that joy in
life is the one Divine commandment.

Before it is too late, he takes pen in hand to transmit the truth, as
he sees it, concerning the incomprehensible and indescribably precious
blessing called life. For it is his secret wish that men after him, whom
his living voice will never reach, may face life with truth as their
banner and with a song in their hearts.

> Go, then, eat your bread with joy,
> And drink your wine with a glad heart,
> For God has already approved your actions.
> At all times let your clothes be white,
> And oil on your head not be lacking.
>
> Enjoy life with the woman you love
> Through all the brief days of your life,
> Which God has given you under the sun,
> Throughout your brief days,
> For that is your life's reward
> For your toil under the sun.

Whatever you are able to do, do with all your might, for there is neither
action nor thought nor knowledge nor wisdom in the grave toward which
you are moving. (9:7–10)

Doubtless Koheleth would have been the first to confess that in taking
such pains to urge the enjoyment of life upon man, at a time when he
himself had already passed his prime and reached the days in which
there is no pleasure, there lurked more than a little of vanity—in
both senses. Fortunately, however, the need for self-expression
triumphed over the dictates of logic, and so a masterpiece was born.

C. The Book

When the book of Koheleth is read without preconceptions, its thoroughly natural reaction to life is completely intelligible. Yet it is not really strange that it has been widely misunderstood. Since the book is in the Bible, most readers turn to it with more devoutness than alertness, and expect to be edified rather than stimulated by its contents. In general, this attitude of mind, however praiseworthy in intent, is harmful to an adequate appreciation of the Bible. In the case of Koheleth, it is fatal. The time is long overdue for recognizing, as A. B. Ehrlich observed, that the Bible is not a collection of religious texts, but rather "a national literature upon a religious foundation." Only from this point of view can the reader savor fully the vitality, color and broad humanity of the Bible and comprehend its message without the distortions induced by dogma or prejudice.

For the religious spirit, the Bible is eternally the Revelation of God, but in no superficial and mechanical sense. Rather it must be understood in the spirit of the profound Rabbinic comment on two rival schools, "Both these and the others are the words of the Living God." When the Bible is approached in this spirit and recognized as the repository of men's deepest aspirations for the truth about life, it becomes clear that Koheleth belongs of right in the great collection.

Another difficulty in the understanding of Koheleth is that he was struggling to use Hebrew for quasi-philosophic purposes, a use to which the language had not previously been applied. A thousand years later, medieval translators still found that Hebrew had not yet fully developed the flexibility, precision and vocabulary necessary for the treatment of philosophic themes. Koheleth's comparative success in this respect is not the least element of his literary skill.

His task was rendered still more difficult by two other facts. The Hebrew language has a very simple structure and only a few syntactic devices are available to express all possible nuances of meaning. Thus, to cite two instances, the moods of verbs must be inferred from the context and subordinate clauses of all varieties are externally indistinguishable from coordinate clauses. Obviously, these and similar features complicate the understanding of a text where exactness is essential.

In addition, during Koheleth's day, Hebrew was steadily losing ground to Aramaic, which resembles it more closely than any other Semitic language. Aramaic was rapidly becoming the *lingua franca* of the entire Semitic world. Hebrew, to be sure, was still spoken in the schools, and was utilized in religious ritual and literature, besides being cultivated by the more educated groups. But the all-powerful Aramaic was being spoken by the common people and making inroads even among the scholars. As a result, Aramaic idioms and modes of expression are characteristic of the Hebrew in "Koheleth," as well as in later writings.

Principally, however, the book has been misinterpreted because of a number of special features in its style, which are themselves a reflection of the author's personality.

Like other writers since, who were raised in a religious tradition from which they have broken away in whole or in part, Koheleth uses a *traditional religious vocabulary* to express his own special vision. The modern reader will think of Ernest Renan, Anatole France and George Santayana as manifesting at times a somewhat similar trait. A few examples of this tendency may be cited. Traditional morality declared that he who fulfilled God's will, would be happy. Koheleth declares that he who is happy is fulfilling God's will!

Indeed, every man whom God has given wealth and possessions and granted the power to enjoy them, taking his portion, and rejoicing in his labor, that is the gift of God, for it is God who provides the joy in a man's heart. (5:18)

The Wisdom writers call the sinner a fool. So does Koheleth, but he reserves the right to define his terms. A sinner is he who fails to work for the advancement of his own happiness. The Book of Proverbs promises that the righteous will ultimately inherit the wealth of the evildoer:

He who increases his wealth by usury and interest, is gathering it for him who befriends the poor. (28:8)

Koheleth promises the same to the man who is "pleasing to God," the man who obeys God's will, and seeks to achieve joy:

To the man God favors, He gives wisdom, knowledge and joy, but to the "sinner," he assigns the task of gathering and amassing, only to hand it over at last to the man who is pleasing to God. (2:26)

The Prophets, with unfailing insistence, call upon the people to hear the word of God. So does Koheleth. He, too, calls upon his reader to remember God and His purpose for man, before old age sets in and the time for joy is past:

> Remember your Creator in the days of your youth,
> Before the evil days come and the years draw near,
> Of which you will say, "I have no pleasure in them." (12:1)

This clothing of the hedonistic principle in religious guise is not without analogy in Hebrew literature. The Book of Proverbs counsels:

> Hear, my son, and be wise,
> and walk in the ways of your heart. (23:19)

Ben Sira, whose general moral system is conventional, makes the enjoyment of life a duty:

> My son, if you have the means, treat yourself well,
> For there is no pleasure in the grave,
> And there is no postponement of death. (14:11)

Even more striking are the words of the Talmudic sage, Samuel, of the third century, cited in the Talmud:

Seize hold and eat, seize hold and drink, for this world whence we depart is like a wedding feast. (Babli, Erubin 54a)

Samuel's great contemporary, Rab, expresses the same sentiment in typically religious language:

Every man must render an account before God for all the good things he beheld in life and did not enjoy. (Jerusalem Talmud, Kiddushin, end)

No more perfect analogy could be found to Koheleth's words:

> Rejoice, O young man, in your youth,
> And let your heart cheer you in your youthful days.
> Follow the impulses of your heart
> And the desires of your eyes,
> And know that for all this,
> God will call you to account. (11:9)

Similarly, when Koheleth says, "Go, eat your bread in joy and drink your wine with a glad heart, for God has already approved your actions" (9:7), he is expressing his philosophy of life in a religious vocabulary congenial to his own temper and the spirit of his age.

The second unique characteristic of Koheleth's style, which has already been analyzed in detail above, is *his use of proverbial quotations*. This is undoubtedly the result of his background and occupation as a Wisdom teacher. His speculations on life did not lead him to abandon his interest in the mundane concerns of the lower Wisdom; he merely went beyond them. As Koheleth continued to teach the practical Wisdom to his pupils, he doubtless contributed to its literature, most of which is couched in short, pithy maxims of a realistic turn. Hence, maxims very similar in form and spirit to those in the Book of Proverbs are frequently met with in Koheleth. These are not interpolations by more conventional readers, as generally assumed. They belong, as MacDonald has well noted, to the author's method of keeping connection with the past, while leaving it behind.

Koheleth's use of this folk-material is so varied and individual that it may fairly be described as creative. It is beyond question one of the most charming features of his style. At times he cites a proverb simply because he agrees with it, and he may elaborate upon it with a characteristic comment. Thus the most confirmed cynic will agree that

> Through sloth the ceiling sinks in,
> And through slack hands the house leaks (10:18),

or suggest that it is wise to diversify one's business undertakings:

Send your goods overseas, so that you may get your return after many days. (11:1)

Frequently, however, Koheleth's comment on the proverb that he quotes subtly changes the meaning of the text, shifting the ground from the realm of the matter-of-fact and the practical to the uncharted regions where speculation and skepticism have free rein.

Examples of this use of a proverb as a text with ironic comment are plentiful. Thus one conventional maxim extols the virtues of cooperation. Koheleth approves the sentiment, but for reasons of his own:

"Two are better than one, because they have a reward in their labor." True, for if either falls, the other can lift his comrade, but woe to him who is alone when he falls, with no one else to lift him. Then also, if two sleep together, they will be warm, but how can one alone keep warm? Moreover, if some enemy attack either one, the two will stand against him, while a triple cord cannot quickly be severed. (4:9–12)

The conventional teachers of morality emphasized that love of money does not make for happiness. This idea is expanded by Koheleth through the characteristic reflection that strangers finally consume the substance of the owner.

"He who loves money will never have enough of it and he who loves wealth will never attain it." This is indeed vanity. For as wealth increases, so do those who would spend it, hence what value is there in the owner's superior ability, except that he has more to look upon? (5:9)

In what may perhaps be described as the most "conservative" passage in the Bible, the Book of Proverbs counsels submission to political authority:

Fear, my son, God and king, and meddle not with those who seek change. (Prov. 24:21)

Koheleth repeats this idea, but with his tongue in his cheek:

> I say: keep the king's command,
> And that because of the oath of God.

Submit to the king because of your oath of fealty, but also, he adds as an afterthought:

Since the king's word is law, who may say to him: "What are you doing?" (8:2–4)

because the king is powerful enough to crush you!

Koheleth would undoubtedly agree with the universal view that life on any terms is preferable to death. Yet his general intellectual conviction as to the futility of living impels him to a comment which ostensibly justifies, but actually undermines, the entire proposition.

"He who is attached to the living still has hope, for a living dog is better than a dead lion." The living know at least that they will die; but the dead know nothing, neither have they any reward; for their memory is forgotten. Their loves, their hates, their jealousies, all have perished—never again will they have a share in all that is done under the sun. (9:4–6)

Another noteworthy device by which Koheleth expresses his divergence from commonly accepted views is the use of *contrasting proverbs*. As is well known, proverbs frequently contradict one another, since they summarize the empirical experience of the race. When faced by the need of making an important decision, a man may find himself in a quandary between the warning, "Look before you leap" on the one hand, and "to hesitate is to be lost" on the other. The beautiful sentiment "Absence makes the heart grow fonder" is bluntly negated by the callous saying, "Out of sight, out of mind."

The compiler of Proverbs was aware of this tendency, when he quoted these two maxims in succession:

Answer not a fool according to his folly, lest thou also be like unto him.
Answer a fool according to his folly, lest he be wise in his own eyes. (Prov. 26:4, 5)

Koheleth uses the same device, but for his own purposes. He cites a proverb expressing a widely accepted point of view and then subtly registers his disagreement, not by a lengthy argument, but by citing another utterance diametrically opposed. Where Koheleth's sympathies lie in these debates is easy to determine. In each pair of contrasting proverbs, the latter represents his standpoint.

No theme was dearer to the hearts of the instructors of youth than the importance of hard work. Koheleth expresses his doubts on the subject by first quoting a proverb attacking laziness and then citing another which mocks the gospel of unceasing toil:

"The fool folds his hands and thus destroys himself."
"Better a handful acquired with ease, than both hands full gained through labor and chasing after wind." (4:5, 6)

Like all the Wise Men, conventional or otherwise, Koheleth has a "prejudice" in favor of wisdom as against folly. He himself tells how the wisdom of one poor man proved more efficacious than a mighty army. Yet he knows, too, how little wisdom is honored for its own sake, and how one fool can ruin the efforts of many wise men. These ideas seem to be expressed in some reflections, couched in the form of brief proverbs contradicted by others:

I said "Wisdom is better than prowess," but "the poor man's wisdom is despised and his words go unheeded."
"Wisdom is better than weapons." But "one fool destroys much good." (9:16, 18)

Whether Koheleth is citing other Wisdom writers or is himself the author of these "quotations" can rarely be determined. As a teacher of Wisdom, trained in its schools, he would naturally formulate his own ideas, as well as those he wished to negate, in the accepted form of the *mashal*, or proverb. Sometimes a stylistic peculiarity seems to indicate that the utterance is his own; but even where this clue is lacking, the material may well be original with him.

Naturally these quotations are not as a rule marked by external signs; they must be inferred from a careful study of the text, often based upon technical considerations. To transmit the sense to a modern reader, a translator must use quotation marks or an introductory phrase.

From all that has been said, it is clear that the Book of Koheleth is not a debate, a dialogue, or a philosophical treatise. It is best described as a *cahier* or notebook, into which the author jotted down his reflections during the enforced leisure of old age. They differ in mood, in style, and in length. At times when he grows impassioned, he develops a subtle inner rhythm, as in the majestic opening section of Chapter I. At others, the rhythm is much more pronounced, as in the unforgettable "Allegory of Old Age" in Chapter 12. Generally, however, his medium is prose.

It is possible that these brief essays were collected and edited by Koheleth himself, since the book opens and closes with the theme, "Vanity of vanities, all is vanity," and the first and last sections are the most eloquent and moving of all. Very often, the end of a section can be recognized by Koheleth's reverting, after a discussion of his subject, whether it be wealth, wisdom or corruption, to one of his two fundamental themes—the tragedy of man's ignorance of ultimate truth, and his God-given duty to achieve happiness.

The author's fascinating personality is thus reflected in a style rich in nuance and eloquent in its reticence. Koheleth, to be sure, is a skeptic, but that merely emphasizes the fact that he is a child of an age of tradition, when one world-outlook is dying and another still unborn. The skeptic is essentially a complex personality, the product of diverse and contradictory forces, such as childhood training and education, remolded by adult experience and reflection. No man ever rejects *in toto* the entire heritage of his day. In the soul of every skeptic there are intermingled the completely conventional, the modified old, and the radically new. To simplify Koheleth means to destroy him, but to approach him with understanding means to possess the key to a fascinating personality.

Koheleth's characteristic style helps to explain how the book managed to enter the Biblical canon. Matter-of-fact readers, unaware of his unconventional use of a religious vocabulary or his citation of proverbs for his own special purposes, would find the book replete with sound orthodox sentiments. And all the more would they be predisposed to this conclusion by the fact that Koheleth, in the two opening chapters, calls himself the son of David. His obvious purpose in doing so was to offer reflections on the value of wisdom and wealth, for both of which Solomon was famous. But this literary device stood Koheleth in good stead; it provided his book with the necessary aura of sanctity and antiquity for inclusion in Scripture.

Nevertheless, there was much in the book that was a stumbling-block to the devout. Rabbinic literature, indeed, records many objections to its retention in the Biblical canon. That it was never dislodged may be due in part to the naiveté and lack of historical perspective of many of its readers. But, basically, it is a tribute both to the fascination of the book and to the catholic taste of the Librarian of the Synagogue, who saw in every honest seeker after truth a servant of the one Source of truth. Whatever the motives that led to the preservation of the book, we cannot be too grateful.

Koheleth would have been shocked, even amused, to learn that his note-book had been canonized as part of Holy Scripture. But the obscure instinct of his people was building more truly than it knew when it stamped his work as sacred. In the deepest sense, Koheleth's is a religious book, because it seeks to grapple with reality. The Psalmist had sung:

> A broken and contrite heart,
> O God, Thou wilt not despise.

This cry of a sensitive spirit, wounded by man's cruelty and folly, this distilled essence of an honest mind, unwilling to soar on the wings of faith beyond the limits of the knowable, remains one of man's noblest offerings on the altar of truth.

15. THE SONG OF SONGS

I. A Unique Book

Books have their own peculiar destinies, a Latin proverb informs us. Every student of human nature knows how wide are the fluctuations in fashion and interest affecting men's attitudes toward works of literature, art and music.

In this regard, the Song of Songs is a shining exception. For over twenty centuries it has retained its appeal to men's hearts. To be sure, the book has been variously interpreted during its long career. Earlier ages, more devout than our own, read the Song of Songs as an allegory and saw in it an expression of the ideal relationship of love subsisting between God and man. However, as the full scope and character of Biblical literature became evident, this traditional view, in spite of its inherent charm and religious significance, became less and less popular and is today virtually abandoned. Within the last few decades, the allegorical theory has been revived in a very special form. Some scholars have sought to interpret the Song as the ritual of a pagan fertility-cult, but this effort cannot be pronounced a success, as this study seeks to demonstrate.

Today it is generally recognized that the book is to be understood literally, its theme being human love, a view which was, indeed, adumbrated in ancient times. Yet even now there is no unanimity with regard to the meaning and character of the book. Some scholars have maintained the position that the book is a drama, with either two or three characters. This theory is still frequently encountered in popular treatments of the Song, but it, too, I believe, cannot sustain critical examination.

As the results of archaeological and literary research continue to mount, it becomes increasingly clear that the Song cannot be understood in isolation, however splendid and exalted. The life and faith of ancient Israel is, on the one hand, part of the culture-pattern of the ancient Near East and, on the other, markedly distinct from it. Unless both elements of this ambivalent yet perfectly natural relationship are fully taken into account, we obtain a distorted picture of reality. Only

when the Bible is set within the larger framework of the Fertile Crescent, can we gain an adequate appreciation both of its place in the
world from which it emerged and of its unique character. For the
Bible is both the record of God's revelation to man and of man's
aspiration toward God.

When the Song of Songs is studied without preconceived notions,
it emerges as a superb lyrical anthology, containing songs of love and
nature, of courtship and marriage, emanating from at least five
centuries of Hebrew history, from the days of Solomon to the Persian
period. The Song thus constitutes a parallel, though of considerably
smaller compass, to the Book of Psalms, which is a florilegium of man's
yearning and love for God. If the two basic imperatives of religion are
the love of God and the love of man, the Song of Songs, no less than
the Book of Psalms, deserves its place in Scripture.

Nor is this all. John MacMurray has written that "the Hebrew form
of thought rebels against the very idea of a distinction between the
secular and the religious aspects of life." This acute observation does
not go far enough. Authentic Hebrew thought did not rebel against
the dichotomy; it never recognized its existence. The inclusion of the
Song of Songs in the Biblical canon is evidence of the persistence in
Judaism of the basic conception that the natural is holy, being the
manifestation of the Divine. This insight may well have been the
unconscious motivation of Rabbi Akiba's high praise of the Song of
Songs. "The entire universe is not as worthy as the day on which the
Song of Songs was given to Israel, for all the Writings are holy, but
the Song of Songs is the Holy of Holies."[1] In these passionate words,
Rabbi Akiba was upholding the right of the Song of Songs to a place in
the Scriptures. The warmth of his defense testifies to the vigor of
the challenge to which it was subjected, probably stronger than in
the case of Esther, Koheleth and Proverbs.[2]

The Song of Songs is unique among the books of the Bible in spirit,
content and form. It is the only book in the canon lacking a religious
or national theme, the Divine name occurring only once and then only
as an epithet (8:6). To be sure, Esther also makes no direct mention
of God, but its national emphasis is unmistakable. Even that is lacking
in the Song of Songs. The reason for the doubts as to its canonicity
is not hard to discover. Fragments of secular poetry are imbedded in
the Bible,[3] but this is the only complete work which is entirely secular,
indeed, sensuous, in character.

As in the case of Koheleth,[4] more than one factor helped to win admission for this little book into the canon of Scripture. While the charm and beauty of its contents played their part, if only on the subconscious level, there were two basic factors operating consciously. First was the occurrence of Solomon's name in the text,[5] which led to the attribution of the whole book to him, witness the title: "The Song of Songs, which is Solomon's" (1:1). The several references to "the king"[6] were, naturally enough, identified with Solomon as well. Second was the allegorical interpretation of the book, according to which the love of God and Israel is described under the guise of a lover and his beloved.[7] This seemed reasonable since wise King Solomon would surely occupy himself only with recondite, spiritual concerns. Hence the Solomonic authorship of the book undoubtedly strengthened, if it did not create, the allegorical interpretation of the Song. This interpretation found Biblical warrant in the frequent use by the Prophets of the metaphor of marital love to describe the proper relationship of Israel to its God.[8] This combination of factors overcame all doubts about the sacred character of the Song of Songs, and its canonicity was reaffirmed at the Council of Jamnia in 90 c.e., never to be seriously challenged again.[9]

II. The Allegorical Interpretation

The allegorical view of the Song of Songs to which we owe its inclusion in the canon and therefore its preservation was already well established in the first century c.e. The Apocryphal book IV Esdras uses the figures of "lily," "dove," and "bride" to refer to Israel (5:24, 26; 7:26). While the comparison to a bride might conceivably be based on other Biblical passages, like Jer. 2:2; Isa. 62:5, the references to "lily" and "dove" point unmistakably to our book. The only passage in the Septuagint which may point to a mystical interpretation is the rendering of *mērōsh 'amānāh* in 4:8 as "from the beginning of faith," but this is far from certain, since *'amānāh* has the meaning "faith" in Neh. 10:1. The Mishnah cites the description of Solomon's wedding in 3:11 and refers it to the giving of the Torah and the building of the Temple.[10] The same view underlies the Targum on the book, and the Midrash *Shir Hashirim Rabbah*, as well as many talmudic interpretations of various verses in the book.

Medieval Jewish commentators like Saadia and Rashi accepted its assumptions unhesitatingly. It is possible that the unconventional Abraham Ibn Ezra may be expressing his secret doubts on the subject by the method he employs in his commentary, which he divides into three parts, the first giving the meaning of the words, the second the literal meaning of the passage, and the third the allegorical interpretation.[11] Commentators differed as to details, but the general approach was clear. The book narrates, in symbolic fashion, the relationship of God and Israel from the days of the Patriarchs and the Exodus, extols the steadfast love and protection that God has given His beloved, and describes the fluctuations of loyalty and defection which have marked Israel's attitude toward its divine Lover.

When the Christian Church accepted the Hebrew Scriptures as its Old Testament, it was easy to transfer the parable from the old Israel to the New Israel, though there were variations of attitude. The first known allegorical treatment was that of Hippolytus of Rome, written early in the third century. He precedes Origen, Jerome, and Athanasius, who referred the book to Christ and the Church, while Ambrosius and Cornelius a Lapide identified the Shulammite with the Virgin Mary. Other figurative theories also were not lacking. Some of the older commentators, like Origen and Gregory of Nyassa, saw in it an allegory of the mystical union of the believing soul with God, a particularly congenial view, since mysticism has often expressed itself in strongly erotic terms.[12] Luther saw in it an allegory of Christ and the Soul.

The allegorical theory has been generally abandoned by modern scholars in its traditional guise. Yet a few contemporary Roman Catholic scholars[13] and some Orthodox Jewish writers[14] still interpret the book as an allegory of Israel's history.

Other forms of the allegorical theory have not been lacking. Isaac Abrabanel and his son Leo Hebraeus, basing themselves on the fact that Wisdom is described in *Hokmah* literature as a beautiful woman, who is contrasted with the "Woman of Folly" in Proverbs,[15] interpreted the beloved in the Song as a typological symbol of Wisdom, a view suggested in modern times by Godek and Kuhn. However, the details in the Song of Songs are both too concrete and too numerous to support this or any other allegorical view, which has accordingly found few adherents.

III. The Cult Theory

The most modern form of the allegorical theory regards our book as the translation of a pagan litany. In 1914, O. Neuschatz de Jassy suggested that it is a version of an Egyptian Osiris ritual, while Wittekindt proposed the view that it is a liturgy of the Ishtar cult.[16] The theory was most vigorously propagated by T. J. Meek,[17] who, in 1922, published the theory that the Song is a liturgy of the Adonis-Tammuz cult, the rites of which were undoubtedly practised in Palestine and were denounced by the prophets.[18]

The influence of Mowinckel and others[19] has popularized the view that the poetry of the Old Testament is in large measure cult-material, most of which was taken over from Canaanite religion.[20] Once the theory was set in motion, not merely the Psalms, but also the books of Hosea,[21] Joel,[22] Nahum,[23] Habakkuk[24] and Ruth,[25] have been interpreted, in whole or in part, as liturgies of the fertility-cult, and the end of the process is not yet in sight. Thus Haller declares that the Song of Songs was originally a cult-hymn for the spring festival of Ḥag Hamazzot, which the Canaanites observed with a litany glorifying Astarte as "the beloved" and Baal as Dod "the lover." The Song, we are assured, is part of the widespread Near Eastern ritual of the dying and reviving god.[26] Deuteronomic theologians are then assumed to have profanized the orginally sacred text, so that today it appears as a collection of erotic lyrics of a secular character. The impact of recent archaeological discoveries, particularly of Ugaritic literature, have given this view a new vogue.

Nevertheless, the cult-theory of the book cannot be sustained, we believe, when subjected to analysis.[27] It begins with a hypothetical approach to the Hebrew Bible which is highly dubious. That the Old Testament contains only *Kultdichtung* is a modern version of the attitude which regards the Bible exclusively from the theological standpoint, instead of recognizing it, in A. B. Ehrlich's succinct phrase, as the Hebrews' "national literature upon a religious foundation."[28] Undoubtedly the religious consciousness permeated all aspects of the national life in ancient Israel, but the existence of secular motifs cannot be ignored, particularly in the area of Wisdom, to which the art of the Song belonged, and with which it was identified.

There are other telling objections to the view that the Song of Songs is a liturgy of the dying and reviving god. That the Ḥag Hamazzot was such a festival in Israel is a gratuitous assumption, with no evidence in Biblical or in post-Biblical sources. The proponents of the theory are driven to adduce as proof the synagogue practice of reading the Song of Songs during Passover. The oldest reference to the custom, however, is in the post-Talmudic tractate *Sopherim*, which probably emanates from the sixth century c.e.,[29] at least a millennium after the composition of the book. Its liturgical use at Passover can be explained without recourse to far-fetched theories. It is eminently appropriate to the festival, both in its literal sense and in the allegorical interpretation which has been official for centuries. Its glorification of spring (cf. 2:11 ff.; 7:11 ff.) was congenial to the "festival of Abib" and the Midrash refers many passages in the text to the Exodus, with its moving spirits, Moses and Aaron.

Efforts have indeed been made to find vestiges of the Ishtar-cult in the text, but none of them are at all convincing.[30] The Song of Songs makes no references to this spring festival or any other, or, for that matter, to any ritual observance.

Proponents of the theory are in diametrical disagreement on a fundamental issue, whether the alleged pagan ritual in the Song has remained in its original and unmodified form[31] or whether it has been drastically reworked as part of the JHVH cult.[32] If the former is the case, it is an insuperable difficulty that the entire book makes no references to dying[33] or to weeping for the dead god[34] or to the decay of nature. If the latter alternative is true, there is the additional problem of a JHVH liturgy in which the Divine name is absent, either explicitly or as an allusion.

It is human love, not that of a god, which is glorified in the Song, and that with a wealth of detail, which rules out an allegorical interpretation. The entire book deals with concrete situations, whether of love's repining, or its satisfaction, of lovers' flirtations, estrangement and reunion. Moreover, the frequent references to specific localities in the topography of Palestine effectively rule out the likelihood that this material could have been used for liturgical purposes. For the essence of a liturgy is that it is typological, being concerned with a generalized and recurrent pattern of activity.[35]

One is, of course, at liberty to assume that our book represents a secular reworking of a no longer extant litany of an assumed Israelite cult which has left no record of its existence behind it. Such a complex of unsubstantiated hypotheses recalls the argument that the ancient Hebrews must have known of wireless telegraphy, because archaeologists in Palestine have found no wires in their excavations.

Neither the older nor the more recent allegorical interpretations of the Song of Songs are convincing explanations of the original character of the book. In favor of the traditional Jewish and Christian allegories is the fact that they have their own independent charm, which the cult-theory does not possess.

It may even be granted, as Rowley well says, that "we, for our profit, may rightly find in the images of the Song, as in all experience, analogies of things spiritual," but that "does not mean that it was written for this purpose and that the author had any such idea in mind."[36] The key to the book must be sought in a literal interpretation of the text, as the surest basis for true understanding and lasting appreciation of its greatness.

IV. THE LITERAL INTERPRETATION

While the allegorical view of the Song of Songs early became official, it is noteworthy that the Rabbis were well aware that in many circles it was being interpreted literally. That the allegorical view had difficulty in winning universal acceptance is clear from the warmth of the statement in the Tosefta:[37] "He who trills his voice in the chanting of Song of Songs and treats it as a secular song, has no share in the world to come."

Obviously, too, the literal view of the book lay at the basis of the doubts expressed in the Mishnah as to its canonicity:[38]

The Song of Songs and Koheleth defile the hands (i. e. are canonical). Rabbi Judah says, The Song of Songs defiles the hands, but Koheleth is in dispute. Rabbi Jose says, Koheleth does not defile the hands and the Song of Songs is in dispute. . . . Rabbi Simeon ben Azzai said, I have a tradition from the seventy-two elders on the day that Rabbi Eleazar ben Azariah was appointed president of the Academy that both the Song of Songs and Koheleth defile the hands. Said Rabbi Akiba, Heaven forfend! No one in Israel ever disputed that the Song of Songs defiles the hands. For all the world is not as worthy as the day on which the Song of Songs was given to Israel, for all the writings are holy, but the Song of Songs is the Holy of Holies. If they differed at all, it was only about Koheleth. Rabbi Johanan ben Joshua, the brother-in-law of Rabbi Akiba, said, Both the division of opinion and the final decision accorded with the statement of Ben Azzai, i. e. they differed on both books and finally decided that both were canonical.

Nevertheless, the literal view, which was rejected on the conscious level, won a measure of unconscious acceptance even in Rabbinic circles. That the book deals with human love is implied in the well-known statement:

Solomon wrote three books, Proverbs, Koheleth, and the Song of Songs. Which did he write first ? . . . Rabbi Hiyya the Great said, He wrote Proverbs first, then the Song of Songs, and then Koheleth. . . . Rabbi Jonathan said, The Song of Songs he wrote first; then came Proverbs, and then Koheleth. Rabbi Jonathan proved it from normal human behavior. When a man is young, he sings songs. When he becomes an adult, he utters practical proverbs. When he becomes old, he voices the vanity of things.[39]

In the Christian Church, too, the literal view was known and fought. The position of the fourth-century Theodore of Mopsuestia was declared a heresy by the Second Council of Constantinople in 353. His objections to the book were repeated, in 1544, by Chateillon, who wanted it expunged from the canon as immoral. It is characteristic of the broader conception of canonicity in Judaism that no such demand for its elimination was made, even by the anonymous French Jewish commentator of the twelfth century or by a few other medieval Jewish writers who regarded it as a song written by Solomon for his favorite wife.[40] In the sixteenth and seventeenth centuries various scholars suggested that the book was a collection of eclogues, and analogies with the Idylls of Theocritus were frequently invoked. It was Herder who, in 1778, explained it as a collection of songs extolling the joys of human love. This view, however, receded in popularity for over a century thereafter.

V. The Dramatic Theory

In the eighteenth century, years before Herder, several scholars, like Wachtel (1722) and Jacobi (1771), espoused the view that the book is a drama. This view is perhaps foreshadowed by two Greek manuscripts of the fourth and fifth centuries c.e., which actually supply speakers for the various verses of the book. It is the dramatic theory which was the first to win wide acceptance among modern scholars and readers in two variant forms. According to the first, adopted by Delitzsch, there are two main characters, King Solomon and a rustic Shulammite maiden, and the book consists substantially of expressions of love by the two principal characters. According to the other view, first propounded by J. S. Jacobi and elaborated by Ewald, there are three characters, a beautiful maiden, her shepherd lover, and King Solomon, who on a visit to the countryside discovers her and becomes enamored of her beauty. The luxuries of the royal court and the blandishments of the king are powerless to shake her love. At length the young rustic lovers are reunited, and the play ends with a song on the lips of the maiden and her shepherd lover.[41] It is obvious that the second view has a dramatic tension lacking in the first, and it has been increasingly espoused by those who favor the dramatic theory.[42]

Nonetheless, the theory suffers from several grave drawbacks which must be clarified, since this view is still often taken for granted, particularly in popular treatments of the book:

1. That speakers must be supplied for the various lines would be natural and constitutes no difficulty. The crux lies in the fact that *the entire plot must be read into the book and the natural intent of the words be ignored again and again.* One or two instances must suffice. Thus Driver, following Ewald, attributes the opening section, 1:2–7, to the maiden in these words:

Scene I. (The Shulammite and Ladies of the Court.)—The Shulammite, longing for the caresses of her absent shepherd-lover, complains that she is detained in the royal palace against her will, and inquires eagerly where he may be found.

Now none of this reconstruction is in the actual text. The opening verses 2–4 make no reference to the lover as being absent. Moreover, the complaint in verse 7, which is addressed directly to him, is not that she is detained against her will by the king, but that she can not find him among his fellow-shepherds. Finally, this interpretation does not do justice to the text of verses 5 and 6. The proud words of these verses, in which the maiden praises her own beauty and explains her dark hue, are hardly the words appropriate to one who wants to flee the court and the king's advances, in order to be reunited with her shepherd lover.

The remainder of chapter 1 is assigned to Scene II as follows:

Solomon (9–11) seeks to win the Shulammite's love. The Shulammite (12, aside) parries the king's compliments with reminiscences of her absent lover. —Solomon (15)—The Shulammite (v. 16, aside) takes no notice of the king's remark in v. 15 and applies the figures suggested by it to her shepherd-lover.

Now verses 9–11 might *conceivably* be Solomon's words as he seeks to win her love, but there the plausibility of the reconstruction ends. Verse 12, "while the king sat at his table (or couch), my spikenard sent forth its fragrance" (JV), cannot naturally mean (*pace* Driver) that "while the king *was away from me*, at table with his guests, my love (for another) was active" (italics Driver's). Nor is there anything to suggest that vv. 13–14 *parry* any of the king's compliments or that she has more than one lover in mind at all. Finally, assigning v. 15 to the king and v. 16 to the maiden, who is *referring to her absent lover*, means to divide what is obviously a single literary unit, both in form and in content. The love-dialogue is clear:

"Thou art fair, my beloved, thou art fair, thine eyes are doves."
"Thou art comely, my lover, and sweet, and our couch is fragrant."

There are many other instances where the exigencies of the dramatic theory artifically divide obvious literary units. Thus 2:2 is assigned to Solomon, while 2:3 is again attributed to the maiden as an *aside*.

2. Incidents which in a drama should have been acted out are narrated, as in 2:8; 5:1, 4. This is perfectly comprehensible in a lyric, but not in a play.

3. The climax of the plot is assumed to be 8:11 ff. Here the young lovers spurn the luxury of Solomon's court in favor of the delights of love, contrasting the high financial returns of Solomon's vineyard with the "vineyard" of the beloved's person and charm. But precisely here the dramatic form is totally lacking. Solomon is not addressed at all, which is what one should have expected in a dramatic confrontation of king and commoner as they contend for the maiden's hand. Instead, it is clear from the narrative phrase, "Solomon had a vineyard at Baal-Hamon," that Solomon is *not* present, and the adjuration in v. 12 is therefore rhetorical and not actual.

4. The distribution of the name "Solomon" in the book is worthy of note. Aside from the superscription (1:1), the name occurs six times more—in 1:5, where it is used generically,[43] and in two other sections, i. e. in chapter 3 (vv. 7, 9, 11) and in chapter 8 (vv. 11, 12), and *nowhere else*. The full significance of this fact will be discussed below. Suffice it to note that if Solomon were a principal protagonist of the drama, we should expect a more consistent use of his name throughout the book than the existing pattern. As for the noun "king," *hammelek*, which might conceivably be an epithet for Solomon in the drama, it is also very rare in the book, occurring in only three additional passages (1:4, 12; 7:6) besides its use together with "Solomon" in two cases (3:9, 11).

5. That the book is a drama presupposes that it is a literary unit. This is, however, ruled out categorically by linguistic considerations. The noun *pardēs* (4:13) is of Persian origin, and the passage in which it occurs cannot, therefore, be older than the Persian period (6th century B. C. E.). On the other hand, in 6:4 the lover compares his beloved to Tirzah and Jerusalem. The parallelism makes it clear that the poet must be referring to Tirzah, the old capital of the Northern Kingdom of Israel, which was replaced with Samaria by Omri in the first half of the ninth century B. C. E.[44] A lover does not usually praise his beloved by comparing her to a city ruined centuries earlier! Hence this passage cannot be later than the ninth century B. C. E.[45] It is obvious that if at least one passage in a book cannot be earlier than the sixth century, and another cannot be later than the ninth, the work is manifestly not a literary unit, and the dramatic theory is conclusively ruled out.

VI. SONG AS A BRANCH OF WISDOM

In the Hebrew Bible, the Song of Songs finds its place in the third section, the Hagiographa, in proximity to Psalms and Lamentations on the one hand, and to Proverbs and Job on the other. This third section is not a heterogeneous collection but, on the contrary, possesses an underlying unity, being the repository of *Hokmah* or Wisdom. Wisdom was much more than a branch of literature. It included all the technical arts and practical skills of civilization. The architect and the craftsman, the weaver and the goldsmith, the sailor and the magician, the skillful general and the wise administrator of the state, are all described as *hakāmim*, "wise."[46] In Rabbinic Hebrew the epithet *hakāmāh* is applied also to the midwife.[47]

One of the most frequent uses of the term *Hokmah* refers it to the arts of poetry and song, both vocal and instrumental, for the composition and the rendering of songs, which were often done by the same individual, required a high order of skill. Thus the women skilled in lamentation at funerals are called *hakāmōth* by Jeremiah (9:16).

The relationship between Wisdom and Song was so close that the terms were used interchangeably. Thus in I Kings 5:10–12 we read:

And Solomon's wisdom excelled the wisdom of all the children of the east, and all the wisdom of Egypt. For he was wiser than all men: than Ethan the Ezrahite, and Heman, and Calcol, and Darda, the sons of Mahol; and his fame was in all the nations round about. And he spoke three thousand proverbs; and his songs were a thousand and five.[48]

Ethan and Heman, who are here described as "wise,"[49] are the eponymous heads of the musical guilds in the Temple in Jerusalem. Note, too, that the same biblical passage attributes both "proverbs" and "songs" to Solomon.

The songs of the prophet Balaam are called *mashāl* (literally, "parable, proverb"), perhaps because the poems are replete with comparisons (Num. 23:7, 18; 24:3, 15, 20, 21, 23). But essentially the term is a synonym for "song." Thus the unknown poets, whose military epic is cited in the fragment in Num. 21:27–30, are called *mōshelīm* (literally, "makers of *mashal*"). The term *hīdāh*, "riddle, mysterious saying," together with *mashāl*, is applied to the song played on the *kinnōr*, "the lyre" (Ps. 49:5; 78:2). The recently discovered evidence from Ugaritic sources corroborates the Biblical tradition, previously dismissed as anachronistic, which declares that these guilds of singers are very ancient. In fact, they probably go back to the Canaanite period.[50]

Now Wisdom literature as a whole began on a secular note and only gradually took on a religiou scoloration. This is clear from the chronology of the best attested branch of Oriental Wisdom, that of Egypt, where religious motifs are late in appearing. Similarly in Israel, as Pfeiffer correctly says, "We know positively that the secular school (of Wisdom) flourished before the pious."[51] The oldest popular

Hebrew proverbs and the Wisdom fragments imbedded in the Historical books are all secular in character.[52]

A similar development may be postulated for that branch of Wisdom called *shir*, which includes both poetry and music. The Song certainly played an important role in religious ritual, at sacrifices, processions and festivals, but it was not limited to these areas. Actually, it was coextensive with life itself, dealing with all the normal secular concerns of life, such as combat and victory,[53] the opening of a well, vintage and harvest,[54] feasting and carousing,[55] the glory of nature and the tragedy of death.[56]

Undoubtedly the poems of national significance, like those of war and victory, were given a religious character, as in the "Song of the Sea" (Exod. 15) or the "Song of Deborah" (Judg. 5), since the historical experience of Israel was conceived as reflecting the will of God. But it is noteworthy that many of the briefer snatches of song which are preserved in prose narratives and are explicitly quoted from older collections, like the *Book of the Wars of the Lord* (Num. 21:14) and the *Book of Jashar* (probably the "Book of Heroes," Josh. 10:13; II Sam. 1:18; I Kings 8:53 in the Greek), are purely secular in content. The Song, like Wisdom, as a whole, later developed a religious stamp, but it remained an acquired characteristic.

For self-evident reasons, the secular note would be more likely to be preserved in the area of love and courtship, which has inspired more poetry and music than any other field of human interest. Into this area, where the sensual and the physical play so important a part, the traditional religious coloration would have the greatest difficulty in penetrating. The existence of secular love-songs in ancient Egyptian and Akkadian literature,[57] as well as among contemporary Arab peasants and city dwellers,[58] strengthens this contention, besides offering many a key to the understanding of the biblical song.[59]

VII. The Song of Songs as a Collection

If the Song of Songs be approached without any preconceptions, it reveals itself as a collection of lyrics. This view of the book was taken by a Middle High German version of the 15th century, which divided it into 54 songs. A long catena of modern scholars have adopted the same position, though naturally differing on the division of the book.[60]

A great step forward in the interpretation of the Song was taken in 1893, when J. G. Wetzstein, Prussian consul in Damascus, called attention to the nuptial customs of the Syrian peasants, who have the couple sit on a "throne" during the wedding-meal as "king" and "queen," while the guests sing songs of praise (*wasf*), glorifying the bride and groom. In some cases, the bride also executes a "sword dance" during the festivities. The affinities with several passages in the Song are obvious, and many scholars were accordingly led to interpret the entire collection as emanating from such wedding celebrations.[61]

That the praise of the bride on her wedding day was a regular feature of Jewish weddings in Second Temple days, and that these songs of praise were a technical art and therefore part of Hokmah, is clear from an ancient Talmudic tradition. It reads as follows: "How is one to dance before (i. e. praise) the bride? The Shammaites declare: 'By praising her for the qualities she actually possesses.' The Hillelites say: 'By saying of every one, O bride, beautiful and gracious.' "[62] The same function continued to be performed by the *badḥān* or humorous rhymster at East-European weddings until our day.

On the other hand, it is clear that some of the lyrics in the Song of Songs are not connected with wedding ceremonies or with married love at all.[63] The only justifiable conclusion is that the Song of Songs, like the Psalter, is an anthology, running a wide gamut of its emotions. It contains songs of love's yearning and its consummation, of coquetry and passion, of separation and union, of courtship and marriage.

The division of the songs will depend upon the changes in theme, viewpoint, background or form. These criteria will not always be sufficiently exact to command universal assent. Much will be dependent upon the literary taste and insight, as well as upon the knowledge, of the interpreter. But this is simply a restatement of the truth that exegesis is essentially an art, which rests upon a foundation of scientific knowledge.

VIII. SOLOMON IN THE SONG OF SONGS

If the Song of Songs is an anthology of love poems, how are the seven instances of Solomon's name in the text to be explained? For on this view he is neither the author of the book, as the traditional view claims, nor its hero, as is maintained by the dramatic theory.

Several of these instances are easy to explain. In the opening verse of the book (1:1), we have a later superscription by an editor who had already accepted the theory of Solomon's authorship.[64] In three other passages, the use of the name is authentic. These are in 1:5 ("Solomonic hangings"), where it is a descriptive term like our "Louis XIV furniture," and in 8:11 and 12, where Solomon is used to typify a possessor of great wealth, as the ancients used "Croesus" or as moderns might use the name of a multi-millionaire like Vanderbilt or Rockefeller.

The other three examples of Solomon's name, it is generally suggested, are glosses which were induced by these authentic occurrences of the name in the text, and were reinforced by the tradition of Solomon as the "great lover" (I Kings 11:1 ff.). It would therefore be natural to believe that he was also intended by the word *melekh*, "king," in the Song, though the word actually referred to the bridegroom. Hence "Solomon" was added as a gloss in three more verses (3:7, 9 and 11).

For all its apparent plausibility, however, this approach is not adequate. Not only do we find "Solomon" used without the word "king" in 3:7, but the word "king" occurs several times in the book without the gloss "Solomon" (1:4, 12; 7:6). The clue to the solution lies in the observation that the only three passages in the book in which "Solomon" is apparently unauthentic (3:7, 9, 11) *all occur in the same poem.*

This poem (3:6–11) is generally regarded as a rustic wedding song. But if it is scrutinized carefully, a variety of problems arises:

The poem contains many descriptive traits which, literally viewed, cannot apply to a simple peasant wedding. The pillars of smoke (v. 6) and the sixty heroes trained in war (v. 7) are often dismissed as poetic hyperbole. However, v. 10, "he made its pillars of silver, its top was of gold, its seat of purple, its inside being inlaid with leather,"[65] is much too explicit to be merely the product of a poet's heightened imagination. A country lover might describe the open fields as his fresh couch, the cedars as the walls of his home and the sycamores as his rafters (1:16 f.), but the circumstantial description of a luxurious palanquin, far beyond the reach of a rustic couple, would be a mockery rather than a tribute of praise to the lovers.

Another difficulty is the explicit national note to be found only here. Not only do we have a reference to "the daughters of Jerusalem"

(3:10), which is familiar from other passages in the Song (2:7; 3:5; 5:8, 16; 8:4), but "the daughters of Zion" (3:11) are mentioned in this poem, and nowhere else. Most important of all, while the Palestinian locale pervades the entire book, the only national reference, that to "Israel," occurs in 3:7.

Moreover, the occurrence of Solomon's name in these verses is not easily solved by deletion. In 3:7, "king" does not occur and "Solomon" cannot be removed without leaving a lacuna. Hence the entire stich must be dropped. In v. 11 the deletion of "Solomon" irreparably destroys the rhythm of the verse.[66] Even in v. 9, the excision of the name is not required on rhythmic grounds.[67]

These difficulties, cumulatively viewed, all point to the conclusion that we have here no song for a rustic wedding but, quite the contrary, an epithalamium for a wedding of great luxury, one possessing even national significance. In fact, all the details cited are easily explained by one assumption—*that we have here a song composed on the occasion of one of Solomon's marriages to a foreign princess*, probably an Egyptian.[68]

Such a poem has survived in Psalm 45, in which an Israelite king is marrying a Phoenician princess.[69] Obviously, songs were composed for and sung at different stages of the wedding ceremony. Psalm 45 is addressed to the king (vv. 3–10) and to his new queen (vv. 11–14), perhaps after the marriage rites had been concluded. Our song, on the contrary, is a chorus of welcome addressed to the bride as her procession approaches from across the wilderness which separates Palestine on the east and on the southwest from its neighbors.

All the details of the poem are explained naturally on this simple premise. The princess travels with a large retinue, which encamps at night and sends up pillars of smoke (v. 6). Her palanquin was sent to her by Solomon and is escorted by the royal bodyguard, sixty of the heroes of Israel (v. 7; cf. II Sam. 23:8 ff.; I Kings 1:10). The litter is made of the finest cedarwood of Lebanon, one of the by-products of his commercial relations with Phoenicia. Its decorations of silver, gold, purple and leather (v. 10) are in keeping with Solomon's penchant for luxury, and may well have been prepared by the noble ladies of Jerusalem (v. 11).

All the references to Solomon in the book, aside from the title, are thus authentic, including the three references in this song, which dates from Solomon's reign. The presence of this poem, in the collection, would serve as the nucleus for the tradition attributing the entire book to Solomon.

In connection with this early date for the song, two linguistic problems must be considered. Graetz derived the word *'apirión*, "litter, couch" (3:9), from the Greek *phoreion*, which would imply a period considerably after Solomon's day, but evidence is mounting for contacts between the Greek world and the Semitic Orient both older and more extensive than was previously realized. Hence, a Greek origin for *'apirion* would not automatically rule out a Solomonic date. However, this etymology is far from certain. On independent grounds, many scholars prefer other derivations, the most plausible being from the Sanskrit *paryanka*, "sedan, palanquin."[70] That Solomon had regular commercial relations with India is being increasingly recognized, as scholars re-evaluate the Biblical evidence in the light of new extra-Biblical data.[71] According to our sources (I Kings 10:22), Solomon's imports from the East included ivory, apes (*qōph*) and peacocks (*tūkī*). As the derivation of these words indicates (Sanskrit, *kapi*; Malabar, *toqai, toqhai*), India was the point of origin of these luxuries. In addition, Solomon's ships might well have imported the palanquin, or at least the materials from which it was constructed, from India, together with its native name.

The syntactic construction in 3:7 (*miṭṭāthō šelliš\u1d49lōmō*), which would seem to reflect Aramaic influence,[72] does not represent an insuperable objection to a Solomonic dating for the poem as a whole. Popular songs often tend to be supplemented and modified with time, so that a late phrase may enter an early poem, and inconsistencies result. The composite character of folk-poetry must always be kept in mind. Thus, in a modern Palestinian love-lyric, the girl Fulla is addressed as Jewish, Mohammedan and Christian, all in the course of the eleven stanzas of the song.[73] While she is called Serena, a popular name of Spanish-Jewish actresses (stanza 4), she is described as making her ablutions before prayers, a Mohammedan practice (stanza 6), while the marriage ceremony is described by a specifically Christian term (stanza 9).

Moreover, the evidence is constantly growing that an "Aramaic" usage is not necessarily late in Hebrew. Not only in Northern Israel, but even in the south, the close linguistic affinities of the two languages[74] were strengthened by continuous relations between Israel and Syria throughout the pre-Exilic period.[75] The usage may, accordingly, be older than can at present be documented in our extant sources.[76]

Moreover, related instances of pronominal anticipation occur in Biblical Hebrew and Phoenician.[77] Hence we are not forced to delete the entire clause from the poem, or even to assume that it was introduced later.[78]

Whatever approach be adopted on this detail, the unique features of this poem mark it as a royal wedding-song going back to Solomon's reign. It is at present the oldest datable unit in the book. By contributing to the growth of the tradition of Solomonic authorship, it helped to win inclusion for the entire Song of Songs in the canon of Scripture.

IX. DATE OF THE BOOK

Being lyrical in character, with no historical allusions, most of the songs are undatable. There are, however, a few exception ;, which have already been noted. The song in which Tirzah, the early capital of North Israel, is referred to (6:4), must predate the year 876 B. C. E., when Omri made Samaria the capital of his kingdom, while the use of a Persian word like *pardēs* (4:13) can hardly antedate the 6th century. Yet even this latter inference must be qualified by the consideration already adduced above, that folk songs often undergo many changes with time, so that later words and expressions may well be inserted into much older material. The grounds for attributing one song (3:6–11) to the period of Solomon have already been set forth. Thus the datable material in the Song spans five centuries. The period begins with Solomon's accession to the throne (c. 960 B. C. E.), includes the early days of the Northern Kingdom (c. 920–876), and reaches down to the Persian era (6th–5th century).

The variations in language, which point to a considerable difference in the dates of the different songs, are only one factor, though decisive, in making it impossible to agree with Rowley, who has "the impression of a single hand" in the Song with "a corresponding unity of theme and style."[79] So, too, the varying geographical locales, from the Lebanon mountains in the north to the Dead Sea region in the south, from Transjordan to the central valleys, plainly point to a different provenance for the various songs. The change from rustic simplicity in some lyrics to the sophistication of the city in others points in the same direction.

It is most probable that the other songs in the book fall within the same four centuries as the datable units, with the bulk of the material being pre-Exilic rather than post-Exilic. The freshness of the poetry, the naturalness of the references to the Palestinian landscape, and the unabashed attitude toward love all seem to point to the period before the Babylonian Exile. No national disaster has yet cast its shadow over the temper of the people, and there is no echo as yet of the deepening of the religious consciousness which followed the Restoration under Cyrus and the reforms of Ezra and Nehemiah. That most of the place-names are northern and eastern also points to the pre-Exilic era, in fact to the period preceding the destruction of the Northern Kingdom in 722 B. C. E., since the Jewish settlements were restricted largely to Judah in the south during the Persian and pre-Maccabean period. The book was redacted in the Persian period, the heyday of Wisdom literature, not later than the fifth century.

X. HEBREW ELEMENTS IN THE SONG OF SONGS

Love lyrics are, as we have seen, difficult to date because their basic emotion knows no limit of time. Since the sentiment is not limited in space, love songs are not specifically national. In this respect, the Song of Songs shares the qualities of Wisdom literature as a whole, which is the most secular and least particularist element of Hebrew literature.

Nonetheless, some specific *national* coloring is to be found in the book. The reference to "the heroes of Israel" (3:7) is needed in this epithalamium of a foreign princess to indicate the nationality of her bodyguard. The "tower of David" upon which the shields of the heroes are hung (4:4) testifies to the widespread living character of the tradition of David's band of heroes, which is now embodied in the lists in II Sam. 23:8 ff.

The only other national notes are *geographical*, the cities, hills, and valleys of the country. Principally, the book reflects the background of Northern Israel. It is the northern mountain range which appears in Hermon and Senir (modern Jebel esh-Sheikh) as well as in Lebanon (now Jebel Libnan) and 'Amana (the modern Jebel Zebedâni).[80] The central territory of Northern Israel appears in Shunem,[81] in

Carmel and Sharon, as well as in Tirzah, if its location is to be sought at Tel-el-Fâr'ah. The Transjordan appears in Heshbon (modern Hesban) in the south, in the districts of Gilead, and possibly in Bashan to the north.[82] On the other hand, the territory of Judah is sparsely represented. Aside from the references to the daughters of Zion (3:11) and of Jerusalem (3:5; 5:8), only En-gedi on the Dead Sea is mentioned (1:14).

The preponderantly northern coloring of the book, as already noted, is significant in strengthening the view that the songs are predominantly pre-Exilic. The northern provenance of the songs also explains the Aramaisms in the book, which reflect the close proximity of the pre-Exilic Kingdom of Israel to Syria. Foreign products and articles bear foreign names, whether Sanskrit or Persian.[83]

Attention to the geographical locale is sometimes helpful in delineating the literary unit. The passage 1:9–17 is often regarded by commentators as one song.[84] However, the references to Pharaoh's horses and chariots (v. 9), which were most likely to be seen in Southern Palestine, and the mention of the vineyards of En-gedi on the western shore of the Dead Sea (v. 14), point to Judah in the south. On the other hand, the reference to the lovers' meeting in the forest, their "house walled with cedars" (v. 17), must necessarily reflect a North Israelite locale, since cedars never grew in southern Palestine.[85] So, too, the Aramaized form berōthīm, "sycamores," for the more common Hebrew berōšīm (v. 17), points to the Northern Kingdom, which was more exposed to Aramaic influence. It is therefore clear that the passage consists of two independent songs (1:9–14 and vv. 15–17).

When this is recognized, other divergences which tended to be overlooked or misunderstood receive a natural and unforced explanation. The first song speaks of the beloved as luxuriously decked out in jewels (vv. 9–11), and the lover is called "king" (v. 12) and is therefore the bridegroom. He is probably speaking during the festivities of the bridal week and hence uses the plural (na'aseh, v. 11) in the presence of his friends. Hence, too, the frank reference to sexual intimacy (vv. 12–13). The second song, on the other hand, reflects the simplicity of an outdoor tryst of lovers (note dōd, v. 16), not of the bride and groom, hence the delicate reticence regarding their relationship.

Religious motifs are even rarer in the book than specific national references. In the noun *šalhebbethyāh*, "flame of God" (8:6), the Divine name is used to express the superlative, and the word is equivalent in meaning to "a mighty flame." This usage has many analogies in Biblical Hebrew.[86]

We believe that Hebrew religious attitudes, hitherto unrecognized, lie at the base of a unique phenomenon in the book, the adjuration "by the gazelles and the hinds of the field" (2:7; 3:5), "not to disturb love until it be sated." That the gazelle and the hind were symbolic of love is, of course, clear from Biblical and post-Biblical Hebrew, where they were used as metaphors for a graceful and loving young woman.[87] Ebeling, in his study of Babylonian magic, calls attention to the Babylonian practice of tying a gazelle to the head of the bed and a ram at the foot as a magical rite to induce potency, with the formula, "like that ram may my husband love me."[88]

This is, however, far removed from an oath "by the gazelle," particularly for the strongly monotheistic Hebrews. A closer parallel is afforded by the Greek custom, practiced by no less a figure than Socrates, of swearing by an animal, as e. g. "by the dog," "by the goose," or by any nearby plant or object, such as "by the caperberry," "by the almond" and "by the cabbage."[89] The Greek philosophers defended this usage by asserting that the Greeks never intended to swear by the animals as gods, but used the animals as substitutes for gods. This was no mere apologetics, but a reflection of the widespread fear of the consequence of an unfulfilled oath. Hence arose the desire for an "escape formula."

Another factor, however, often enters into the choice of a substitute, which has been overlooked—*a similarly sounding term, even if irrelevant or virtually meaningless, is often chosen.* Thus the Rabbinic vow-term *ḳorbān* would frequently be replaced by *ḳōnām*.[90] In contemporary colloquial English, this phenomenon can be clearly observed. "Gosh darn" does duty for "God damn," "Gee," for "Jesus," "Jiminy Crickets" for "Jesus Christ," "Holy Cow" for "Holy Christ," etc.[91] Older substitutions of the same kind that entered English literature are "zounds" for "By God's wounds," "Marry" meaning "indeed," for "By Mary," "Dear me," probably for "Dio Mio," "By Cripes" for "By Christ." The German replaces "Gott" by "Potz" in *"Potzwelt," "Potzwetter" and "Pottsblitz."* The Frenchman changes "Dieu" into *bleu* in "Corbleu," "Morbleu," "Sambleu," and avoids the name of God altogether by swearing by "nom de nom."

Of the common speech of the Hebrew populace, little, if any, has reached us, and so the only extant example of this phenomenon is to be found in our book.

The most solemn Hebrew adjuration would be *be'lōhei ṣebhā'ōth* or *be'ēl šaddai*, "by the Lord of Hosts" or "by the Almighty."[92] The deepseated reluctance to use the Divine name, which finds expression in the Third Commandment (Ex. 20:7), became increasingly felt with time. This tendency is mirrored in such Biblical books as Esther and Ecclesiastes, as well as in the editing of Psalms, and finds varied expression in Rabbinic literature.[93] The desire to avoid mentioning God's name would be particularly strongly felt in connection with an oath concerned with the physical aspects of love. Hence, the lover replaces such customary oaths as *bē'lohei ṣebhā'ōth* or *be'ēl šaddai* by a similarly sounding phrase *biṣebhā'ōth 'ō be'ayelōth hassādeh*, " by the gazelles or the hinds of the field," choosing animals, which symbolize love, for the substitutions. It is likely that the Septuagint retained some recognition of the oath by rendering the unique Hebrew phrase "in (or, by) the powers and the forces of the field."[94] The Midrash also recognized the irregular character of the oath in the Song and identified "the gazelles and the hinds" with "the hosts of heaven and earth."[95] Here, as elsewhere, the homily rests upon a fine perception of the essential meaning of the text.

In this reticence with regard to the use of the Divine name, particularly in the context of sensual love, as well as in its pervasive delicacy of expression, which will be discussed below, the Song reveals itself as authentically within the Jewish tradition.

At times, the differences between the Hebrew poet and his Oriental confrères prove highly revealing of the Hebrew *ethos*. Moreover, what the Song does not say is often as significant for its Israelite outlook as any overt Hebrew element.

Thus, hunting was a favorite sport in Egypt and Mesopotamia, as literary sources and archaeological discoveries abundantly indicate.[96] In a love-song emanating from "the Golden Age" of Egyptian lyric poetry in the 18th dynasty,[97] the maiden expresses the yearning for her lover:

> How good it would be,
> If thou wert with me
> When I set the trap.

She is referring to a small trap set for bird-catching. It is noteworthy that in all the references to nature in the Song, hunting is not mentioned. Nimrod and Esau were hunters, but the taking of animal life for sport was not popular in ancient Israel,[98] an attitude crystallized further in Rabbinic Judaism.[99]

Even more characteristic of the Hebrew spirit is the absence of the personification of nature in the Song. In the Egyptian poem "The Tree in the Garden" the poet goes on to say, "The tree speaketh."[100] For the Hebrew poet, nature serves as the glorious background for human love, but never as more, exactly as nature is the manifestation of the creative power of God for the Psalmist and for Job.[101]

The age-old relationship of wine, women, and song finds its reflection, of course, in the Song, for wine-drinking was widespread in Israel. Nonetheless, references in our book to the first member of the triad are very few.[102] Nothing is to be found resembling these lines of an Egyptian love song:[103]

> Her lover sitteth at her right hand,
> The feast is disordered with drunkenness.

The absence of this theme in the Song may, of course, be the result of the choice of poems in the collection. It is at least equally likely that it reflects a negative attitude toward drunkenness, which became traditional in Judaism.

Another common aspect of love-poetry, virtually missing here, is the motif of faithlessness and jealousy.[104] On the other hand, the Egyptian maiden complains.[105]

> What meaneth it that thou wrongest another heart and me?

To be sure, coquetry and the maiden's resistance to the lover's advances occur as themes,[106] but no "love triangle" is to be met with in our book. This absence, however, must be accidental, or the result of the editor's choice—the human emotion involved is ubiquitous and must have existed in ancient Israel.

XI. EXTRA-HEBREW PARALLELS TO THE BOOK

The universality of love as an emotion and an experience, which is responsible for the absence of any considerable degree of specific Hebrew coloration in the book, should make us wary about postulating

direct borrowings from other peoples in these songs. Mere resemblances of theme are not sufficient. What is methodologically required
is a special sequence of theme or some other unusual feature, not
explicable in terms of Hebrew background. A few centuries later, the
Palestinian city of Gedera was the home of the gifted Greek poets
Meleager and Philodemus the Epicurean, who flourished in the 1st
century B. C. E. It is a purely gratuitous assumption that the lyric
gift was limited to the Greek inhabitants of the country and that the
Hebrews were congenitally incapable of love-poetry.

With the all but universal rejection of a Greek date for the book
today, scholars have turned instead to the Egyptian culture-milieu
in seeking evidence of borrowing in the Song of Songs. Thus, it has
been argued that the use of 'āḥōth, "sister," for "beloved" is an
Egyptian usage. Being unhebraic, the word was glossed by kallāh,
"bride," everywhere except in the last passage (4:9, 10, 12; 5:1, 2).[107]
Actually, the assumption of glossing is not supported by the meter.
Of the five passages where the term occurs, it is not accompanied by
kallāh in one (5:2), and it can not be a gloss in two others (4:9, 12),
because its deletion would destroy the rhythm of the text.[108] In the
other two passages (4:10; 5:1), metric considerations cannot be
invoked at all, since either the retention or the deletion of 'āḥōth
would produce an acceptable rhythmic pattern.[109]

The entire assumption that the usage is unhebraic, however, is
unjustified. The Hebrew nouns rē'a and ra'yāh (re'ūth), which are
common in the meanings "friend" and "neighbor," also signify
"beloved."[110] Similarly, the synonyms 'āḥ and 'āḥōth, "brother,
sister," develop the parallel meanings of "friend, neighbor" and
"beloved."[111] Aḥōth therefore means "beloved" in the Song, when
the lover, in an outburst of emotion, heaps up terms of endearment,
coupling "sister" either with "bride" or with "friend."[112] So too, the
Hebrew and Arabic word for "daughter," bat, bint, means "girl" and
is not restricted to the specific family relationship.[113]

Nor is there any objective ground for assuming that the feeling
for nature was an exclusively Egyptian trait. The God speeches in
Job manifest a loving insight into nature unparalleled elsewhere,
and the prophets and psalmists disclose a love and observation of the
external world which needed no foreign influence or literary borrowing.[114]

Of direct borrowings in the authentic sense, there is no evidence.

Nonetheless, since love is the same anywhere, the reactions and forms of expression of love-lyrics everywhere will resemble each other. Accordingly, Oriental love poetry, ancient and modern, often sheds light upon the background of the Hebrew poem. Because of the close relationship of love to magic and religion[115] which modern psychology and anthropology have revealed, ancient incantation texts also add considerably to our understanding of the Song.[116]

Tur-Sinai has called attention to the background underlying 8:9:[117]

> If she be a wall,
> We will build upon her a turret of silver;
> And if she be a door,
> We will enclose her with boards of cedar.

Charms warding off all types of perils were couched in this form. Thus, for example, the Assyrian charm against a crying baby was as follows:

If it is a dog, let them cut off morsels for him!
If it is a bird, let them throw clods of earth upon him!
If it is a naughty human child, let them adjure him with the oath of Anu
    and Antu!

Even more apposite, because it demonstrates that *homah*, "wall," and *deleth*, "door," "bar," in 8:9 are synonymous and not antithetic, is the following charm against an enemy:[118]

> If he is a door, I will open thy mouth,
> If he is a bar, I will open thy tongue.[119]

Obviously there is no incantation implied any longer in the Song, but the formula has survived as a love motif.

While several *wasfs* in praise of the beloved occur in the book, only one *wasf* praising the lover is to be met with (5:10–16). In part the description is highly extravagant and goes beyond the limits of metaphor. Thus, for example, 5:11, 14, 15:

> His head is fine gold . . . .
> His hands are rods of gold, set with topaz . . . .
> His thighs are pillars of marble
> Set upon sockets of gold . . . .

Perhaps these phrases are more than mere poetic hyperbole. This

is suggested by a Babylonian adjuration for the recovery of a sick
person from illness:[120]

> Like lapis lazuli I want to cleanse his body,
> Like marble his features should shine,
> Like pure silver, like red gold,
> I want to make clean what is dull.

The Biblical *wasf* may therefore be extolling the health and potency
of the lover.

A long-standing difficulty in the Song is presented by 5:1. The
first four stichs of the verse speak of the lover enjoying the myrrh,
honey, wine and milk that symbolize the delights of love. The fifth
stich of the verse is couched in the plural:

> 'ikhᵉlū rēʿīm šᵉthū vᵉšikhᵉrū dōdīm

"Eat, friends, drink abundantly, O loved ones." It is, of course, inconceivable that either the love-struck youth or the maiden would
invite others to enjoy the same pleasures as the loved one, and the
stich has therefore been emended either to the masculine singular[121] or
to the feminine,[122] either procedure requiring no less than five changes.
Some have regarded the stich as a misplaced fragment of an independent song[123]. A solution to the problem through an illuminating parallel
is offered by an Arab song, widely known all over Palestine and Syria,
which would indicate that the poet may address the individual lover
in the plural, as well as in the singular:

> Examine me,
> O physician,
> As to what I suffered
> On behalf of the beloved one.
>
> By God, O Lord!
> This is a wondrous thing;
> Yet my heart melted
> For the beloved ones.[124]

The Hebrew text of 5:1 is therefore in order and the stich is in place.

XII. Motifs and Patterns in the Collection

Because of the degree of subjective judgment which must enter into the delimitation of the songs, unanimity is not to be expected. Our own study of the book indicates that it contains twenty-eight songs and fragments, which fall into several patterns, though they often overlap. To mark each basic theme, we have added descriptive titles:

A. Songs of Yearning

The Call to Love (1:2–4)
The Rustic Maiden (1:5–6)
Tell Me Where My Love (1:7–8)
Love's Proud Proclamation (2:4–7)
Would Thou Wert My Brother (8:1–4)
Let Me Hear Thy Voice (8:13–14)[125]

B. Songs of Fulfillment

Love's Barriers—a Duet (4:12 to 5:1)
How Delightful Is Love (7:7–10)
The Beloved's Promise (7:11–14)[126]
Love Under the Apple-Tree—a Duet (8:5)
Surrender (2:16–17)

C. Songs in Praise of the Beloved

Bedecked in Charm—a Duet (1:9–14)
My Beloved Is Perfect (4:1–7)
Love's Enchantment (4:9–11)
The Power of Beauty (6:4–7)
The One and Only (6:8–9)

D. Duets of Mutual Praise

Our Walls Are Cedars (1:15–17)
Who Is Like My Love (2:1–3)
The Lover's Welcome (2:14–15)

E. Love in the World of Nature

The Time of Singing Is Come (2:8–13)
Call From the Mountains (4:8)
Love's Dawning (6:10–12)[127]

F. Dream Songs

The Dream of the Lost Lover (3:1–5)
Love's Trial and Triumph (5:2 to 6:3); see below.

G. The Greatness of Love

The Seal of Love (8:6–7)
The Finest Vineyard (8:11–12)

H. Songs of Courtship and Marriage

A Wedding Song for Solomon (3:6–11)
The Maiden's Dance (7:1–6)[128]
The Ramparts of Love (8:8–10)

I. Love's Sorrows and Joys

Love's Trial and Triumph (5:2 to 6:3)

This, the most elaborate and perhaps the most beautiful song in the collection, is a blending of several patterns: (a) the *dream motif* (5:2), which incorporates the themes of coquetry (5:3) and longing (5:4 ff.); (b) the *waṣf* in praise of the lover (5:10 ff.); and (c) praise of the delights of love (6:2 f.).

In several instances, the units seem very short and we have merely fragments,[129] perhaps only titles of songs, which are no longer extant in their full form. On the other hand, it must always be remembered that in these charming lyrics we lack the music to which they were invariably sung. The number of words and lines required for a song would therefore generally be fewer than in the case of poetry designed to be read. One has only to compare the few words in the popular Israeli song or traditional Hasidic melody with the longer texts of modern poetry in Hebrew or any other language to see the difference.

The longest lyric in the book (5:2 to 6:3), which consists of eighteen verses, is, as has been noted, a highly complex blending of several literary motifs.

In a collection such as this, it is to be expected that phrases and verses will reappear more than once.[130] Glosses are, of course, not to be ruled out *a priori*, but deciding which words are secondary is a particularly precarious undertaking in a collection of popular folk-songs, where additions are natural.[131] Thus the two dream-songs (3:1–5 and 5:2 ff.) repeat the theme of the city watchmen, but the second passage introduces a variation, which is in thorough keeping with the more elaborate development of the song as a whole.

XIII. Symbolism and Esthetics in the Song

It is of the essence of poetry that it employ *symbolism* to express nuances beyond the power of exact definition. This is particularly true of love poetry, where the reticences imposed by social convention add both urgency and piquancy to the use of symbols. Hence the beloved will be compared to a flower (2:1 f.), and the lover to a tree (2:3). The delights of love will be described as fruit (2:3), wine (1:4; 5:1), or perfume (5:1), as milk and honey (5:1), as a garden (4:12; 5:1; 6:2), or a vineyard (8:12). The maiden's resistance to the lover's advances will lead to the metaphor of a sealed fountain (4:12) or a high wall (8:9),[132] and the beloved "enemy" will be attacked with the power of charms (8:8 ff.). The invitation to the lover will be couched in the form of a call to enjoy the vineyard (2:15), the fountain (4:15), or the garden (4:16), while the confession that love's demands have been met will be expressed by the figure of a vineyard unguarded (1:6) or of a gazelle upon the mountains of spices (2:17; 8:14).

Symbolism is much more profound than allegory. In allegory, the imaginary figures that are chosen as equivalents for the real characters and objects involved have no independent reality of their own. The language of symbolism, on the other hand, is superior to literal speech as well, because its elements possess both existential reality and a representational character. When, for example, the maiden, in 2:4 f., announces that she is faint with love and asks to be sustained with raisins and apples, she is calling for concrete food, to be sure, but *at the same time*, by her choice of fruits that are symbolic of love, she is indicating that only the satisfaction of her desires will bring her

healing. To cite another instance, when the beloved speaks of awak-
ening her lover who is asleep under the apple-tree (8:5), the tree is real
enough, but, at the same time, it symbolizes her wish to rouse the
dormant desire of her lover. When the girl declares, "I am a wall and
my breasts are towers" (8:10), the simile is especially apt, because it
expresses both her inaccessibility to the many suitors who are besieging
her, and her maturity and readiness for love when her true lover
appears.

Nor is the potency of symbolism exhausted by this trait alone. It
is characteristic of the delicacy of the songs that the woman in each
case expresses her desire for love by indirection. While a blunt avowal
would repel by its crassness, the use of symbolism, which conceals
as it reveals, heightens by its subtlety the charm of the sentiments
expressed. Psycho-analytic theory has offered a highly plausible
explanation for this powerful appeal of symbolism to the human spirit.
According to psycho-analysis, the "unconscious" persistently seeks
some avenue of expression which will elude the "censor" who stands
guard over the conscious mind. Symbolism performs this liberating
function for the unconscious admirably, because, in its very nature,
it expresses far more than it says; its nuances are at least as significant
as its explications. Its overt meaning has nothing in it to arouse the
vigilance of the censor, and meanwhile its deeper content is able to
cross the threshold of consciousness.

Modern psychological research has also shed considerable light
on the intimate relationship between love and pain. This connection
is expressed in the great "Dream-Song" (5:2 to 6:3). When the
love-sick maiden wanders through the city, in search of her lover, the
watchmen beat her (5:7).

Stephan cites an old *haddâwiyye* from Jaffa, which affords a striking
parallel:[133]

> The quarrel rose between me and him:
> They dragged me to the *sarai*;
> They beat me a thousand strokes;
> They beat me on my ankles.

An Egyptian love song of the New Kingdom[134] expresses the same
theme of the lover's devotion in the face of physical attack:

> I will not let go of thy love
> Even if I am beaten,

As far as the land of Palestine with *shebet* and clubs
And on to the land of Ethiopia with palm-ribs
As far as the hills with sticks
And unto the fields with cudgels.

The variations in date and geographical provenance do not exhaust the variety to be found within this small book. The songs reflect the simplicity of rustic scenes, the sophistication of the great city, the poverty of the shepherd's hut, and the luxury of the royal palace. Hence it is possible for one scholar to find in the book "the simplest kind of ballads scarcely touched by the polishing efforts of the self-conscious poet,"[135] while another declares that the Song is to be classed "as belles-lettres rather than as folk-songs," and finds them "only less artificial than the idylls of Theocritus."[136] Actually, the book contains both the simple and unrestrained outpourings of un-tutored love and the elaborated literary expressions of the same basic impulse.

Frequently the point is made that the boldness of expression in the book with regard to sexual intimacy and bodily description is not in keeping with modern taste. It is true that the description of the maiden's charms in 7:3 is more explicit and franker than has been custom-ary in Occidental poetry, but this passage is unique in the Song. Elsewhere, the description of physical beauty is frank without crass-ness. To evaluate it fairly, the Song should be judged against its Oriental background. Actually, its delicacy is at least as striking as its lack of inhibitions. The symbolism used in describing the mani-festations of love throughout the book adds piquancy without offending. It should also be noted that some of the most outspoken passages are to be found in songs relating to married love.[137] Yet even here we have none of the crassly physical references to be found in the Akkadian love-charms,[138] in Sumerian love-poems,[139] or in contemporary Arabic love-songs.[140]

Esthetic standards are notoriously prone to change. In describing the beauty of a woman today, we would not think of her as resembling a city or a mare (1:9), yet we do compare a city to a woman,[141] and we refer to a beautiful horse by the feminine pronoun. A horse was, of course, not a beast of burden, but the cherished comrade of kings and nobles.[142] Sociological and economic factors undoubtedly in-fluence tastes in feminine pulchritude. The ancients liked their women large, as the Venus de Milo demonstrates and as is clear from the Song, even after allowance is made for poetic hyperbole (see 4:4; 7:5). Undoubtedly this taste for an ample woman reflected the emphasis upon child-bearing as woman's chief task. On the other hand, the modern preference for thin, "stream-lined" figures testifies to the present position of women as associates, and even as competitors, with men in all fields of activity in a society of small families, where child-bearing plays a considerably less important role. Yet in this area the French proverb has particular cogency: "Plus ça change, plus c'est la même chose." The love of a man for a maid is a perennially fresh theme in literature, because it is a constant of human nature.

XIV. SOME STYLISTIC TRAITS IN THE SONG

Our understanding of the Song of Songs is helped considerably when certain characteristics of style are kept in mind. One of these is the *use of quotations*, without any external formula or phrase to indicate that the words are being quoted. We have demonstrated above how widespread this usage is in biblical, rabbinical and Oriental literature generally.[143] Several passages in the Song are best explained as instances of this use of quotations.

In 1:7–8, Tur Sinai[144] plausibly explains v. 8 as the words of the shepherds who want to draw her affections away from her lover:

> Tell me, O thou whom I love,
> Where dost thou feed and rest thy flock at noon?
> Why should I be a wanderer
> Among the flocks of thy friends,
> *Who would mock me and say, if I asked about thee:*
> "If thou dost not know, O fairest among women,
> Go forth in the tracks of the flocks
> And feed thy kids near the shepherds' tents."

The closing verses of the Song, 8:13 f., are explained by Haller as containing the words that the lover wishes to hear from his beloved:

> O thou who sittest in the garden
> With friends listening,
> Let me hear thy voice
> *Saying to me,*

> "Hasten, my beloved, and be as a gazelle,
> Or as a young hart
> Upon the mountains of spices."

In 1:4, the third stich, "We will rejoice and be merry with thee," may well be the quotation of the words of the bridegroom to his beloved, who responds in the following stichs, "We shall inhale thy love more than wine."

This use of quotations without a *verbum dicendi* is illustrated in a popular modern Palestinian Arab song, current in several versions:[145]

"If you should visit me one night, O perfection of my happiness,
I would rejoice and mortify the envious (saying:), "My friend regales me."

The use of similes and metaphors in the Song also requires a word of explanation. When the poet uses a figure of speech, he often continues to elaborate upon it for its own sake, without reference to the subject for the sake of which it was invoked. The figure, so to speak, develops its own momentum and has its own independent existence. Thus, in 4:2,

> Thy teeth are like a flock ready for shearing
> Who have come up from washing,

the second stich describes the sheep, without being related back to the teeth. Similarly, in 4:4,

> Like the tower of David is thy neck,
> Built as a landmark,

the second stich likewise refers not to the neck, but to the tower of David.

The difficulties and obscurities of the Song are due, in large measure, to the fact that it is an expression of a segment of Israelite life, which is largely unknown to us otherwise. Reference has already been made to variations in esthetic standards. These factors should caution us against facile emendations and transpositions in the text.[146] Only in a small number of passages does emendation of the Masoretic text seem justified on the basis of our present state of knowledge.[147]

XV. The Song of Songs in Holy Writ

Undoubtedly, the allegorical interpretation of the Song of Songs, aided by the ascription of the book to King Solomon who is mentioned in the text, led to its inclusion in the Biblical canon. That Pharisaic Judaism admitted the book into the canon because it was "an ancient book, a religious book, and one that had always been religious"[148] as part of a pagan fertility cult, is unlikely to the point of impossibility. Had there been any recollection of such a use of the material, those who objected to the canonicity of the book would not have hesitated to mention it, and its chances for inclusion would have been nil.

The view against which Rabbinic Judaism levelled its strictures and which led to lengthy discussions as to its canonicity was the widely held literal interpretation, with which the Rabbis were very familiar, as has been noted. That all objections were overridden and the Song admitted into the canon indicates that on the subconscious level, at least, another factor operated, as was the case with Ecclesiastes:[149] a genuine affection for the book. It was this attitude which refused to permit its exclusion from Scripture, an act that would have spelled its ultimate destruction. As Jastrow well says: "It entered the canon not by vote, but because of its inevitable human appeal. Love is sacred even in passionate manifestations, when not perverted by a sophisticated self-analysis."[150]

The physical basis of love is extolled in the Song without shame or pruriency. Yet it serves as the foundation for the spiritual relationship, which is adumbrated in many an incidental phrase and reaches its climax in the great paean to love[151] in 8:7:

> Many waters can not quench love,
> Neither can the floods drown it.
> If a man would give all the substance of his house for love,
> He would be laughed to scorn.

It is in this sense that the modern reader, who is not likely to read it as an allegory, will echo Akiba's passionate description of the book as "the Holy of Holies," for it is, in Herder's words, "holy as a song of pure natural love, the holiness of human life."

Over and beyond its eternal youthfulness and inherent charm, the Song of Songs, precisely because it is within the canon of Scripture, serves to broaden the horizons of religion. It gives expression, in poetic and hence in deathless terms, to the authentic world-view of Judaism, which denies any dichotomy between body and soul, between matter and spirit, because it recognizes them both as the twin aspects of the great and unending miracle called life.

NOTES

1. For the entire passage in M. Yad. 3:5, see note 38 below.

2. On the canonicity of these contested Biblical books, see F. Buhl, *Canon and Text of the O.T.* (Edinburgh, 1892) pp. 3–32; H. E. Ryle, *Canon of the O.T.* (2nd ed., London, 1909); as well as the suggestive treatments of Max. L. Margolis, *The Hebrew Scriptures in the Making* (Philadelphia, 1922), pp. 83–96, and S. Zeitlin, "An Historical Study of the Canonization of Hebrew Scriptures," in *Proceedings of the American Academy for Jewish Research*, vol. III (1932), pp. 121–58. See also R. H. Pfeiffer, *Introduction to the O. T.* (New York, 1941), pp. 50–70.

3. See below, sec. VI.

4. See R. Gordis, *Koheleth—The Man And His World* (New York, 1951), chap. IV (later referred to as *KMW*).

5. In 1:1, 5; 3:7, 9, 11; 8:11–12.

6. In 1:4, 12; 7:6.

7. Professor H. H. Rowley's book, *The Servant of the Lord and other Essays on the O. T.* (London, 1952) contains a characteristically thorough study of "The Interpretation of the Song of Songs" (pp. 189–234), incorporating two earlier papers of the author in *JThS*, vol. 38 (1937), pp. 337 ff., and *JRAS* (1938), pp. 251 ff., and supplemented with valuable references to recent literature. On p. 232, note 3, he cites the older surveys of the history of the interpretation of the *Song*, from C. D. Ginsburg and Salfeld to Vaccari and Kuhl, to which he acknowledges his own indebtedness.

8. Cf. Hos., chaps. 1–2; Jer. 2:2; 3:1–3; Isa. 50:1 f.; 54:5; 62:4 f.; Ezek., chaps. 16, 23; II Esdras 9:38; 10:25 ff.

9. In Christian circles, Theodore of Mopsuestia, who opposed its place in the canon, was excommunicated as a heretic.

10. Cf. M. Ta'an. 4:8.

11. To be sure, in dealing with a similar procedure by Origen in his *Commentary* on the Song, Rowley (*op. cit.*, p. 200) denies that it implies any adherence to a literal meaning of the text. But what may be true of the 3rd century Church Father is not necessarily true of the medieval Jewish commentator, who frequently felt compelled to disguise his adherence to heterodox views, and even to polemize against ideas that he found attractive.

12. Cf., for example, R. A. Nicholson, *The Mystics of Islam* (London, 1914); G. Scholem, *Major Trends in Jewish Mysticism* (New York, 1946).

13. Cf. P. Joüon, *Le Cantique des Cantiques* (1909); A. Robert, "Le genre

littéraire du Cantique des Cantiques," in *Revue Biblique*, vol. 52 (1943–44), pp. 192 ff.; E. Tobac, "Une page de l'histoire de l'exégèse," in *Revue d'histoire ecclésiastique*, vol. 21, part 1, 1925, pp. 510 ff., reprinted in *Les cinq livres de Salomon* (1926); G. Ricciotti, *Il Cantico dei cantici* (1928).

14. Cf. J. Carlebach, "Das Hohelied," in *Jeschurun*, vol. 10 (1923), pp. 97 ff., especially pp. 196 ff.; R. Breuer, *Das Lied der Lieder* (1923).

15. Cf. Prov. 8:1 ff.; 9:1 ff., 22 ff.; B. S. 14:23; 15:2; Wisdom of Solomon 8:2 ff., and see *per contra* Prov. 9:13 ff.

16. Cf. Neuschatz de Jassy, *Le Cantique des Cantiques et le mythe d'Osiris-Hetep* (1914); Th. J. Meek (see the following note for references); W. Wittekindt, *Das Hohe-lied und seine Beziehung zum Istarkult* (Hanover, 1925); L. Waterman, in *JBL*, vol. 45 (1936), pp. 171–87; Graham and May, *Culture and Conscience* (1936), pp. 22 f. The same theory underlies the excellent commentary of M. Haller, *Die fünf Megillot* (Tuebingen, 1940).

17. Cf. his papers, "Canticles and the Tammuz Cult," in *AJSL*, vol. 39 (1922–23), pp. 1 ff.; "The Song of Songs and the Fertility Cult," in W. H. Schoff ed., *The Song of Songs, a Symposium* (Philadelphia, 1924), pp. 48 ff.; "Babylonian Parallels for the Song of Songs," in *JBL*, vol. 43 (1924), pp. 245 ff. In private correspondence he later informed Professor Rowley that he had modified his views, without indicating in what direction. Cf. Rowley, *op. cit.*, p. 213, note 5.

18. Cf. Isa. 17:10 f.; Ezek. 8:14; Zech. 12:11. On the other hand, it is doubtful whether Jer. 22:18 refers to the ritual, and Isa. 5:1–7 surely is not connected with it.

19. S. Mowinckel, *Psalmenstudien*, vol. 2 (1922), pp. 19 ff.; Hempel, *Die althebraeische Literatur und ihr hellenistisch-juedisches Nachleben* (Wildpark-Potsdam, 1930–34), pp. 24 ff.; O. Eissfeldt, *Einleitung in das A. T.*, pp. 94 ff.; E. H. Leslie, *The Psalms*, pp. 55–62.

20. Cf. L. Kohler, *Theologie des A. T.* (Tuebingen, 1936), pp. 169, 182; G. Hoelscher, *Geschichte der israelitischen und juedischen Religion* (Giessen, 1922), pp. 62 ff.

21. Cf. H. C. May, "The Fertility Cult in Hosea," in *AJSL*, vol. 48 (1930), pp. 73 ff.

22. Cf. I. Engnell, in *Svenske Biblikst Uppslagsverk*, vol. 1 (1948), col. 1075 f.

23. Cf. P. Humbert, in *ZATW*, NF, vol. 3 (1926), pp. 266–80; *idem*, in *RHPR*, vol. 12 (1932), pp. 1 ff.

24. Cf. E. Balla, in *Religion in Geschichte und Gegenwart*, 2nd ed., vol. 2 (1928), col. 1556 f.; E. Sellin, *Einleitung in das A. T.* (7th ed., 1935), p. 119.

25. Cf. W. E. Staples, in *AJSL*, vol. 53 (1936), pp. 145 ff.

26. The difficult נִדְגָּלוֹת in 6:4, 10, he regards as a textual error for *Nergal*. This emendation, which creates a *hapax legomenon*, is unnecessary. For the meaning of this crux = "these astonishing sights," see the textual commentary in Robert Gordis, *The Song of Songs* (New York, 1954), pp. 90, 92 and *idem*, "The Root *degel* in the Song of Songs" in *Journal of Biblical Literature* vol. 88 (1969), pp. 203 f.

27. Cf. the trenchant criticism of N. Schmidt, "Is Canticles an Adonis

Liturgy?", in *JAOS*, vol. 46 (1926), pp. 154–64; and H. H. Rowley, in *JRAS* (1938), pp. 251–76, now amplified in his *The Servant of the Lord*, pp. 219–32.

28. Cf. his *Kommentar zu Psalmen* (Berlin, 1905), p. V.

29. Cf. Sopherim 14:16 (ed. Higger, p. 270), which apparently refers to its reading on the *last* two days of the festival, as observed in the Diaspora: בשיר השירים קורין אותו בשני לילי ימים טובים של גליות האחרונים חציו בלילה אחד וחציו בלילה שני: . On the date of the tractate, see Higger, *op. cit.*, Introduction. The reason is indicated in *Mahzor Vitry*, p. 304: ולכן אנו אומרים בפסח על שם ששיר השירים מדבר מגאולת מצרים שנא' לסוסתי ברכבי פרעה וכל הענין מדבר מארבע גליות למבין: The medieval *piyyutim* which have entered the Passover liturgy are largely based on the *Song of Songs*, as in the cycle of hymns which begins with ברח דודי (Cant. 8:14).

30. It has been argued that *zāmīr* in 2:12 must mean a "ritual song" (cf. Meek, in Schoff, *op. cit.*, pp. 49 f.). Actually, the root *zāmar* means "sing, make music," generally used in the Bible of ritual song, to be sure, but only because of the Bible's preoccupation with religious themes. The noun is used in a secular sense in Isa. 25:5, זְמִיר עָרִיצִים, "the tyrants' song of triumph"; note the parallelism. See also Isa. 24:16; Job 35:10. It is noteworthy that the Talmud interprets Ps. 119:54, זְמִרוֹת הָיוּ־לִי חֻקֶּיךָ, in a specifically secular sense and criticizes David for treating God's laws as mere song: מפני מה נענש דוד בעוזא מפני שקרא לספר תורה זמרות היו לי חקיך "Why was David punished in the incident of Uzzah (II Sam., chap. 6)? Because he called the scroll of the Law mere 'songs'" (B. Sotah 35a; Yalkut Shimeoni, Psalm 119, sec. 480d). Actually, זֶמֶר is cognate to the noun זָמִיר (cf. קֶדֶם, קָדִים; זֶרֶם, זָרִים, Jer. 18:14, on which see Gordis, in *JThS*, vol. 41, 1940, pp. 37 ff.). The root is used to refer to a secular song *in direct connection with our book*; cf. Tos. Sanh. 12:10: רבי עקיבא אומר המנענע קולו בשיר השירים בבית המשתאות ועושה אותו כמין זמר אין לו חלק לעולם הבא, "He who gives his voice a flourish in reading the Song of Songs in the banquet-halls and makes it a *secular song* has no share in the world to come."

The 10th century agricultural calendar of Gezer lists ירחו זמר, "two months of vine-pruning." The Vav is best taken as a dual, status construct (so. I. G. Février, in *Semitica*, vol. 1, 1948, pp. 33 ff.; W. F. Albright, in J. E. Pritchard, *Ancient Near Eastern Texts*, Princeton, 1950, p. 320a), rather than simply as the old nominative ending (so D. Diringer, *Le iscrizioni anticho-ebraiche Palestinesi*, 1934, p. 5; Th. C. Vriezen-J. H. Hospers, *Palestine Inscriptions*, Leyden, 1951, pp. 12 f.). However, *yrhw zmr* comes after ירחו קץ קץ and therefore, as Dalman (*PEFQS*, 1909, p. 119) points out, "it cannot be the first pruning which comes in March, but the second, in June or July." Rowley (p. 229 f.) follows him in interpreting Song 2:12 as a reference to this second pruning. But this is very unlikely, since, according to the poem, the winter and the rain are just over and the first bloom is taking place. For this, June-July is too late. So, too, the parallelism with "the voice of the turtledove" strengthens the view that *zāmīr* refers to "singing." Accordingly, there is no basis for interpreting it either as ritual song or as meaning "pruning," which is against the parallelism and the context.

Another *locus classicus* of the cult-theory has been מַה־דּוֹדֵךְ מִדּוֹד (5:9), which is rendered, "Who but Dod is thy beloved?" (Meek, in Schoff, *op. cit.*, p. 55; Wittekindt, *op. cit.*, p. 82). Meek argues that *mah* means "who" in Babylonian, or that it is a textual error for מִי. But even this assumed correction does not suffice to yield the required sense, which would have been expressed by some such phrase as מִי דוֹדֵךְ כִּי־אִם דּוֹד; cf. Isa. 42:19, מִי עִוֵּר כִּי אִם־עַבְדִּי, "Who is blind but My servant?" Actually, there is no real evidence for Dod as a divine name used in Israel. Conversely, Meek's objection to the usual interpretation is not valid. He argues that the rendering "What is thy beloved more than another beloved?" requires the addition of "other." I do not know of an exact analogy in Hebrew for the construction, on either view, but supplying "other" is justified. Cf. Gen. 3:1: וְהַנָּחָשׁ הָיָה עָרוּם מִכֹּל חַיַּת הַשָּׂדֶה, "The serpent was wiser than all *other* beasts of the field"; cf. *ibid.* 3:14; 37:3; Deut. 7:7; 33:24, בָּרוּךְ מִבָּנִים אָשֵׁר, "Blessed above all *other* sons is Asher"; Judg. 5:24; Ps. 45:3. The usual rendering, literally, "What is thy beloved above (the class of) lover," is therefore eminently satisfactory.

The difficult כַּנִּדְגָּלוֹת (6:4, 10) is emended to כְּנֵרְגַּל, "like Nergal," the Babylonian god of the underworld, who was the partner of Ninurta, the summer sun, and "whose powerful gaze is contrasted with the milder light of the dawn and the moon (Haller)." Even if this attractive suggestion be adopted, if offers no real support to the cult-theory. Ritual texts and mythological allusions may employ the same figures, but they are worlds apart in their outlook, as Homer and Milton, or Vergil and Dante, abundantly attest. Biblical writers use Leviathan, Tehom, Mot, Rešeph, and other elements of pagan religion, but for them, unlike the Babylonian and Ugaritic epics, these are mythological references, not religious verities. This is particularly true with regard to astronomical phenomena. Cf. the Babylonian names of the months in the Hebrew calendar, which include the god Tammuz himself, or the modern names of the planets, the days of the week and the months. Actually, there are some important objections to the emendation. For these and for an alternative interpretation, see the reference in note 26.

31. So de Jassy, *op. cit.*, p. 90.

32. So Meek, in *Song of Songs—a Symposium*, p. 53.

33. "Death" and "Sheol" are mentioned in 8:6 purely as similes.

34. As, e. g., in Ezek. 8:14 ff., where it is clearly condemned as a foreign rite.

35. This consideration, incidentally, disproves the hypothesis that Psalm 2 is part of a liturgy of enthronement. The historical background is clearly that of a revolt of subordinate rulers, much too specific a situation for a recurrent litany of royal enthronement.

36. *Op. cit.*, p. 201.

37. Cf. Tos. Sanh. 12:10. The text is quoted in note 30 above.

38. Cf. Mishnah 'Eduy. 5:3; Tos. Yad. 2:14. In M. Yad. 3:5, the final decision in its favor is registered: שיר השירים וקהלת מטמאין את הידים ר׳ יהודה אומר שיר השירים מטמא את הידים וקהלת מחלוקת ר׳ יוסי אומר קהלת אינו מטמא את הידים ושיר השירים מחלוקת ר׳ שמעון אומר קהלת מקולי בית שמאי ומחומרי בית

הלל אמר ר׳ שמעון בן עזאי אני מקובל אני מפי שבעים ושנים זקנים ביום שהושיבו את
ר׳ אלעזר בן עזריה בישיבה ששיר השירים וקהלת מטמאין את הידים אמר רבי
עקיבא חס ושלום לא נחלק אדם מישראל על שיר השירים שלא תטמא את הידים
שאין כל העולם כולו כדאי כיום שניתן בו שיר השירים לישראל שכל הכתובים
קודש ושיר השירים קודש קדשים ואם נחלקו לא נחלקו אלא על קהלת אמר ר׳
יוחנן בן יהושע בן חמיו של ר׳ עקיבא כדברי בן עזאי כך נחלקו וכך גמרו:

39. Midrash Shir Hashirim Rabba 1:1, sec. 10. רבי יונתן אומר שיר השירים
כתב תחילה ואחר כך משלי ואח״כ קהלת ומייתי ליה ר׳ יונתן מדרך ארץ כשאדם
נער אומר דברי שיר הגדיל אומר דברי משלות הזקן אומר דברי הבלים:

40. Cf. Rowley, p. 206, n. 4.

41. The division of the book according to both views is conveniently set forth
by S. R. Driver, *Introduction to the Literature of the O. T.* (New York, 1906), 12th
ed., pp. 437–43.

42. Thus only the older commentators, Hengstenberg, Keil, and Kingsbury,
favor the first. The second is accepted by Driver (*op. cit.*). The catena of commentators who share this view is given in R. H. Pfeiffer, *Introduction to the O. T.*
(New York, 1941), p. 715.

43. יְרִיעוֹת שְׁלֹמֹה means "Solomonic curtains," being parallel to "Arab
tents," like our phrases "Louis Quatorze furniture," "Queen Anne fashions,"
and the like.

44. Cf. I Kings 16:23 f. Oesterley-Robinson, *History of Israel* (Oxford, 1932),
p. 463, dates the accession of Omri to the throne as 886 B.C.E. W. F. Albright, in
L. Finkelstein, ed., *The Jews* (New York, 1949), p. 33, places it as circa 876
B.C.E.

45. The grounds for maintaining that there is even older material in the book,
going back to the 10th century B.C.E., will be presented below.

46. Cf. Gen. 41:8; Ex. 28:3; 35:25, 31; 36:1; Isa. 10:13; 29:14; 44:25; Jer.
9:16; 10:9; 49:7; Ezek. 27:8; Ps. 107:27.

47. Cf. M. Shab. 18:3; M. R. H. 2:5; B. 'Er. 45a.

48. Or, "five thousand," with the Septuagint.

49. Cf. I Kings 5:10–12 with I Chron. 15:19 and the superscriptions of
Psalms 88 and 89, and see Gordis, *KMW*, p. 17.

50. So W. F. Albright, in an unpublished paper, "The Canaanite Origin of
Israelite Musical Guilds."

51. Cf. Pfeiffer, *op. cit.*, p. 650.

52. Cf. I Sam. 10:12; 24:14; II Sam. 14:14; I Kings 20:11; II Kings 14:9; Jer.
23:28; 31:29; Ezek. 16:44; 18:2.

53. Cf. Gen. 4:23; Judg. 15:16; I Sam. 18:7.

54. Cf. Num. 21:17 ff.; Isa. 16:10; 22:13; 27:2.

55. Cf. Amos 6:5; Isa. 5:12; Job 21:12; Ps. 69:13.

56. II Sam. 1:19 ff.; 3:33; cf. Amos 5:16; Jer. 9:16 (מְקוֹנְנוֹת, חֲכָמוֹת
יֹדְעֵי נֶהִי).

57. Cf. A. Erman, *Literature of the Ancient Egyptians*, tr. by Blackman
(London, 1927); J. B. Pritchard, *Ancient Near-Eastern Texts Relating to the O.T.*
(Princeton, 1950); S. Schott, *Altaegyptische Liebeslieder* (Zurich, 1950).

58. For a collection of these songs, containing text, translation, and notes, see the extremely valuable study of St. H. Stephan, *Modern Palestinian Parallels to the Song of Songs* (Jerusalem, 1926).

59. Cf. Gordis, *KMW*, pp. 16 ff., and note R. H. Pfeiffer's judicious statement on the subject (*Introduction*, p. 712): "There must have existed in Palestine during the last centuries of our era a considerable amount of erotic poetry of which our book alone survives by accident."

60. Jastrow and Budde each finds 23 songs, though they differ on the subdivisions. Haller finds 26, Bettan 18. We divide the book into 28 songs, several of which are fragmentary and some of which may be doublets. Popular songs frequently circulate in many versions.

61. So Wetzstein, Budde, Stade, Cornill, Kautzsch, Jastrow, Cassuto, Goodspeed, and others. Cf. Pfeiffer, *op. cit.*, p. 716.

62. B. Ket. 16b: כיצד מרקדין לפני הכלה בית שמאי אומרים כלה כמות שהיא בית הלל אומרים כלה נאה וחסודה.

63. At the same time, Gebhardt's objection to the view *in toto* is much too extreme. The doubts which have been raised by H. Granquist as to the existence of such a custom as a "king's week" among the Arabs of Palestine overlook the clear-cut references in Jewish practice to שבעת ימי המשתה, "the seven days of feasting" following the wedding, which are observed to the present day with a repetition of the Seven Nuptial Blessings first recited at the marriage. Moreover, Rothstein's objection that the bride is never called "queen" in the Song loses part of its force when it is recalled that while rabbinic literature cites and elaborates on the proverb חתן דומה למלך, "The bridegroom may be compared to a king" (Pirke de Rabbi Eliezer, chap. 16), there is no corresponding phrase about the bride. However, the Sabbath is described as both "queen" and "bride" in Talmudic and post-Talmudic sources; cf. Shab. 119a and Solomon Alkabetz' famous hymn *Lechah Dodi*.

64. Hence the use of the relative, *'ašer,* instead of *še,* and the high valuation on the book expressed in the title. See the Commentary *ad loc.*

65. This appropriate rendering of *'ahᵃbhāh* was proposed by G. R. Driver, who called attention to the Arabic *'ihabatᵘᵐ*, "skin (human or animal)," *'ahibatᵘᵐ*, "soldier's equipment, leather)" in *JBL*, vol. 55, 1936, p. 111. This definitive solution of the difficulty disposes effectively of the need to emend the *MT* to a word meaning "ivory," either *hōbhᵉnim* (so Graetz and most moderns) or *habbim* (so Tur-Sinai).

66. The meter of the verse is 2:2:2 || 3:3:3:. *B'yōm hᵃthunāthō* receives three beats, both because of its length and the exigencies of the meter. On this procedure, as well as on the technique of longer stichs at the end of a poem, cf. above, chap. 3, esp. pp. 70 f.

67. The *kinah* rhythm is not limited to the 3:2 pattern, its basic trait being a longer stich followed by a shorter. Scholars have been led astray here by the conjunctive accents linking *hammelekh šelōmōh*, when actually the words belong to separate stichs, with a 4:3 meter for the verse, which is in climactic or complementary parallelism. Similarly, in Num. 23:7 the words *bālāq melekh mō'ābh*, though linked by conjunctive accents, belong to separate stichs. For a full dis-

cussion of the meter of the verse, cf. Gordis, "A Wedding Song for Solomon,"
in *JBL*, vol. 63 (1944), especially pp. 266 ff.

68. On Solomon's foreign marriages in general, cf. I Kings 11:1 ff.; on his
marriage to the Egyptian princess, cf. I. Kings 3:1.

69. The dating of Psalm 45 has been the subject of wide difference of opinion.
While it has been referred to Solomon (Kirkpatrick), to Jehu (Briggs, ICC), to
Ahab and Jezebel (Hitzig, Buttenwieser), or to Jehoram and Athaliah
(Delitzsch), Pfeiffer's judgment that the king's name can not now be determined
is the soundest view. Evidently, such compositions must have been common,
though only one has survived in the Psalter. The preservation of another example in the *Song of Songs* is perfectly natural, in fact even more appropriate.

70. So Robertson-Smith in Yule, *Glossary of Anglo-Indian Words*, p. 502;
Brown-Driver-Briggs, *Lexicon*, s. v. Tur-Sinai (in his paper, p. 4, n. 1) adduces
an Akkadian parallel *ap* (*p*)*aru*, meaning "hut of reeds" and also "head cov-
ering." Erbt and Wittekindt read *'appidyōn*, from Babylonian *'aphad*="come as
messenger." Zapletal reads *appadan*, Babylonian "tent," which occurs in Dan.
11:45. Tur-Sinai makes a new suggestion in *Halashon Vehasepher* (Jerusalem,
1951), p. 389, where he argues that a litter is too small an object and suggests
that the word is actually a scribal combination of אף, "also," and an unknown
word ריון.

71. The technical term "ship of Tarshish," which the book of Kings applies
both to Solomon's vessel that sailed with Hiram's navy and brought back "gold,
silver, ivory, apes and peacocks" (I Kings 10:22) and to the ships of Jehoshaphat
which sailed from the southern port of Ezion-geber (I Kings 22:49), has been
regarded as a generic term for a large vessel, no matter what its destination, like
our English "Indiaman." Thus it could be used of vessels going eastward to
Arabia, Africa, or even India. This, in spite of the fact that the place-name
"Tarshish" has been generally equated with some port west of Palestine, such as
Carthage (LXX on Ezek. 27:12), the Roman province of Africa (Targum on I
Kings 22:49; Jer. 10:9), Tarsus in Cicilia (Josephus, *Antiquities*, 1, vi, 9),
Etruscan Italy (Cheyne), Tharsis on the Black Sea (Desnoyers), Tharros in
Sardinia (Covey-Crump), or, as is most generally accepted, Tartessos in Spain
(first proposed by Eusebius and revived by Bochart; cf. W. Max Müller,
Dictionary of the Bible, vol. 4, pp. 683 f.; Galling, *Biblisches Reallexikon*, pp.
510 f.).

On the other hand, it seems clear that the book of Chronicles thought of
Tarshish as lying to the east of Palestine, since it uses the phrase "ships going to
Tarshish" in its account of these same nautical enterprises of Solomon and
Jehoshaphat (II Chron. 9:21; 20:36). This was long dismissed as another example of the unreliability of the Chronicler. Recent scholarship has, however, gone
far in rehabilitating his credibility (cf., for example, Von Rad, *Die Geschichts-
bildung der Chronistischen Werke*, Stuttgart, 1930; Martin Noth, *Ueberlieferungsgeschichtliche Studien*, Halle, 1943; W. F. Albright, *From the Stone Age to
Christianity*, Baltimore, 1940, p. 268). It is, therefore, not impossible that the
Chronicler's view of Tarshish is another example where his value was unduly
discounted in the past. Thus Bochart's old attempt to validate the Chronicler's

references by assuming that there were two localities referred to as "Tarshish," one in the Western Mediterranean, the other in the Indian Ocean, was dismissed summarily by scholars (cf. W. Max Müller, *Dictionary of the Bible*, vol. 4, p. 684n). On the other hand, J. Hornell contends vigorously that Tarshish refers to "a great mart on the west coast of India," from which gold, spices, pearls, and other gems were shipped westward (cf. his paper, "Naval Activity in the Days of Solomon and Rameses III," in *Antiquity*, vol. 21, p. 72). This view is favorably considered by Salo W. Baron (*A Social and Religious History of the Jews*, 2nd ed., New York, 1952, vol. 1, p. 321, n. 3.).

Whatever the identification of Tarshish, the Oriental provenance of *'apiriōn*, rather than the proposed Greek etymology for the word, becomes increasingly more plausible.

72. Cf. Dan. 3:26; 4:23, and such frequent Mishnaic locutions as רבונו של עולם.

73. Cf. Stephan, *op. cit.*, pp. 35 f.

74. That this affinity involved not only the vocabulary, but also the phonetic and morphologic structure of Hebrew, was conclusively demonstrated by Max L. Margolis. Cf. E. A. Speiser in *Max L. Margolis, Scholar and Teacher*, edited by R. Gordis (Philadelphia, 1952), pp. 31–34.

On the various categories of "Aramaisms," see *KMW*, pp. 59, 362 f. Cf. also Driver's judgment (*op. cit.*, p. 440) that "*še* and many words common in Aramaic are part of the northern dialect." They represent part of the North-West-Semitic vocabulary, common to both Aramaic and Hebrew, except that some words became common in the former and were used only sporadically in the latter. To this category of a common *Wortschatz*, we may assign, in addition to the relative (cf. Judg. 5:7; 6:17; 7:12; 8:26; II Kings 6:11), בְּרוֹת (1:17, instead of בְּרוֹשׁ; cf. סַבֹּלֶת for שִׁבֹּלֶת in Judg. 12:6) and שַׁלְמָה (1:7), a Hebraized form of the Aramaic דִּלְמָא.

Many others have classical Hebrew parallels: לכי (2:13 Kethib, cf. II Kings 4:2 Kethib); נטר (1:6; cf. Lev. 19:18; Amos 1:11, reading וַיִּטֹּר for וַיִּטְרֹף; Jer. 3:5, 12, etc.); קפץ, "leap" (2:8; cf. קפץ, "close, clench," Deut. 15:7; Isa. 52:15) הרהיב (6:5: cf. Isa. 3:5; *Rahab* the mythological monster mentioned in Isa. 30:7; Job 9:13, etc.); Lamed accusative (2:15; 8:13; cf. Lev. 19:18, 34; II Sam. 3:30).

Authentic Aramaic borrowings seem to be חרכים (2:9); כתל (2:9); סתו (2:11); סמדר (2:13, 15; 7:13); פג (2:13); טנף (5:3); סנסנים (7:9); and סוגה (7:3), though new texts may change the picture.

75. Cf. A. T. Olmstead, *A History of Palestine and Syria* (New York, 1931).

76. Thus the word *'ašīāḥ* occurs only in the Hebrew of Ben Sira (50:3) with no Biblical parallel, but it is found in the Mesha Inscription (Line 9) as *'ašūah*. The late Biblical and Mishnaic word *nekhasim* occurs once, in Josh. 22:8. The root *kibbel*, occurring only in Job 2:10 and Esth. 9:27, and generally regarded as a late Aramaism, was recently found by Albright in the Tel-el Amarna Letters (*BASOR*, 89, Feb., 1943, pp. 29 ff.). On the conjunction *še*, once regarded as a "late Aramaism," see note 74.

77. In Biblical Hebrew, pronominal anticipation occurs a) with a verbal

suffix (Ex. 2:6; 35:5; Jer. 9:14; Ecc. 2:21); b) with a nominal suffix, which resembles our usage more closely (Ezek. 10:3; Prov. 13:4; Job 29:3; Ezra 3:12; possibly also Num. 23:18; 24:3, 5) and c) after the preposition Lamedh (Ezra 9:1). That the usage is early in origin is attested by its occurrence in Phoenician in the Karatepe Inscription of Azitawadd (9th or 8th century B.C.E.); cf. Text C, I, lines 17–18, לשבתנם דדנים lit. "for the dwelling of them, of the Danunians"; III, line 4, לתתי בעל כרנתריש lit. "for the giving of him, of Baal Kalendris (?)". Cf. C. H. Gordon in *JNES*, vol. 8, 1949, pp. 113 f.; N. H. Tur-Sinai in *Leshonenu*, vol. 17, no. 4, p. 9.

78. So Jastrow, H. L. Ginsberg (orally, to the writer), Haller.

79. *Op. cit.*, pp. 212 f.

80. On the modern identification of these sites, see Wright-Filson, *Historical Atlas to the Bible* (Philadelphia, 1945), pp. 107 ff. While Deut. 3:9 informs us that Senir was the Amorite equivalent for Hermon, the Song (4:8) treats them either as distinct mountain peaks or as a wider designation for the Anti-Lebanon range.

81. The equivalence of "Shulammite" with "Shunemite," long maintained, is attested by *Sulem*, the modern Arabic name of *Shunem*. On other recent theories, see the Commentary *ad loc.*

82. If כְּמִגְדַּל הַשֵּׁן in 7:5 is to be read as הַבָּשָׁן, in view of the other geographical similes in the *wasf*.

83. Thus פַּרְדֵּס (4:13) is not a garden, but a park. Of the spices mentioned, קִנָּמוֹן, אֲהָלוֹת and כֹּפֶר are probably Indian, like אַרְגָּמָן and אַפִּרְיוֹן. אֱגוֹז may be Persian. See the Lexicons of Brown-Driver-Briggs and Baumgarten-Kohler, *s. v.*

84. So e. g., Jastrow, Haller. Pfeiffer (*op. cit.*, p. 710) regards vv. 12–17 as a unit.

85. Cf. *Enzyklopedia Miqrait* (Jerusalem, 1950), vol. 1, p. 554b.

86. Cf. מַאְפֵּלְיָה, "deep gloom" (Jer. 2:31); מֶרְחַבְיָה, "great enlargement" (Ps. 118:5); גִּבּוֹר צַיִד לִפְנֵי ה', "an exceedingly mighty hunter" (Gen. 10:9); אַרְזֵי אֵל, "mighty cedars" (Ps. 80:11).

87. Cf. אַיֶּלֶת אֲהָבִים וְיַעֲלַת חֵן (Prov. 5:19). These and similar terms are frequent in the love poetry of Jehudah Halevi, Immanuel of Rome, and other medieval Hebrew poets.

88. Cf. J. Ebeling, "Liebeszauber im alten Orient," in *Mittheilungen der altorientalischen Gesellschaft*, I (1905), pp. 27, 33.

89. Cf. the discussion in S. Lieberman, *Greek in Jewish Palestine* (New York, 1942), pp. 125–27, who cites some of the abundant material assembled in P. Meinhardt, *De forma et usu iuramentorum*, pp. 77 ff., and Hirzel, *Der Eid*, p. 96, note 2.

90. Cf. Lieberman, *op. cit.*, p. 129, note 106.

91. Cf. Burgess Johnson, *The Lost Art of Profanity* (New York, 1948); esp. pp. 26, 101, 116, 117. I am indebted to Professor Mario A. Pei for this reference. I was unable to consult *A Dictionary of Profanity and Its Substitutions* by M. R. Walter, on deposit in manuscript form in the Princeton University Library, to which Johnson refers.

92. The most popular oaths naturally invoked the God of Israel: a) חי ה׳, "As JHVH liveth" (I Sam. 14:39, 45; 19:6, and often; I Kings 1:29; 2:24, and often; Jer. 4:2; 5:2, and often; Ruth 3:13); נשבע בה׳ (אלהים) (Josh. 2:12; 9:19; I Kings 1:17; 2:8, etc.). b) חי האלהים (II Sam. 2:27); נשבע באלהים (Gen. 21:23). c) (rarely) חי אל (Job 27:2). d) חי ה׳ אלהיך (I Kings 17:12; 18:10); נשבע לה׳ (Zeph. 1:5; Ps. 132:2).

Additional solemnity undoubtedly attached to oaths with more elaborate formulas as a) חי ה׳ אלהי ישראל (I Sam. 25:34; I Kings 17:11); b) חי ה׳ צבאות, "As JHVH, Lord of Hosts, liveth" (I Kings 18:15; II Kings 3:14); ונשבעות לה׳ צבאות (Isa. 19:18). A possible double oath occurs in only one poetic passage: חי ה׳ וברוך צורי, "God liveth and my Rock is blessed" (II Sam. 22:47 = Ps. 18:47). So also the oath בְּחֵי הָעוֹלָם, "By Him who liveth eternally" (Dan. 12:7).

To avoid mentioning JHVH, oaths by His name became common: בשם ה׳ (Isa. 48:1); בשמו (Deut. 6:13; Jer. 12:16); בשמי הגדול (Jer. 44:26); בשמי (Jer. 12:16).

Joint oaths invoking God and a human being also occur: a) חי ה׳ וחי נפשך, "As God lives and as does your soul" (I Sam. 20:3; 25:26; II Kings 2:2; 4:30); b) חי ה׳ וחי אדני המלך, "As God lives and as does my lord, the king" (II Sam. 15:21).

The Lord Himself swears by His own being: a) חי אני, "As I live" (Num. 14:21; Jer. 22:24; Ezek. 5:11; 14:16, and often; Zeph. 2:9). b) חי אנכי (Deut. 32:40); בי, "By Myself" (Gen. 22:16; Isa. 45:23; Jer. 22:5; 49:13). c) בקדשו, "By His holiness" (Amos 4:2); בקדשי, "By My holiness" (Ps. 89:36). d) בנפשו, "By His essence, literally, soul" (Jer. 51:14; Amos 6:8). e) בימינו, "By His right hand" (Isa. 62:8). f) בגאון יעקב, "By the glory of Jacob," an epithet for God (Amos 8:7).

93. Cf. the illuminating study by S. S. Cohon, "The Name of God, a Study in Rabbinic Theology," in *HUCA*, vol. 23, 1950–51, Part I, pp. 579–604.

94. Reading ἐν ταῖς δυνάμεσι καὶ ἐν ταῖς ἰσχύσεσι τοῦ ἀγροῦ. Cf. Siegfried *ad loc.*

95. Cf. Midrash Shir Hashirim Rab. 2:7: במה השביען ר׳ אליעזר אומר השביען בשמים ובארץ· בצבאות בצבא של מעלה ובצבא של מטה׃. "By what did he (*sic*) adjure them? R. Eliezer says, 'He adjured them by heaven and earth. Biṣᵉbhā'ōth means by the host (Ṣᵉbā') above and by the host below.' "

96. Cf. K. Galling, *Biblisches Reallexikon* (Tuebingen, 1937), pp. 286 ff.

97. Cf. J. A. Wilson, in Pritchard, *op. cit.*, p. 468a.

98. Cf. W. H. Bennett, in Hastings, *Dictionary of the Bible*, vol. 2, pp. 437 f.; K. Galling, *Biblisches Reallexikon* (Tuebingen, 1937), pp. 286 ff. On the other hand, killing animals in self-defense was naturally practised (cf., for example, Judg. 14:6; I Sam. 17:34 ff.), and some game animals were used for food (Deut. 12:15, 22; I Kings 5:3).

99. The Jewish laws of *shehitah*, which prescribed slaughter with a knife, effectively ruled out the use of birds or animals killed in the hunt.

100. Cf. Erman, *op. cit.*, p. 249.

101. Cf., *inter alia*, Psalms 19 and 105; Job, chaps. 38–41.

102. Note that in 1:4 and 7:10, wine is used merely as a comparison, while in 1:6 and 8:12, the vineyard is a symbol for love. The difficult closing phrase of 5:1 is the only direct reference to heavy drinking in the Song (šikhᵉrū, literally "become drunk"). See the Commentary on this passage.

103. Erman, *op. cit.*, p. 251.

104. The noun *kin'āh* in 8:6, as the parallelism indicates, means "passion." The possibility of other lovers is raised in 1:7. See the Commentary *ad loc.*

105. Erman, *op. cit.*, p. 248.

106. As e. g. 2:14; 4:12 ff.; 5:2 ff.; 8:8 ff.

107. Cf. Pfeiffer, *op. cit.*, p. 711. As a matter of fact, *'āḥōth* occurs in the meaning of "beloved" with no gloss, in another song, 8:8. See Commentary *ad loc.*

108. The MT in 4:9 has a 3:3:3 meter. The deletion of כַּלָּה would create 2:3:3, a rare, if not impossible, pattern, since as a rule closing stichs are longer than the opening ones only at the end of a literary unit, for the purpose of creating a strong close. See the following note for an example, and cf. chapter 3 in this volume. In 4:12, the rhythm is 2:2:2:2, which would also be destroyed by deleting כַּלָּה, to create a 3:4 meter.

109. In 4:10, the MT is 4:3:3, a common form of the *kīnāh* rhythm. With the deletion it would be the frequent 3:3:3 meter. In 5:1, the MT exhibits the 4:3:3:3 pattern; with the deletion of *ahōtî*, it would be 3:3:3:3. The closing stich, אָכְלוּ רֵעִים שְׁתוּ וְשִׁכְרוּ דּוֹדִים, which is widely regarded as out of place, is in 2:3 rhythm, normal at the close of a poem. See note above on the metric principle involved.

110. On רֵעַ as "friend," cf., *inter alia*, Gen. 38:12; as "fellow, neighbor," cf Ex. 2:13; Lev. 19:18; as "lover," cf. Jer. 3:1. On רַעְיָה (רְעוּת) as "friend," cf. Judg. 11:37 *Kethib*; as "fellow, neighbor," cf. Ex. 11:2; Jer. 9:19; Esth. 1:19; as "beloved," cf. Song 1:9, 15; 2:2, 10, 13; 4:1, 7; 5:2; 6:4.

111. On אָח as "friend," cf. II Sam. 1:26; I Kings 9:13; as "fellow, neighbor," cf. Lev. 19:17. On אָחוֹת as "fellow, neighbor," cf. Ex. 26:3, 5, 6, 17; Ezek. 1:9, 23; 3:13.

112. On the equivalence of אָח and רֵעַ, cf. Ps. 35:14, כְּרֵעַ כְּאָח־לִי הִתְהַלָּכְתִּי; Job 30:29, אָח הָיִיתִי לְתַנִּים וְרֵעַ לִבְנוֹת יַעֲנָה.

113. Tur-Sinai calls attention to this fact, *op. cit.*, p. 367. This usage is not restricted to Biblical Hebrew (Gen. 30:13; Isa. 32:9; Prov. 31:29), but is common in modern Israeli Hebrew as well.

114. Cf., on the appreciation of beauty in the Bible, the eloquent presentation of S. Goldman, *The Book of Books*, vol. 1 (New York, 1948).

115. Cf., *inter alia*, J. G. Frazer, *The Golden Bough* (New York, 1922); A. E. Crawley, *The Mystic Rose* (New York, 1927); B. Z. Goldberg, *The Sacred Fire* (New York, 1930).

116. Cf. J. Ebeling, "Liebeszauber im alten Orient," in *Mittheilungen der altorientalischen Gesellschaft*, vol. 1 (1925); *idem*, "Aus dem Tagewerk eines assyrischen Zauberpriesters," in *MAOG*, vol. 5 (1931). It is the merit of N. H. Tur-Sinai, in his paper "Shir Hashirim," now reprinted in his *Halashon Vehasepher*,

vol. II (Jerusalem, 5711), pp. 351–88, to have utilized this material for the interpretation of our book with great brilliance. At times, however, his deductions,
like his basic view of the *Song* as part of a gigantic prose-poetic history of Israel
(cf. p. 388), do not carry conviction.

117. *Op. cit.*, p. 367. We are, however, unable to accept his interpretation
(p. 368) that *šey^edubbar bāh* (8:8) means "when incantations are pronounced
upon her."

118. Ebeling, "Aus dem Tagewerk," p. 19.

119. Ebeling's rendering "seine Zunge" is a *lapsus calami*. The Akkadian is
lisânaka.

120. *Ibid.*, p. 37.

121. Ehrlich reads: ‏אֱכֹל רֵעִי שָׁתֵה וּשְׁכַר דּוֹדִי‎.

122. Haller reads: ‏אִכְלִי רַעְיָתִי שְׁתִי וְשִׁכְרִי דוֹדִים‎.

123. So Budde, who deletes the stich entirely, also Jastrow.

124. Cf. Stephan, *op. cit.*, p. 80. The text reads as follows:

> Ykšif 'alayya
> Ya tabîb
> 'Ala-lli atâni
> Min il-ḥabîb
> Wàllah ya râbb
> ha-l-àmru 'ajîb
> Wàna 'albi dâb
> 'Ala l-aḥbâb.

Stephan (note 3) suggests that the plural *aḥ-bâb* is used for the sake of the
rhyme (with *dâb*). That is hardly a compelling reason, since the singular *ḥabîb*
would be an excellent rhyme for *'ajîb*, and the second and fourth lines of the
stanza would be in rhyme, exactly as in the preceding stanza, *ḥabîb* rhymes with
tabîb.

125. V. 14 is best taken as a quotation of the words which the lover wishes to
hear (‏הַשְׁמִיעֵנִי‎: ‏בְּרַח דּוֹדִי‎), an invitation to enjoy the delights of love (so Haller;
slightly differently Bettan).

126. The entire passage 7:7–10 and 11–14 may constitute a single song in duet
form, the first portion being spoken by the lover, the second by his beloved.
However, there is no direct plea to the beloved in 7–10, which is essentially a
poem of praise, and vv. 11–14 do not constitute a direct answer. We therefore
prefer to regard these passages as two independent poems.

127. It is possible that these verses may be independent fragments. V. 12 is
completely untranslatable in its present form.

128. That this is a dance is clear from the fact that the description of the bride
begins with her feet. That the occasion is a wedding is highly probable, both
from the frank description of her physical charms, by far the most outspoken in
the book, and from the reference to the "king," i. e. the bridegroom, in v. 6.

129. Cf., for example, 8:5 or 8:13 f. Albright has made the suggestion that
Psalm 68 may contain the titles of a collection instead of being the text of a
single poem.

130. Such are the three adjurations of the daughters of Jerusalem (2:7; 3:5; 8:4), the first two of which include the reference to the hinds and the gazelles of the field. So, too, the same text is repeated in 2:5 and 8:3; the phrase seems less relevant in the second passage. The two dream songs (3:1–5 and 5:2 ff.) repeat the theme of the city watchmen (3:3; 5:7) with a variation in the latter.

131. Cf. Pfeiffer, *op. cit.*, p. 710, for a list of alleged glosses. Some are essential to the text and need only to be interpreted correctly (as e. g. 5:6). Most rest upon considerations of meter which of themselves do not suffice to justify excisions in the text. Not only is there great uncertainty concerning all theories of Biblical meter proposed (cf. W. H. Cobb, *A Criticism of Systems of Hebrew Meter*, Oxford, 1905), but our lack of the accompanying music makes it impossible to tell what words were repeated or lengthened in the chanting of the songs.

132. Thus, in Palestinian Arabic, a girl deprived of her virginity is described as *maftûḥa* (see Stephan, p. 16). Cf. also the Talmudic phrase פתח פתוח מצאתי (Ket. 9b) as a charge of unchastity.

133. *Op. cit.*, p. 18.

134. Cf. A. Erman, *op. cit.*, p. 241.

135. Cf. Jastrow, *op. cit.*, p. 13.

136. Cf. Pfeiffer, *op. cit.*, p. 711.

137. Thus 1:12, 13 and 7:3 f. both occur in poems where the lover is "king," i. e. the bridegroom (1:12; 7:6).

138. Cf. Ebeling, "Liebeszauber," *passim*. See especially the direct references to the *membra* (pp. 11, 33) and to sexual congress (pp. 21, 43).

139. See the Sumerian "Love Song to a King" (S. N. Kramer, in Pritchard, *op. cit.*, p. 496).

140. Cf. Stephan, *op. cit.*, pp. 21, 39, for examples of such crudity in modern Arabic poetry.

141. A striking instance where a city is compared to love occurs in Egyptian poetry:

> I will go to Memphis and say, "Give me my sister tonight,
> Memphis is a dish of love-apples, set before the Fair of Face."

(The last epithet is a name of Ptah, god of Memphis). Cf. Erman, *op. cit.*, p. 245.

142. See the description of the horse in Job 39:19 ff. and Horace, *Odes*, III, 2.

143. See the study "Quotations As a Literary Usage in Biblical, Oriental, and Rabbinic Literature," in this volume.

144. *Op. cit.*, pp. 365 f.

145. Stephan, *op. cit.*, p. 60:

> *lô zurtani fard lêle yâ kamâl saʿdi*
> *afraḥ vʾakîd il-ʿazul—"ḥubbi mhannîni."*

146. For a telling instance of unnecessary emendations and deletions, apparently supported by comparative religious data, cf. the references cited in note 26 above.

147. The following changes from the Masoretic text appear necessary:

1:2 For יִשָּׁקֵנִי read יַשְׁקֵנִי (doubtful)

3:6 For כְּתִימְרוֹת read בְּתִימְרוֹת (doubtful)

4:15 For גַּנִּים read גַּנִּי

5:13 For מִגְדְּלוֹת read מְגַדְּלוֹת

     For עֲרוּגוֹת read עֲרוּגַת

6:12 For שָׂמַתְנִי מַרְכְּבוֹת read שָׁם תְּנִי מֹרֶךְ בַּת (so Tur-Sinai).

7:14 For דּוֹדָי read דּוֹדִי

8:2   For תְּלַמְּדֵנִי read וְאֶל חֶדֶר הוֹרָתִי (see the Commentary)

For details see the textual commentary in our book *The Song of Songs* (New York, 1954).

    148. Cf. Meek, in Schoff, *op. cit.*, pp. 52 f.

    149. Cf. Gordis, *KMW*, pp. 121 f.

    150. *Op. cit.*, p. 16.

    151. Tur-Sinai, *op. cit.*, pp. 383 f., refers the "love" which is the subject in 8:7 not to the relationship of a maiden and her lover, but to the effort of an interloper to steal the affections of a married woman from her husband. The passage is interpreted to mean that it is impossible to make monetary restitution for this heinous sin. This is highly ingenious, but we find it unconvincing. There is a clear-cut reference to the wronged husband in Prov. 6:27 ff., which Tur-Sinai adduces as a parallel, but it is entirely lacking here.

1. GENERAL INDEX

2. INDEX OF BIBLICAL PASSAGES

a. *Old Testament*

14:4 — 227
14:14 — 35, 389
14:17 — 213
15:2 — 60
15:21 — 394
17:13 — 227
19:36 — 199, 206
22:6 — 65
22:14 — 158
22:47 — 394
23:8 — 366, 369
24:11 — 315

I Kings

1:10 — 366
1:17 — 394
1:29 — 394
2:8 — 394
2:24 — 394
3:1 — 391
3:9 — 213
5:2 — 394
5:3 — 394
5:10-12 — 33, 362, 389
8:1 — 59
8:5 — 50, 56, 59
8:53 — 33, 363
9:13 — 395
10:22 — 367, 391
11:1 — 365, 391
11:18 — 93
11:31-39 — 20
12:3 — 56
12:20 — 51
12:21 — 56, 59
13:6 — 18
14:6-16 — 20
14:8 — 245
14:16 — 245
14:24 — 213
15:12 — 213
16:23 — 389
16:34 — 252
17:to 21 — 32
17:11 — 394
17:12 — 394
17:21 — 18
18:10 — 394
18:15 — 394
19:1 — 278

19:3 — 220
20:11 — 389
22:11 — 21, 231
22:19 — 24
22:23 — 220
22:47 — 213
22:49 — 391

II Kings

2 to 9 — 32
2:2 — 394
3:14 — 394
4:2 — 392
4:30 — 394
4:33 — 18
5:10 — 278
6:11 — 392
7:1 — 252
7:16 — 252
8:11 — 278
14:9 — 35, 389
14:23 to 15:7 — 32
15:8 — 243
17:27 — 253
23:1 — 58
23:7 — 213
24 — 12

Isaiah

1 to 35 — 223
1:4 — 67, 150, 214
1:15 — 157
1:16 — 260
1:21 — 68
1:24-28 — 187
1:26 — 73
1:27 — 259
2:1-5 — 268
2:1 — 265
2:2 — 195
2:3 — 266
2:12 — 195
3 — 187
3:5 — 392
3:10-11 — 304, 313, 338
3:16 — 261
4:6 — 247, 265
5:1-7 — 386
5:1 — 237, 251
5:5 — 237

5:6a — 237
5:6b — 237
5:8-17 — 187
5:8 — 190, 261
5:12 — 389
5:16 — 259
5:20 — 306
5:24 — 219
6 — 7, 277
6:3 — 259, 277
6:5 — 226, 233
7 — 207
7:3 — 231
7:5 — 207
7:14 — 199, 231
7:15-16 — 214
7:16 — 215
8 — 207
8:1 — 232
8:3 — 231
8:4 — 207, 215
8:6 — 207
8:8 — 231
8:10 — 231
8:16 — 24, 219
8:19 — 154
8:20 — 219
8:23 — 227
9:5 — 278
10 — 323
10:1-2 — 261
10:2 — 264
10:5-6 — 263
10:7 — 153
10:12 — 263
10:13 — 33, 389
10:15 — 256
10:21 — 231
11:1 — 278
11:2 — 158, 264
11:6 — 266
11:9 — 267
14:13 — 52
14:14 — 158
14:20 — 214
15:1 — 151
16:1 — 277
16:7 — 251
16:10 — 389
17:10 — 386
18:7 — 277-78

55:24 — 110
57:8 — 301
59 — 71
59:8 — 121
60:7 — 248
60:8-12 — 227
62 — 71
63 — 70-71
66 — 71
67 — 71
68 — 396
68:31 — 51
69:13 — 389
69:33 — 112, 150
69:36 — 252
71 — 70
71:20 — 248
73 to 83 — 59
73 — 70, 189
73:17 — 189
73:25-28 — 189
74:22 — 301
75 — 41
75:10 — 112
78:2 — 362
78:37 — 301
80:11 — 393
81 — 41, 70
82 — 41, 59, 70, 212
82:1 — 52
82:6 — 200
84 — 71
84:11 — 124
86 — 71
86:14 — 51
88 — 389
89 — 70, 389
89:6 — 51
89:36 — 394
90 — 70
91 — 70
91:1 — 158
91:9 — 158
92:2 — 158
92:10 — 74
94 — 70
94:1 — 74
94:8 — 189
94:12 — 189
94:21 — 189
95:7 — 112

95:9 — 149
98 — 70
103 — 70
103:14 — 250
104 — 44, 70
104:11 — 93
104:20 — 93
105 — 394
106 — 70
107 — 84
107:6-8 — 84
107:13-15 — 84
107:19-21 — 84
107:27-31 — 84
107:27 — 32, 389
108:2 — 301
108:7 — 248
109:2a — 150
109:3b-5a — 150
109:5-20 — 111
109:6-19 — 150
109:6 — 150
109:15-18 — 150
109:16-19 — 150
109:19-20 — 150
109:20 — 150
109:25 — 150
109:28-29 — 150
109:29 — 150
109:31 — 150
110 — 83
110:10 — 189
111 — 70, 82
111:1 — 51
112 — 33, 189
112:2 — 189
112:5 — 189
112:9 — 189
113 — 71
113:7 — 186
113:9 — 252
116 — 70
117 — 71
118:5 — 393
118:17 — 153
119 — 70, 83, 189
119:54 — 387
120 to 134 — 76
121 — 77
123 — 71
125 — 70

127 — 189
128 — 33
129 — 70, 235
129:2 — 149
132 — 77
132:2 — 394
133 — 189
138:6 — 158
139:11 — 155
145 — 71, 83
147 — 71
148 — 70
149 — 70
150 — 70

Proverbs

1:4-5 — 164
1:13 — 194
2:1-4 — 190
2:5-8 — 190
2:16 — 193
3:1-4 — 190
3:5-12 — 190
3:9 → 182
3:15 — 193
3:16 — 173
3:19 — 161, 336
3:28 — 169
4:24 — 134
5:7 — 183
5:9 — 193, 195
5:14 — 50
5:15 — 193
5:18 — 195
5:19 — 393
6:1-5 — 193
6:6-11 — 157, 193
6:24 — 164, 183
6:27 — 398
6:30 — 194
7:5 — 183, 193
7:14 — 183
7:16 — 169
8:1 — 35, 386
8:11 — 193
8:15-16 — 164
8:22 — 35
9:1 — 35, 386
9:10 — 158, 195
9:13 — 386

b. *Apocryphal Passages*

c. *New Testament*

3. INDEX TO TALMUDIC AND MIDRASHIC PASSAGES

a. *Mishnah*

d. *Palestinian (Jerusalem) Talmud*

e. *Minor Tractates*

f. *Midrashim*

4. INDEX OF AUTHORS